Church, Religion and Society in Early Modern Italy

EUROPEAN STUDIES SERIES

General Editors	Colin Jones, Richard Overy, Joe Bergin, John Breuilly and Patricia Clavin

Published

Robert Aldrich	Greater France: A Short History of French Overseas Expansion
Nigel Aston	Religion and Revolution in France, 1780–1804
Yves-Marie Bercé	The Birth of Absolutism: A History of France, 1598–1661
Christopher F. Black	Church, Religion and Society in Early Modern Italy
Susan K. Foley	Women in France since 1789
Janine Garrisson	A History of Sixteenth-Century France, 1483–1589
Gregory Hanlon	Early Modern Italy, 1550–1800
Michael Hughes	Early Modern Germany, 1477–1806
Matthew Jefferies	Imperial Culture in Germany, 1871–1918
Dieter Langewiesche	Liberalism in Germany
Martyn Lyons	Napoleon Bonaparte and the Legacy of the French Revolution
Hugh McLeod	The Secularisation of Western Europe, 1848–1914
Robin Okey	The Habsburg Monarchy, c.1765–1918
Pamela M. Pilbeam	Republicanism in Nineteenth-Century France, 1814–1871
Helen Rawlings	Church, Religion and Society in Early Modern Spain
Tom Scott	Society and Economy in Germany, 1300–1600
Wolfram Siemann	The German Revolution of 1848–49
Richard Vinen	France, 1934–1970

Church, Religion and Society in Early Modern Italy

CHRISTOPHER F. BLACK

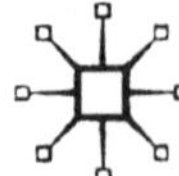

First published 2004 by
PALGRAVE MACMILLAN
Houndmills, Basingstoke, Hampshire RG21 6XS and
175 Fifth Avenue, New York, N.Y. 10010
Companies and representatives throughout the world

PALGRAVE MACMILLAN is the global academic imprint of the Palgrave Macmillan division of St. Martin's Press, LLC and of Palgrave Macmillan Ltd. Macmillan® is a registered trademark in the United States, United Kingdom and other countries. Palgrave is a registered trademark in the European Union and other countries.

ISBN 0–333–61844–0 hardback
ISBN 0–333–61845–9 paperback

This book is printed on paper suitable for recycling and made from fully managed and sustained forest sources.

A catalogue record for this book is available from the British Library.

Library of Congress Cataloging-in-Publication Data

Black, Christopher F.
Church, religion, and society in early modern Italy / Christopher F. Black.
p. cm. — (European studies series)
Includes bibliographical references and index.
ISBN 0–333–61844–0 – ISBN 0–333–61845–9 (pbk.)
1. Christian sociology – Italy. 2. Catholic Church – Italy – History.
3. Italy – Church history. I. Title. II European studies series (Palgrave Macmillan (Firm))

BX1543.B55 2004
274.5'06—dc22 2004050022

10 9 8 7 6 5 4 3 2 1
13 12 11 10 09 08 07 06 05 04

Printed in China

For my Mother Roma Black

In memory of departed children

With gratitude for consolation from 'the playthings of the Holy Spirit'

Contents

List of Tables and Maps

Tables

Maps

Preface

Preliminary words are desirable about the book's title, its coverage, and orientation. While the title is similar to Helen Rawlings' on Spain,[1] my book was conceived differently long ago, and does not follow hers in structure and coverage. This book derives from a project – too grandiose – envisaged 30 years ago, to write a very full study of the pre- and post-Tridentine Italian church, including its religious culture. One drafted chapter became my *Italian Confraternities in the Sixteenth Century* (1989; reprinted 2003), which led to more studies on confraternities, and indirectly to my *Early Modern Italy. A Social History* (2000–01). This book takes up part of that original challenge. In the intervening years much has changed, and a huge amount more material is published to complicate life for a single author trying to tackle all of Italy.

Originally this book had 'Counter Reformation' in the title, though 'Catholic Reform', as an increasingly current alternative concept from the 1970s, would have been highlighted as an alternative thread. Both terms have been rejected as unhelpful and outdated overarching concepts; though both phrazes may occasionally appear later as minor descriptors. 'Counter Reformation' implies that what the Roman Church was doing and recommending was primarily negative, and reacting against Protestant threats and criticisms. 'Catholic Reform' ties in with theories that reforms of western Christendom were attempted before the Luther-Zwingli-Melanchthon challenges surfaced, including in geographical areas such as Italy and Iberia which remained loyal to the central Roman Catholic authority. It postulates a common Christian reform background that affected Luther, Loyola and Calvin – and men like Seripando, Contarini, Giberti, Pole,

Miani and others active in Italy. 'Catholic Reform' can also be attached to persons and policies in the post-Tridentine period that aimed at continuing earlier ecumenical reform trends, without having a key focus on the Protestant challenges. John O'Malley's arguments for using a more neutral 'Early Modern Catholicism' are persuasive. He concludes:

> Early Modern Catholicism suggests both change and continuity without pronouncing on which predominates .... This term seems more amenable to the results of 'history from below' than the four just discussed (Counter Reformation; Catholic Reform or Catholic Reformation; Tridentine Reform and Tridentine Age; The Confessional Age or Confessional Catholicism), all of which indicate more directly the concerns and actions of ecclesiastical, political, or politico-ecclesiastical officialdom. Early Modern Catholicism more easily allows consideration of the resistance to control attempted by any social, ecclesiastical or intellectual elite. It allows for the negotiation that seems to have occurred at all levels – between bishops and Rome, between pastors and bishops on the one hand and pastors and their flock on the other, between accused and inquisitors – with even illiterate villagers emerging as effective negotiators when their interests were at stake. [and the term] has space for the new roles played by Catholic women, lay and religious.

However that term can cover from the late fifteenth century to the French Revolution.[2]

Partly because of word limits, I focus on only part of 'early modern' Catholicism: on the post-Tridentine period till the mid- or late seventeenth century. The closure of the Council of Trent in December 1563 was a defining moment for Italy, if not for all parts of the Catholic world. The period before this is covered in Chapter 1 in terms of the religious crises, and discussions throughout Italy of heterodox ideas; and in other chapters when considering developments of institutions, policies and ideals that fed into the multi-faceted reformation of Italian church and society. Tridentine legislation set some programmes and norms for further reform, but many other agencies of change were at work. The book balances descriptions of church organisation and social life, with assessments of the problems of restructuring. Discussion and overall analysis is complicated by Italy being politically divided into about 17 significant states, and 290 or more bishoprics. Church and cultural leaders saw 'Italy' as a single entity for some purposes, but the other divisions militated against a monolithic or uniform Church. We are in the pursuit of 'local knowledge', in the words of Simon Ditchfield's pertinent survey article.[3] This suggests many churches, rather than one Church. Part of my stress is on the positive and negative interactions between centre and periphery, but also between people and institutions locally, and even conflict within the centre – Rome.

The chosen title points to a selective bias in my coverage, affected by word limits, personal interests and expertise. Predominantly, I am concerned with the interactions of the church institutions and their clergy with the wider lay public – 'society' – within the Italian peninsula; and with the position of the laity not only in the parish structure, but in relation to 'good works'. Famous church intellectuals (like Roberto Bellarmino and Cesare Baronio) appear, but for their impact on wider society, rather than brilliant writings on theology, history, philosophy and science. The recent production of Anthony Wright's very valuable study of the Papacy, allows me to limit consideration of Popes, and largely to roles within Italy.[4] The Religious Orders are discussed primarily for their general religious educational and philanthropic contributions, not for higher scholarship and education or internal life. Nuns and nunneries have a broader consideration because Tridentine attempts to enforce strict enclosure constitute a major revolutionary attempt, with wide social implications. Visual and musical attempts to overwhelm and entice the faithful are deemed highly significant. Colour plates and high quality black and white photos are not feasible in the series book; but the notes suggest readily accessible illustrations in art books and CDs for the music.

[1] Helen Rawlings, *Church, Religion and Society in Early Modern Spain* (Basingstoke, 2002).
[2] O'Malley, *Trent and All That*, 141.
[3] Ditchfield, ' "In search of local knowledge": Rewriting early modern Italian religious history'.
[4] Wright, *Early Modern Papacy.*

Acknowledgements

Research on this book has been built up intermittently since the mid-1970s, interwoven with other projects. For enabling research visits to Italy, and giving papers at international conferences, I am grateful to the following bodies: the British Academy, the Arts and Humanities Research Board, the Carnegie Trust, the University Court and the Arts Faculty Planning Unit of Glasgow University, as well as my own Department research fund.

Many intellectual and personal debts in pursuing this subject have already been acknowledged in my two previous books. The late Eric Cochrane personally provided encouragement in the early 1970s, fostering a sceptical approach to much past and then current writing on the Italian Church. Special thanks are owed to Danilo Zardin, who since taking a very supportive interest in my book on Confraternities, has been a major supplier of books and offprints, notably on confraternities, and on the religious-social history of Lombardy. His research work and interpretations have affected much discussed below.

My interest in, and knowledge of, the fascinating Friuli region, has been fostered by Maria Bortoluzzi, a family friend from Spilimbergo, and Aldo Colonello of the Circolo Culturale Menocchio in Montereale Valcellina who have not only been friendly guides to their region, but providers of interesting books. Jenny Greenleaves Manco has been a kind host in Fiesole, recently facilitating research in Florence, as well as being a guide intermittently since student days to Florence, the city of her birth, and remoter parts of Tuscany. Among many other academic colleagues, and some former students, who have helped me (possibly long past their recalling in some cases), with advice, encouragement, references, books, offprints, conference invitations etc., I would particularly like to thank Tricia Allerston, Charles Avery, Elizabeth Black, Michael Bury, Sam Cohn, Bruce Collins, Nick Davidson, Andrea Del Col, Niki Dialeti, Simon Ditchfield, Simon Dixon, John Durkan, Konrad Eisenbichler, Mario Fanti, Giovanna Farrell-Vinay, Costas Gaganakis, David Gentilcore, Olwen Hufton, Mary Laven, Lance Lazar, Oliver Logan, Richard Mackenney, Eilidh MacLean, Adelina Modesti, Thomas Munck, John O'Malley, Giorgios Plakotos, Irene Polverini Fosi, Paolo Prodi, Brian Pullan, Helena Roach, Roberto Rusconi, Nick Terpstra, Marcello Verga, Andrea Vianello, Susan Verdi Webster, Anthony Wright. Mike Shand helpfully developed the Maps, as for my *Early Modern Italy*, though responsibility for any errors of course remains mine.

List of Abbreviations

AABol	Archivio Arcivescovile, Bologna
AAF	Archivio Arcivescovile, Florence
AdiSP	Archivio di Stato, Perugia
ASB	Archivio di Stato, Bologna
A.S.Pietro	Archivio di S.Pietro, Perugia
APV	Archivio della Curia Patriarchale, Venice
ASV	Archivio di Stato, Venice
ASVR	Archivio Storico del Vicariato, Rome
BCP	Biblioteca Comunale, Perugia
S.	San, Sant', Santo, Santa. Meaning Saint or Holy (in the singular). Abbreviated when a prefix to names of churches, confraternities and institutions.
SS.	Santi (plural, Saints or Holy); Santissima, Santissimo, Santissimi (Most Saintly, Most Holy). Similar usage.
SU	Sant'Uffizio (Section of Inquisition records in ASV)

The Early Modern Popes

Papal name	*Papal Reign*	*Name*	*Home city/ town*	*Papal 'nephew', or other family aid*
Adrian VI	1522–23	Adrian Dedal	Utrecht	
Clement VII	1523–34	Giulio de' Medici	Florence	
Paul III	1534–49	Alessandro Farnese	Rome	Card. Alessandro Farnese
Julius III	1550–55	Ciocchi del Monte	Rome	
Marcellus II	1555	Marcello Cervini	Montepulciano	
Paul IV	1555–59	Gian Pietro Caraffa	Naples	Carlo Carafa
Pius IV	1559–65	Giovanni Angelo de' Medici	Milan	Card. Carlo Borromeo (St)
Pius V (St)	1565–72	Michele Ghislieri	Bosco	Card. Michele Bonelli
Gregory XIII	1572–85	Ugo Buoncompagni	Bologna	Card. Filippo B. (nephew) and Giacomo B. (bastard son)
Sixtus V	1585–90	Felice Peretti	Grottommare (Ancona)	Card. Alessandro Peretti
Urban VII	1590	Giov. Batt. Castagna	Rome	
Gregory XIV	1590–91	Niccolò Sfondrati	Somma (Lombardy)	

(Continued)

Papal name	*Papal reign*	*Name*	*Home city/ town*	*Papal 'nephew', or other family aid*
Innocent IX	1591	Giov. Antonio Facchinetti	Bologna	
Clement VIII	1592–1605	Ippolito Aldobrandini	Fano	Card. Pietro Aldobrandini
Leo XI	1605	Alessandro de' Medici	Florence	
Paul V	1605–21	Camillo Borghese	Rome (and Siena)	Card. Scipione Borghese
Gregory XV	1621–23	Alessandro Ludovisi	Bologna	Card. Lodovico L.
Urban VIII	1623–44	Maffeo Barberini	Florence	Card. Carlo (brother); Taddeo, Card. Antonio (nephews)
Innocent X	1644–55	Giov. Batt. Pamphili	Rome	Card. Camillo Pamphili
Alexander VII	1655–67	Fabio Chigi	Siena	Card. Flavio Chigi
Clement IX	1667–69	Giulio Rospigliosi	Pistoia	
Clement X	1669–76	Emilio Altieri	Rome	
Innocent XI	1676–89	Benedetto Odescalchi	Como	
Alexander VIII	1689–91	Pietro Ottoboni	Venice	Card. Pietro Ottoboni
Innocent XII	1691–1700	Antonio Pignatelli	Spinazzola (Puglia)	
Clement XI	1700–21	Francesco Albani	Urbino	

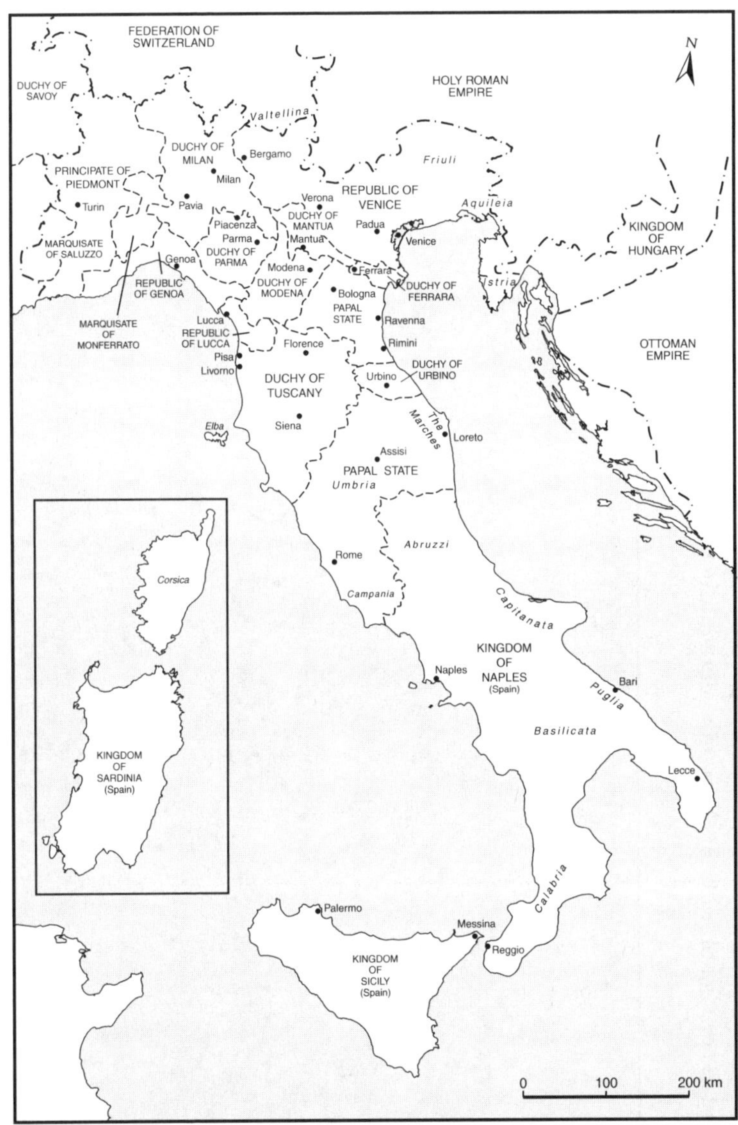

Map 1 Map of Italy: Political divisions, 1559

2–4 Italian bishoprics

The following maps indicate the location of most of the seats of the Italian Bishoprics, and relate to the Appendix on the Bishoprics. We have not managed to record every single one, especially in the areas around Naples. (To be considered in connection with the Appendix on the Bishoprics. Locations guided by Jedin *et al.* (eds), *Atlas d'histoire de l'Eglise.*)

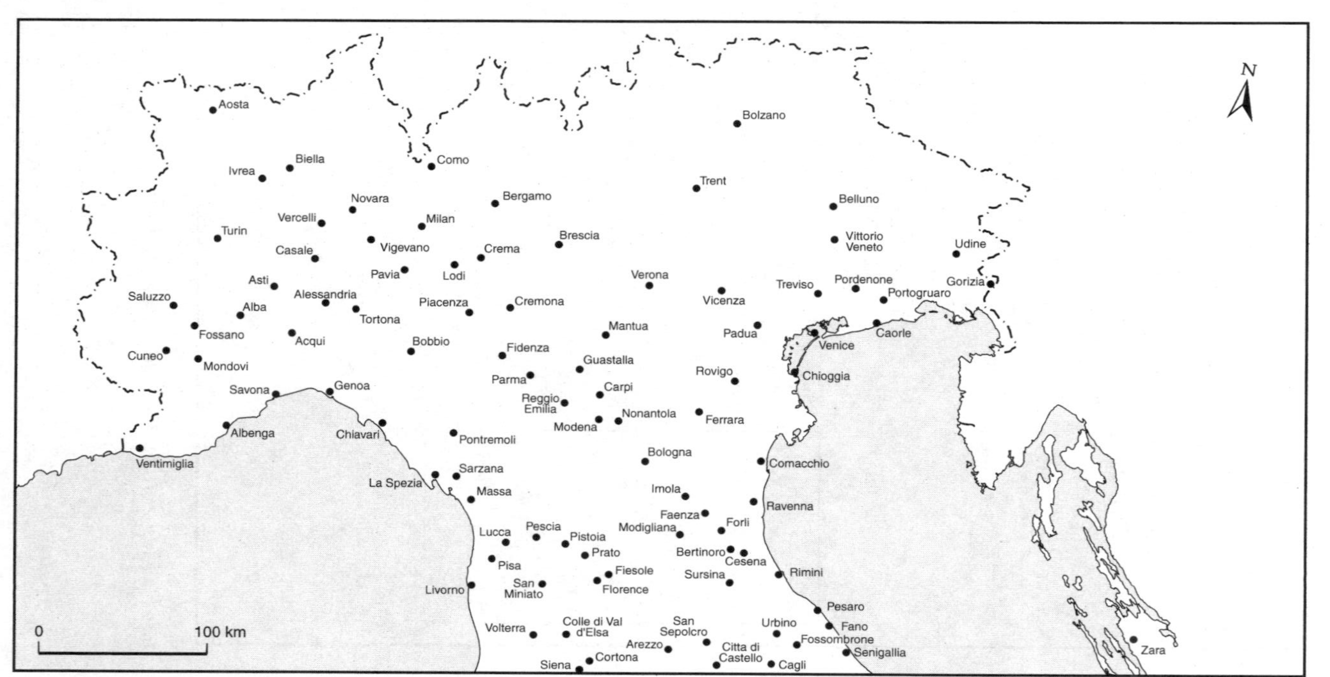

Map 2 Northern Italian bishoprics

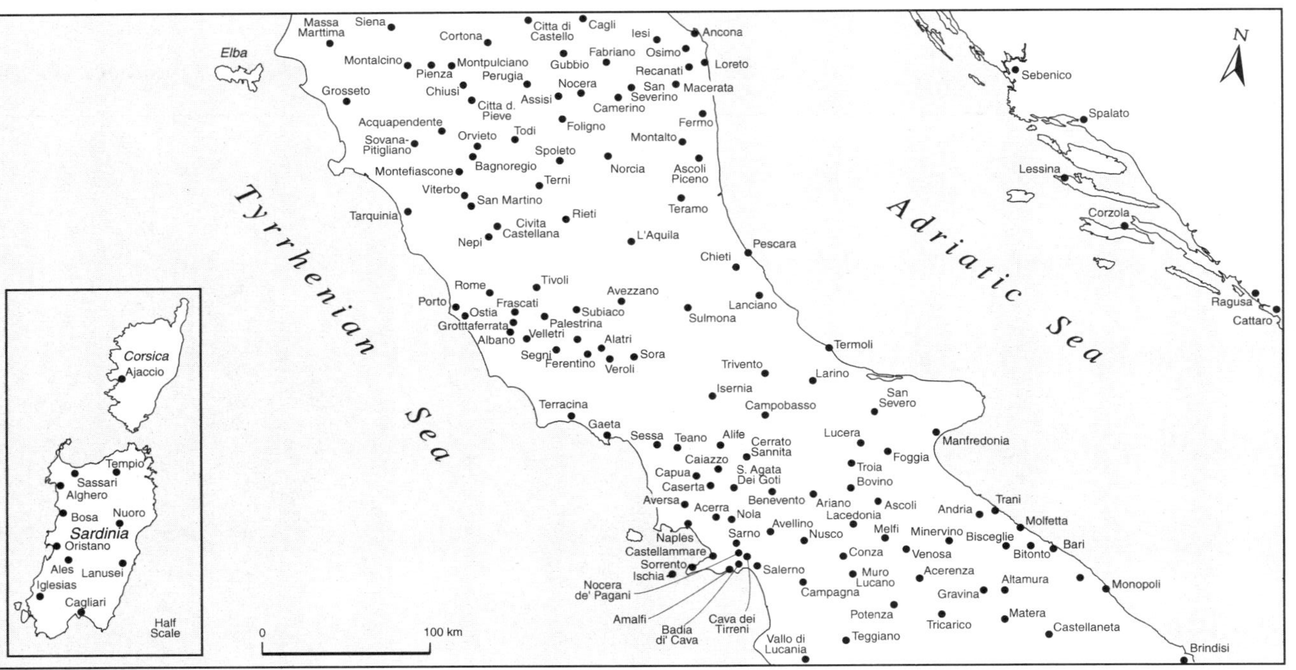

Map 3 *Central Italian bishoprics, with Corsica and Sardinia*

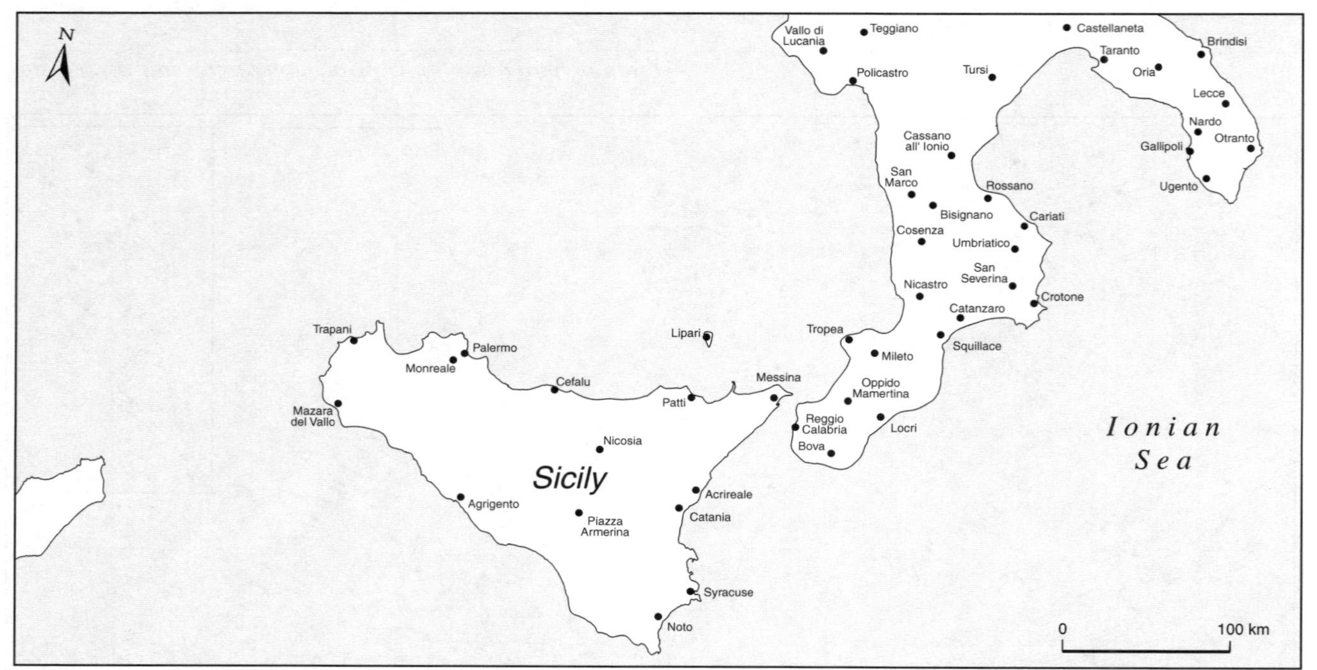

Map 4   Southern Italian and Sicilian bishoprics

Map 5 Places where groups of Protestant sympathisers were revealed, 1540s–1560s (• indicate major centres of interest ∘ indicate lesser centres of interest)

1 Religious Crises and Challenges in Early Sixteenth-Century Italy

This book is primarily concerned with the period after the closure of the Council of Trent, and the response to the reformations once the Council had set guidelines. However, the impact of the Reformation ideas and attitudes earlier has to be considered to understand the real or perceived threats in the eyes of the hierarchies, or lesser anti-Protestant campaigners. The impact and perceptions affected the course and rulings of the Council, the activity of control and repression independent of the Council, and policies post-Trent, whatever their relationship to Trent. Also an understanding of the real extent of Protestant appeals within Italy up to the 1560s will help us comprehend the nature of the 'success' of the Tridentine Reform.

The religious crises have to be seen in a wider context of other crises affecting the Italian peninsula from the late fifteenth century, which conditioned reactions to religious challenges and debates.[1] The relative peace of Italy was shattered by King Charles VIII of France's invasion in 1494 to claim the Kingdom of Naples from the Spanish. This produced a period of warfare and conflict, involving French, Spanish and German Imperial forces, with Swiss and German mercenaries. Italian states frantically changed sides for survival – until the European peace settlement of 1559 at Cateau Cambrésis, which left the Spanish King Philip II as the dominant outsider (see Map 1). He ultimately controlled the Viceroyalties of Naples and Sicily, along with Lombardy and Sardinia; though the local elites in all these areas hàd considerable powers and influences. The period of the Italian wars, 1494–1559, witnessed disruption from actual battles, sieges and sacks of cities (most spectacularly of Brescia, Prato and Ravenna in 1512, and Rome in 1527), with the dispersal of vulnerable surviving populations. Famine conditions resulted, populations were afflicted by various plagues, and syphilis was spread through the land. The calls for philanthropic 'good works' in response were considerable. The adverse war-induced conditions, partially explain the seemingly desultory reaction of church and Italian state leaders to the religious challenges launched in the north from Luther and Zwingli from 1517–19.

Reactions were also conditioned by the Ottoman Turkish threat, and an initially greater fear of Muslim challenges through the Mediterranean and along the North African coast. Turkish naval forces harried coastlines, Sultan Suleyman seriously contemplated adding Rome to his empire, while Popes sometimes prioritised a Crusade over settling religious and political disputes in western Europe. Holding a Council of the Church was affected. In 1535 Pietro Paulo Vergerio reported to King Ferdinand I of Bohemia and Hungary (Holy Roman Emperor from 1558), a conversation he had had with an envoy to Pope Paul III, who had said: 'I certainly want this Council to be held, but first I should like to make peace between his imperial Majesty and the King of the French … I also want to restrain the Turk.' In 1551–52 when the second stage of the Council of Trent was active, Turkish forces raided Sicily in July 1551 (burning Augusta), and in 1552 had an armada off Naples, which then landed and pillaged around Gaeta. Papal troops were put on alert for an assault on Rome, but the Turks retired.[2]

The cultural impacts of the physical crises were considerable and varied. The 1527 Sack of Rome shattered moods of complacency and humanist overconfidence. It scattered to the north and south some of the moving spirits for both Religious and cultural reform, beneficially affecting the growth of new Religious Orders, congregations and confraternities. It induced religious pessimism in some, possibly making Lutheran ideas of salvation by faith more appealing. Others sought moral reform to appease an angry God or salvation through good works.[3]

The leadership of the Roman Church, and the conduct of church affairs, was regularly challenged. The political and economic crises from the 1490s, mentioned earlier added stimuli, but also inhibited some responses. Calls for reform of abuses within the Catholic Church in Italy, or for reformation of its institutions, teachings and practices, building on strengths from the past, came before Luther or Zwingli launched what we generically call Protestantism. Fra Savonarola, burned as a heretic in Florence in 1498, leading an overt and strident challenge to papal immorality, and calling for a new spirituality, epitomised the crisis.[4] His continuing influence on Catholic reformers, which needs better recognition, will be noted through this book. As the northern debates developed, much interest in them was shown within Italy, at all levels of society – from intellectuals, bishops and princes to urban artisans and 'peasants'. Debates remain lively among historians as to the extent of the Italian Protestant movement or movements, over which strands were most predominant, and why 'Protestantism' was defeated in Italy.

Modern historians of Italian Protestantism tend to be strongly biased towards Protestants, whether from a religious conviction (Protestant or liberal Catholic, seeing Tridentine Catholicism as a form that should not have 'won'), or from a left-wing political viewpoint, supporting the underdogs suppressed by an authoritarian and cruel Catholic Church. Many such historians seemingly assume the Protestantism that would have prevailed, would have been 'better', intellectually and democratically. But a victory for certain forms of Protestantism – such as Genevan and Scottish-style Calvinism – would probably have generated more repression and been 'unpopular' for greater numbers. Just as in Britain philo-Catholic historians have stressed the popularity of the old religion, so for Italy historians need to recognise that Protestantism was conveyed by minorities, even if a majority of Catholics could find plenty to criticise and satirise in the Roman Catholic Church.

Through much of Italy certain Protestant ideas were discussed, written about, preached, at many levels of society through to the 1560s. Salvatore Caponetto's *The Protestant Reformation* is a mine of information, though sometimes confusingly organised and short on helpful explanations.[5] While he follows Delio Cantimori in stressing Calvinist influences, he covers the prior enthusiasm for Erasmus (who visited Venice, with mixed impact and enthusiasm), the rapid interest in some of Luther's ideas, especially on salvation by faith alone, a greater knowledge of northern ideas through Melanchthon. The Italian scene is complicated by the impact of the Spanish exile Juan Valdes with a network of contacts operating out of Naples, bringing in key figures such as Vittoria Colonna, Reginald Pole, Pietro Carnesecchi to create what may be seen as an Italian Protestantism.

Italy also had maintained heretical communities of Waldensians, both in the north-west and (more obscurely) in the south in Calabria and Puglia. Some of the Waldensians soon saw Calvinism as offering compatible beliefs, and sought to make common cause (with disastrous results in the south). Calvinism's influence in Italy was made greater by the French influences in Piedmont, and by the court of Ferrara and Duchess Renée de France, a notable Calvinist, wife of Duke Ercole II d'Este.

While stressing that Protestantism was known and debated in Italy, Silvana Seidel Menchi calls Italian Protestantism a 'non-event' and 'marginal phenomenon', since no state committed itself to a Protestant faith. While networks of Protestant contacts existed, no major communities were established, and the Spanish–Italian movement of Valdes was not coherent enough to make a major European impact. Even in major cities with attested Protestant sects, Lucca and Venice, only about 0.5 per cent could be judged to be committed. If sympathisers – not in trouble or reported to authorities – are included, less than 2 per cent are deemed philo-Protestant. She argues that what needs more explanation is the solid 0.5 per cent, not why Protestantism failed.[6]

The limited Protestant support and its solidity are both relevant for what happens later. In terms of the reactions – overreactions for those preferring a more ecumenical or Erasmian outcome – myth and perceptions were more important than 'real' support. A small minority could generate a reformation change, but it needed the commitment of an urban ruling elite or a Prince, which was not fully forthcoming in Italy. Caponetto argues that the failure of the Republic of Venice – however anti-Papacy at times – to back a Protestant cause, doomed Italian Protestantism.[7] The Republic demonstrated that many forms of Protestantism were offered and discussed, but could not produce a common cause against the Roman Church.[8] Reform traditions and intellectual debates, native to the Republic and embracing outside movements for strong Catholic reform, could foster a re-formed Catholic Church, which might avoid a full breach with Rome, but maintain some autonomy. A panic over networks spreading the more radical ideas of Anabaptism in 1550–51 led the Venetian political leaders, hitherto fairly tolerant of debates and books about salvation by faith alone, marriage of priests, rules of fasting or the power of Popes, to decide on cooperation with the Roman Inquisition.

Many parts of Italy were well prepared to receive reform ideas – over theological interpretation, liturgy, or the reform of morals – but unlikely to show a commitment to a single non-Roman dogmatic or institutional approach. The humanist intellectual tradition encouraged textual exegesis and debate; the Italians were in the forefront of producing vernacular (essentially Tuscan Italian) translations of the Bible, or at least major parts of the New Testament.[9] An active printing industry in the north, with transmission networks across the Alps, could rapidly circulate some texts, but without being committed to a particular confessional line. A variety of views was good for business, in Florence, Milan or Venice. Italy had a long tradition of dynamic popular preaching that was socially critical, and could be anti-papal. Anticlericalism was standard in literary discourse. Northern and central cities had urban communities with literate artisans, and with a tradition of confraternities and guilds that encouraged their lay control of religious life. Despite the physical geography of mountainous Italy, with few navigable rivers, much of Italy had a mobile and communicative society – and not just between the major cities. Those with ideas as well as goods to distribute, to proselytise, as well as those wishing to escape threats, could move quite readily. But the multi-state system made it hard for policing and prosecuting authorities to catch and curb. The Inquisition tribunals faced and partially overcame, such challenges.

Committed Protestants, though few, communicated and influenced each other. They could also be antagonistic and uncooperative. The early reformers, Erasmian, Lutheran/Melanchthonian, Waldensian and Valdesian were inclined to be canny, evasive and 'nicodemist', refusing to commit themselves in broad daylight, as Calvin complained.[10] Many avoided full confrontation, would reconcile themselves, or skilfully argue with investigators and inquisitors, securing exoneration and release. But some like Pietro Carnesecchi and Aonio Poleario were to lose the argumentation, and their life, in the 1560s–1570s. They did not work for the overthrow of the Roman Church – at least not yet. The wholeheartedly Calvinist became more confrontational, seriously subversive, dangerous; so alienated other groups.

Juan de Valdes, inspirational for many Italians, but ambiguous in his theology, probably stood most for Erasmian irenicism and tolerance, and nicodemism. Commenting on John 16:2 (with Jesus saying 'the hour is coming when whoever kills you will think he is offering service to God'), he declared:

> In this statement I learn this, that everyman must be careful never to become passionate about things which pertain to religion – I mean

> defend this or attack that with passion – so that passion should not blind him in such a way that he should come to err against God out of ignorance born of malice.[11]

This attitude reflected that of many Italian philo-Protestants, both from the elite and artisans, in the early years. Thomas Mayer's recent challenging study of Reginald Pole indicates that Pole – however confrontational he was against Henry VIII – crucially shied away from clear religious conflicts, and retreated into ambiguous writing.[12] But the 1540s saw more confrontational and intolerant positions on various sides.

Much of the above explains why Italy did not see a Protestant victory in any state; but also helps explain later authoritarian reactions. The numbers of 'heretics' might be small, but they were in influential positions – at petty courts, in the preaching Orders, and among the mobile, vocal and literate artisans. For the suspicious, small influential groups could soon infect the many. For somebody as paranoid as Cardinal Gian Pietro Carafa, to become Pope Paul IV, the few constituted huge dangers, especially if they were not only on the streets of Lucca, in the bars and *palazzi* of Venice, but within the Curia in Rome, or in courtly circles based in Viterbo linked to key ecclesiasts. Hence, extreme reactions and overreactions, notably through the Inquisition, which under Carafa was a decidedly persecuting institution, and not the corrective or re-educational one it became later.

The initial official reactions to both 'Lutheran' ideas from the north (with 1518 seeing the first Italian edition of a Luther work),[13] and the circulation of Juan de Valdes's works in the 1530s from Naples, were laid back or ambivalent. First at political levels the threats from the Muslim Ottomans were more serious, as were the political designs of Spain, France and the Empire on Italian states.[14] But at theological and philosophical level some new religious ideas had much to offer; and they were not necessarily heretical. Luther was not the first to argue that a reading of St Paul, especially in *Romans*, and St Augustine, could lead to a belief in salvation by faith alone. A greater emphasis on God's mercy and grace, on Christ's sacrifice, on the benefit of Christ, on man's worthlessness, on God's foreknowledge, could all appeal, and be found worth considering and debating. Praiseworthy thinkers, church diplomats and practical episcopal reformers like Girolamo Seripando, Gasparo Contarini, Reginald Pole, Pier Paolo Vergerio and Giovanni Grimani saw merits in some of the Lutheran and/or Valdesian ideas, and ways of reaching a compromise with the northern

Protestants through a Church Council. Seidel Menchi points to philo-Protestants who wanted to 'conquer the Catholic Church from within' (naming Patriarch Giovanni Grimani of Aquileia, Bishop Pietro Bonomo of Trieste, and Bishop Vittore Soranzo of Bergamo);[15] in other words to have a modern Lutheran theology within a Rome led Church. Some of the philo-Protestant ideas were spread and discussed surreptiously among the elite, in personal contact, in letters and in poems. Other communicators were major preachers, in the traditions of Italian preaching, confronting social problems, calling for moral reform and repentance; but with some moving to Lutheran positions on faith and salvation. Much of this prepared the ground for more dangerous discussions. Some bishops and cardinals were ready to protect such preachers, even when it was sensed they were treading on dangerous ground, until the mid-1540s.

In the 1520s and 1530s significant interest in, and debate about, 'Lutheran' ideas was evident, though with a rather restricted knowledge of Luther's actual writings.[16] Italians were open to new ideas, ready to debate them but without making too categorical statements of their own beliefs, feeling their way. The knowledge that Luther and others had interesting ideas would have affected many more than those who had a clear idea of what it meant to be 'Lutheran', or were committed. By 1528 the Venetian dramatist Ruzzante could assume that his carnival audience for *La Moscheta* knew that Luther had raised controversies over free will, in reply to Erasmus.[17]

Paul Grendler stressed there was a mood of religious restlessness in Italy through the early sixteenth century, and by the 1530s a number of 'adventurers of the pen' were willing and able to enter the fray, and stir up debate; for example, Pietro Aretino, Ortensio Lando and Anton Francesco Doni. Aretino, famous for pornographic poems and dialogues, vituperative journalism, anticlericalism, and for attacking the nudity in Michelangelo's *Last Judgment* painting on the Sistine Chapel's altar wall, also encouraged a basic faith in simple Christian messages, including the Virgin birth. Ortensio Lando greatly admired Erasmus, and new scriptural analysis, apparently followed Zwingli on the Sacraments, but then reacted against the excesses of German theological debate. His bitter anticlericalism fostered discontent in urban classes, and his writings (notably his 1552 *Dialogo della Sacra Scrittura*) encouraged a reliance on scripture, and salvation through faith not works. A.F. Doni, a Florentine weaver, became a popular writer in Venice, possibly associated himself with Anabaptists, but dabbled in a whole range of beliefs, before settling by the early 1550s on a utopian dream of a simple reformed Catholicism. Though all might have been charged with heresy, their impact probably more assisted reformed Catholicism. Doni's utopian dialogue, *I Mondi*, with only minor emendations, (keeping its messages of social equality) was a major commercial success in the later sixteenth century.[18]

By the 1540s however, Gian Pietro Carafa and others considered that the Italian irenic and tolerant attitude was dangerous, that 'our Italy' was seriously imperilled – just as some philo-Protestants thought 'our Italy' was ripe for a victory against an unreformable and unconvertible Rome hierarchy. The Italian scene was rapidly polarised. The open-minded or the ditherers had to decide what were the touchstones of belief and practice; how much issues like 'faith alone', the cult of saints, transubstantiation mattered to them. Some opted for exile as open Protestants, others to be nicodemists, hiding their true beliefs. Alternatively, many retained loyalty to a Roman church increasingly emphasising the most conservative interpretations of St Paul, and anathematising almost all that Luther, Zwingli or Calvin wrote, but which answered some of the criticisms of immorality and lack of care for ordinary souls.

In 1542 the medieval Inquisition system was reformed or replaced, and what we might consider as the early modern Italian Inquisition created. The Holy Office of the Inquisition was established in Rome as a permanent bureaucratic institution under the Pope, and negotations started to establish permanent dependent tribunals in other Italian states, as well as in other cities of the Papal State. The prime mover was Gian Pietro Carafa, who had knowledge of the Spanish Inquisition as a diplomatic envoy, and had noted the efficacy of this papal-sanctioned but royal controlled institution in pursuing and curbing heretics – Judaisers, Lutherans and mystical Alumbrados (who had influenced Juan de Valdes). Through the 1540s and 1550s the Inquisition developed its activities from the centre and in some localities, as more and more groups of Protestants were revealed in Italian towns, and revelations came about the real or alleged beliefs of leading preachers, and of the *spirituali*. Some indication of the spread of anti-Roman groups and sects is given on Map 5, which makes some distinction between major and minor 'heretical' centres in the 1540s–1560s. These were areas which worried the Inquisition. The following discussion and some in Chapter 9, will clarify the types of philo-Protestants involved, or *spirituali*.

The term *spirituali* covers networks of philo-Protestants or Catholic reformers who showed interest in ideas from Erasmus, Luther,

Melanchthon and Valdes. A text most emblematic of their interests is the *Beneficio di Cristo* (of which Benedetto Fontanini da Mantova was the main author, if amended by others),[19] a best-seller with support in high places in the early 1540s, but to be seized and eradicated by the Inquisition when some decided it was heavily Calvinist in inspiration. Its popular appeal was however its overall language about a religion of love (*carità*), and images of the metamorphosis of the sinful soul into the perfection of Christ.[20] Increasing knowledge of the *spirituali* heightened the sense of crisis for the conservatives in Rome, for the networks included leading people like Cardinals Contarini, Pole and Giovanni Morone, or court-culture leaders like Vittoria Colonna (marchioness of Pescara, poet friend of Michelangelo and closely connected with Pole), and Eleonora Gonzaga, duchess of Urbino, supporter of the Capuchin preacher Bernardino Ochino and Pier Paolo Vergerio, Bishop of Capodistria. Giulia Gonzaga (1513–66), as a young widow ran the lordship of Fondi; after meeting Valdes in Naples in 1536 she became a key supporter of his ideas, and of many *spirituali.* The investigation of her widespread correspondence confiscated at her death was to provide evidence of the long-term serious heresy of many people, and led to the final trial and execution of Pietro Carnesecchi in 1567[21] (see Chapter 9). Some of these died before they could be unmasked and condemned as 'heretics' by Carafa and his successors. Pole came very close to being tried. In 1540–41 Viterbo, where Pole was papal governor, became a refuge centre for many Valdesians (from Naples, Florence and elsewhere), and Carafa was soon to see this as a pernicious trouble centre, protected by Pole.[22] Cardinal Morone, on the other hand, survived lengthy Inquisition investigations to become the key figure in the third phaze of the Council of Trent, bringing it to an effective conclusion.

Philo-Protestant support became obvious in other circles. The flight of the General of the Capuchins (then the most dynamic branch of the Franciscans), Bernardino Tomassini alias Ochino (1487–1563) from Siena, in 1542 was one of the crisis turning points. This spectacular preacher, with contacts in leading northern cities, decided that salvation by faith alone was a touchstone belief, and he would not risk defending it to inquisitors. From Geneva, Ochino appealed to the Venetian Signoria to make its Republic the Italian doorway for Protestantism. A forlorn hope. A like-minded Capuchin, Girolamo Galateo (1490—1541), had died in a Venetian prison; for preaching on faith and works he had been tried by Carafa, sentenced to death by the Pope, but the Venetian Council of Ten had commuted this to imprisonment, then house arrest. But, he was rearrested when his *Apologia* (Bologna, 1541), called for the Venetian Republic to 'return to the Word and to the truth of Sacred Scripture ... [and to] defend that part of your crucified Christ and his Gospel and his Word'. Galateo's stimulation led to the formation of artisan groups that became openly known through the trial of a carpenter, Antonio 'marangone' in 1533. Antonio owned a vernacular Bible (probably Antonio Brucioli's 1530 translation of the New Testament), Luther's *Centum gravamina*, and various other books. He had talked in many Venetian churches, visited artisan workshops, and used a bookshop as a focus for discussions, attended by Tuscans and Germans as well as Venetian artisans. This was an early sign that Protestant ideas, communicated by preaching, books and shop-based discussion was affecting the urban populace. Small communities were also infected; Lutheran groups were discovered through Istria in 1534, thanks to Franciscan preachers and German contacts working through Trieste. Ironically, the papal legate seemingly, enthusiastically involved in pursuing this 'plague' was P.P. Vergerio, who in 1547 was himself to flee to Calvinist Switzerland.[23]

Another significant development was the spread of Calvinism in the little Republic of Lucca, primarily fostered by Pietro Martire Vermigli (1499–1562), leading the Lateran Canons at San Frediano as prior from June 1541. Earlier he had imbibed Erasmian and Bucer ideas in Bologna (1530–33), Valdesian ideas in Naples (1537–41), becoming fully committed to the central doctrine of salvation by faith alone. Lucca provided a significantly receptive audience, helped by many monks and patrician support. Eventually, Cardinal Bartolomeo Guidiccioni persuaded or threatened the republican government to curb heresy. Ahead of any trials leaders, including Vermigli, fled to Geneva and further afield. Vermigli infected England. However, remaining enthusiasts contaminated peasants through Tuscany and Emilia, in the Garfagnana, Lunigiana, in small towns like Càsola and Fivizzano, from where prohibited books circulated; as Jesuit missionaries later found.[24] The Luccan episode contributed to Carafa's persecution mania and the creation of the Holy Office. Lucca as 'the republic contaminated with heresy', as Cardinal Guidiccioni noted it in 1542, was the most worrying threat because of the social and political quality, rather than the quantity, of its supporters. The republican government itself in 1540 had banned most religious festivals, including that of the Volto Santo, central to Luccan civic religion, which honoured a statue of the Holy Face, supposedly carved by Joseph of

Aramathea. Bernardino Ochino's sermon attack in 1538 on excessively expensive and time-consuming Luccan feasts possibly triggered the government's confrontation, allegedly to save the poor from superstition.[25]

From earlier heretical struggles Italy had its own Waldensian communities in north-west Italy, Calabria and Puglia. From about 1526 the northerners had decided to learn about the new movements; by September 1532 Waldensians from Calabria and Puglia had representatives meeting in Chanforan (valley of Angrogna), with the northerners, to make some common cause with Guillaume Farel and the Genevan reform movement. As a result Waldensians became more open in their beliefs – ultimately leading to serious persecution in the 1560s. The Locarno region was infected especially by Franciscan preaching during 1549–55, which established philo-Protestant networks linking the north-west through the valleys to Switzerland and France. Heretical enclaves survived there well into the post-Tridentine period. Some preachers from this area had carried their messages far south, to Palermo, Naples, as well as more closely to Genoa, Florence, Mantua, Milan and Venice. Ochino had already in 1539–40 introduced Sicilians to 'the benefit of Christ', and salvation through faith.

The strength of Lutheran interest in the Brescia–Verona region, where Lutheran books were being sold from about 1524, was revealed in the Brescian patrician, Giovan Andrea Ugoni's trial in 1546. He linked with small traders and artisans critically, discussing free will, purgatory and papal power. His book collection included works by Zwingli and the now condemned *Beneficio di Cristo.* He was released, arguing that trial procedures contravened the Venetian Council of Ten's 1521 orders. The worried Inquisition, however managed a second trial in 1552, successfully securing Ugoni's public abjuration, (but we meet him again). This encouraged the Inquisition to secure better cooperation with state authorities. Bishop Vittore Soranzo of Bergamo's arrest in 1551, revealing his correspondence with Bucer and Ochino, is seen by Caponetto as ending the Bucerian middle way policy.[26]

The final noteworthy crisis came in 1551 with Pietro Manelfi's revelations about the networks of Anabaptists through Venetian territory and beyond. A priest from near Senigallia, he had become an Anabaptist leader, but in October 1551 he went voluntarily to the Bologna Inquisitor, Fra Leandro degli Alberti, allegedly wishing 'to return to the bosom of the Holy Roman Church', and rejecting Lutheranism and 'Anabaptist perfidy'. The investigation was transferred to Venice, as the presumed epicentre, and Rome made clear its deep worry. A certain 'Tiziano' was cited as the leading proselytiser from 1549–51, with a Swiss version of Anabaptism, rather than the more radical and potentially violent Thomas Müntzer teaching. He had established a group in the delightful hilltop town of Asolo (with local elite support), and having fostered other groups in Cittadella, Gardone, Rovigo, Padua and Vicenza, he proselytised through the Ferrara state, and Florence. The Paduan enterprise brought contacts with exiled Valdesians from Naples (under abbot Girolamo Busale, who turned Anabaptist). When some argued that the soul was mortal, and Christ was mere man, conflicts and splits developed, aired in a 'council' meeting in Venice. Manelfi decide on recantation and betrayal of Tiziano and others. One of the group, Benedetto del Borgo had earlier been arrested in Rovigo and executed in March 1551, and a more complex associate, the Sicilian visionary Giorgio Rioli (alias Siculo) had been executed in May 1551; but Manelfi's indications of a much larger network rang alarm bells in the Venetian state as well as in Rome. Further worrying was Manelfi's claim that his group: 'considers all Christian magistrates to be enemies of God, and insists that no Christian may be emperor, king, duke, or hold any office whatsoever, and the people are not obliged to obey them'.[27] It was one thing to challenge papal monarchy, another to challenge all political rule. Essentially, this episode persuaded the Venetian Republic to take a full offensive against major heresies, and to cooperate with the Roman Inquisition, provided it was agreed that the Venetian tribunal should be a church–state dyarchy.

By the mid-1550s Protestant and Valdesian ideas had been aired very widely, and small groups existed in such cities and towns as: Asolo, Bologna, Bergamo, Brescia, Cremona, Ferrara, Florence, Gardone, Genoa, Lucca, Mantua, Milan, Modena, Naples, Padua, Palermo, Rome, Rovigo, Siena, Treviso, Udine, Venice, Vicenza and Viterbo. Groups existed in the valleys and foothills of Piedmont and Friuli, in Istria, in the Garfagnana and Lunigiana, and in Calabria and Puglia, if one includes the old Waldensians. The social profiles are puzzlingly varied. Upper class support was strong in Brescia and Lucca (131 from about 400 identified Protestants 1530–1600), but artisans were the main support in Bergamo, Vicenza or Udine. Of 774 Venetian philo-Protestants identified for the period 1547–83, 189 were in the top group of artisans, involved in luxury goods. Women featured as elite leaders, but rarely among the artisans classes, and then largely as related to male leaders.[28]

Elite leaders could be challenging in counter arguments and evasive over their true beliefs; as with the major Florentine figure Pietro Carnesecchi. Many however could be persuaded to recant, and many philo-Protestants were reluctant to pass over to the extremes of Calvinism and Anabaptism. The circulation of the vernacular Bible or portions thereof was considerable, and the discussion of the Gospel widespread among literate artisans, as well as by preachers. Artisan workshops, retailing outlets and print-bookshops were useful meeting places, and locations to see copies of the Gospels or Paul's epistles. Such evidence helps explain the powerful attack on the vernacular Bible, in the Indexes of Prohibited Books (Chapter 9). For theologically trained preachers and high churchmen the doctrine of salvation by faith alone was a major consideration; but might be less so among the artisan-based sects. In Udine, Modena and Istria the cult of saints, fasting laws, and the Real Presence in the Eucharist were the targets.[29] These aspects remain part of the agenda, or targets in denunciations in Venetian Inquisition cases, for example, in the later period (Chapter 9).

For many philo-Protestants in Italy, it was often very much a pick-and-mix procedure; each man or woman selecting doctrine(s) and practices, or hate targets to suit their needs, or according to whom or which books they were exposed. This meant moving and variable targets for Catholic defenders, and difficulties in directing their campaigns; but it rendered the overall threat less, because philo-Protestants were not united. If the Catholic reform movements turned to re-education, and to making some beliefs and practices more explicable and appealing, they might create a more acceptable, and willingly accepted Catholic Church. The variability and ambivalence of the heretical targets, and success in getting recantations, help explain a less crisis-minded attitude from the Inquisition by the 1560s, and a shift of targets.

However, a deep crisis situation was still perceived when the Council of Trent entered its third stage (1562–63), and the final codification of responses to the religious challenges. Some events and policies in Venice and the Veneto might exemplify a range of problems to be faced, and possible approaches to control. Venice as the most cosmopolitan city, and centre of world trade, had the greatest mix of religious opinions (Jewish and Muslim added to the diverse Christians), and probably the freest discussions at all levels of society. It had the largest printing industry, assisting the dissemination of ideas. The wider Veneto territory could readily be affected by the movement of people and books, and oral discourse. The upper valleys and mountains protected the deviant from pursuit. Venice and the Veneto could readily be influenced by ideas from German, Swiss and French lands. Republican leaders were likely to be hostile to Spanish influences, and many wanted to maintain a considerable distance from direct papal power.

For the remoter area of Aquiliea, Andrea Del Col has revealed a remarkable document: a confession of faith in 1559 from three critics of Catholic orthodoxy.[30] From June 1559, Angelo Peruzzi, the bishop of Feltre's vicar general, conducted a Visitation of part of the diocese, bordering Austrian lands. As Chapter 3 will discuss, Visitations were tours of inspection designed as a key to episcopal control. Peruzzi and his team started in the Valsugana. Unusually, in a Visitation he was joined by the inquisitor of Feltre (Fra Antonio dal Cavolo, a Feltre noble). A *processo* against a priest in Strigno had indicated that the valley had notable Reform adherents, protected by an Austrian captain, Gaspar Genetto in Castel Ivano, whose brother Andrea was parish priest of Strigno. Peruzzi in Strigno summoned three known Reform supporters, the notary Zuan Battista Rippa, a shoe-tanner Matteo Coppa Zudei and Zuane Vacharo. Peruzzi turned the session into a kind of colloquy, both sides explaining and debating their positions. Despite the Inquisitor's presence, Peruzzi indicated that there would be no trial; but he wanted the three to record afterwards a declaration of their faith, which duly appeared, and survives. This was a learning exercise for the hierarchy, and for the historian: a clear indication of local reform views, presented to the hierarchy, but free from the constraints of an episcopal or inquisition investigation. The testament shows that one at least had considerable Biblical knowledge, quoting an Italian translation, notably from Pauline epistles, but also the Psalms. Rippa submitted a copy of Antonio Brucioli's Bible translation. Thanks, presumably to this notary's wider knowledge, some specified canons from Gratian's *Decretum*, a major legal text, were cited – against the idea that social and hierarchical distinctions on earth can be repeated in heaven; arguing that an excommunicate can only do good through grace. Del Col detects the influence of the *Beneficio di Cristo*, the *Somma di tutta la Sacra Scrittura*, and Ochino's sermons; prohibited books which were known to be in circulation in the area.

The testament said they had no disagreement with the vicar general and inquisitor on the Eucharist. However, they challenged the existence of purgatory: Paul in Hebrews talked of Christ sitting at

God's right, purging our sins, and St Augustine found no Biblical support for any place but paradise and hell. They attacked the argument about the intercession of saints, as only God can know our hearts, though we can imitate the lives of saints 'as true friends of God'. They argued that the Pope had no special powers above other priests and bishops. They followed St Paul who: 'in many places teaches that all our salvation comes from the passion of Christ through the grace of God blessed, without our merits and without our good works, only through mere liberality', though they agreed that good works characterised a Christian, because one cannot call a tree good that does not make and produce good fruits. 'The works then are fruits of grace and signs that we are saved (*della salute*).' The trio found no Biblical justification for oral confession, which the Greek Church did not accept. Our sins can only be remitted by the blood of Christ, not the hands of a priest. The Council of Trent's 1551 decree on penitence was specifically attacked. They challenged the Pope's power to ban eating meat on prohibited days, which went beyond what the Gospel says. Popes and bishops should not add laws, but preach the Gospel and administer sacraments as God instituted them. The testament concludes by saying that the writers are making a kind of confession, praying for Christ's compassion; but if the reverend vicar and the inquisitor can show the truth otherwise, through the Gospels, they hope they will be able to understand their errors.

> We pray God that his Holy Spirit inspires in our hearts the knowledge of his truth, which may guide and govern all our actions, so we may together with the other elect enjoy the celestial country (*fruir la patria celeste*), promised to every believer in his only born Son.

This bold challenge showed the authorities that they were dealing with a well-read and thoughtful group, challenging much of the current teachings of the Catholic Church. The views might be judged as essentially 'Italian' reform, rather than transalpine (though books by Bucer and Melanchthon were locally available). In the same month Rippa wrote another letter to the Vicar General, with a summary of the false opinions of the Anabaptists. He also disassociated himself from the other two, because they were banished by the Venetian Republic and he did not wish 'in any way to unite with them on account of the faith and religion'. He then glossed what was said about papal authority, and now considering St Paul's views on obeying good and bad lords and magistrates, he confessed he would obey papal laws and constitutions 'while they are not directly contrary and repugnant to the sacred gospel of Jesus Christ'. So the notary reduces the confrontation and slides into accepting a compromise position.

Peruzzi's 'soft' and seemingly open educational approach was already paying dividends, and potentially better than a very confrontational one, especially in a mountainous border area. If the fathers reassembling in nearby Trent three years later were aware of this kind of information, they had evidence of well-read and thoughtful 'heretics' through the valleys. That access to the vernacular Bible could generate many arguments against orthodox Roman teaching was fully evidenced. Not unconnected, a long battle ensued within the hierarchy before the ultimately disastrous decision to ban totally vernacular translations of the Bible, in the 1596 Index of Prohibited Books (see Chapter 9). Interestingly, in 1576 Captain Gaspar Genetto of Castel Ivano resurfaces, being denounced as 'luterano', holding religious services in his castle where Luther's sermons were read, and protecting heretics banished from the Venetian Republic.[31]

For Venice itself, and its wider contacts, revelations arise from studies of Francesco Spinola and his associates. The Venetian Inquisition had him drowned off the Lido on 31 January 1567.[32] Born in Como in 1520, he became a notable humanist scholar and poet, moving about and developing contacts in Brescia, Padua and Venice. He was a great arguer and debater, even in prison. While his own *processo* record has been lost, we know much through references in many other investigations, and the writings of a French humanist and prophet, Dionisio Gallo, who shared Venetian prison cells with him 1566–67. Witnesses suggest that Spinola had variously taught that only two sacraments were valid (baptism and marriage), that purgatory did not exist, Indulgences had no value, Christ was the only intercessor, and that salvation came through faith alone. Spinola in the 1560s moved around the literary circles of Venice, writing adulatory poems, teaching various young persons including the sons of Leonardo Mocenigo and corrected books for the powerful printer Gabriele Gioliti. Spinola called his followers *fratelli* or *evangelisti*, distinguishing them from *ugonotti* (French Calvinist Huguenots). But according to a fellow prisoner in the prisons of the Venetian Council of Ten, he was in the pay of the Huguenot leader, the Duke of Condé, and part of French schemes to destabilise the Venetian religious scene. Spinola moved between various meeting places and discussions; sermons given at San Matteo di Rialto and open air scenes near the Rialto, discussions in Domenigo Gottardo's apothecary shop near

San Fantin (where donations were collected to support the proselytisers or accused in prison, and where Spinola may have encountered Pietro Carnesecchi), and a *ridotto* (gambling den), organised for patricians by Andrea da Ponte, who was to flee to Geneva.

Among Spinola's contacts was a fellow poet, Andrea di Ugoni (see above). Between then and his recantation in 1565 in Venice, Ugoni was moved by reading the works of Zwingli, Bullinger and Calvin, by sermons heard at San Matteo, and by events in France, about which he wrote to Queen Catherine de' Medici and the King of Bohemia. Ugoni on recantation – and on revealing many names of religious controversialists in Brescia, Vicenza and Venice – was leniently treated, being released to house confinement – in rooms rented from the painter Titian, who seemingly preferred renting the floor below him to the religiously suspect rather than common prostitutes (*meretrice*). Key patricians influenced by Spinola, also treated leniently by the inquisitors, included Giacomo Malipiero a lawyer, whose *processo* in June 1565 was revealing of Spinola's views, and Antonio Loredan.

Spinola's informative prison companion Dionisio Gallo played a complex role. A Frenchman from Gisors and the College rector in Lisieux in the early 1560s, he became a mystical prophet, moved by the Virgin, and an admirer of St Brigid of Sweden. He badgered the French court of Charles IX and his mother Queen Catherine de'Medici to promote a crusade to convert Turks and Jews. Unwelcome in Paris, he moved by late 1565 to Turin and Duke Emmanuele Filiberto's court. Later he was welcomed by Duke Cosimo in Florence, but after a public row in the Duomo with the papal Nunzio (Bernardino Brisegno), he was imprisoned on the Nunzio's order (in Cosimo's absence). Released but banished, Dionisio visited the Ferrara court, then Rome, before reaching Venice in mid-1565, hoping that Venice would lead a real reformation and crusade. Here he was supported by leading patricians, like Giusto Morosini, and young men from the Corner, Mocenigo, Miani, Da Canal, Contarini and Emo families. These patricians seemed to want a reform of the church from within. Some like Antonio Loredan were influenced by Savonarola, and notably his *Oracolo, il qual trattava de renovatione Ecclesiae*, which Dionisio was later to reformulate.[33] A reforming prophet like Dionisio could be welcomed by them. He preached reform in the courtyard of the Doge's palace and, when failing to obey the Inquisition's order to desist as an unlicensed preacher, he was imprisoned. He initially found himself in the civil police prison of the Signori di Notte. Other prisoners objected to his praying and singing litanies through the night, and severely beat him. On petitioning to be moved to prisons of the Ten in the Doge's palace (which also then served the Inquisition tribunal), he found himself sharing a cell with Spinola – but also with a Turk, who claimed to have been a torturer back home, and who proceeded to make life hell for Dionisio Gallo and Francesco Spinola. They both, however continued to preach and pray loudly, to the annoyance of other prisoners. On Dionisio's evidence he and Spinola had a complex relationship; they shared some ideas about a need for reform of the church, a basic anticlericalism, which saw the impiety of the clergy as the root of problems, and for a while Dionisio seemed to reject purgatory. But Dionisio accused Spinola of giving false testimony against him (probably under torture), implying he shared more heretical views. He ended up pleading for Spinola's life, claiming that given time he could turn him into a true Catholic reformer. His pleas for Spinola were in vain; he himself was released but banished and fled to the protection of the D'Este Duke of Ferrara.

We will return to the Inquisition later. In this above case-study the person drowned, Spinola, was the one who was seemingly most outspoken, who argued with, and influenced a wide range of people in various cities and who propounded a full range of heretical beliefs. This also highlights that in the 1560s, as official reform moved into a new phaze, northern Italy saw much reform advocacy and discussion in high circles. The hierarchy's problem was detecting the extent of the networking and open discussion, the differences between major heresiarchs (like Spinola) in sympathy with Luther, Zwingli or Calvin and more traditional internal reformers distrustful of lax clergy and a too intrusive papacy, some of whom (like Dionisio) might be dangerous as crowd pullers if not as heterodox subversives. The threat of French influences was taken seriously, given that both the Florentine and Ferrara courts had significant links with the French royal families.

2 *The Council of Trent and Bases for Continuing Reform*

The Council of Trent, operating in three separate periods (1545–47, 1550–51 and 1562–63), was one of the major Councils of the Church, but historically one of the most significant attempts to produce a body of legislation. It was and is important, whether one criticises or praises it for what it did or did not do. It has been heavily attacked on all sides. For some, a general council of the Church was inaugurated to attempt reconciliation between 'Protestants' and the Roman Catholic Church. It certainly concluded in general as an affirmation of the most conservative theological doctrines, intransigent against doubters, and with norms for ensuring that such views and practices prevailed in its aftermath. Protestants might have deemed it irrelevant as well as a betrayal, but they had to take cognisance of it as it guided the Roman Catholic opponents' behaviour against them, and philo-Protestants within the Catholic areas. Catholics have diversely criticised the legislation for being too weak or too authoritarian.

Background and Criticisms

Much criticism past and present has been unrealistic and counterfactual. My main concern here is with the Council's decrees as foundations or guides for continuing re-formation of the institutional church, with what it taught and believed, how Catholics at all social levels might subsequently behave. The conclusion of the Council in December 1563 (too hurriedly, from the unrealised fear that the

Pope would imminently die, rendering all the decisions null), and the ratification, printing and circulation of the decrees at least in Italy by June 1564 did mark a crucial stage in a longer process of reforming church and society. Irrespective of the merits or defects of what went into print, the church and its supporters had norms as a basis for reform; or as means to stop change.[1]

The Council of Trent met intermittently over 18 years, in 3 stages; and such a Council had been seriously considered from about 1530. The Council thus lacked continuity of purpose and personnel. Between stages, forward planning was lacking on how the renewal might proceed; understandably since few were certain that the Council would be recalled, and in what form. For the third and final stage, 1562–63, it was bitterly disputed whether this was a new Council, or a continuation. If seen as a new Council, as French and Imperial representatives argued, various decisions and decrees from 1545–47 and 1551–52 might be revisited and changed. If a continuance, which Philip II of Spain and most in the Curia argued, some more ambivalent declarations might not be reviewed. In particular Philip and Cardinal Inquisitors feared reconsideration of the 1547 Decree on Justification, as was made clear when the Patriarch of Aquileia, Giovanni Grimani, who was under deep suspicion for having supported the views of *spirituali* and sheltered some heretics, asked to have his case heard before the assembled fathers at Trent in 1562. Pius IV fudged the issue whether the Council was new or not, but in effect it was a continuation, and little was 'revisited'. Technically, none of the decrees were canonically fixed until the whole collection was ratified by the Pope in 1564; but some decrees were clearly treated as definitive by inquisitors and others in the interim.

A general Council of the Church was considered through the 1530s, with conflicting motives; to reach accommodation with some of the various Protestant factions, or to clarify what the Catholic teaching was on controversial issues such as Justification and Salvation, the interpretation of Scripture, the role of good works, the number and nature of Sacraments, and/or as a way of reforming behaviour and morals, to remove targets of anticlerical criticism. Hindsight indicates that the failure of discussions with Lutherans at the Colloquy of Ratisbon in 1541 ended the hopes of a compromise and reconciliation, but some attending the Council from 1545, when it finally started genuinely sought compromise, and that dim hope remained in 1550–51. By the third stage it was clear to virtually all that the Council was an affirmation of orthodox Catholic teaching, based on the more 'traditional' or conservative interpretation of St Paul and St Augustine's teachings; and a platform for disciplined reform of members of the church, under papal leadership. The validity of the Council was challenged, notably outside Italy, for this papal triumphalist conclusion, and for it being essentially an 'Italian' council. Particularly in 1545–47 and 1550–51, the decisions were made by a small group, mainly Italians under papal influence. Part of the delay in calling a Council and getting it started had been to answer such a fear. Trent was finally agreed upon as a city lying in the jurisdiction of the Holy Roman Empire under the Emperor Charles V, but primarily Italian speaking, and in the diocese of a fairly independent-minded episcopal family (Madruzzo), whose leading members, whether as bishop or coadjutor were mostly absent! A plague scare encouraged most of the Council Fathers to move in March 1547 to Bologna, the second city of the Papal State, which Charles V's supporters considered illegitimate. Some useful debates took place there (till September), but no formal decrees were agreed, in deference to this view.

The accusations that the Council was flawed by the paucity of attendees, and that too many were Italians and papal voting-fodder need some comment. The ambivalent Spanish attitude is relevant for 'Italy', since Philip II and his successors ruled in the Kingdom of Naples and Lombardy. About 400 to 500 clergy could have attended and voted: Diocesan Bishops from 'loyal' areas, Generals of Religious Orders, and leading Abbots – no Abbesses of course. When the Council finally opened in Trent in December 1545, 30 participants were able to vote: 4 Archbishops (Aix, Armagh, Palermo and Uppsala), 21 Bishops (16 of them Italian), and 5 Generals. More drifted in, so that 60–70 voted on the major issues, three-quarters of them Italian. The 1550–51 sessions saw similar numbers and biases. The third period in 1562 opened with 109 Cardinals, Archbishops and Bishops (85 Italian), 4 Abbots and 4 Generals. The rousing ratification of the Council's work in December 1563 named 216 prelates: 6 Cardinals, 196 Patriarchs, Archbishops and Bishops, 7 Abbots and 7 Generals.[2] The Spanish, French and Imperial presence, and influence had been more significant. There were *zelanti* Italians voting at the behest of the Papal Legates, but it is hard to gauge the extent of this; as with the pressure of Italian and non-Italian secular figures. That such pressure was perceived as a problem, but one that could be overcome, and that an individual could be subject to conflicting pressures, is indicated by the Bishop Pietro Camaiani of Fiesole, writing to Duke Cosimo of Tuscany:

> I have voted according to my conscience , and I cannot change it even if it were to cost me my life. I am devoted to the Pope, and I remain obedient to you, my Duke, in all worldly matters, but I value the salvation of my soul too highly to be able to vote against my convictions at the council. I am a grown man and I know what I have to do ... But I have no doubt that the prelates who are upright and do not behave in a sycophantic servility are in the long run performing a better service to the authority of the Holy See and the papacy than the others.[3]

Cardinal Legates Girolamo Seripando and Giovanni Morone in fact found the Italian *zelanti* claque a hindrance to effective business as they tried to conclude the Council effectively.

The 'national' issue can be exaggerated. Italians bulked large in the main formal votes in sessions held in the Trent Cathedral, but much discussion took place elsewhere in committees, where non-Italians played significant roles, and where 'Italians' showed divided views. Andrè Duval and Hubert Jedin, studying evidence on debates behind the scenes on Justification, the origins of episcopal authority, Extreme Unction, Confession, or Clandestine Marriages show lively discussion and complex voting or advocacy patterns.[4] Though not able to vote in open Council sessions, numerous theologians advised and made verbal or written contributions more privately. At the beginning in 1545, 42 theologians were in attendance, 16 of them Spanish; and between 50 and 80 joined in the deep theological debates in 1547. In the small committees and congregations intellectual weight came from Spanish theologians like the Dominican, Thomist Melchior Cano (notably on the Eucharist), Domingo de Soto and Alfonso de Castro; and the Jesuits, Alfonso Salmerón and Diego Lainez; from the Germans, G. Gropper and E. Billick.

Most theological issues had received serious discussion, often with an input of considerable historical scholarship, though arguably, with at times some blinkered and conservative views of early church beliefs and practices, or even more recent norms (as with married clergy, or the enclosure of nuns). Tridentine rulings had weight behind them, even if then and since Catholics have regretted the final verdicts. As important for our focus is a recognition that the 'Italian' input was divided. During the 1546–47 debates on Justification, Bishop Pietro Bertano of Fano took the imperial side rather than Rome's. In 1562, Cardinal Seripando and the bishop of Modena joined the Iberian Archbishops of Braga and Granada in a minority group opposing the proposition on the nature of the Mass. The Venetian Bishops were heavily divided in the hot debate about the validity of clandestine marriages – with Bishop Daniele Barbaro (often a supporter of the French Cardinal Charles Guise of Lorraine, to the annoyance of Patriarch Trevisano), arguing that marriage should be considered rationally and that a clandestine marriage was irrational. In the fraught discussions on whether episcopal residency was by God's law (*ius divinum*), as heavily argued by powerful figures from France and Spain (but also Domenico Bollani of Brescia), or by human law (*ius humanum*), Cardinals Seripando and Gonzaga were both very reluctant to push the latter view, as demanded by the papacy, and earned the wrath of Pius IV, who curbed the debate. Here Italian clergy were heavily split.[5]

Giuseppe Alberigo has argued that throughout the Council, Italians held a multiplicity of views, and that powerful Italian clerics played strong minority roles, even if threatened (sometimes physically), by the overzealous papal claque of lesser bishops (who had greater need of the right promotion!)[6] Divided views and conflicts were to continue among Italians running the early modern Italian churches.

The Council's Main Work

My concern here cannot be with the long story of the Council and its debates for which well-balanced digests are readily available, as in Michael Mullett's *The Catholic Reformation*, but with key aspects of the three periods of meeting, with particular reference for immediate developments within Italy, and effects on post-Tridentine reform. The decrees, on ratification in 1564, were accepted by all states within Italy; unlike with Catholic states outside Italy, where some rulers gave no official recognition of the decrees, or hedged them with qualifications. Through the three stages of the Council, discussion and decision-making were on two strands: first, theological definitions, teaching and doctrine, to counteract heresy (decrees *de extirpandis haeresibus*), and second, the reorganisation of the church, the conduct of its members, and the reform of abuses (decrees *de moribus reformandis*). In the first two periods, 1545–47 and 1551–52, the first category had priority, though foundations were made for the second; the final period, 1562–63, consolidated some doctrinal positions, but the debates and conflicts over the nature of the church, over its organisation and how to reform abuses predominated.

The 1545–47 sessions early on ratified with little trouble the Nicene (or Nicaeno–Constinopolitan) Creed from the Council of Nicaea as a basic statement of faith and devotion. This was a stance with which Lutherans at least could agree; and so far there were few anti-Trinitarians to worry. However, room for compromise was lessened when it was ruled that in interpreting the Bible, the texts of the Bible and Tradition (the long history of interpretation) were equally valid, 'with the Holy Spirit dictating'. In practice subsequent debates about access to the Bible in the vernacular led to the ban on such translations in the 1596 Clementine Index, with the effect that for most Italians, Tradition (mediated through the clergy) became more important than scripture itself. By the summer of 1546 the fathers were focusing on the thorny problems of original sin, justification, grace, free will and predestination; they thus entered the central theological battle ground. As a positive declaration (in Session 6) the Council decided:

> Man is justified by faith and freely; these words are understood in that sense in which the uninterrupted unanimity of the Catholic Church has held and expressed them, namely, that we are therefore said to be justified by faith, because faith is the beginning of human salvation, the foundation and root of all justification, without which it is impossible to please God, and to come to the fellowship of His sons; and we are therefore said to be justified gratuitously, because none of those things that precede justification, either faith or works, merit that grace of justification.[7]

Elaboration was often by anathemas; that is, condemnation of opinions deemed unacceptable, some of which reflected the genuine views of Protestants, while others were imaginary or a considerable distortion. Crucially, in terms of relations not only with German and Swiss Protestants, but also with Italian philo-Protestants and *spirituali*, the Council anathematised the belief that 'the sinner is justified by faith *alone*', castigating Luther's crucial interpretation of *Romans* 3. While the Council also anathematised the view that 'man can be justified before God by his own good works, whether done by his own natural powers or through the teaching of the law, without divine grace through Jesus Christ', it emphasised the value of good works as signs of grace received. The 'good works' defence had a significant impact on the subsequent philanthropic work of Religious Orders and lay confraternities. Interestingly, the great modern theologian, Hans Küng, who has his own problems with Pope John Paul II, commented: 'The decree on justification, which is the glory of the Council, accepts what is valid in the Reformers' position to a surprising degree'.[8]

Discussion and rulings on the sacraments followed, and further consolidation of the lines between the Roman position and 'Reformers' came when the Council ruled that seven Sacraments had been instituted by Christ and his apostles: Baptism, Confirmation, the Eucharist, Confession/Penance, Ordination, Extreme Unction and Marriage. Many Protestants had decided that the only Sacraments were Baptism and the Eucharist (or for them, the Lord's Supper). Through the Tridentine and post-Tridentine periods Italians were to challenge the number and validity of the Sacraments. The subject of the Eucharist was a major feature of the 1550–51 sessions, leading to the crucial decree (October 1551) on Transubstantiation, that

> Through consecration of the bread and wine there comes about a conversion of the whole substance of the bread into the substance of the body of Christ our Lord, and of the whole substance of the wine into the substance of his blood. And this conversion is by the Holy Catholic Church conveniently and properly called Transubstantiation.[9]

The decrees in the 1545–47 and 1550–51 periods covering the organisation of the church and ways of reforming morals and behaviour, laid considerable stress on the roles of bishops, to ensure reforms through their personal residence, and through visitations of their dioceses and parishes, in some control over Religious Orders, in the proper examination of candidates for ordination. Sessions in 1551 spent considerable time trying to ensure suitable priests in the first place, and their proper behaviour subsequently. The ground was laid for the later decision that diocesan seminaries should be established to train them (see Chapter 6).

When the Council Fathers reassembled in January 1562, much had changed, and this final stage became significantly different.[10] The central papal scene, and the situation in Italy had been profoundly affected by the rigorist, at times brutal, attitudes, of Gian Pietro Carafa, and his reign as Pope Paul IV (1555–59). Ideas of compromise with Protestants, and Italians sympathetic to some Lutheran doctrines, were essentially removed. The Council determinedly consolidated traditional Catholicism, to counteract 'the pest of heresy and schism', as Pius IV stressed in calling for the Council.[11] The Peace of 1559 brought hope that the Council could progress with some urgency; but is also meant that the politico–religious interests of Spain and France in particular would be more rigorously pursued. In the event 'nationalist' interests and prejudices (in central political terms, and cultural ones as well), produced intense conflicts between the 'Spanish', 'French' and 'Italian' interests, not just verbally, but in street struggles between adherents. While theological discussions and rulings continued, much more was said and done about 'reforming' church organisation and behaviour than in the two previous periods. I will concentrate on aspects that most affected the socio-religious situation in Italy, and conflicts in the post-Tridentine period.

In doctrinal elaboration, past positions on the Mass or Eucharist, purgatory and prayer were reinforced. The laity would not normally receive communion in both kinds, but only the bread; they would be denied the chalice, except where the Pope gave very special permission for its use – as in parts of the Empire where the Emperor and Duke of Bavaria wanted concessions to keep certain areas Catholic. The justification for the bread-only communion was that the bread contained both the body and blood of Christ, (as ruled by the Council of Constance). Denying the chalice to the laity marked a distinction between clergy and laity. This particular view of communion was not apparently a major contentious point subsequently among Italians, though possibly an issue in the Inquisition's questioning of Paolo Veronese's *Last Supper* painting (Chapter 10).

The Council reinforced the view that the Mass is the representation of Christ's passion (not just a commemorative act). Those present at the Mass 'obtain mercy and find grace in seasonable aid. For, appeased by this sacrifice, the Lord grants the grace and the gift of penitence and pardons even the gravest crimes and sins.' In relation to Christ's sacrifice on the Cross 'the fruits of that bloody sacrifice ... are received more abundantly through this unbloody one, so far is the latter in any way from derogating from the former'.[12] Guidelines and rules about the Mass followed from this attitude, and led to significant policies. The Mass was to be celebrated in Latin, not the vernacular, said or sung without distortion, or improper music. The laity were encouraged to be penitential witnesses rather than participants in the liturgy. The Host came to be emphasised, put on display in a monstrance, adored as a symbol of Christ's sacrifice. The altar area was set apart, and up, from the laity; to give the celebrant respectful room for celebration. Internal architecture and altar decoration was adapted and developed to add emphasis, and create the scene for theatrical display (see Chapter 10). The laity were to have a good view, so impeding screens and tombs were to be removed. When masses were well celebrated this might give an emotional charge, but congregational participation was even further reduced, in contrast to the reformed churches. Modern Catholics have criticised or regretted this, but Hubert Jedin defended this approach, for creating a clear distinction from Protestants. Non-Tridentine policies, however encouraged the laity to participate in many other ceremonies and devotions, especially offices of the Virgin, and to confess and receive communion more often than the Tridentine minimum of Easter confession and communion. Confraternities promoted such lay participation.

In the context of Sacraments, but with major social implications, the discussion and rulings on marriage proved very lively and fraught, especially in the final sessions, though issues of clandestine marriages, and marital indissolubility had been raised back in August 1547.[13] Much debate focused on clandestine marriages: whether a marital agreement between a couple was a valid marriage, if the promises had been made secretly by them, without parental permission or public and legal recognition. The November 1563 decree canons resolved that marriage was a sacramental act performed by the couple concerned (as Adam and Eve had set the precedent). Provided they were physically able, and not barred by laws of consanguinity, their promises made a valid sacramental act in the eyes of God. It was the only Sacrament not requiring the active participation of a priest. Such an interpretation left open the social problem of clandestine marriages. Some contributors worried about couples who would thus create a marriage in a secret deal, which was subsequently deemed unacceptable as a social misalliance by one or both of the wider families involved. Others were concerned that after a couple had consummated a private wedding sacrament, one (usually the male) would renege, and deny the 'wedding' had occurred. The famous, or infamous Canon, *Tametsi dubitandum* ruled that secret marriages of consenting couples were valid, even if opposed by parents.[14] The Council's resolution amounted to a bold legal claim by the church to being the final and sufficient arbiter of a valid marriage, and to a double validity concept. Hitherto marriages had as much, or more (depending on the area and locally operative laws), to do with civil contracts and social recognition, as a religious arrangement. Marriages could readily be organised without resort to any clergy or religious ceremony or blessing. Now all was supposedly standardised under church law.

Under normal circumstances a couple (or their representatives) must give public notice that they wanted to marry (possibly formally exchanging betrothal vows (*de futuro*), and have such intention made public by banns. Assuming no impediments were found, the ceremony of the couple exchanging vows (*de praesenti*) must be conducted before two witnesses, in church, and in the presence of a priest, though he need not express his consent, or be an active participant. A blessing should follow, though this might be delayed if in Lent or Advent, before consummation completed the sacrament. Under episcopal authority concessions might be given to avoid a public declaration of the banns, or having the ceremony in the parish church. If these rules were not followed, and no dispensations given, the church could rule that the sacrament was valid in the eyes of God (preventing any other marriage while both were alive), but the wedding was invalid, so the couple could be separated and prevented from acting as married – unless and until they conformed to the rules with due ceremony.

The Council opposed the pleas of some that parental consent be required; though some states, such as Piedmont, tried to impose this as a secular adjunct for validity. However, the church leaders at Trent had been intent on protecting couples acting in good faith, from being bullied by parents or overlords into marrying somebody against their will, or preventing them marrying their desired partner. In its theological and social claims in relation to marriage the church was making a dramatic stance. As Gabriella Zarri has stressed marriage was sacralised (raising its status), clericalised (at least initially), and made a greater part of the church's social disciplining. However, educating the public about the new marital systems, and enforcing them, was to prove one of the most time- and paper-consuming aspects of post-Tridentine episcopal legislation, preaching and decision-making, as we shall note again (see Chapter 5).[15]

Another major struggle at Trent, publicised in (un)diplomatic exchanges and in the streets, concerned the position of bishops. In July 1563 the Council ruled that bishops were entrusted with the care or cure of souls (*cura animarum*), by divine right (*ius divinum*) and not just by church law. This ruling had various implications, particularly that the bishop on being ordained was obligated to reside and exercise his pastoral role, and not be called away for long periods to serve the church elsewhere, or be a pluralist; and once a consecrated bishop always a bishop. However the papal faction, against the Spanish, secured a decision that while a consecrated bishop was wedded to the Church, his bond with a particular diocese was not inalienable, and he could be moved on papal order, or be left unallocated.[16] This was seen as a papal victory over bishops, as was lamented by Philip II at the time, and in the early seventeenth century by Paolo Sarpi, the Venetian Servite friar who led the Republic's propaganda campaign against the Papal Interdict in 1606, and who went on to write (and have published in London), a brilliant polemical History of the Council.[17]

Despite this verdict, much Tridentine legislation (largely pushed through in November and December 1563), and recommendations backed the pastoral and discipline roles of bishops.[18] Bishops were expected not only to be resident most of the time, but to exercise leadership through regular preaching, and control over parish priests, when the parochial system was to be reformed and strengthened. In theory bishops were to hold annual diocesan synods of their leading clergy to sort out problems and give instructions. The metropolitans were to hold provincial councils every three years.[19] Reality fell well short of such ideals, (Chapter 4 and Appendix). Bishops were to organise regular Visitations of their diocese, whether personally or through suffragan bishops and vicars general. Because the educational levels of many parish priests were recognised as defective, bishops were to create diocesan seminaries to provide better trained clergy, unless other educational institutions such as universities or colleges provided by Religious Orders were adequate. The selection of priests for parishes was expected to be open, if possible subject to competition, and with bishops checking on credentials, suitability, and that pluralism was not involved. Bishops were to exercise more control over hospitals, 'pious places' such as orphanages, lay confraternities, Monti di Pietà pawn-broking institutions. The justification for this episcopal involvement in institutions which had hitherto often jealously guarded lay independence, was that it was necessary to ensure that the last wills and testaments of donors were being fulfilled. Bishops should also insist on checking and ratifying the constitutions of lay confraternities and hospitals, even if they could not supervise regular practice. More vaguely bishops were told to ensure that churches were in good condition, that their decoration was seemly and not 'lascivious' (a favourite description); that the subject matter of paintings followed biblical texts, or well-established stories of the lives of Saints; that music was seemly, did not evoke lascivious thoughts (by echoing love songs), and that the word texts of the Mass and Offices were not rendered unintelligible by polyphonic excesses.

Tridentine legislation on the enclosure of nuns was to launch social battles. Stories, real or imaginary, about the immoral conduct of nuns, their relations with friars, priests or lay visitors, had provided propaganda ammunition for Protestants; this needed remedying. The Tridentine answer was to insist that all girls and women on taking their vows as nuns, should be firmly enclosed in convents, not venturing forth, and with very strict controls over who might visit the convent. This proved highly contentious and hard for bishops and heads of Orders to enforce, and had wide social implications, with adverse effects on the religious roles of women (Chapter 8).

Facing another Protestant criticism, the Council reinforced the doctrines of purgatory and of indulgences, but recognised that abuses had and did exist. Bishops were to ensure as they checked on their dioceses, that offering of indulgences for relief from a period in purgatory should be carefully controlled, and the whole doctrine of purgatory be clearly explained (or avoided) when dealing with the less educated. The Council also reinforced the importance and efficacy of invoking the intercession of Saints, in praying for the salvation of souls. While this had been and remained a significant area of attack for Italian reformers, as revealed in Inquisition denunciations, the post-Tridentine teaching and visual display was to add emphasis to the cult of the Virgin and Saints.

One of the late issues decided by the Council was the support for public penance, as part of the reconciliation process in the Sacrament of Penance (the central discussion of which had been in 1551). The push for public over merely private penance came apparently in 1562, largely from northern Italian bishops of rigorist disciplining inclinations. It won the day because the author of a 1562 history of confession, Mariano Vittori, which emphasised the role of public penance in church history, joined Cardinal Legate Morone's circle of advisors. Bishop Gerolamo Ragazzoni in celebrating the achievements of the Council as it concluded in December 1563 emphasised public penance as being the way 'to reinforce the staggering and nearly crumbling church discipline'.[20] The extent to which this was implemented connects with a current debate (to which we will return), on the extent to which confessors, linked with parish priests and inquisitors, using humiliating public penance, together created a coercive disciplining society.

The Council was concluded rather hurriedly, with some of the decrees rushed through in November–December 1563. Various reform matters were skimped or ignored, notably control over male Orders and monasteries, the reform of Princes, with their intrusion into church jurisdiction (which had been on the agenda). Hopes of some that the Council itself would modify Paul IV's notorious Index of Prohibited Books were not fulfilled, and this led to revision in Rome. Similarly, the papacy was left to produce major official texts: the Missal and Breviary, and a suitable Catechism for use by priests for the basic teaching of doctrine (even if other catechisms might also be sanctioned).

Genuine euphoria accompanied the closure of the Council in Trent cathedral. But it was not till June and July 1564, when the Pope had formally approved the Decrees, and copies of them had been printed for distribution, that reforming supporters of the Council could feel free to treat the work of the Council as the basis for action. Some in the Curia, worried that the implementation of certain decrees would affect their income, had delayed publication until 30 June 1564. However, surprisingly, the Venetian Senate moved fast, and by 22 July 1564 sent out orders for the decrees to be implemented generally, telling bishops in the Republic to publish them as soon as possible.[21] The papal ratification came with powerful provisos, to the alarm of conciliarists and secular rulers: no glosses on the texts of the decrees should be made without permission, and papal authority was needed to interpret for the implementation of decrees. This seemed like papal absolutism. In practice a Congregation of the Council became the chief vehicle for this process of interpretation; and diocesan synods could effectively produce their own decrees that might be seen as glosses or interpretations, without being necessarily vetted in Rome.

Whatever the criticisms of the Council procedures, its decrees or omissions, the outcome was impressive as a legislative activity. Statutes do not in themselves solve problems, but the published decrees provided some norms for future conduct, a general climate in which reform might take place, and doctrinal rulings to be used against opponents, or to enthuse adherents of the Roman Catholic Church. The potentially most effective decrees for post-Trent implementation were those concerning episcopal power in relation to their clergy and parishioners; for the creation of seminary education; for regularising Christian marriage; for enclosing nuns. Implementation was another matter; and personal views of modern commentators affect verdicts on whether the failure to fulfil certain reforms was disastrous (when episcopal and clerical control was limited), or beneficial (when diversity could remain, new initiatives be undertaken, and the laity have more roles to play).

Whatever the criticism of the Council, it speeded action. Once a council had been mooted as an or *the* answer to the Protestant challenges and Catholic reformers' own analyses of faults in the teaching and organisation of the Church, some reformers did lead the way in episcopal reform, as with G.M. Giberti (1495–1543) in Verona or Ercole Gonzaga (1505–63) in Mantua. But much potential reform was delayed while doctrine and practical reform measures awaited official sanction. Once the Council's work was ratified there was a call for action, and a stimulus, based on Tridentine norms. Reformers were likely to be selective in what they chose to implement, but further waves of action are detectable for the rest of the 1560s, and slower, steadier, reforms followed, while new forces joined those set in motion by Trent and the Tridentine generation.

General Problems over Implementation

Subsequent chapters will discuss how reform of church and society was or was not achieved in different aspects, because of or despite Trent. It is worth emphasising here some general factors that affected the speed and efficacy of post-Tridentine reform; personnel, money and jurisdiction.

While the character and attitudes of Popes and their immediate circles in Rome were important, dynamic reforming bishops and local enablers were essential. The quality of the episcopacy will be discussed in Chapter 4. Much depended on their willingness and ability to implement policies and utilise financial and human resources beneath them. The Venetian ambassador Giacomo Soranzo soon commented on the young papal nephew Carlo Borromeo: 'He gives a unique example to everyone, so one can reasonably say that he alone has more effect on the Court of Rome than all the decrees of the Council together'.[22] Cardinal Carlo Borromeo's own dynamism as Archbishop of Milan (as well as activity in the closing stages of the

Council as nephew of Pope Pius IV), and his inspiration to many others who became vicars general and bishops, made a considerable difference.

The Milan diarist Giambattista Casale enthusiastically recorded on 29 August 1564, how Borromeo (who was detained in Rome by his papal uncle), had sent his Vicar General Niccolò Ormaneto 'to publish in Milan and the whole diocese of Milan the decrees of the Holy Council of Trent and to see that they were put into execution up to every iota, by order of his Holiness'. On that day Ormaneto summoned all the clergy who had a benefice to submit to obedience. He also organised a major celebratory procession, including children from the Christian Doctrine schools. He then held a three-day *Concilio* of the clergy to discuss implementation. Additionally, he had the credentials of confessors checked. This was a dynamic Vicar General, later a notable Apostolic Visitor of other dioceses, and then Bishop in his own right (Padua). As we shall elaborate this was rapid model reaction to the reform call; but hard for many to follow.[23]

But even with personal dynamism, money was a key problem. Money was needed to establish and run the desired seminaries and colleges; to restore and develop churches that were often in a dilapidated state outside the wealthy cities and parishes; to fund enclosed nunneries, and the philanthropy of hospitals and confraternities; to support suitable clergy in remoter dioceses and parishes. The available wealth was very unevenly distributed, and making it fairer was extremely difficult. Reform tended to move faster in the wealthier parts of Italy, though some bishops did wonders in poor remoter dioceses. But a theoretically wealthy diocese might not derive full benefits, since that wealth might be siphoned off to reward or support papal relatives, cardinals, and friends of secular rulers. Some of the efficacy of reform depended on the ability of a bishop, abbot, General of a Religious Order to secure the patronage and wealth from others to boost the resources of their own institution. As Olwen Hufton's work is showing, funding Catholic reform was very complex.[24] Some of this connected with jurisdictional rights.

The jurisdictional situation was fraught. Who had the right to reform and discipline whom? Raise money from whom? Or enter what properties? An unclarified area in the Trent legislation was the relationship of church and state, or clerical and lay institutions. Even where the church made specific claims – to control some hospitals or lay confraternities, city councils, princes or lay organisations readily challenged the bishop or his agents. Many were very protective of their patronage rights – over institutions or parochial benefices. Those kinds of jurisdictional confrontations one might expect, but within the church many jurisdictional struggles also developed as soon as any side wanted to change anything; as I have shown for the diocese of Perugia, which had several reforming bishops after Trent. Religious houses disliked interference from bishops, whether over their own convents and monasteries, or over their control of some parishes – as in the case of the great Benedictine house of San Pietro on the edge of Perugia. They objected to diverting revenues to a seminary or college not run by themselves. When reforming bishops wanted Rome's backing for their policies and jurisdictional claims, even within the Papal State, it was not necessarily forthcoming. The Pope might not wish to alienate a ruler or city council that opposed the bishop's reform. He might prefer to support a leading cardinal acting as protector of a Religious Order (and/or having a pension as a temporary administrator of a House), rather than his opposing bishop.[25] Archbishop Carlo Borromeo battled together with Rome against the Spanish Governor over the threat to introduce a branch of the Spanish Inquisition into Lombardy, but was on his own in other struggles to discipline religious houses, or control Carnival processions. The legal path to effective reform was lined with political obstacles. In interstate relations, the papacy had to be mindful of short and long-term political concerns. Did it keep the secular government content to secure support over Inquisition needs, or alienate that government by supporting the reforming bishop? Within the Papal State the Pope could be torn between the secular interests of the state, and the spiritual-ecclesiastical policies of an episcopal reformer; the latter might well lose. But the Pope might agree to appoint an Apostolic Visitor, with more powers than an ordinary bishop, when the latter needed help against resistant convents or confraternities, or when the ordinary was lax or scared to take initiatives.

With the Council concluded, the Italian Church or churches had to combine various policies. The call was there to reorganise church structures from central government to parochial consolidation. This was, as the controversial liberal theologian Hans Küng put it in 1961, 'an armaments programme and a plan of campaign'.[26] Various key documents had still to be produced: a standard Roman Missal, Breviary and Catechism, and a revised Index of Prohibited Books. But there were also huge worries about remaining heretical groups, with more key inquisitorial investigations underway or imminent. Within a short time the Calvinist campaigning out of Geneva, which had increased as the European wars were being brought to an end (and finished in 1559), was to add to religious and secular conflict in the Spanish Netherlands, as it had already done in France. The Papacy needed to create barriers, or counter propaganda, to prevent further infection of the Italian peninsula.

Crisis management of perceived heresy trouble spots might impede structural reform. Roman authorities were concerned in the aftermath of Trent that heretical beliefs persisted and were still well embedded in artisan classes in some cities. Pius V campaigned between 1566 and 1568 to eradicate evangelical remnants, both by some harsh punishments, and by persuading people to reveal their past errors, promising pardon if they appeared voluntarily before inquisitors – as in Modena. Investigations in 1567–68 showed that Modenese urban groups had been heavily influenced by writings such as the *Beneficio di Cristo* and the *Sommario della Santa Cristiana*, which stressed salvation by faith alone, not by works. Men like Giovanni Maria Maranelli (alias Tagliadi), and Geminiano Tamburino confessed to having owned and read such works back in the 1540s, though claiming they had put them aside once the Index or the bishop had indicated they were heretical. Whether they had genuinely retreated to orthodoxy, it was clear from some others, like Pietro Curione and Antonio da Cervia (who fled from Modena and was captured and sent to the stake in Bologna in 1567), still maintained their 'Lutheran', evangelical and congregationalist beliefs, and remained strongly anticlerical. The Roman authorities had evidence that they had much to eradicate or argue against.[27]

Ready for Action?

Given continuing problems within Italy, and threats or distractions elsewhere – whether in Europe north of the Alps, or in confronting the Ottoman Turks in the eastern Mediterranean and north Africa – how well placed was the Catholic Church in the mid-1560s? The central papacy was consolidating itself, and moving closer to an absolute position. The Carafa papacy had proved very contentious, ending in some chaos in 1559 on Paul IV's death. Prestige and equanimity had been largely restored by Pius IV. Improved relations with Spain (whatever the tensions over the Council), as the major political power in the Italian peninsula, made for a somewhat easier position in promoting reforms outwith the Papal State. Control over the Papal State had been consolidated, with elites of major cities like Bologna, Perugia, Viterbo being persuaded that it was more profitable to work with Rome than against it. However, rural banditry was distracting, and worsened through to the 1590s. Within Rome, papal domination over the organs of government had increased, the power and influence of cardinals in concistories had declined; and the Pope increasingly worked through specialist groups and institutions. By the mid-1560s the Inquisition at the centre and in tribunals elsewhere was fairly well established to coordinate assaults on remaining heretical centres and key individuals. By August 1564 a Cardinals' Congregation of the Council was in place to interpret and seek to implement Council decrees. The number of bishoprics in Italy was vast (Chapter 4 and Appendix), but already in place were influential exemplars who could develop programmes and inspire others. The reform precedents of early Catholic reforming bishops like Giberti in Verona or Ercole Gonzaga in Mantua, could be carried forward by men they inspired, like Niccolò Ormaneto.

Alongside the bishops, as both allies and contestants, were the new Religious Orders. By the mid-1560s the Jesuits, Oratorians, Theatines, Ursulines and Barnabites were recognised and consolidated for action through the cities and rural areas. Even what was to be the most dynamic branch of the Franciscans, the Capuchins had made some recovery from the setback and scandal of the defection to Protestantism of their preacher and leader, Ochino in 1539. The scene was set for the implementation of Tridentine reform within Italy, with a range of suitable personnel and institutions. How far they could overcome the general obstacles already outlined, and work their way through conflicting policies and agenda will be discussed through the rest of the book.

We must next turn to a fuller consideration of the nature and efficacy of central Roman organisations to conduct both normative reform of members, and to curb the remaining threats to orthodoxy.

3 *Centre and Peripheries: The Papacy, Congregations, Religious Orders*

The processes involved in implementing Tridentine decrees and wider Catholic reforming agendas required leadership from the Papacy and its central government – of the church generally and of the supporting Papal State – and cooperation of secular authorities, the episcopal system, Religious Orders and lay religious organisations; what we might loosely call the peripheries. This chapter will consider aspects of the central system under the Papacy as far as they are concerned with the Italian scene. A system of Congregations was developed and reformed, supposedly to offer leadership, to coordinate the work of church personnel and institutions, and exercise discipline (as notably with the Inquisition). The new Religious Orders, most of which developed a central organisation in Rome, were products of reform attitudes and policies; they also could have central roles as coordinators, trainers, disseminators of spiritual guides to the peripheries in Italy and further afield. This chapter focuses on the structures and some policies at the centre. Other chapters will reveal in passing problems and complicated reactions in different peripheries, whether meant geographically or in institutional extensions from the hub. It is easiest to outline the emergence and general nature of the new Religious Orders here, and exemplify their different and varied activities as they associated and cooperated with other institutions; discussed in several subsequent chapters. Many tensions existed between central institutions and personnel, which were replicated in conflicts in localities.

Bishops, local monasteries, lay confraternities learned to adapt, under pressures coming both from the centre, and from rivals, ecclesiastical and secular, on their doorstep. Jurisdictional conflicts abounded. The frustration of attempts to exercise more control, quasi-absolutist, from the Papal centre, crossing into rival political territory, was most notably encountered in Paul V's conflicts with the Venetian Republic, leading to the Interdict Crisis of 1606–07. For lack of space, this high profile conflict must stand for many lesser conflicts between church and state elsewhere. It was a clear warning against excessive papal bids to control the periphery.

The Papacy

While the power of the Catholic Church and of the Papacy was diminished in geographical terms for Europe because of the Reformation, arguments continue over the remaining powers of the Papacy, politically, diplomatically spiritually, and the priorities of post-Tridentine Papal policies. Popes wore many hats or tiaras.[1] They were the spiritual and pastoral head of the Catholic Church for all those recognising that apostolic succession from St Peter. They had ultimate responsibility for church doctrine, even if the overriding doctrine of Papal Infallibility was not imposed until the nineteenth century (Vatican Council 1870–71). The Pope was bishop of the diocese of Rome, he was political sovereign of the Papal State. Through his diplomatic services he could exercise varying influences on international diplomacy and warfare, even if his own military and naval powers were limited. In so far as he controlled or influenced Religious Orders, especially the Jesuits, he could exercise worldwide influences from South America to the East Indies. There is little doubt that Papal control over the remnant of the Catholic Church and over the Papal State protecting it in central Italy, was more centralised and 'absolute'. Some of us have argued that the Papal State was at the forefront of political absolutism, which developed in the sixteenth century as a positive political doctrine to enhance state control in the interests of most subjects, and override selfish factionalism of overmighty barons or municipal elites. Of course practicalities limited that absolutism.[2]

Recent analysts of the post-Tridentine Papacy have debated the priorities and motivations behind the power and policies. Paolo Prodi has emphasised the political interests of Popes, and their family concerns as rulers of Papal State and Church, with secular interests increasingly overriding measures to implement Tridentine policies for the reform of members of the Church; they impeded the pastoral work of bishops, Religious Orders and clergy. However, the process was accompanied by an increased clericalisation of church government. Adriano Prosperi has concentrated on the repressive and dictatorial side of post-Tridentine religious policies, and emphasised the Popes' roles and particular interests in the operation of the Inquisition and, from 1571 the allied Congregation of the Index, emphasising that a number of Popes had previously played leading roles as Cardinal Inquisitors (Paul IV, Pius V). Others had been inquisitors or Holy Office consultants (Marcellus II, Sixtus V, Urban VII, Innocent IX, Clement X). Prosperi also sees modified policies towards the sacraments of confession and penance as adjuncts to imposing a conscience and thought control over the people. Having highlighted and outlined the Prodi emphasis on the 'Papal Prince' and Prosperi's equation of Papal Office with the Holy Office in control of tribunals of conscience, A.D. Wright draws attention to papal concerns for pastoral care, within their own diocese of Rome, but also more widely in church policies. Most post-Tridentine Popes were concerned to make Rome a city fit to lead the Catholic Church, a theatre displaying the spirituality, philanthropy and cultural vitality of a revived Church; a city that could attract both the mighty who could influence worldwide policies, and humble pilgrims. Alexander VII most consciously redeveloped and propagandised Rome as a Theatre for the Church.[3] (See Chapter 10) To characterise the post-Tridentine papacy as being narrowly in any one mould seems dangerous, as William Hudon underlines. Most Popes had family political interests, a concern for political power, interest in key Inquisition activities, pastoral care, and the image of Rome. One could shift the prioritisation between them for any given Pope, but I am not sure any Pope serving for any length of time ignored any aspect. The major changes of priority probably concerned the wider, non-Italian, world, rather than the Italian scene of our concern.

The Pope, once elected, had considerable power within the Church over spiritual and organisational affairs. The combination of spiritual power (if not 'infallible'),with some temporal power in an increasingly centralised Papal State after about 1540, could make the Pope seem the most 'absolute' of European rulers. But many limitations existed. Through the period Popes had for political reasons to be wary of pushing doctrinal decisions (as over Jansenism or the

Immaculate Conception of the Virgin), when leading Catholic rulers had decided and conflicting views of their own. We are more concerned here with the power of the Popes to implement reform policies within Italy. The power of Spain within mainland Italy, ruling the Duchy of Lombardy and the Kingdom of Naples (even if theoretically the latter was a feudal dependency of the Pope until the eighteenth century), was restraining. Other states within Italy could prove extremely troublesome to Popes, as in the Venetian Interdict Crisis.

Conclaves that elected the Pope could be very lengthy and fraught with tension.[4] Deals might be done, and obligations incurred, that could inhibit the behaviour and policies of the man elected; and the winner might need both luck and acumen to be able to change policies. In our period conclave voters tried to secure commitments from those in contention for future action and support once elected, but these were evaded. Some of the most *papabile* candidates in the eyes of contemporaries or later church historians – whether for intellectual and moral qualities, or diplomatic skills – were not elected. Most notably the Oratorian Cesare Baronio was vetoed by the pro-Spanish faction in 1605 because his historical scholarship challenged Spanish pretensions in Sicily. This was a great relief to him, because like Reginald Pole he had no wish to be Pope; and he had even been 'forced' to accept the Cardinal's hat.[5] Many Popes were elderly, and sometimes sickly, possibly inhibiting dynamic reform – though Sixtus V, elected as an elderly compromise candidate while more powerful Cardinals reconfigured their support, proved to be one of the most energetic Popes: as administrative reorganiser, hammer of troublemakers in the Papal State, and a major urban planner for Rome. Paul V (1605–21), elected in his mid-50s, was as irascible, if not as personally dynamic (leaving much to the notorious Cardinal nephew, Scipione Borghese). Innocent XII elected when 76 had a longish and not too disastrous reign, (1691–1700). One or two of the most potentially able elected died quickly: Marcellus II (1555: only in his mid-50s), Urban VII (1590, aged about 70), Gregory XIV (1590–91), Gregory XV (1621–23).[6] Counterfactually, one might argue that had Marcello Cervini lived longer, Catholic–Protestant relations might have become easier, and internal Catholic reform and theology more open-minded, given his reputation as a thoughtful humanist and pragmatist, when diplomat and bishop, and milder member of the Inquisition.[7]

Popes ruled theoretically through the College of Cardinals, having been elected by those Cardinals who could get to Rome in time.

Supporters had to be rewarded to some extent, which could drain resources.[8] Few powerful Cardinals could be fully trusted, since they would have an eye on the succession. This led to the use of key family members, the 'Cardinal nephew' (*nipote*), though he was not always in precisely that relationship (see List of Popes). The position, developed through the Renaissance period, was retained during the reforming post-Tridentine period, as a practical solution to political and administrative problems, even if it incurred adverse publicity. Cardinal nephews might be most important in running secular aspects of papal power, in diplomacy, in the Papal State, in financial affairs, as with Michele Bonelli (for Pius V), Pietro Aldobrandini (Secretary of State for Clement VIII), Scipione Borghese (multi-active for Paul V), Lodovio Ludovisi (for Gregory XV), or Camillo Pamphili (for Innocent X). R. Po-Chia Hsia cites Cardinal Lodovico Ludovisi as one of the most notorious examples of a nephew who accumulated benefices to make a mockery of the Tridentine rules and philosophy: with the benefices of the Archbishopric of Bologna, control of 23 abbeys, the vice-chancellorship of Church, and headship of the Segnatura (a lucrative office granting dispensations from church regulations). His case is interesting in that his power and influence continued after his papal uncle's death (1623), until his own in 1632.[9] Scipione Borghese was, as V. Reinhardt has exhaustively shown, an even more scandalous pluralist, and leech on church incomes, whether from abbeys left vacant, or offices of the Papal State. Some such income went to renovating or building churches, and sponsoring new art, as from Pietro and Gian Lorenzo Bernini.[10]

More constructively for reform, Cardinal nephew Carlo Borromeo was the outstanding exemplar, working at Trent and in its aftermath for Pius IV; but he resented this role, and wanted to lead as Archbishop of Milan. Maffeo Barberini as Urban VIII utilised his family for power, influence and great cultural patronage; with his brother Cardinal Carlo, and three nephews in action.[11] By the end of the pontificate the Barberini family had created much scandal, and damage in the Papal State, though Cardinal Antonio Barberini was a good churchman. While the abuse of power by papal families, to the detriment of serious reform and improvements for the majority, might scandalise some, many contemporary Italians expected Cardinals to be lavish patrons and high spenders; to serve the interests of the city or locality from which they originally came, and provide job opportunities in Rome and the Papal State; to have a large household, protecting scholars and artists, and training future church bureaucrats and leaders. They spent money on renovating their titular churches (like Baronio), or helping built new ones for the Religious Orders, or assisting hospitals and nunneries. Some of the expenditure might be on alms-giving for the poor, though that was certainly a meagre percentage of Scipione Borghese's overall expenditure (about 3 per cent).[12] The newsletter reports (*Avvisi*) sent out of Rome would often comment on the huge debts of Cardinals when they died, and see the 100 000 scudi debts of a Medici, Bentivoglio or Farnese Cardinal as a good sign. What might be seen as morally reprehensible, might also be judged as improving the spectacular image of the Church, its churches and decoration; and also oiling the wheels of government and administration when a well-paid and organised civil service was not part of the early modern scene.

The Borghese and Barberini families undoubtedly tarnished the papal reputation in the eyes of many, if not immediate beneficiaries. Later Popes could, however, restore the papal reputation, and prove re-invigorators of spiritual and organisation reform, such as the Blessed Innocent XI (1676–89), judged by Eamon Duffy as 'by any standards a very great pope'.[13] A model Bishop of Novara and educational reformer, and another reluctant and ascetic Pope, Innocent tackled the papacy's disastrous financial and economic situation, fostered poor relief, encouraged missionary work at home and abroad, tried to restrain both Louis XIV's assault against Calvinist Huguenots, and James VII/II's unpopular Catholic policies in Britain.

The family Cardinals, with a small group of other favoured figures, could be the key to efficient papal government, temporal and spiritual. The full College of Cardinals came into its own for the conclave to elect a Pope, but otherwise the power of the full body was limited. Consistories of Cardinals as an advisory or legislative assembly of those Cardinals available in Rome, and usually presided over by the Pope, diminished in power and influence. As Cardinal Gabriele Paleotti of Bologna complained by the 1590s, freedom of discussion was limited, and Popes were reluctant to take advice outside their immediate circle. Clement VIII completed a major process of diminishing the role of the Cardinalate as a group. It was certainly kept in the dark over foreign affairs, possibly understandably as Rome was (and is), a great gossip-shop, and this Pope was conducting a diplomatic revolution in his pro-French policy. [14] In a consistory in March 1632, Urban VIII demonstrated the authoritarian position by peremptorily slapping down the Spanish Cardinal Gaspare Borgia, who was trying to defend the role of the Spanish

King; and declared:

> cardinals in private (*secreto*) consistory do not speak openly unless previously licensed on matters, or questioned, and while we seek counsel, this we are not held to follow. You as an orator do not have a place in this session (*consessu*), for here there are no parts for princes' orators, but we heard you, and hear you in a place which is convenient for orators.[15]

Borgia claimed to speak as a Cardinal Protector, but was ruled out of order.

For Italian church affairs much horse-trading went on between cardinals behind the scenes, or in making representations to the Pope or his cardinal Nephew, as cardinals acted as Cardinal Protectors – to Religious Orders or particular houses, to hospitals, national churches.

Congregations

Increasingly the central organisation of the Church was focused on Congregations. These evolved from earlier tribunals and administrative bodies, such a the Datary, Segnatura, Rota (between them dealing with dispensations from church rules, concessions, appeals from various courts, and so forth), or the Apostolic Chamber as the main financial institution. New Congregations of the Inquisition (with a subsidiary offshoot that of the Index), and of the Council in 1564, for interpreting the decrees, appeared. A Congregation of Bishops was established in 1573, inspired by Carlo Borromeo, for more personal goading or assisting of individual bishops.[16] Sixtus V's rationalisation and restructuring programme in 1588 produced 15 Congregations. The Congregations were headed by a small group of Cardinals, with a bureaucracy of curial officials, directly responsible to the Pope, though the Cardinal Nephew or another relative might be a driving or influential force. Sixtus V and Clement VIII often had them meeting formally in their Palace to ensure control. The Congregations could become competing power houses, serving personal interests of rival cardinals. In 1592, the Congregation of Good Government (*Buon Governo*) was created to consolidate control over the Papal State, especially over financial and economic issues, approving local budgets, and attempting a single balance sheet. By 1629, it had

14 Cardinals and a General Treasurer, with a sizable bureaucracy below; it superseded in part, but not completely the old Camera Apostolica. More Congregations were added through the seventeenth century. The famous Congregation of Propaganda Fidei (the spreading of the Faith), was formed in 1622 to control and pursue overseas missionary work. 'Propaganda' was then a neutral word, and only later took on a pejorative tone, implying excessive spin-doctoring. The Congregation for Apostolic Visits in 1624, and that for the Residence of Bishops in 1634, as an expansion or reinvigoration of a simpler 1605 Congregation[17] took responsibility for reform activities hitherto part of that of the Congregation of the Council. In 1649, a Congregation for Convents was the answer to some years of worry about supervising and rationalising the proliferation of male and female convents, when many were very small and underfunded.

The Congregation approach to church government had mixed effects. The chaos and corruption of past church administration called for better central control; the 1588 major reform was partly to deal with scandals in the Datary, which had become the centre of the venal 'sale of office' system, also well known in many secular states. As A.D. Wright points out, the Datary of the seventeenth century continued to combine the 'more truly ecclesiastical income', from some allocation of benefices, dispensations and revenues of 'the venal office market'; it was a key to much papal financing.[18] The 1588–1630s reforms were probably beneficial in immediate central efficiency. A divide and rule policy, playing off Congregations and different groups of Cardinals, could enhance a Pope's authority, as with Sixtus V, Clement VIII, Paul V, especially with able and ruthless (if corrupt) Cardinal Nephews. For reforming at the periphery, a bishop had a number of different powerhouses and bureaucracies to overcome; or select to help him positively. Those resisting change at the periphery had a choice of Congregations and Cardinals to whom they might resort for vetoes. This could mean protection against abusive and dictatorial episcopal power; or the frustration of reforms planned in the interests of morality, education, philanthropy and control of consciences.

As potential agents of Church reform, the Cardinals' qualities and reasons for elevation, were very mixed; not changing dramatically in the Tridentine and post-Tridentine period. Tony Antonovics studied 243 Cardinals from 1534–1590, to test H.O. Evennett's assertion that the post-Trent period saw a significant shift in quality and typology.[19] As before, the new appointments were affected by relationship to the incoming Pope, by being compatriots of the Pope, by rewarding leading political families from states within Italy, whose cooperation was needed (the Gonzagas, D'Este amd Medici in particular), as well as mollifying Philip II of Spain or the Venetian Republic. Thereafter Curial experts, lawyers, administrators were rewarded, as were diplomats. Elevation because of depth of theological knowledge seems a limited consideration. Few came from Religious Orders. The situation was affected by various factors. Three types of Cardinal existed; those attached to titular churches in Rome, or a few suburbicarian dioceses;[20] these would be expected to serve central government, in Rome or a part of diplomacy, and would not have significant pastoral roles. A few Cardinals would be non-Italians and part of political structures elsewhere (as most famously Cardinals Richelieu and Mazarin in seventeenth-century France). Third the bishops of leading sees were named Cardinals. Some of these episcopal Cardinals had a full episcopal career moving up the ladder from poorer to wealthier sees. Some might have other careers within the Church (or, as with Venetians, in secular diplomacy), and end up as a Cardinal Archbishop or Patriarch. For this third category the tension existed between serving the diocese or metropolitan see, or the central government. This tension existed for the two leading episcopal 'models', Carlo Borromeo and Gabriele Paleotti (see Chapter 4). Different qualities (if fitness for purpose was a consideration in the elevation beyond family needs) were to some extent needed, depending whether central government or the episcopal see had priority.

The Cardinals were predominantly Italian; 43 out 58 in 1563. Of the new creations between 1566 and 1605, 106 (72 per cent) were Italians, with 38 of them born in the Papal State. From 1605 to 1655, 152 (82 per cent), were Italian, though there were some powerful Cardinals from Spain and France.[21] The imbalance offended non-Italian rulers, who sometimes reminded Popes of the Tridentine view that the choice should better represent the Catholic world. But when 'foreigners' were given the title, it was more a political honour, and rarely brought a foreign decision-maker into the Roman citadel. Popes reckoned they needed Italians at the centre of Church affairs in Rome. A strong Italian majority would guarantee an Italian Pope in the next conclave. The last non-Italian Pope, Adrian VI (Jan. 1522–Sept. 1523, originally from Utrecht), was deemed (by Italians) a disastrous precedent – too devout, puritan, stringently economic minded against Roman public interest, diplomatically incompetent, and the choice of the young Emperor Charles V.

The character profile of cardinals, as of bishops, was affected by the reluctance of some worthy figures in the Religious Orders to accept the roles of bishop and/or cardinal. Several Theatines (who were targeted for bishoprics in the South in particular), evaded the call to a see (and so potentially an episcopal Cardinal), though Paolo Burali, after various refusals, was persuaded to be bishop of Piacenza, then Cardinal Archbishop of Naples. He was an energetic reforming bishop, austere, and regularly corresponding with his mentor, Borromeo.[22] Cesare Baronio, the great church historian, and most famous Oratorian after Philip Neri, successfully declined bishoprics, but was forced to accept a Cardinal's hat in 1596. This made him eminently *papabile*, but as already noted his candidacy in 1605 was vetoed by the Spanish faction. Jesuits were seldom made cardinals, because of the attitude of the Order, and possibly a fear of them by successive Popes. Cardinal Roberto Bellarmino, also deemed *papabile* in 1605, was the exception as a powerful Jesuit Cardinal, a major theologian, but also highly energetic bishop of Capua.[23]

The powerhouses of central church government were probably the Congregations of the Holy Office, of the Index, and of the Council; for secular affairs those of the Camera Apsotolica, then the Buon Governo, and for 'influence', the Datary. Struggles developed both institutionally and personally between Cardinals and officials in the Holy Office and Index (though personnel overlapped), to the detriment of coherent policies – and excessive rigour! (Chapter 9).

The Sacred Congregation of the Council was initially a key institution for coordinating post-Tridentine reform. It conducted a very healthy correspondence with the dioceses; the Vatican series 'Liber Litterarum' has 38 volumes of letters for the period 1564–1902, copying the letters sent out. And this does not include letters specifically relating to the Visitation *ad limina* reports that bishops produced, and brought, or sent, to Rome (see Chapter 4). They dealt with holding episcopal Visitations (inspection tours), synods and councils, with parochial reconstruction, appointments to benefices, with the bishops' (non)-residency, and so forth. This epistolary activity lessened from about 1606.[24] Some of the Congregation's letters to lay bishops could be tart and rude, as with a 1587 letter to Archbishop Cesare Marcelli of Palermo (a royal nominee), for not organising diocesan visitations. In 1607, the bishop of Parma was chastised for his poor record of residence and that of many of his clergy; effectively, since by 1611 complaints arose that he was excessively rigid about granting licences for clergy to be absent. Reactions to this Congregation from reformers at the periphery were not necessarily favourable. Carlo Borromeo, who had been instrumental in creating the Congregation in the first place, later complained that the responses to his questions, or ratifications of the orders and conciliar decrees he wanted to promulgate, were too slow, and so frustrated his work. He sent the proposed decrees arising from the 4th Provincial Council in 1576, and had no relevant response by May 1579, when he called for his 5th Council. He went to Rome to get the Pope to approve his decrees. He challenged the right of the Congregation to revise his legislation; as he and his resident bishops knew local conditions best. In July 1581, he irately protested at the Congregation challenging the right of his dependent bishop of Bergamo to appoint a vicar to deal with some issues concerning nuns. He asked his agent to protest to Cardinal Carafa, who spoke for the Congregation, stressing 'that this puts in doubt similar matters concerning the deputations of vicars, which the Council of Trent, freely remitted to the judgement, and to the decision of bishops.' Congregational slowness might have been a deliberate way for Gregory XIII and others in Rome to restrain Borromeo, who was seen as too rigorous, and undiplomatic in Milan, given Spanish susceptibilities.[25]

While the Congregation of the Council was the interpreter of the decrees, in practice it faced competition from other Congregations, not only the Inquisition, but that of the Rota, according to the diary of a leading Frenchman in the Rota and Datary, Séraphin Olivier-Razzali. Most cases just concerned delegated powers for lesser cases (as the Rota itself claimed), with only the most serious issues moving from the Rota to the Congregation of the Council, as in 1583 over interpreting the Tridentine decree on marriage.[26]

Central Roman government had to deal with other states and city governments within the Papal State if ecclesiastical reform was to be implemented. The Papacy through the Renaissance period had developed diplomatic procedures and skills, with permanent or temporary ambassadors and agents. The most crucial figures could be the permanent ambassadors, Nunzios, in the key cities; for the peninsula in Naples, Turin and Venice. While primarily involved in secular church–state relations, they became significantly involved in ecclesiastical affairs, over episcopal appointments, jurisdictional issues, the powers and activities of Apostolic Visitors, problems of heresy and the roles of the inquisitors. Nunzio Riccardi in Turin in the 1580 and 1590s was an important figure, especially in campaigns to bring orthodox belief and behaviour to remoter areas. The Venetian Nunzios played prominent roles in basic church–state relations, but they were also part of the

Venetian Inquisition Tribunal. Nunzio Alberto Bolognetti, heavily criticised the state of the Venetian Church, and the reluctance of Venetian patricians to take action, as in investigating scandals in nunneries, or fraudulent friars. In the 1590s Antonio Maria Graziani had a hard time negotiating with the Venetian government over the imposition of the Clementine Index and its impact on the book trade. Paul Grendler, while noting Graziani's strong advocacy of papal rights, judges him the wrong appointee, failing to understand Venetian susceptibilities over intrusions on lay rights. The Papacy had to make many concessions to the Venetian Senate for the benefit of the local bookmen. Graziani was never employed again in a diplomatic position, though whether a more sensitive diplomat would have done much better over the Index issue remains doubtful. The Nunzios in Naples possibly had the hardest time, in negotiating with the Viceroys, to allow ecclesiastical matters, unofficial inquisitorial investigations, to proceed.[27] Nunzios, empowered as legates *de latere*, could act effectively over appointments to benefices, inquisitorial investigations, allowing parish priests to absolve sins normally reserved to the bishop; thus they could undermine the ordinary bishop's authority and control.[28]

Within the Papal State an arm of central government was the Cardinal Legate for provinces like Umbria or Bologna-Romagna, and governors or lieutenants sent to the cities. While their roles were primarily secular, coping with local politics, economic and financial problems, they dabbled in narrow ecclesiastical affairs. They implemented papal bulls, and decrees sent from different congregations and offices in Rome. They issued their own edicts to improve the moral welfare of the inhabitants; and could ordain priests, so challenging the bishop's role. These papal liaison figures might be seen as useful assistants in the 'disciplining' or 'social control' policies (see Chapter 9). Governor G.D. De' Rossi of Perugia on 24 December 1587 issued an edict positively urging all good Christians to contemplate the Mystery of Christ's birth; but warned that the vigil must be kept fittingly, without singing through the streets at night, and without distractions from neighbouring inns, or prostitutes appearing enticingly in churches.[29]

The Venetian Interdict Crisis

Nunzios had to sort out major and minor jurisdictional conflicts with other states (and between competing church institutions locally). They could not quietly resolve all conflicts. The Venetian Interdict crisis of 1606–07 was the most publicised jurisdictional confrontation between the central church (more personally Paul V), and any secular state. It tested and set limits to growing claims for papal authority in secular matters. The immediate cause was the Republic's arrest of three notorious characters (accused of parricide, rape and poisonings between them), who claimed clerical status, and so outwith the secular courts. One was Abbot of Nervosa, another a canon, the third Count of Valdemarino. Church authorities had done nothing, so the Republic finally took action, to the grand ire of the Pope. Prior to this, however other tensions had arisen. For years the Republic had been worried that too much land and property was passing into church hands, with tax exemptions, so reducing the tax basis for the Republic. The government sought to ban (starting with the city in 1561), transfer of property in *mortmain*, inalienably into church hands. In the papal view this was illegitimately interfering with testamentary dispositions. In March 1605, a law had greatly extended the scope of the ban; and from 1603 nobody in the Republic was to build a new church, convent or hospital without Senate permission. The Republic has also stopped allowing the papal Nunzio to imprison Venetian clergy without approval from a secular official. In 1605, trouble between the Republic and Rome had arisen over the new Patriarch of Venice – Venice and Aquileia entitled their bishop as Patriarch. Traditionally the Republic produced three candidates from which the Pope selected one, preferably the first choice. The candidates were usually from the patrician elite of Venice, had served state as well as church (sometimes having been ambassador in Rome); in minor orders, but not necessarily a deacon or priest. A nominee for a bishopric was theoretically expected to have a theological qualification, or be able to prove his fitness in theology. This had not happened with Patriarchs. In 1605, the Pope asked the front-runner, Francesco Vendramin, to present himself in Rome to have his theological knowledge tested. The Republic was offended. Tensions were thus high when the Republic arrested the criminous clerks. The newly elected Doge, Leonardo Donà, had long stood against Papal incursions, and had helped resist some implementation of the 1596 Index. When the Republic would not give way, Paul V excommunicated the Doge and Senate, and imposed an Interdict on the Republic, meaning that all religious services and comforts should cease until the Pope's will was fulfilled.[30]

The struggle was verbal rather than physical; the Pope would not back his cause militarily, but by spiritual sanctions, and a propaganda war. The Jesuits were ordered to lead the war of words, arguing that the Pope had the right to interfere in another state to enforce clerical disciple, and protect clerical privileges. The Republic selected a brilliant Servite friar, Paolo Sarpi, to lead their written defence against such interference in anything more than the most spiritual affairs of individuals. The war of words was extensive and erudite (Cardinals Cesare Baronio and Roberto Bellarmino were recruited by the Pope to oppose Sarpi), involving defences of 'liberty', state 'sovereignty', and 'absolute' rights, backed by investigations of the early church, and of Venetian church life, past and contemporary.[31] The Interdict essentially failed in Venice itself. The government's orders for all churches to remain open, services continue, Christian burial still be conducted, were obeyed by virtually all clergy. The local Jesuits, made to opt for the papal side, were driven out, along with a few others. The lay confraternities (*Scuole*) were called on to stage processions favouring the Venetian church, loyal to St Mark and the Virgin, and to lampoon the Pope. The most spectacular procession, with representational scenes on carts, was for Corpus Christi 1606, described by the English ambassador Sir Henry Wotton (a great admirer of Doge Donà) as:

> the most sumptuous procession that ever had been seen here ... (designed) first, to contain the people still in good order with superstition, the foolish band of obedience. Secondly, to let the Pope know (who wanteth not intelligencers [spies]) that notwithstanding his interdicts, they had friars enough and other clergymen to furnish out the day.[32]

Reactions on the mainland were more varied, with some bishops and clergy backing the Interdict. In the end, the French helped produce a fudged settlement; the Interdict and personal excommunications were lifted. The two original accused clergy were handed over for trial by the French; the religious who had been expelled could return – except the Jesuits. The recent rules about property transfers in the mainland would remain, but not be enforced. The Jesuits were not allowed to return for some time and then never fully re-established themselves in the city.

The wider importance of the crisis was that its showed an Interdict was not a workable weapon for the Pope, that compromises over jurisdictions with secular states would have to be made. Papal 'absolutism' had its limitations. The hopes of James VI/I and his English diplomats like Wotton, that Venice would break with Rome and become like Anglicans were dashed. This had not really been likely, even if Sarpi and some other Venetians were happy to correspond with French Huguenots. Venetians were pleased to remain Catholic, but very much with local variations. They would, however, call on papal support, and the Rome Holy Office if desirable for their own purposes.

The Inquisition

For many the chief weapon of centralising Counter Reformation control was the Holy Office of the Inquisition, already noted in action dealing with early heretics (Chapter 1). The early modern Italian version of the Inquisition, or the Roman Inquisition, was developed following the Bull *Licet ab initio* of July 1542.[33] Various local inquisitions had shown increasing alarm about Lutheranism and other heresies, and signs of increasing debate about theological matters. Events in Ferrara, and the link between that Duchy and France, led Paul III in 1536 to declare that Italy was being affected by a plague of heresy; and this inspired the establishment of a central, papal directed, system. Various scandals and several steps followed before the Bull put six cardinals under the Pope in charge of a permanent institution to eradicate 'heretical depravity'.[34] A crucial input into the character and early stringency – and undue persecutory fervour – of the Roman Inquisition came from Gian Pietro Carafa, a conservative Theatine Catholic reformer. He had witnessed the operations of the Spanish Inquisition, praised its activities, and was ready to make an Italian version effective. Paul III gave him the lead role, which he was to continue more intensely as Paul IV. In 1555 he made the Holy Office the pre-eminent Congregation. 'We are of the opinion that no tribunal acts with more sincerity, nor more with a view to the honour of God, than this one of the Inquisition', he told Venetian ambassador Bernardo Navagero in July 1557, when he announced that profane swearing, sodomy, 'simoniacal heresy' (so abolishing the sale of benefices and of sacraments he supposed), would be added to its remit, 'forbidding all other tribunals ... to interfere with those matters for the future'.[35]

Unlike medieval Inquisitions, which were essentially local adjuncts to, or substitutes for, episcopal investigations of particular heresies, the Roman Inquisition became a permanent institution, based on a

central bureaucracy in Rome under Papal leadership, ready to deal with all kinds of heresy, though obviously initially focusing on the new Protestant threats from the North, and local support within Italy.

However impressive the Holy Office's central system, striking fear into the unorthodox, it had many anomalies and limitations in controlling through Italy. It lacked the central control, or autonomy, that the Spanish Inquisition enjoyed. Outside the Papal State its operation had to be negotiated with the rulers of each state. Philip II of Spain wanted the Spanish Inquisition to have tribunals in his Italian possessions; this he had in Sicily and Sardinia, but the Popes refused to allow this in the Kingdom of Naples and Lombardy. Philip II and his successors forbad the Roman Inquisition to operate openly in the Kingdom, and so inquisitors worked more in a medieval fashion linking archbishops and bishops with Rome more informally and secretly, with impediments imposed by the Viceroys. The Roman Inquisition could operate more readily in Lombardy, though not without frustrations from the Spanish Governors. Varying arrangements were made with other secular rulers. In the case of Venice, after much fraught negotiation, the central Venetian Inquisition became a shared church – state operation from 1547. In the wider Republic, on the mainland, local inferior tribunals operated with less secular control, though both the central Venetian tribunal and the Holy Office in Rome might insist on consultation, and issue commands.[36]

Though local political situations might restrict the operation of inquisitors, as individuals or in tribunals, correspondence with Rome was often very active, and mutually cooperative, even with the most independent tribunal of Venice.[37] The Congregation of the Holy Office legislated to control the tribunals' procedures, and interpreted the rules, issued manuals to assist investigations and trial procedures (as most notaby Eliseo Masini's *Sacro arsenale*, first published in 1621, but reprinted several times), and supervised the work of local inquisitors and tribunals.[38] The Bologna Inquisitor in the later sixteenth century was constantly pressed to keep Roman Inquisition Cardinals informed about suspicions and suspects, in city and the rest of the archdiocese – with strict secrecy imposed.[39] The local officials were expected to consult over serious cases, forward copies of the major testimonies, give detailed descriptions of suspects or accused who had escaped from prison, and to send the most notorious or difficult accused to Rome for investigation and trial there – as in the case of Giordano Bruno (from Venice) or Galileo (from Tuscany). It was Rome's decision not that of the more lenient trial tribunal in

Portogruaro, that the now famous heretical miller in Friuli, Domenico Scandella (or Menocchio), should be executed following his second trial in 1599 for propagating strange cosmological ideas (explaining creation, as angels and men emerging like worms from fermenting cheese), attacking the Trinity and sacraments, for reading prohibited books, and much else. Rome decided he should be executed this time as 'a relapsed person, who reveals himself to be an atheist in his interrogations'.[40]

Roman authorities undertaking their own investigations sought support from the local inquisitors, to chase up contacts, find more witnesses, or track those who had escaped capture. Thus, Rome sought Bologna's assistance over Baron Albert Schenk of Limburg, a suspect German Lutheran in 1589, or with possible associates of Marco Samuel of Antivari whom the Holy Office was investigating in 1587 for necromancy. Correspondence shows sometimes lively cooperation directly between local tribunals (as with Bologna, Modena, Florence, Venice, Udine), or with Rome acting as intermediary. The flow of information could become overwhelming, and the triviality of some reporting to Rome, or some questions sent to the Holy Office might impede serious investigations, as the Bologna inquisitor Innocenzo da Modena was warned in 1573.[41]

Rome did not fully control inquisitors or even their selection, especially in the early years. Inquisitors came mostly from the Religious Orders, predominantly Dominican, and the Order often chose the nominee. The Congregation did not itself nominate the inquisitor in Ancona till 1566, Florence till 1572, or to Milan until 1587.[42] Local officials might have different views from the central Cardinals and Inquisitor General, whether over the seriousness of certain 'heresies', the danger of some individuals (as with Menocchio), or the extent to which dubious books might be eradicated. Personality clashes, revealed, for example, in surviving correspondence in Bologna, probably reduced the efficiency of central–local cooperation. The main regional inquisitors and tribunals worked through networks of local agents and assistants. The Bologna tribunal seems to have superintended 17 vicariates, with fairly well regulated vicars reporting to Bologna. The limited surviving records for Tuscany suggest a variety of clerics who served as inquisition agents and investigators, supplementary to their other tasks.[43]

The Inquisition system was a key weapon for control and education; but it was not monolithic, grossly tyrannical. Political and jurisdictional considerations impeded efficiency, as did the limitations of manpower, problems of sorting out relevant denunciations and information, divided priorities over different 'heresies', and variable support for the inquisitions work. Over the period the targets shifted (Chapter 9).

Religious Orders

The Religious Orders, especially the most eminent New Orders, can be mentioned first as part of the central direction of reform and spread of reform ideas and spirituality, though obviously their individual houses were part of the peripheral community. Most were directed from Rome, and had Cardinal Protectors promoting their interests before Popes and Congregations.[44] The importance, for my predominantly socio-religious study, of the male members of the religious orders is the way they contributed to the wider community, alongside – with friendship or animosity – the secular leaders and institutions. Life within the male monasteries, their devotions or scholarship, their scandals, has largely to be ignored here, for space reasons. The nunneries will receive a lengthy discussion on their own (Chapter 8); the Tridentine campaign to enclose them fully had major social repercussions, about which some vigorous and fascinating studies have recently emerged.

'Religious Orders' covers a variety of situations and organisations, from vast and rich monastic houses of confined monks to solitary friars spending most of their time on their own (organisationally), either as itinerant preachers or as recluses. Under this loose heading are included some congregations and ambiguous associations of clerics and laity, not receiving full recognition and discipline of an Order. The focus is on new congregations and Orders, emphasising active service in the wider community, rather than on cloistered prayer, scholarship and farming, as with old monks. But monks, notably Benedictines, might also publicly serve parishes and organise farms; while Dominicans ran Inquisition tribunals, or were bishops in remote dioceses, along with Theatines (Chapter 4). The new Jesuits were almost everywhere – and have not let posterity forget it. For Mark Lewis there arose 'a new religious style of life found in the clerks regular', partly arising out of medieval confraternities and a 'new articulation of the priesthood'.[45]

The new Religious Orders and congregations originated in the early years of the century, though the steps and time till full canonical recognition varied. Priority in time belongs to the Clerks Regular of Theatines (effective from 1524), deriving in part from the Divine Love confraternity, and named after Gaetano di Thiene, (1480–1547), Bishop of Chieti. Their first superior was the unlikely Gian Pietro Carafa, later the rigid Pope Paul IV, who as Pope exercised unprecedented direct control over the Order when he uncoupled it from the Somaschi (see later). The Theatines were initially noted for personal asceticism, preaching, and social welfare (though hospital and education work dropped from their priorities from the 1550s); they were often of well-to-do backgrounds, able to obtain funding from southern nobility, but personally maintaining their poverty. Favoured by Spanish Kings and their officials as well as Neapolitan nobles (including powerful and wealthy females), they prospered in the south especially, served in parishes and bishoprics and developed some splendidly decorated churches (as in Naples and Lecce), through others' largesse. An early historian, Giovanni Battista Del Tufo, in 1609 boasted of and defended the creation of lavishly decorated churches for the glory of God, and education of the people. In the seventeenth century Theatines developed an important base in Rome at Sant'Andrea della Valle, but numerically it remained a small community. They had 46 communities in Italy by 1650, but with restricted membership – only 1111 religious; the 13 communities in the Neapolitan province had 341 members. As Von Pastor stressed their best reform contribution might have come as 'a seminary of bishops', based on earlier parish work. They produced and utilised a devotional guide, *Il Combattimento spirituale*, by Lorenzo Scupoli (1530–1630), to rival the Jesuit *Spiritual Exercises*.[46]

Also the Divine Love movement, with Theatine support, fathered Somaschi, or Servants of the Poor (as called in 1531), named from a group based in Somascha (near Bergamo), led by Girolamo Miani, a friend of Carafa's. Papal recognition came in stages from 1531. They were annexed to the Theatines 1547–55, then established an independent congregation. Miani and his friends had reacted to the miseries of plague epidemics and war damage, leading to major contributions in social welfare. While Miani produced a clerical order, others as lay men and women fed into the wider philanthropic movements of confraternities, conservatories and hospitals (Chapter 7).

Under similar impetuses developed the Clerks Regular of St Paul, or Barnabites, with Antonio Maria Zaccaria (1502–47), noble doctor from Cremona who turned to theology and the priesthood, as a key figure. Officially recognised as a congregation from 1530, the

Barnabites become famous for hospital and prison work, notably in northern Italy. Later as an Order they were exempted from episcopal service. Like the Jesuits they had a special attachment to the Popes. The Barnabite fathers cultivated wide intellectual interests, but maintained a strong popular touch in organising impressive religious meetings, open-air sermonising, liturgical displays such as Forty-Hour Devotions (Chapter 10).

All was not easy for the early Barnabites. Zaccaria and others had many female followers, and sought to create an associated female organisation, which would evangelise in the world alongside their male associates. Along with Countess Ludovica Torelli (1499–1569), who led a religious and literary court at Guastalla, and Virginia Negri of Cremona (1508–55), he helped create the Angeliche (Angelicals of St Paul), recognised by Paul III in 1545, based on the nunnery of San Paolo in Milan. Unfortunately for them, a key influence on Torelli and Negri – who became Paola Antonia on taking vows – had been the Dominican Fra Battista Carioni da Crema (d.1530), who came under suspicion for Protestant sympathies and teaching, and who did not disguise his Savonarolan sympathies. Added to an air of theological suspicion for his followers, was the scandal for some gentlewomen parading penitentially through Milan streets doing good, helping and advising priests. By the early 1550s 'Divine Mother' Negri was seen as acting like a priest herself, and was denounced for such after visiting Venice, leading to an Inquisition investigation in Rome. Fra Battista's writings were posthumously condemned by Julius III as 'scandalous in several parts, rash in others, and heretical in many'. Negri was forced from her role in the nunnery, and died confined in a convent of Poor Clares, while the Barnabites were made 'to reinvent themselves in a more conservative form'.[47] The Barnabites had to disassociate themselves from the San Paolo nunnery, and the female inhabitants were driven into ever tighter enclosure – to become all the same a rich power house under the Sfondrati family. The male Barnabites survived to flourish worldwide, even if more circumspectly. The 'scandal' of the Angelics depressingly sabotaged widespread movements in northern Italy for an open 'third way' role for women in the public expression of active Christianity. It fuelled at Trent and subsequently the campaigns to impose strict enclosure on professed nuns. The worry about female 'living saints' (*Sante vive*) or 'Aspiring Saints' having undue influence over priests, and acting like priests, was to surface in inquisition investigations of several women through the later sixteenth and seventeenth century.[48]

The Ursulines (Orsoline), similarly attempted to satisfy female religious aspirations. The heroine of this foundation was Angela Merici, lay spinster, then tertiary, of Brescia (1474–1540). Inspired again by the Oratory of Divine Love, and its work for 'incurables' (often syphilis sufferers), she gathered other women, married and unmarried, to contribute to philanthropy, religious education, spiritual devotions. Between 1535 and 1544 she secured official recognition from the Bishop, then the Pope, for her group, with a status between Third Order and confraternity. Later the Ursulines were pushed into more disciplined hierarchical control as a congregation. From 1567, when Archbishop Carlo Borromeo called them to Milan, they were both promoted and controlled by this dominant male. He was particularly keen on their teaching of girls, and wanted all his diocesan bishops to foster a branch. Despite Borromeo's penchant for strict enclosure of women, he and later papal authorities never successfully subjected the Ursulines to full enclosure rules. While some Ursulines lived communally, others remained with their families. Most came from humbler families, unlike the Angeliche, and they avoided a public high profile. This was the most popular female congregation, providing a path that women could follow in religious service outside a nunnery or family enclosure.

The Jesuits were the central Religious Order – both positively for the ubiquity of their contributions, and negatively for the jealousy and political ire they could generate.[49] The Jesuits had a special vow of obedience to the Pope, which was called on in the Venetian Interdict crisis of 1606–07. Ironically, papal suppression of the Jesuits was one of the most significant papal acts of the eighteenth century.

The Jesuits had started modestly with limited ambitions, with Ignatius Loyola (1491–1556), his Iberian, French and other friends aiming for Jerusalem as pilgrims. Coming from Paris and seeking Paul III's blessing in Rome on the way in 1537, they were persuaded to make Rome their Jerusalem, especially as war with the Turks made such a pilgrimage nigh impossible. By 1540, ten such friends constituted the new Order, the Society of Jesus, which became Rome centred, and often suspect to Spanish Kings and church leaders, whatever its worldwide roles later. Mystical meditation in a Spanish tradition (which came to alarm the Spanish Inquisition), and self-examination had been the early contribution of Loyola as spiritual leader. From this role he developed *The Spiritual Exercises* (finished in 1548), the most famous devotional guide of the period. Early versions won him keen friends; the published work, developed through interaction with his associates and reading of past writings, became a path to spiritual renewal for many from all levels of society. While it was 'the spiritual drill-book' for the Society,[50] it was also a manual to help Jesuits take others – according to whatever level of intellect, education and devotion – through a self-examination and meditation. An increasing stress on its flexibility and away from the early emphasis on a path to asceticism, both affected its popularity, and attacks on Jesuit moral accommodation to the penitent's position. *The Spiritual Exercises* could also be a self-used manual – as with Gian Lorenzo Bernini;[51] though in this role and as literature it might not have the appeal of the rival Theatine devotional manual, *The Spiritual Combat* by Lorenzo Scupoli, which likewise remains in use. *The Spiritual Exercises* was a Christocentric text, following various influences on Loyola, but has also been seen as 'a kind of Rosary without beads', based on narrative scenes foregrounding Christ rather than Mary.[52] Penitents were encouraged to visualise episodes, or potential pilgrimage scenes. This mental visualisation was to be annexed to the use of the visual in paintings by the turn of the century.

The Jesuits developed a large worldwide organisation, headed by the General in Rome. Of all Orders, their members had the longest training, probably the fullest and widest education, with an efficient communication system, linking distant groups and individuals to the centre, or each other. The Society of Jesus was not a monolithic or narrow organisation; consultation with Rome about designing churches or colleges did not lead to uniform creations, nor to a 'Jesuit style'. Diversity, according to local needs, physical resources (stone or brick), was encouraged. Diversity characterised many of their activities. In fact excessive adaptation to local customs and beliefs was one of the charges in the eighteenth century that produced campaigns to abolish the Order. While Ignatius Loyola had modest ambitions for his original society and Order, once Peter Canisius won the argument that they should combat heresy through education, they moved to the central position in much post-Tridentine reform activity. Their help was soon requested by reforming bishops, and the Generals in Rome sought to supply the needs.

By the turn of the century, Jesuits in Italy were running universities and colleges, assisting in diocesan seminaries, founding clerical congregations and lay confraternities, and giving advice to independent confraternities. They were leading missionaries, from the previously mentioned campaign against Waldensian beliefs in southern Italy, targeting the South as the 'Indies' of Italy or Europe, and some slum areas. Jesuits helped in hospitals and prisons, and (following an early concern of Loyola), assisting repentant prostitutes and vulnerable girls or women, especially in Rome, with the influential Casa Santa Marta (from 1542–43).[53] Not far into the seventeenth century they moved from a puritanical approach to art, to patronise ostentatious propaganda art, and art for the glory of God – in buildings, paintings, music and theatre. Thus the Jesuits will be mentioned in most chapters to follow. By 1615, Jesuit colleges seem to have been established in 59 places on the Italian mainland, with 15 in Sicily, 1 in Corsica and 4 in Sardinia; and the Jesuits had another 7 residences, without full college status.[54]

From central Rome's viewpoint, the second most important new male Religious Order was that of the Oratorians, founded by Philip Neri (1515–95).[55] Though of Florentine origin, it became a Roman confraternity, congregation of priests and finally a fully recognised Order in 1575, albeit with a continuing Florentine input in membership and spirituality, including the processional singing of Lauds. The Oratorians did not develop like the Jesuits. Neri and other early post-Tridentine leaders, like Cesare Baronio, were reluctant to expand the Order, geographically, numerically or in activity. Where Jesuits tried to answer episcopal calls for help, the Oratorians often declined them, including one from Borromeo in Milan. They wanted the Order to serve the spiritual needs of Rome – from Cardinals down to local Romans who wanted joyful and penitential processions between basilicas. Oratorians would serve scholarship, and test the dedication of potential recruits to full membership by tending the sores and wounds of the poor in Roman hospitals.Their headquarters church, Santa Maria in Vallicella (the Chiesa Nuova), and a growing complex of buildings including the Oratory chapel (with Borromini as the exciting and adventurous architect), became the centre of much that was vital and experimental in the spiritual life and religious culture of Rome. Much was done for clerical-lay interaction and understanding. Churches elsewhere established affiliations, and imitated its services and worship. But when it was finally agreed to open a second House, in Naples, the experience was contentious and unhappy. The Rome–Naples confrontations by 1612 led to Paul V agreeing that Oratories should be self-governing, and subject to the local bishop. By 1650, 35 Oratorian centres had been established – as in Perugia (1615), Bologna (1616), Fermo and Turin (1649) – but no network in Italy of multi-purpose activities to rival the Jesuits, (The French Oratory, an imitator in part, but apart, had a fuller role in French Catholic reform.)

Other Religious Orders and congregations of lesser import had emerged and continued to be founded through the post-Tridentine period, responding to new and old needs. A few can be briefly named here. The Clerks Regular of the Mother of God (also called Leonardini or Matritani), developed by the Lucchese apothecary turned priest, Giovanni Leonardi (1541–1609), was recognised as a congregation from 1574. As well as promoting Marian devotions, they preached, visited hospitals, and from about 1609 under Paul V's encouragement ran schools. Besides Lucca and Rome they had major centres in Naples (1632) and Genoa (1669). Briefly in 1614 they were linked with the budding Piarists, which José de Calasanz (or Calanzio, 1557–1648), had developed as group providing alms and education for poor slum children in Rome and later elsewhere (Pious Schools or Scuole Pie). Calasanz' followers became a separate group again from 1617, and a full congregation under Gregory XV's support, to become better known as Scolopi, dedicated to teaching. By 1634 they had opened schools in about 14 Italian cities, from Carcere (near Genoa) to Messina, Cosenza to Norcia.[56] Another specifically dedicated Order (from 1586), was that of the Ministri degli Infermi (Ministers for the Sick, or Camilliani), founded by Camillo de Lellis (1550–1614), a soldier inspired by having his foot cured in the Roman hospital of San Giacomo. This nursing Order became famous for battlefield work. Close to them in practical Christianity were the Hospitalers of S. Giovanni di Dio, hovering between lay confraternity and clerical Order. Better known as Fatebenefratelli after their half-sung greeting 'Fate bene fratelli, per l'amor di Dio', (Do good brothers, for the love of God), they were much praised in Camillo Fanucci's 1601 guide to Roman philanthropy, and expanded to run and assist in many hospitals throughout Italy. They had 30 convents spread through the Kingdom of Naples by mid-century.[57]

From the old also came new; pre-eminently the Capuchins, as a reforming branch of the Conventual Franciscans. They had been in trouble in the early decades of the sixteenth century for flirtations with Protestant ideas, and the scandal of their General Ochino's flight. However, they recovered their reputation as missionary preachers of the most dramatic kind, and in this rivalled the Jesuits. While less concerned with formal education, or philanthropy, and rarely becoming bishops or central church administrators, the Capuchins deserve major credit for assisting in religious revival through preaching. They also provided guidance on preaching and mission work for others from bishops to parish priests, as notably did Girolamo Narni.

Their prevalence in Italy is remarkable. By 1596 they had 586 convents, organised in 22 Provinces through the mainland and islands, claiming a total of 6420 members. By 1678 they numbered 11 863 in 833 convents; by 1761 they had reached 15 682 brothers in 866 houses. From 1621, Paul V freed them from control by the general of the Conventual Franciscans.[58]

As Gigliola Fragnito stresses the old Mendicant Orders, while criticised and found wanting by many in the early sixteenth century, regained popularity from the second half – for both spiritual and less honourable social reasons (connected with strategic family planning, limiting marriages). The papal inquest of 1650 (which led to the closure of some smaller monasteries), revealed 5200 Mendicant houses, of which 1083 had been founded since 1580, containing some 60 000 religious, with 34 000 from the various Franciscan groups.[59] Their monastic houses were part of the urban and rural scene, not just retreats from the world, contributing to wider society through supporting confraternities, providing services and sermons in their churches and chapels open to the public, sending out preachers, helping educate would-be secular priests, offering hospitality to travellers. As with many new Orders, the old still appealed to members of upper society with a vocation.

New and revitalised Religious Orders and congregations were reactions to the challenges of the religious and social crises of the early and mid-sixteenth century. They could make a profound impact on the religious and social life of Italy. While rivalries and tensions existed between them and some bishops at the periphery, and Roman authorities at the centre, these religious groups interlocked with the history of episcopal-led reform, parish revitalisation, the spiritual and social work of lay confraternities, as revealed in subsequent chapters.

4 *Episcopal Leadership*

The success and failure of post-Tridentine reform, as guided by that Council, was heavily dependant on the power and influence of bishops. The Council itself has been judged the most *episcopal* Church Council.[1] Bishops had dominated the formal council procedures and decision-making, whatever theologians did behind the scenes. One of the last major battles had been over the rights of Bishops. The insistence on the residence of bishops, to be absent for no more than six months, which had first occasioned strong debate in 1546–47, was ratified. G. Alberigo celebrated episcopal residency, with activity for the salvation of souls (*salus animarum*) as the Council's practical ecclesiology.[2] The spirit of St Augustine as Bishop as well as theologian inspired the ideology of reform. Therefore, bishops were expected to lead reform campaigns, as organisers and preachers inspiring clergy and laity below them. In practice episcopal leadership proved very variable. Various models of episcopal leadership existed, from the autocratic to the liberal and consultative. Many bishops scarcely approached a model – through incompetence, indifference, conflicting career needs and powerlessness against rival jurisdictions. A.D. Wright once argued that one of the great failures of the Council was its assertion of episcopal authority, which was then accompanied by 'insufficiently stringent reform of princely privileges', and a failure to curtail the princely nomination of bishops (though this was more significant outside Italy).[3] This chapter will explore the complexities of episcopal geography, the problems of recruitment and appointment, career pressures, and the tensions over jurisdictions. It will consider how bishops operated in their dioceses, the functions of institutions under them, and the ways in which bishops worked with lesser clergy and laity. The individual bishop's approach moulded the types of reforms that did – or did not – follow down the line, as I showed with Perugia's bishops.[4]

The Diocesan Map

The diocesan map for Italy was complex. (Maps 2–4, locating most operational episcopal seats, though not all, and Appendix, listing bishoprics.) At the closure of the Council of Trent, 'Italy' had about 280 to 290 operative dioceses, depending which one includes on the islands and along the Dalmatian coast. The count was constantly changing, with creations, amalgamations, splits and suppressions, which my list tries to record. France only had 131 dioceses, and Iberia 68. Some of the Dalmatian bishoprics, where the Venetians had dominated, were now largely inoperative because they were under Turkish threat or control. Where they still received Italian appointments, they can be counted as part of the ecclesiastical career structure. This book concentrates on the Italian peninsula, paying little attention to Sicily and Sardinia (with strong Spanish domination), or Corsica (though Genoese controlled); but they are included in surveying the episcopal scene here, if Italians were appointed. Aosta was suffragan to a French province, but had Italian bishops, influenced by the Piedmontese rulers out of Turin. Bressanone, suffragan to Salzburg in the County of Tyrol is sometimes counted as 'Italian', though most bishops were German: Christopher Madruzzo, bishop of Trent also held Bressanone 1542–65, and it was actively served by an Italian suffragan, B. Aliprandini, from 1558 to 1571.

Of the Italian dioceses about 120 were independent (directly responsible to the Pope); whether as archdioceses headed by patriarchs and archbishops or as dioceses directly dependent on Rome. The others were suffragan dioceses attached to archbishops, as notably in the South, or to the Patriarchate of Aquileia in the north-east. Through the post-Tridentine period a few changes occurred in the episcopal map, as new bishoprics were created, others suppressed or amalgamated. Crema was created in 1580, Colle Val D'Elsa in 1592. Pienza and Montalcino formed a joint bishopric 1563–99, then separated. Prato and Pistoia were united in 1653. The Patriarchate of Aquileia, in imperial Roman days based on a great trading city now ruined, effectively operated out of Portogruaro and Udine (as for inquisition activities or synods), and the latter officially replaced it in

1752. In 1582 Bologna, independent from Ravenna since 1518 or so, was elevated to a metropolitan archepiscopate under the model reforming bishop Gabriele Paleotti, with Cremona, Modena, Parma, Piacenza and Crema now made suffragan to it, though that situation changed again.

The geographical size and wealth of the dioceses varied considerably. Milan, Naples or Padua were populous and wealthy; as also smaller dioceses like Catania, Monreale, Piacenza, Ravenna, Salerno and Verona. Melfi and Torcello, though small, could provide a reasonable income. The extent to which the incumbent bishops enjoyed that wealth or used it for reforming purposes, depended on whether pensions for other clergy were also derived from such episcopal 'tables' (official incomes for the diocese). Cardinal Archbishop Girolamo Della Rovere in 1590 complained to Rome of the 'aggravation' of pensions taken from his income, detrimental to his (vigorous) activity.[5] In the case of the bishopric of Iesi, Cardinal Cesare Baronio received a significant pension from its 'fruits', and Cardinal Camillo Borghese (later Pope Paul V), profited also from its income after his brief incumbency (1597–99).[6] Hardly examples of good resource management for bishoprics, this practice was heavily attacked by Paolo Sarpi, Servite friar, defender of the Venetian Republic against Paul V's Interdict, and critical historian of the Council of Trent.[7] Many Italian dioceses were extremely small and poor, and hardly distinguishable from a *pieve* parochial complex (Chapter 5). Many of these were in remoter parts of southern Italy. The diocese of Nicotera consisted of a *città* of 50 families or households, and a few scattered villages; Lavello and Montepeloso were just *città* of 500 and 800 households. In 1611 Montemarrano covered three small parish towns. But northern Italy could have small bishoprics, such as swampy Comacchio near Ravenna. Arguably serious reform after Trent should have rationalised the diocesan boundaries, diminished the number of bishoprics, and spread the financial resources so that diocesan seminaries could be created to train suitable priests, networks of vicars general be established to supervise the parochial clergy. Though dioceses were amalgamated, or new ones created, it was for political reasons, not organisational efficiency. Secular rulers and cities were loath to lose the status of a bishopric, and see a Duomo (cathedral) degraded; and some might want to elevate self and city to such a status. Popes liked to have even dysfunctional bishoprics with minor incomes available to reward clergy serving the papacy as diplomats, administrative officials in the Roman Curia, or a personal assistant. The attractive little town of San Miniato in Tuscany became a *città* and diocese, separated from that of Lucca, in 1622–24, thanks to Grand Duchess Maria Maddalena d'Austria, who on the death of her husband Cosimo II, ruled this little territory in her own right, 1620–31. The Lucchesi strongly resented this loss. San Miniato was able to afford its own modest seminary in 1650, and develop to have a spectacular building dominating a whole piazza. This act of princely promotion proved reasonably successful in ecclesiastical terms.[8]

For an understanding of the post-Tridentine Italian episcopacy I surveyed fairly closely those appointed from 1560 to 1630; about 2000 episcopal appointments in all (see Appendix). Some bishops successively held a number of sees, so fewer than 2000 individuals were involved. Some dioceses, especially in the South, had a rapid turnover conditioned by remoteness, poverty and insalubrious conditions. San Marco (Calabria) had 19 bishops of whom 13 died in residence, while Strongoli, Crotone (both in Calabria) and Chioggia (near Venice), had 12 bishops. Strongoli was, however later to have a long-serving incumbent Alessandro Ghislieri (1601–21). Such rapid succession was hardly conducive to planned, consistent reform. Poorer dioceses received members of Religious Orders, who might be presumed to tolerate poverty more than career curialists accustomed to more palatial accommodation in Rome. The Theatines were increasingly selected; at least 30 sees had one or more Theatine bishop in the 1590s to 1620s, notably in the South, favoured by the Spanish Government and the Viceroys of Naples. Wealthier northern dioceses such as Bergamo and Crema also had Theatine bishops, and this Order provided one of the leading model episcopal reformers, Paolo Burali who served Piacenza (1568–76) and then became Archbishop of Naples (1576–78).

The re-emphasis on episcopal preaching encouraged the appointment of members of Orders who prided themselves on preaching, such as the Dominicans and Franciscans as well as Theatines, both to poverty-stricken dioceses, and more prestigious sees for star preachers. Members of preaching Orders were sent to sees like San Marco (G. Naro, Dominican, 1613–23), Naxos and Paros, Suda (suffragan of Naxos), Stagno (Stanj in Dalmatia), or Montemarrano (under Benevento). Ambrogio Salvio of Bagnoli, a leading preacher against heresy, was rewarded with the Bishopric of Nardo. Some major touring preachers were appointed as well. Examples included

Francesco Panigarola from the Order of Minims, an elaborately 'baroque' preacher who was bishop of Asti 1587–94. The Dominican Vincenzo Ercolani, a scholarly and popular preacher (see below), was successively bishop of Sarno, Imola and most effectively of Perugia (1576–86).[9] Another Perugian Domincan preacher and correspondent of Ercolani, Ignazio Danti was bishop of Alatri (1583–86). The *cattedra* and pulpits of Mantua and Venice were to be filled by powerful preachers – respectively, Francesco Gonzaga of the Minims (1593–1613) and Patriarch Giovanni Trevisano, former Benedictine abbot (1560–90), who however became more noted – with favour or distrust depending on the target – for his legislation.

Many episcopal appointments went to diplomats and stalwarts in the administration of the Papal State or central Roman government. These were likely to be recalled for further central duties, to the detriment of their local flock, unless they made provision for good service by suffragans or vicars general. When Antonio Maria Galli, an administrator serving Sixtus V was rewarded by being made Cardinal Bishop of Perugia (1586–91), and sought to use his administrative skills in the interests of standardised reform, he encountered the animosity and resistance of the very powerful Benedictines of San Pietro.[10] Antonio Marchesani, Datary under Pius V, was rewarded with the reasonably prosperous see of Città di Castello (1572–81). Theological expertise seldom led to an Italian bishopric, except possibly in the Veneto. Among the exceptions were Cesare Lippi, a professor of sacred theology in Padua who was made bishop of Cava (1606–22), near Salerno; and Paulo Pico, a Dominican doctor of theology who served for 27 years as consultant to the Congregation of the Index, and ended his life as Bishop of Volturara (under Benevento), 1613–15. In 1613 Volturara had a Cathedral and about 150 houses – not a rich reward.[11] Adriano Berezio (alias Bereti, and Valentico) held the chairs of Metaphysics (1543–51) and Scripture (1551–64) at Padua University, and was a pontifical theologian at the Council of Trent. He served as Inquisitor in Venice 1564–66, before being made bishop of Capo d'Istria (1566–72). One of his writings argued for the Eucharist against Calvin's teaching. In this bishopric he succeeded Tomasso Stella, a notable Dominican theologian, who had preached in Trent in 1546, and more publicly in Bologna when the Council sat there. He moved from the bishopric of Lavello to Capo d'Istria in 1549, from where he could descend on Venice to preach and advise. Another Venetan or Istrian bishopric, Cittanova, was held (1570–81) by Gerolamo Vielmi (1513–81) – but he was seldom if ever resident.

The Dominican Vielmi had taught metaphysics and theology at Padua, and then (1560–65) at Rome's Sapienza University. There he taught Carlo Borromeo and Agostino Valier, who were to become leading pastoral bishops. Vielmi himself served as suffragan to the Bishop of Padua (Alvise Pisani) from 1563–66, while lecturing on Scripture. As suffragan he functioned fully as a bishop. Influentially he composed an oration *De optimo episcopi munere* in 1565 (published Venice, 1575), which reinforced a message that bishops should preach and teach.[12]

Interestingly the unfortunate, much-manned, Calabrian Bishopric of Strongoli received Claudio Marescotti (1587–90); a doctor of theology from the Monte Olivetan Congregation – who was not suitable for teaching, probably for reasons of dubious theology rather than pedagogical and rhetorical ineptitude. Presumably he was deemed safer there as bishop with an illiterate peasant flock than near urban scholars.[13] The Servite Paolo Sarpi, a great scholar in philosophy and theology, assistant to Carlo Borromeo, initially friend of Roberto Bellarmino, failed in his and friends' pleas to be given a bishopric. Probably judged too dangerous for his contact with foreigners of Protestant leanings, alleged challenges to certain doctrines, and love of new sciences, had he been so satisfied, he might not have been the Venetian champion in the Interdict crisis, and later author of an anti-papal history of the Council of Trent.[14]

'Model' Bishops

If one studies the 'best-practice' of reforming archbishops and bishops, several models might be detected. Three exemplary leaders can illustrate different episcopal roles, and what could and could not be achieved. Within the historiographical debates Carlo Borromeo is judged the hero or villain of 'The Counter Reformation', while Gabriele Paleotti represents 'Catholic Reform'. My third example, Vincenzo Ercolani has not been included in such debates, but can represent another strand of Catholic Reform, harking back to Savonarola.

The most influential 'model' for Tridentine reform was Carlo Borromeo (1538–84).[15] He arose from an aristocratic pre-Tridentine background: Milanese noble family, beneficed at 12, studying civil and canon law from age 14, with little sign of deep religiosity. His career and transformation, started with his uncle, Pope Pius IV, summoning him to Rome in 1559, in the papal nephew tradition. In 1560 he was made Cardinal Archbishop of Milan – under age at 22. He became an active, sometimes troublesome figure at Trent, 1562–63, most notably working on the Catechism (published in 1566). He was instrumental in establishing two Congregations, of the Council (1564) and of Bishops (1573), to foster reform through Italy, but came to battle with both when they restricted his own activities.[16] To avuncular annoyance, in 1565 Carlo insisted on becoming a resident archbishop in Milan, and so implementing the Tridentine reforms there rather than in Rome. He led the way in holding provincial councils and diocesan synods, and publishing the legislation profusely, backed with many more printed documents. In print, letter-writing and orally he was ready to instruct on all matters, from marriage to architectural design. He organised networks under his suffragan bishops, vicars general, local vicars (*vicari foranei*), to control and guide parish priests and confessors. He led Visitations touring his diocese and archdiocese, personally trekking through the mountains to remote villages to preach, observe and interrogate. He instituted several seminaries to educate new priests, bringing in Jesuits and Barnabites as helpers, also using their own colleges. He assiduously promoted parish confraternities – Holy Sacrament, Rosary and Christian Doctrine – with the last (about 500 of them for the 750 odd parishes of his Milan diocese) helping the parish priests teach the basics of Christian Doctrine through the catechism, to children and ill-informed adults about to marry. He made many enemies, from Spanish governors of Milan (such as the Duke of Albuquerque who tried to stop him publishing the Trent decrees), and fellow Milanese nobles, to recalcitrant priests, nuns and laity who resented his dictatorial ways and puritanism. Resistance grew against attempts to discipline wealthy monasteries and nunneries, to curb carnival activities, to check personally on booksellers selling prohibited books, to press people to self-denounce to inquisitors or to his own curial court.[17]

Bitter enemies matched admiring supporters. In October 1569 a group of clergy, resenting his upsetting interference, plotted his assassination, with one firing a crossbow at him while praying during a service in the oratory within his episcopal palace, superficially wounding his back. According to the admiring diarist Giambattista Casale, Borromeo would not allow ‘the rogue’ to be seized until the cantors had finished singing a motet. The four provosts were hanged or beheaded after being defrocked, in August 1570; with the shooter having his hand cut off first at the door of the palace. Casale admired Borromeo's introduction in 1567 of the Ambrosian carnival, honouring Milan's great bishop St Ambrose and his liturgy, and arousing city pride against Roman liturgical ways, 'to get the people of Milan to observe a wholly spiritual and holy carnival', bringing in procession to the well-adorned Cathedral, for communion or blessings, the major confraternities and the schools of Christian Doctrine (for which Casale taught), 'with male children dressed in wings and shirts'. So 'it seemed that through all Milan there was to be seen nothing but angels, as if Paradise had been opened. So edified was the whole of Milan that everyone forgot about the usual ribald carnival (*ribaldo carnevale*) and talked thereafter only of the holy things of Paradise.' Rather wishful thinking. Some missed the secular fun, but it showed Borromeo was trying to entice and uplift, not just ban what he saw as sinful.[18]

To local relief however, he successfully resisted Philip II's attempt to impose the Spanish Inquisition on Lombardy, and instead operated a Rome-linked tribunal. Borromeo could have difficult relations with Rome; when it thought he was being too undiplomatic in dealing with Spanish authorities, competing Religious Orders or other vested interests, and when he thought Roman Congregations were too slow in ratifying his legislation, or backing his initiatives. Though feared and hated by some, especially in the early years, he earned respect and admiration notably during the major plague epidemic of 1576–77, remaining in the city, indefatigably giving comfort, holding masses in the streets so that those quarantined in their houses could observe and distantly participate. Such *caritas* (love and charity), and his undoubted moral rectitude and asceticism, facilitated the campaign for his canonisation, rewarded in 1610; his asceticism and charity was publicly lauded rather than episcopal leadership. Yet his episcopal legislation was widely influential.[19]

Carlo Borromeo represents for many the 'Counter-Reformation', for his intransigence against heresy, his puritanism, dictatorial controls, as well his implementation of Trent recommended institutions and procedures. He subjected himself to an ascetic regime of fasting, flagellation and mortifications; and expected others so to do. He essentially operated a moral police force, and imposed public penances and humiliations on the immoral, as well as fines (which helped poor communities). Minor peccadilos received harsh punishments; as an early biographer, Carlo Bascapé, noted.[20] When Borromeo heard of a priest who drank too much and kept the wine for Mass in iced water, he had him shut up in a room in the archbishop's palace for some days, living only on water, which was kept warm in the sun. Borromeo had a narrow vision of the laity's place in the Church, with limited organisational roles, to be seen, to see, but not be heard. If they fulfilled a role, as in teaching Christian Doctrine, it was to be under strict clerical supervision. He followed Cardinal Inquisitor Ghislieri's view that the laity should not have access to the vernacular Bible, and personally hunted down bookshop and library copies. His rigidity and intransigence, however could be attacked by other church reformers, including Gregory XIII and Gabriele Paleotti, a correspondent, almost friend, and rival episcopal model. Paleotti wrote to Borromeo on 5 December 1566:

> I do not wish to stop telling you, because of my indebtedness to you, what I understand; one thing, that you never spare yourself, and never cease, and you cannot go on in this way. The other thing is that towards others you are too austere and rigorous, and you mingle with it little clemency and leniency, which I detect from all your pronouncements. Further I doubt whether you consult with others very much, but act on your own and from your own opinion on these matters, even with the holiest zeal. However they would wish that you communicated with experienced people because their opinion at least might calm others a lot. I see that I have passed the limits of modesty, but all is said for the good, not only of yourself, but of myself, so that the more I need light and warnings, the more I shall be helped by your most prudent opinions.

Borromeo replied at the end of December:

> You more especially make me understand the means I might take to govern myself discretely, both me personally and in my governing of others. Nevertheless my intention is never to pass the limits of discretion, although perhaps I can be given a different opinion by men, and with some reason for the method of my procedure in this principle since my coming here to Milan, having found everything wooded and overgrown. This has made me remain in a way oppressed that I have not seemed to be able to pardon myself with a good conscience; and it has been proper for me at least externally to show some severity towards others, to extirpate from them evil habits and to sow some good seeds of discipline and religion;

although as to the effect of carrying this out, it does not appear to me that I have trespassed past the limits of benignity.[21]

Gabriele Paleotti (1522–97) came from a Bolognese senatorial family of substance, studied and taught law at Bologna university – and wrote a work in 1550 defending the rights of bastards. He came to prominence as an auditor of the Rota tribunal in Rome, and was sent to the Council for 1562–63, to work alongside Cardinal Morone. He made a mark in securing compromises and agreements over reform decrees.[22] He was made Cardinal in 1565, and sent to Bologna as bishop in 1566. Old and unwell he moved to the suburbicarian bishoprics of Albano (1589), then Sabina (1591), to be nearer the Roman Curia, but still fulfil some pastoral duties. Against Paleotti's scruples and protests, the Pope had him retain Bologna.[23] Unlike Borromeo he started modestly, with just a diocese; it was not till 1583 that Bologna was upgraded to a metropolitan archbishopric, with suffragan bishops to supervise as well (see Appendix). Paleotti had a fine record of holding synods, aimed at mutual encouragement more than dictatorial instruction and allowing discussion. He was an assiduous preacher, and organiser of Visitations. He willingly delegated responsibilities to vicars general, suffragan bishops, congregations of local clerical assemblies, allowing them financial roles and controls (to Borromeo's chagrin). Local archpriests outside Bologna could operate without constant hounding by rural vicars (in contrast to Lombardy). Laymen helped supervise Bologna parishes, with some representatives elected by the community to work with his own nominees. Lay confraternities were encouraged to promote their public roles, to hold religious processions, have Forty Hour devotions. He encouraged Name of God (*Nome di Dio*) confraternities to work with the episcopal curia to reconcile disputes and bring peace to neighbourhoods – though records do not survive to indicate their detailed operations. He assiduously fostered religious education, using Congregations for teaching Christian Doctrine in the city, and Corpus Christi confraternities in the rural areas teaching the catechism and some elementary reading skills. Within the University he used a Congregation of Perseverance to foster Christian values among students, and to encourage the best minds to enter the Church.

While Borromeo showed much interest in church architecture and the design of altars and chapels, Paleotti focused on promoting a revived religious art, as the Bible for the illiterate, and aid to devotion. Well acquainted with Bolognese painters and their works, he wrote an uncompleted art treatise (*A Discourse on Sacred and Profane Images*), first circulated in manuscript and partly published in 1582[24] (see Chapter 10). In this, as in other writings and preaching, he encouraged debate, some experimentation, and open-mindedness. Paleotti's understanding and relatively emollient approach, fostering cultural interests, inspired some other leading Catholic reformers, including Philip Neri and the Oratorians, and some French episcopal attitudes. He resented excessive Roman centralisation, which impeded some Bologna plans, but would not back him against local opposition. When in Rome he was sufficiently upset by papal domination of the College of Cardinals and lack of discussion in consistory that he wrote a treatise in 1592 arguing that the College should operate as a proper senate, and 'showed that it was the office of the Pope to take counsel from the college of cardinals', as the Venetian ambassador reported it.[25] This may help explain why Paleotti was a better promoted model for non-Italians than those closer to Rome. That his emollient, open-minded and more lay centred approach had fewer followers has been seen by some historians as a failure for Catholic Reform, and Paleotti himself.[26]

Vincenzo Ercolani (or Herculani), successively Bishop of Sarno, Imola and most notably Perugia (1578–86), stands as another Catholic Reform model. From a Perugian noble family he was influenced by one of Ochino's sermons (before his defection) to change from studying medicine to theology. He entered the Dominican Order, and had a great impact as a teacher of scripture and theology, but also as a popular preacher. Surviving copies of correspondence (made by his nephew-secretary Timoteo Bottonio, later his biographer), shows that he was a part of a wide network of Dominicans, nuns and lay people, who exchanged and discussed books, provided each other with spiritual advice and comfort, and wrote religious poetry.[27] His correspondents included Bonsignore Cacciaguerra, a leading Neapolitan advocate of frequent communion for the laity, the ascetic Florentine nun and spiritual adviser Caterina de' Ricci, and the Salviati family (dominant in both Florence and Rome). Savonarola's influence as spiritual adviser remained strong among this network, and Ercolani with friends at S. Maria sopra Minerva in Rome struggled to keep his works off the Index. Ercolani in 1558 (when he was Prior at the Minerva), defended Savonarola as orthodox, and criticised the Inquisition for thoughtless and careless work on the Index. Fortunately, the often hard-line Inquisitor Michele

Ghislieri (later Pope Pius V), admired Ercolani – who had first attracted him to the Dominican Order.[28] In 1562, Ercolani wrote from Rome to Portia Masssimi de'Salviati, in S. Lucia, Florence, that she should be mindful of Savonarola's seven spiritual rules.[29] Ercolani became a bishop much against his will (distracting him from scholarship and prayer), but once enthroned he fulfilled episcopal duties. From remote Sarno he was called to conduct Visitations elsewhere, to involve himself in Dominican business, and be a Legate to Iberia and France (1571–72). He treated Carlo Borromeo's synodal legislation as guide to activity in Sarno, but went on to hold two of his own synods in Perugia, printing the outcome of his two-day synod in 1582. That year he published a new Ritual for his diocese, with glosses on the holy sacraments. He developed a reputation in Perugia for charity towards the poor, prisoners, repentant prostitutes, and those in hospital, bringing in the congregation of Fatebenefratelli to help in Perugia's main Misericordia hospital.

Bishops at Work and Diocesan Organisation

The summaries of 'model' bishops demonstrate most aspects of what could be done. This section will elaborate on some procedures and the organisational systems below bishops. Numerous appointees were far from able to imitate the models, even if willing. Many bishops were called to Rome, or found reasons for being in Rome, rather than in their dioceses. Pius IV after Trent tried to diminish the Rome-based bishops, sending them back to their dioceses, but this policy did not survive. Both Popes and bishops had interests in significant numbers of bishops being at the heart of the Church. According to Eugenio Sonnino, the annual average of bishops residing in Rome between 1600 and 1619 was 46, falling to 37 through 1620–59, and rising to 54 for 1660–79.[30]

How did or should bishops run their diocese or province in the early modern period? They were expected to preach, to the public on major occasions, to their assembled clergy in synods, to parishes, monasteries, confraternities on Visitations. They might preside over major Masses, processions, important ceremonies such as the Maundy Thursday Washing of Feet, Forty-Hour Devotions, or confirmation. For overall command, under Tridentine rules, the metropolitan archbishops were to guide their provinces via triennial provincial councils, gathering together their senior clergy, while individual archbishops and bishops were to hold annual synods for their subordinate clergy, including parish priests and confessors. Both councils and synods might produce printed statutes and edicts, but increasingly edicts and printed guides or admonitions flowed out under episcopal licence to parish priests' personal consideration, or for public reading out and display. Bishops were expected to organise official Visitations, tours of inspection, of their dioceses – led by themselves or vicars general – investigating property, personnel and behaviour of clergy and parishioners. These might then inform and dictate more legislation and edicts. Much official business came their way; dealing with manifold appointments, with interrelationships (and jurisdictional disputes), with central Roman authorities, the heads of Religious Orders, with inquisitors, with secular rulers and councils, with local patrons and holders of patronage rights and privileges. Ecclesiastical courts had to be administered and presided over, petitions heard and answered.

Bishops were not alone; their effectiveness depended not just on their own abilities, but those of effective subordinate officials: vicars general, sometimes coadjutant bishops, *vicari foranei* coordinating groups of parishes and *pieve*, and cathedral and Chapter canons. Such substructures of officials could compensate for the lack of episcopal leadership – whether the incumbent was inoperative through incompetence, indifference, or calls to serve elsewhere in central church government or diplomacy. Episcopal led reform and organisation was at its best when an active archbishop or bishop had a faithful and competent team of vicars general and lesser vicars, cooperative Chapters, enthusiastic available Jesuits, Theatines or Barnabites; and had family wealth to deploy, including on a cultured entourage or court. We cannot point to many such ideal situations under current knowledge.

The realities about Provincial councils, diocesan synods and Visitations seldom matched ideals. As the Appendix indicates Provincial councils were rare events. Three early post-Trent ones – Milan 1565, Benevento 1567 and Ravenna 1568 – were models, both in their organisation, and in the published legislation. But the subsequent history is patchy, with no metropolitan archdiocese having a full record through to the mid-seventeenth century. The southern provinces within Calabria, Campania and Puglia had 31 provincial councils before the close of the century, but only nine in the seventeenth, and only Benevento meeting in the eighteenth (1729). Provinces in the Abruzzi, Basilicata and Molise held no councils

1564–1799.[31] This is unsurprising. Many reformers soon realised that assembling the suffragan bishops (and Benevento had up to 17 from a large area of difficult terrain), along with abbots, priors, vicars, and other selected clergy for one to two weeks was administratively difficult, and costly. The metropolitan had limited control over reluctant bishops, and was probably adequately in touch with the enthusiastic and cooperative anyway. Legislation deriving from the council decisions (or archbishop's dictatorial orders), had to be ratified by the Congregation of the Council. This was often slow in coming, even for as frenetic, powerful and influential an archbishop as Carlo Borromeo – and decrees might be vetoed. More positively however, once printed, the legislation might remain in print, be reprinted, and be influential on both synodal legislation, and episcopal decrees and edicts for years to come. The provincial and synodal legislation flowing from Carlo Borromeo remained influential till the twentieth century, in France and Ireland as well as Italy.[32]

Diocesan synods were simpler, more acceptable, and more frequent. No long-serving bishop could keep up an annual record, though Gabriele Paleotti seems only to have missed two years while bishop and archbishop of Bologna. Milan, Bologna and (more surprisingly) Reggio Calabria have the best record over a long period, while Ferrara had regularity through the 1590s (see Appendix). Vincenzo Maria Orsini, Archbishop of Benevento 1686–1724 seems the first bishop holding an annual synod and publishing the results; he became Pope Benedict XIII. For very small dioceses a synod might be deemed pointless, as Galeazzo Morone, Bishop of Macerata argued to the Congregation of Bishops in 1583, when it chivvied: it only had two parishes, both within the walled city, and he had only about ten clergy under him. Synods usually lasted a day, occasionally two or three. The basic programme involved a Mass with the bishop (or organising vicar general) preaching, then discussion of 'cases of conscience' – the basic moral and canon law questions arising from confessions or ecclesiastical court cases and appeals. The attending clergy might be reminded of Tridentine decrees – as on marriage or confessions – and sent away with more printed decrees and notices to be imparted to their local congregations. A composite set of decrees, even a substantial volume, might be printed and distributed later. It is hard to tell how much real discussion took place, though Gabriele Paleotti in Bologna seemed to encourage this. Some synods had a huge attendance, precluding much discussion; 1284 clergy participated in Gregorio Barbarigo's Bergamo 1660 synod.[33] Both the episcopal pep talks and the published legislation probably were stimuli to better parochial practice. The survival of printed decrees has been the main guide to the frequency of these meetings;[34] but local diocesan studies keep on revealing cryptic references to more meetings. Cesena had at least eleven synods 1564–1607, but only two produced extant printed decrees. Napoleone Comitoli of Perugia (1591–1624), combined his own and predecessors' work in a composite printed collection in 1600; and held probably four more synods afterwards without formal publications.[35] Preparatory work could be as valuable as the actual meetings, as with Archbishop Girolamo Colonna of Bologna, 1632–43. In advance parish priests and licenced confessors, individually or through meetings with *vicari foranei*, were asked to alert the bishop to local problems, difficulties with parishioners, cases that ought to be reserved and referred to the bishop and his court (*curia*). The evidence from Visitations would link with synodal work and publication.[36]

Synodal legislation ranged widely across social issues as well as recondite confessional problems. Legislatory pronouncements need careful treatment as evidence, whether of episcopal mentalities, or the socio-religious problems of the faithful. A particular clause or decree (as warning the priest to avoid blessing the umbilical cord along with the baby, because it might be used in magical medicine), might result from a single case in a remote parish, or be reflecting a widespread local custom. Decrees might be repeated over several years in the same diocese; or a bishop copy a decree from legislation in a totally different area, possibly from laziness. Repetition could suggest that episcopal and vicarial control over malpractices was ineffective.

Perugian publications can exemplify concerns. In his first synod (1564, published 1566), Fulvio Della Corgna (bishop 1550–53 and 1564–74), concentrated on the proper celebration of Mass and other sacraments; he raised issues about witchcraft and the position of Jews, and made book recommendations for the libraries of parish priests. He reiterated the Tridentine rules on marriage – a leitmotif through much Italian synodal legislation and one-off decrees (see Chapter 5). There were only two topics for his second synod (1567, but known through a 1587 reprint); the celebration of Mass, and the payment of tithes. Notably, he wanted Masses to be timed for the convenience of the general public, and not to suit a local patron or big-wig. Bishop Ercolani in his 1582 synod (and its 1584 publication), ranged widely. Like others he re-emphasised Tridentine decrees (as again on marriage), reprinted a number of papal Bulls, including Pius V's March

1566 one banning begging in church, demanding the better observation of feast days, and fulminating against the concubinous, sodomites and blasphemers. Ercolani himself wanted a proper investigation of holy images, to be restored if damaged (and suitable); new images were to be vetted by him. He pressed the clergy to teach Christian Doctrine to children and ignorant adults. Such publications were in Latin, so their impact was dependent on the Latin competence of the parish priests – not something to be fully relied upon, especially beyond service Latin. Bishops however produced versions of key orders and recommendations in Italian. Increasingly through the seventeenth century bishops used Italian for public communication to general clergy, and well as for the laity.[37]

Much legislation and more informal pronouncements, were based on the fact-finding Visitations.[38] Various types of Visitations existed, and can cause confusion. First we have the episcopal Visitation of the diocese, conducted by the bishop himself, sometimes shared with or delegated to his coadjutor bishop or a vicar general. This was designed to investigate all the churches and religious institutions of the diocese; conducted under normal episcopal powers, the bishop could face jurisdictional conflicts with Religious Orders, lay confraternities and hospitals, nunneries, or private princely chapels. Second an Apostolic Visitation, conducted under somebody from outside the diocese concerned, operated with extra jurisdictional powers and authority from the Pope. This was used when the incumbent faced jurisdictional difficulties, or was deemed lax by his metropolitan or the Pope. In the first decades after Trent some notable apostolic visitors appeared; such as Francesco Bossio (or Bossi). An active, austere bishop of the Borromean model in own sees of Gravina (1568–74), Perugia (1574–79) and Novara (1579–84), he was also employed as an Apostolic Visitor, including by Borromeo in suffragan bishoprics in Lombardy, as well as in Genoa and Siena. For the last in 1575 the Congregation of Bishops gave him special powers and instruction to enable effective visitations of hospitals and pious places (confraternities), and obtain their account books. His aggressive procedures led to protests from the Grand Duke of Tuscany. When Borromeo himself encountered jurisdictional troubles, in Milan diocese itself Gerolamo Ragazzoni (titular Bishop of Famagosta) was summoned as a trouble-shooting (and – creating), apostolic visitor.[39] Venice strongly resisted an apostolic Visitation in 1580–81; 'the State's honour would be impugned', and 'they feared that the Visitation would threaten the Freedom of the Republic', as the Nunzio Bolognetti irately summarised it. What Visitors might say, and then order, about nunneries, and the conduct of noble nuns and their families, was the most sensitive point, as he noted. In the end the Visitors kept away from the nunneries.[40] A secular ruler could be happy to call in a special Visitor, as Duke Vincenzo Gonzaga of Mantua did with the leading Jesuit Antonio Possevino, whom he sent in 1594 into his territory of Monferrato involving the dioceses of Acqui, Alba, Casale, followed by parts of the Mantuan Diocese.[41]

A pioneering Apostolic Visitor was Tommaso Orfini, when Pius V gave him this role in October 1566 on his way to his own bishopric in Strongoli. He had had prior experience in Rome itself, but he now entered difficult territory, because he was unwelcome to state and local political powers. He visited 10 dioceses, from Terracina to Aversa, before he reached Naples to clear his position with the Viceroy, Alcalà. The Pope threatened the Viceroy with an Interdict if Orfini was not allowed to continue his work, and Philip II granted an ambivalent permission, telling the Viceroy to deal with the Pope 'with all the modesty that is just and owed'. In all – by late 1568 – Orafini visited 25 localities, involving 16 episcopal seats including Archbishoprics of Naples and Bari. The reports were inevitably brief, but he provided the Vatican with a sample of the deep problems of the South against a background of poverty and ignorance – economic, sexual, doctrinal. He managed to give a range of instructions, general and particular as he progressed. The bishops of Conversano, Molfetta, Monopoli and Ostuni were praised as active residents, preaching and so forth, though some of their Cathedral clergy were scandalous. The bishops of Ferentino and Anagni were concubinous and had children, and the latter's Cathedral services were confused and thoroughly deficient. The bishop and clergy of Bitetto were too involved in commerce. Orfini found a scandalous nunnery of Santa Chiara in Barletta (with nuns' children running about), supposedly supervised by Franciscans who spent their time playing cards and games with laity. The confraternities and hospitals of Naples were praised for their charity; while the seminary at Avellino had completed its first year happily under a good Christian master, for 14 boys. He had time to investigate and find a gentleman's allegation of Lutheranism against his own brother to be false. Orafini was hardly tested as a southern bishop himself, as he was moved to Foligno.[42]

Another kind of Visitation was the Visitation *ad liminem.* This was essentially a paper exercise, though physical Visitations might provide evidence for it. It was a report on the state of the diocese, which the bishop was supposed to compose every three years, and take in person to the Pope. By the turn of the century the production rate was reasonably high, though exemptions from personal attendance were not too difficult to obtain. Accumulating the information for these reports required some diligence within the episcopal system to secure information, as with Cardinal Girolamo Della Rovere's report on his Turin diocese, March 1590.[43] Historians have obtained some valuable information from them, as on hospitals, confraternities, pawnbroking institutions, as well as the holding of synods or conduct of an episcopal Visitation.[44] Caution is however needed, because one bishop might wish to stress his achievements (to stay put, or be promoted to a better see), or excessively highlight the impossibility of his diocese (as against uncooperative secular authorities), its poverty or insalubrity, hoping to get moved, or justify staying in Rome or Naples and not reside in a remote southern diocese.

The diocesan and Apostolic Visitations were very diversely conducted, and are variable as historical evidence. Though much used for Italian university theses, their systematic analysis has been slow and difficult. As both David Gentilcore and Simon Ditchfield have warned, Visitation evidence needs careful handling, best linked with the *ad limina* reports and synodal legislation.[45] Surviving records can be voluminous, with pages for each church or institution; or they might amount to a half a page per church.[46] In general terms the Visitations, as with the rarer medieval ones, gave priority to the physical state of churches and their chapels, of nunneries and their buildings, and to the condition of separate fraternities or hospitals; whether buildings were properly roofed, and had windows, whether the altars were suitably erected, with the necessary accoutrements for the proper celebration of the Mass; whether subsidiary altars were properly provided with priests to fulfil mass obligations, and again fittingly equipped. The Visitors checked on the proper keeping of the reserved sacrament and of holy oil; whether crucifixes and altar pieces were in good condition, if they existed. These were the priorities of the early – often rapid – post-Tridentine visitations; and remained essential aspects all through the period, whether for later quick visits, or as part of some very thorough inspections. Trent emphasised that visitations should be pastoral as well as good housekeeping. Some seemingly did come to involve a significant amount of sermonising.

Increasingly the reports indicate that the bishop or deputy checked whether the priest was properly licenced, how often he was present, and if covered by a curate when legitimately absent; whether record books of births, deaths, marriages and confession–communion were being kept, and checked by the centre; whether the priests and curates had necessary books such as missals and breviaries. Clearly less time and effort was spent on checking more deeply on the suitability of the clergy, educationally, spiritually or morally; even less on the conditions of the parochial laity, or the brothers and sisters in a confraternity. Some visitors checked, and reported on clergy in detail, their competence in Latin, ability to preach suitably, their knowledge of confessional procedure, and what cases were reserved for the bishop, their knowledge of the Tridentine rules on marriage; what sort of library they possessed. Their moral position might be fully investigated, especially if the parishioners expressed worries; whether they had a concubine and bastard children; if they had a housekeeper, was she a close relative, or sufficiently old not to be sexually dangerous? The visitors might more helpfully want to know if the priest was adequately housed close by, and push the parishioners to help fund a suitable parish house. Scrutinising the laity was more time consuming and rare. The priest might be asked to indicate how many parishioners were ineligible for Easter communion, because concubinous, practicing prostitution, failing to make peace with neighbours grievously offended. How far those denounced were pursued or persuaded to reform remains obscure. Laity as well a clergy might be quizzed on how well Christian Doctrine was imparted, how frequently Masses were celebrated, whether clergy conducted funerals properly. Confraternities came under increasing scrutiny, not only for the condition of their chapels or separate oratories, their financial situation and fulfilment of bequests, but also whether they attended the sick, escorted the sacrament and holy oil to the dying and attended funerals. The reports basically summarise, and how much questioning in detail went on is hard to tell. A rare example of almost verbatim reporting appeared in the record of the 1636 visit to the rural *pieve* of San Piero in Bossola (Florence diocese); four parishioners were questioned – complaining about how the parish priest mismanaged and left uncultivated the land for which he was responsible![47]

At their best the visitation records provided a major knowledge basis for episcopal government; 'to know is to govern', as suggested by the title of Cecilia Nubola's model analysis of the very full Visitation surveys of the Trent diocese by Ludovico Madruzzo, 1579–81.[48] With such information a bishop could legislate, provide more guidance and instructions, allocate vicars for greater supervision in rural areas, set them to check back on deficient churches or incumbents, demand documentation from priests or confraternity officials, summon clergy or laity to the ecclesiastical court for questioning and trial. Even if the frequency of visitations was not as great as wanted, and follow-up limited, their fairly regular occurrence in most dioceses at a minimal level, was enough stimulus – as Francesco Cesareo concludes – to improve the religious formation of the clergy and laity, recover their spirituality, so 'there was a general renewal taking place which signified a decisive turning point in the life of the Italian Church.'[49] The fear of Visitation and associated investigations could at least inhibit more publicly scandalous clerical behaviour, whether positive sexual conduct, or gross neglect of duties. Lay attendance at a Visitation is hard to deduce. Some official records read as if nobody from the wider community was there in the church, though that is unlikely. The impact of a Visitation might have been greater in remote areas than in a city parish, because rarer. Some Visitations involved heroic efforts on the part of the bishop and his team, trekking through mountainous areas seeking out remote villages and isolated oratories, as for Paolo Burali through the Piacenza mountains. Borromeo's early biographer and former assistant, Giovanni Pietro Guissani, commented on the arduous climbs through the Lombard mountains, often without benefits of horses so that 'the good Shepherd [*Pastore*] was forced to go many miles on foot, with staff in hand, like one of the poor mountain people, even in the cold or excessive heat. Thus he went to very many places where the face of a bishop had never been seen before, to the astonishment and marvel of those who saw him.'[50] The appearance of a feared archbishop like this, followed by lecturing and quizzing, which often revealed gross ignorance and miserable church conditions, must have had a considerable local impact.

Various lines of personal communication existed between the diocesan centre and the parishes, hospitals and fraternities; notably through various kinds of vicars or rural deacons, in rural areas, or through canons and archdeacons in urban communities. Carlo Borromeo's Milan archdiocese probably pioneered with the most widespread network of contacts, but others (including Madruzzo's Trent), soon followed in expanding networks, giving rural deacons and the like more duties and powers. In particular *pievani* of remaining collegiate 'parishes' (see Chapter 5), parish priests, confessors, sometimes lesser curates, were brought together in regular meetings under vicars or rural deacons, formally to discuss cases of conscience, but also to give information and receive instructions. Wietze De

Boer's recent revealing study demonstrates that the Milan system could foster a disciplining confessional society, creating some fears for the unconventional and less moral, though encouraging the enthusiastic. However, ways existed for less committed clergy and laity to evade or resist excessive dictatorship.[51]

Episcopal reform was thus to be made effective by the interaction of the different levels of clergy. Borromeo seemingly more than most considered confessors as crucial. Traditionally many or most confessors came from the Regular Orders. Given that jurisdictional and discipline difficulties could arise between bishop and heads of Orders, Borromeo tried to rely as much as possible on secular confessors, working closely with parish priests. He desired that absolution be not made easy, that reserved cases be properly referred to him or suffragan bishops, and that in potentially serious heresy cases the penitent be made to report him or herself to the Inquisition (since under the secrecy of the confessional the confessor himself was not meant to disclose such matters). Confessors were also instructed in Borromeo's own edicts and most notably his 1574 *Avvertenze ai confessori*, to check that parishioners were fulfilling parochial duties and observing Christian life styles. Under the Borromean regime 'Confessors thus became quite literally the law enforcement officers, who were to use their privileged access to the soul to assist in the application of church law.'[52] On present evidence Borromeo established the strongest episcopal control network. Other bishops did not necessarily have the same determination for such rigid control, nor the enforcing structures.

The vicarial system – Vicars general and *vicari foranei* – could penetrate into seemingly mundane matters of fairly remote institutions; as revealed by records for the sacrament and rosary confraternities in Bagnacavallo (diocese of Piacenza, archdiocese of Bologna). The vicar general and the *vicario foraneo* liaised in checking on confraternity officials, their relationships with and payments of Franciscan preachers, and building activity. In 1649 the Monsignore Vicario rejected a certain Francesco Maria Vittelloni as *massaro* (a finance official) for the sacrament confraternity, elected by the members, and forced a new selection or ballot. The reasons are not given, but Vittelloni (first spotted as a member in 1637) proves to be a key confraternity member until 1702, serving as *priore*, the presiding official, on several occasions from 1651 – so the veto did not inhibit him for long. Intermittent checking might be seen as keeping institutions on edge and wary, when resources for constant surveyance were lacking.[53]

Bishops could be heavily involved in jurisdictional battles, and their powers severely circumscribed, when competing with the Religious Orders, princely and city patronage rights, or pious institutions. Their control over secular clergy could be very limited, as in the appointment to benefices, ranging from those of parish priests and curates, canons, rectors of hospitals, down to minor chaplains. The right to appoint to benefices on a vacancy – the *giuspatronato*[54] – had over the centuries been granted to princes, powerful families, monasteries and local communities. The right might not be just restricted to nomination, but include rights to construct chapels, decorate them, control incomes attached to them. In return obligations existed to maintain all in good order, and ensure the appointee fulfilled his functions. The patrons could be ecclesiastical or lay; in general the former would be assumed to be more attentive to their duties, whereas the laity had less time to commit to fulfilling obligations, as Gaetano Greco points out. Lay patrons might be more interested in prestige and economic aspects of their patronage, than fulfilment of purpose. Patronage rights in the hands of princes, feudal lords, cardinals and abbots, or civic authorities were also part of the political patronage scene, ways of rewarding subordinates (or family members), and fostering clientele networks. Episcopal attempts to erode these in the interests of religious reform were strongly resisted. The failure of bishops to have full control over benefices, whether simple or with cure, was generally a major setback. However, where on occasions ordinary parishioners had the patronage rights over parish priests, attitudes might be more ambivalent. Local appointment of parish priests and chaplains might foster good priest–parishioner relations; but in the eyes of the rigourist reformers, as when Rome battled against Venice's norm of local householders naming their *pievano* (head priest of the parish), this could be bad for discipline on all sides – and lead to the toleration of clerical fornication and priests' bastards.[55]

The extent of episcopal control and of alienated patronage varied considerably, where known.[56] In Pisa in the sixteenth century the laity controlled 65 per cent of city benefices, 60 per cent of the rural; with five of the city parishes the appointment of the parish priest was in the hands of householders and local institutions. In Florence in the early century 27 of 52 parishes had lay patrons, mainly patricians; half of the 50 *pievi* (collegiate parishes, discussed in Chapter 5) had lay patrons, and more than 80 of the 333 rural parishes had popular patronage. A 1542 Neapolitan pastoral Visitation suggested that virtually all the benefices escaped ecclesiastical authority, and this is supported by detailed modern analysis of the church structure in a large area around Vesuvius. In the 1590s, Bishop Montesanto of Teramo (Abruzzi), could only freely appoint 40 of his 140 benefices; feudal families like the Acquaviva nominated others.[57] Figures for the eighteenth century show that bishops had not made inroads into such lay and non-episcopal control. By Grand Duke Peter Leopold's reforms in Tuscany in the late eighteenth century only about 37 per cent of the parishes were under free episcopal collation. Similar points apply to dioceses as varied as Lodi, Matera, Modena or Verona. Gaetano Greco cites as a rare example the successful campaign by Cardinal Vincenzo Maria Orsini (later Benedict XIII), in the Benevento diocese to test the patronage claims of others, and reclaim episcopal control.

The lives of bishops could be harsh and dangerous. Health hazards, poverty, jurisdictional antagonisms, threats of violence could all deter bishops from residency and activity. From 1635 (and until 1668) a Congregation on the Residence of Bishops specifically confronted this situation, pressurising bishops to be resident, or investigating reasons to licence absence, with a provision for adequate substitute leadership. It fined – lightly – some transgressors. Much of its work concerned dioceses in the Kingdom of Naples, in a period of considerable disturbance and violence, with the 1647 Masaniello revolt in Naples being the highpoint. In the first year 69 Italian bishops (35 of them in the Kingdom) sought dispensations from residency. Getting suitable candidates to accept a southern diocese, and reside, was difficult; and those that did could cause or receive serious trouble. Gerace (Calabria) had no resident bishop from 1622 to 1650, and those who later took up the place were no models. Stefano Sculco (1670–86) was accused of violating a young nun, was forced to resign and confined to a Roman monastery. Bishop Pietro Paulo Russo nominated to Nusco (near Salerno) in 1649 found that a *vicario foraneo* had been killed leaving a threatening atmosphere, and asked for a transfer; but without it he was killed, along with another *vicario*, in 1657. From nearby Lacedonia Bishop Benedetto Bortoli's 1682 *ad limina* relation reported how as a sick man he had been attacked and robbed in his palace by local brigands, who had taken him hostage; after 32 days semi-frozen and near death he had been released after a huge ransom had been paid (over eight times his episcopal income). He sought transfer to a quieter see, and to be replaced by a more powerful incumbent capable of controlling brigands.[58]

This chapter has exemplified the diversity of the episcopacy, and of the conditions under which bishops might bring beneficial changes, or be unable and unwilling to do so. Good leadership, backed by a suitable diocesan structure utilising cooperative contributions from parish priests, confraternities and Religious Orders could bring much reform. But many stumbling blocks existed. It is time to look closer at religious and social life in the parochial localities.

5 *Parish Priests and Parishioners*

Reforming the Parochial Systems

In early modern Italy the parish was not a standard fixed concept, or unit, controlling the religious life of people within a clearly defined area. The Council of Trent aimed to create this, from a mess of systems.[1]

Session 24 of the Council stipulated that bishops should aim to create fixed and clear parish boundaries:

> For the greater security of the salvation of souls committed to them, they divide the people into definite and distinct parishes, and assign to each its own and permanent parish priest, who can know his people and from whom alone they may licitly receive the sacraments ... They shall also take care that the same is done as soon as possible in those cities and localities where there are no parish churches; any privileges and customs whatsoever, even though immemorial, notwithstanding.[2]

Various parochial systems had developed through the middle ages in Italy; more diverse than in most of Europe.[3] In the centre and parts of the south an approximation to a modern parish existed; a church with single parish priest exercising cure of souls over the village, or a manageable portion of the city. This church would have a baptismal font to which local babies would be brought, unless to a Cathedral. However, through the peninsula two collegial systems had developed, with a large baptismal district. The better known and more prevalent system was developed in the north under the Lombards, the *pieve* structure. Baptismal churches (*pievi*) were the focus of a network of lesser churches that would conduct other rites and services; baptisms would take place at this mother church (except under emergency conditions), and sometimes funeral rites had to be held there. The leading priests were based on the *pieve*, travelling to exercise full cure over the lesser churches, which would have curates unless very minor. In many cities the Cathedral (Duomo) might be one of the baptismal churches, even the only one. In parts of southern Italy, but notably in Puglia, another collegiate system had developed, based on mother churches called *chiese ricettizie*. Under this a college of priests collectively exercised control of a network of churches, for cure of souls, and for the common control of the property. In the *pieve* system bishops could exercise significant control, even if others had some patronage rights; with the *chiese ricettizie*, bishops found it very hard to exercise control and jurisdiction. The Tridentine legislation was designed to break down these collegiate systems, and to restructure by creating more equal (in terms of population size and income) independent parishes directly responsible to the bishop and his diocesan team.

Pre-Tridentine reformers like G.M. Giberti of Verona and then post-Tridentine bishops were accelerating an existing process of erosion of the *pievi*, and move to more focused self-contained parish churches. The southern system seemed to be harder to change, which some historians have judged a major frustration for episcopal reform.[4] The ideal was for the parish priest to have a manageable flock to guide and protect, knowing them well, but not being too close to them that he became reluctant to discipline. Much facilitated this, including the Tridentine and subsequent requirements for the parish priest to keep records of births, marriages, deaths and of those to be confessed and to receive Communion at Easter (the *status animarum* registers); the norm that marriages should be concluded in the parish church; that the Easter obligation be celebrated there. However, dismantling all the *pieve* mother church system was often resisted. Archpriests accustomed to controlling a network were reluctant to abandon such influence and power. Patronage rights over appointments to dependent churches, and control over incomes discouraged change. Cathedrals like Pisa and other collegiate churches were loath to give up calling all baptisms to their location, and allow fonts in parishes churches.[5] In Rome itself in the 1620s only 11 parish churches had the right to conduct baptisms. However, discounting this fixation on fonts, by the seventeenth century the modern parish system was generally working, with the emphasis on a resident parish priest (or his officially appointed curate). The rural vicars, *vicari foranei*, provided some linkages between churches as in the *pieve* system, but without undermining the improved cure of souls by the resident priest. The terms *pieve* and *pievano* confusingly remained in use through the seventeenth century as alternative words for parish (*parrocchia*) and parish priest. In Venice the leading priest of the parish was called the *piovano*. Usually elected by the parish householders, he seldom served alone but led a group of priests and curates (*titolati*), within his own parish.[6]

The restructuring in terms of equally sized and funded parishes was problematic. Visitation records after Trent and through the seventeenth century, show that urban parishes varied considerably in population size and resources. In cities such as Perugia, Lecce, Reggio Calabria, Naples and Rome itself we find campaigns to reduce the number of small parishes, break up large ones, and create new ones where the population was expanding. In Naples Archbishop Gesualdo struggled hard to increase the number of parishes from 25 to 37 to serve a population of over 200 000 persons in the 1590s. Perugian bishops between 1564 and 1656 reduced the number of city and suburban parishes from 40 to 36, as the population fell from about 20 000 to 16 000; but in 1656 two parishes were as small as 78 (suburban), and 98 (city), while the largest had 1143 souls. Rome readjusted its parochial system, so that where 85 000 persons were divided between 132 parishes in 1566, 115 000 were distributed across 85 parishes in the 1620s.[7] The 'lost' small parishes enabled little churches to be allocated to new Religious Orders or confraternities. Restructuring in the rural *contado* areas was harder to implement. Dependent pievan churches might become parish churches, and have more functions, without gaining extra resources from the former *pieve* church. But in mountainous areas amalgamations of hamlets and villages with one parish priest made little sense, because of communication difficulties. The diocese of Novara added 43 parishes between 1616 and 1763, mostly in the mountains and around Lake Garda; often under petition from remote communities, wanting resident pastoral care.[8]

The answers for poor remoter parishes were to retain them still as part of a *pieve* or *ricettizie* collegial system, or to use members of Religious Orders, supposedly used to poverty, who would be sent out from the monastery to serve stints as parish priests. But they were hardly susceptible to episcopal control. The Perugian Benedictine monastery of San Pietro claimed control of 28 benefices with cure of souls (i.e. effectively parochial) in the Perugian or neighbouring dioceses, and including one city parish (San Costanzo). When Bishop Della Corgna during his 1564 Visitation found that the priest at the latter did not preach at Sunday Mass, and did not understand Transubstantiation, he launched a campaign to gain full control over these Benedictine benefices; with no success. He and successive bishops found the abbots backed by Roman Cardinals, who ensured the abbey retained its jurisdictional rights. It was not until 1651 that San Pietro surrendered most of its parochial benefices to episcopal control; when the economic depression in Umbria hit their farm incomes. This threw the burden of funding the parishes onto the bishop's financial table – similarly under strain.[9]

Despite these failed campaigns, by the mid-seventeenth century the parish church was a more coherent organisation unit for religious and social purposes, better served by priest and/or chaplains and confessors, and providing the community with a greater sense of Christian values and better knowledge of basic doctrines. The number of clerics in relation to laity increased; those given cure of souls were generally better educated, and were providing more religious knowledge to their flock – often helped by lay men and women in confraternities, and by the Religious Orders. Orthodox Christian reformers had been partly successful. The obverse was that for the immoral, those with more quizzical views on certain Christian Doctrines, or interests in a more 'natural' religion, life might be more dangerous and frustrating.

Finding Suitable Priests

Finding enough suitable priests for the parishes was a major challenge. The increased numbers of educated priests were unevenly distributed through Italy, but overall literacy, knowledge of doctrine and liturgy improved over the period – thanks to some success stories in the creation of diocesan seminaries, colleges run by the Religious Orders, and other institutions, (discussed in Chapter 6). The ratio of priests to city inhabitants increased, possibly implying better spiritual care, but straining fiscal resources. Naples had about 1000 priests for 200 000 inhabitants in 1574; 3849 for 337 075 in 1706. Rome's ratio of secular priest to inhabitants changed from 1 : 81 in 1592 to 1 : 55 by 1760. Reggio Calabria more dramatically changed from only 1 : 250 in 1595 to 1 : 144 in 1642, thanks probably to two very active and long-serving archbishops, G.R. Dal Fosso (1564–92), and A.D. Afflitto (1593–1638), both intent on improving clerical education. Distinguishing between fully titled parish priests, others with cure of souls, and more foot-loose priests is often hard. In the diocese of Novara the number having cure of souls was 309 in 1616–18, with 280 being titular parish priests, for the 186 244 inhabitants. By the mid-eighteenth century for 230 512 persons, 389 had cure of souls, with 332 being parish priests. However, the total of secular priests rose from 485 to 1460. In some cases more priests helped widely in the parish, but many were serving simply as special chaplains and Mass priests.[10]

The better educated clerics were not guaranteed to end up as parish priests, or remain such for long. They might not have taken orders for vocational reasons. Families might pressurise some sons to enter the church as part of family strategies, whether 'political', social networking or economic, as in the Trent diocese.[11] Seminaries offering free places for those from poor backgrounds could be tempting, especially under economic depression. In 1630 Bishop Alessandro Bicchi of Imola, while Nunzio in Naples, complained to Cardinal Francesco Barberini about too many young men seeking ordination to secure tax exemptions.[12] While bishops were not meant to ordain to the priesthood unless a benefice was available, that one need not be a parochial benefice. A poorly funded parish priest might soon seek preferment as a priest attached to establishment figures in the church or in high society; as secretaries, personal chaplains, officials in the episcopal curia. As people continued to leave large sums in their wills for Masses for the dead, it might be more lucrative to serve as a Mass priest than as a parish priest.[13] Men with family money and well educated in universities, colleges or seminaries might prefer to remain in minor orders, and purchase a potentially lucrative position as a *chiericato* in a church administrative office, such as in the Camera Apostolica and Datary, where about 4000 posts were available.[14]

As indicated in Chapter 4 bishops did not always have the power to appoint parish priests, because of others' patronage rights. The bishop could veto, but attempting to do could be fraught with difficulties if the patron was powerful, or if the Bishop faced awkward household electors – as in the system operating in most Venetian parishes, and at least five Paduan ones.[15] However, in trying to improve the situation and battle against the old patronage systems, bishops could have local support. Borromeo and his team in 1564 found the commune of Montorfano (within the Gagliano *pieve*), ready to reject its parish priest, because he was never there to celebrate, and 'so rightly he should be deprived of every benefice'; an encouraging sentiment for reformers. Later, in 1583, the commune of Limido rejected their priest because he would rather play cards and seduce women during confession, than confess the dying (who thus died unabsolved); and he would not support the work of the lay confraternity, Corpus Domini. 'We do not wish him, not because we are not ready to obey, but because the scandals are great.'[16]

Visitation records suggest that over the decades those appointed parish priests were better educated, through a variety of systems, not just seminaries. That education did not guarantee better morality, or pastoral care (Chapter 6). How much checking on the suitability of candidates for the priesthood, and for a benefice was effected, is unclear. The Spanish contingent at Trent in particular had wanted all such appointments to be through a *concorso*: the bishop examining those responding to a general appeal. Its operation in Italy is patchily revealed, for example, in Rome, and in Pisa where examiners, *Essaminatori Sinodali*, were appointed to impose a *concorso* even on benefices under lay patronage. In areas where priests moved about and applicants were not local, it was hard to test qualifications, or be sure of the legitimacy of licenses and testimonials. However, the *concorso* system was used fairly rigorously in Marche dioceses, 1570s to 1590s, with members of Orders helping the bishops. Applicants' weaknesses were revealed, their lack of Latin, inability to preach sensibly and their ignorance of the Gospels. But a good winner of an Ancona *concorso* in 1592 declined the offer when he found that the parish was burdened by a pension, leaving him little income. Others who could read well also were unwilling to serve. Economic difficulties worked against getting the best candidates outside the leading cities.[17] Some bishops, as in Faenza, preferred to settle for candidates with a good reputation, and an ability to administer the sacraments properly and frequently, over formal education. Visitors, as in 1574 to the poor diocese of Comacchio, which could not afford its own seminary, recognised that the bishop would have to accept poor quality parish priests and canons.[18] Bishops might be pressurised over appointments, by canons, powerful families or Roman dignitaries. Incumbents might bargain their resignation for naming their successor (a relative) and with a right to reclaim if desired.[19]

Incomes for parish priests were usually meagre, and theoretically adequate incomes could be plundered for pensions for a patron or others. Further, well-qualified priests might be appointed and then appoint less suitable deputies on a fraction of the income, and themselves pursue other lucrative careers in the church, or elsewhere. A Venetian patrician, who was an absentee titular parish priest of Saletto (in the Padovano), with a supposed income of 260 ducats, paid his deputed chaplain just 30 ducats (when 100 ducats was an adequate level of remuneration).[20] Poor parish priests might supplement incomes by saying special masses elsewhere (to the detriment of their main flock), or by teaching. Many had to have secular-based incomes. Paduan Visitation records from 1560 to 1594 show priests as also being merchants and farmers; and records for southern dioceses indicate the same later, with priests notably involved in the olive oil business. Sometimes bishops, recognising the financial realities, licenced such extra-curial activities. The financial position often worsened in the seventeenth and eighteenth centuries; priests' incomes based on rents from long leases could not be readily updated for inflation, and parishioners under their own pressures might strike against tithes, as in the Kingdom of Naples.[21] Playing a secular role alongside parishioners could limit their disciplinary powers, and moral leadership, as well their time for pastoral care.

The origins of parish priests, again from still limited analysis, are shown to be very variable. The seminary system (and allied colleges), encouraged recruiting both from upper echelons of society (with families paying for places), and from poor but honest families, with free places. An analysis of 188 pupils in the Milan seminary 1568–76, whose parental origins are known, suggests that 40.9 per cent came from the upper classes (18 per cent nobles, military and investors; 22.8 per cent from liberal professions and merchants), while 10 per cent were agricultural and 7 per cent labouring. Artisans dominated the middling sector, with some others being teachers and *scrivani* (letter and document writers). But as the official Milanese documentation noted, only about 20 per cent of its diocesan clergy by 1599 was coming with a seminary background. The others would almost certainly have had a middle-lower social background.[22] Seminarians and priests from upper levels of society might find it harder to adjust to small town or rural parishes, while the long period spent in a seminary away from the family through teenage years might inhibit dealings with secular families in the parish. The hierarchy in the Bologna archdiocese at least recognised with some compassion that their priests might be intellectually and socially isolated, as well as physically, in the remoter parishes.[23]

The geographical origins of priests varied. Under the southern *ricettizie* system priests were likely to be from local families, utilising the patronage system. In the north Pisa, Trent and Novara are known to have recruited locally; Novara had about 90 per cent of its parish priests born in the diocese, with significant numbers from well-off families. Novara was good at clerical training. The Venetian household electoral system chose clerics from fairly humble backgrounds in the Veneto, if not the city itself. For much of Italy clerical appointments involved long-distance moving, with Rome scattering many. Reformers had to balance between having priests who were 'distant', who could exercise discipline and not show favouritism, but not too alien to have no understanding of the local community; against recruiting locals who might comprehend individual or family issues, but become compromised by them. This affected local attitudes to the priest's moral conduct, and notably continuing concubinage (see below).

The Duties of Parish Clergy

Following Trent the duties of parish priests and their assistants increased considerably, both in strictly religious obligations, and wider social and administrative roles imposed by secular as well as church authorities. They were under pressure to have a major parochial Mass every Sunday and on major feasts, when they were to give a sermon, or at least read from some religious text. Normally, baptisms and marriages were to be parochial church events. With or without the assistance of confraternities or Regulars, they were to teach Christian Doctrine regularly to children, and adults found too ignorant of basic doctrines (tested before marriage). While it was only obligatory to confess and receive communion at Easter, religious reformers encouraged more frequent confession and communion, with many confraternities, and increasingly lone women from the upper levels of society, being enthusiasts. Such added priests' duties, and encouraged the fuller use of licenced confessors, whether Regulars or other secular clergy. Priests were pressed to be assiduous in visiting the sick and dying at home, taking them the sacrament and holy oil. Given reformers' desire to locate lay confraternities in parish churches under parochial supervision, the parish priests had to spend more time saying masses for them, hearing confessions, attending meetings, even if these societies also paid for other non-parochial clergy (see Chapter 7).

The parish clergy had to keep fuller records on their parishioners – and report on them. While the church had expected priests to register births, baptisms and deaths, Tridentine rules and subsequent episcopal policies helped ensure their being kept, and shown to Visitors and vicars general. Given the new rules on marriage (see below), marriage registers were added to the cupboard. More intrusively priests were now required to keep *status animarum* (literally state of the souls) records. Primarily these were household registers indicating who should be confessing and communing at Easter, who was not yet of age, and who, though of age, was ineligible (and under religious penalties), because living in concubinage, being prostitutes, or refusing to make peace with neighbours, as in a vendetta, or after manslaughter (as a prerequisite for absolution). Such investigations by the parish priest and his assistants could obviously be intrusive; but also beneficially lead to better pastoral care of those in trouble and need, as sampled Roman parish records demonstrated.[24] Detailed sampling proves that the clergy varied considerably in their enthusiasm for recording or omitting the moral backsliders, even if thorough in counting each household unit. The clergy in cities like Bergamo, Bologna, Rome and Venice utilised the information to help decide which parochial poor and sick at home needed assistance (Chapter 7).

The diocesan system both pushed and pulled the parish clergy into reform; through formal and informal visits, calls to meetings for confessional problems or synods, and through printed instructions. From the mid-sixteenth century the expansion of printing assisted the new parochial regimes, provided the priests and chaplains could read – though my viewing several editions of Missals, Breviaries and Catechisms of the later sixteenth century indicates that their small, cramped format was hardly user friendly. The clergy were expected to have a basic library – how basic depended on episcopal views. If Bishop Comitoli of Perugia in 1600 did not want the priest to 'read books, letters or other writings beyond what was necessary for saying the Offices',[25] Bishop Signicelli of Faenza in his 1569 synod had an optimistic list of recommendations: a bible with commentary by an approved author, the Roman Catechism, a Ritual and a Ceremonial for celebrating Mass, a homily book for Sunday and feast day instruction, manuals about the sacraments, a guide (*prontuario*) for solving moral cases. He should also have a *Summa* manual for guiding him through confessions (preferably one of the old favourites, the *Armilla* or *Antonina*), along with the pastoral rule of Gregory the Great and St John Chrysostom's dialogue on the priesthood. The constitutions of the 1568 Ravenna Provincial Council were also required. The 1615 Faenza synod shortened this list: Bible, Catechism, Trent decrees, a Life of Christ and the Saints, and a *Summa* for cases of conscience. Archbishops and bishops like Borromeo (as in his 1569 Brescia synod), Paleotti, Bollani, Della Corgna, Panigarola all produced similar recommendations, while Paleotti stressed that for those weak in Latin a vernacular manual by St Antonino would suit.[26] Panigarola when bishop of Asti attached a simple Italian guide for being a good priest to his formal synodal decrees; and bishop G.B. Costanzo of Cosenza in 1606 produced a guide (*Avvertimento per l'offitio del Rettor Curato*), which by 1609 he sent out to all parish priests for their library.

Inevitably the actual size and content of parochial libraries varied considerably – from 22 to 225 volumes in Rimini's urban parishes in the 1570s and 1580s – though some cupboards might be bare. In poorer areas monastic libraries could assist the local priests.[27] What puritan reformers did not want was the more interesting library of a Paduan parish priest in 1559. He had useful and acceptable works, such as Missals, Breviaries, St Antonino's *Confessionale*, St Jerome's Epistles, works on marriage, on confessing nuns, on the spiritual life and a good death. He had Malerbi's vernacular Bible of 1502 – not yet completely banned. But he also possessed Dante's *Divine Comedy*, Ariosto's *Orlando Furioso*, Pulci's *Morgante*, Bernardo Accolti's *La Virginia*, works by Poliziano, Martelli, Pietro Aretino (on Genesis), and a history in Castilian.[28]

Few parish priests can be brought to life, and good examples deserve more space than is available here. I have previously cited Valentino Giovio in Perugia as an example of the reform of priestly conduct through the 1560s and 1570s, serving parish, confraternities and bishop.[29] Wietze De Boer has noted Hieronimo Di Basti, the curate of Malgrate in Lombardy, on a learning curve under Borromean reform.[30] That a remote area could long hold an educated and dedicated priest is exemplified by Father Matteo Pinelli (1577–1669), who served as parish priest in Cerliano in the remote Tuscan Mugello 1606–69, in succession (by popular vote of the parish householders) to an uncle who had brought him up. His own surviving writings show him musical (especially as organist), literary (admiring Petrarch, and composing a poem attacking tobacco), dedicated to repairing and embellishing his parish church, educating children through a confraternity he created in an oratory he helped have built, and sustaining his flock through plague and economic crises. At parishioners' request he rejected an invitation to move to a better parish. He ran a large household of relatives (10 in 1649). From his seeming remoteness he could contact other educated clergy, including friends and mathematical correspondents of Galileo and a leading Florentine counsellor.[31]

The Parish Church as Focus

From the laity's viewpoint the parish church and its clergy became more important as reforms were imposed, sometimes lessening loyalties towards the religious houses and lesser chapels, though the faithful having fulfilled duties within the parish church were free to attend services elsewhere. The parish church and its environs (such as porticos), as a significant public space, had been used for secular purposes – business meetings, trading, petitioning, and social encounters licit and illicit. It provided sanctuary from the law – if not always respected. Such uses were discouraged, though not fully eliminated, while more frequent religious usage was fostered or enforced. Public Masses on Sundays and feast days, with sermons or at least homiletic readings, should have been regular. Baptisms and weddings were normally now to be in the parish church. Some teaching of Christian Doctrine to children and some adults was to take place in church on a regular basis (Chapter 6). The number of lay confraternities based in the parish church increased, especially in smaller communities, which brought at least select parishioners into church more often for prayers, saying the rosary, attending Vespers and Offices of the Virgin (Chapter 7). Through such confraternities the laity often played significant roles in improving the physical conditions of the churches, their decoration, their sacred vessels, and providing organs and music.

While normal daily or weekly practice is hardly documented, the supposition is that the ordinary Sunday Mass was better conducted on average than before, with better instructed priests, curates and acolytes, guided by the printed official literature. The number of feast days supposedly of obligation, necessitating abstention from work, increased. Sometimes bishops voluntarily or under pressure reduced local feasts, so that people could have enough days to work for themselves, and not just for landlords. They were exposed to more sermons, but these could attract and cause interaction, being in the vernacular, as Jean Delumeau argued. The main service in Latin had limited congregational participation, without singing or vocal prayer. More attention was given to the Eucharist, the display and honour of the Host, with churches cleared of impediments to viewing the high altar. The Visitations checked that altars were equipped for the respectable, even showy, celebration of the Mass. Seating was limited, encouraging perambulation, though some Visitors and bishops tried to ensure that partitions kept males and females separate to reduce distractions.[32] Wealthier parish churches increasingly had organs. Confraternities might use them for *laude* singing in other ceremonies than the Mass. Some parish churches might be elaborately decorated for major Church feasts, have Christmas cribs, or elaborate scenic structures and lighting for the Forty-Hour (*Quarantore*) celebrations – though these were more the speciality of confraternities and Jesuits (see Chapters 7, 9 and 10).

The laity continued to use churches and their environs for their own celebrations beyond official church services, and came under attack for doing so, as indicated in synodal legislation. Carlo Borromeo had campaigned vigorously against dancing on Sundays and feast days, in or anywhere near a church; in the 1570s he made this offense a reserved case, punishable even by excommunication, and liable to public penances. The Jesuits weighed in with relentless sermon campaigns, such that in one village in Lent 1575 'the peasants were too frightened to dance and dress up in costume, and so regretted their numerous sins committed at that time that they began to call on (the Jesuits) to confess their sins'. However, parish priests regularly asked Milan to be able to absolve this offence. A Senator Scipione Suarez di Canova attacked the Vimercate provost for threatening dancers with excommunication and banning unmarried women participating from marrying for two years; these were 'scandalous words, contrary to all reason'. In 1579, Gregory XIII was told by Milanese secular leaders that attacks on dancing undermined time-honoured procedures by which 'many marriages are born'.[33] The extreme form of the campaign seems to have petered out, though bishops everywhere may have tried to keep dancing out of the church itself. Bologna was still condemning dancing in church in 1698.

Vigils of major feasts remained occasions for entertainment and superstitious practices; for eating, drinking, great noises to frighten away evil spirits, as on Holy Thursday or – in Perugia and Cortona – all through Holy Week early in the morning. The celebration of John the Baptist's feast (24 June) remained popular, with bells ringing through the night, ritual bathing for purification and renewal, young persons in particular collecting special herbs for prognosticating love matches or medicinal remedies. Southern dioceses had such festivities in and out of church at Christmas as well. Local clergy were probably complacent about such activities, if not complicit.[34] More alarmingly, churches continued to be used as refuges for criminals and bandits.[35]

Tridentine reform sought greater parochial control over the rites of passage, involving a major struggle over marriage, if not baptism and burial. Baptisms were to be registered through parochial records, and unless the child's life was in danger the baptism should be in the recognised baptismal font (in Cathedral, *pieve* or parish). In an emergency a lay person, such as the midwife, could baptise the baby. Registering births had been more common pre-Trent than any other church recording, so this was easier to enforce.[36] The reforming church required the recording of godparents, who were held responsible for registering the birth; and it sought to limit the numbers of godparents to two or three. In the past for social reasons, such as 'protection' and networking, families named many protecting godparents. Godparenting, however created spiritual relationships inhibiting marriage alliances, and this could be a serious complication in closely knit communities. Even with limits on godparents, post-Tridentine bishops, as in Piedmont, found themselves under pressure to give dispensations for marriages that otherwise broke rules of spiritual relationship as well as consanguinity, because of a shortage of eligible partners. In dealing with baptisms practices varied as to whether still-births and early post-natal births should be recorded, whether illegitimacy should be noted (with the formula 'ex damnato coitu'). Episcopal legislation attacked various unacceptable popular practices associate with baptisms, such as ringing bells to ward off evil and preserve the child's life – supposedly a Venetian habit. Priests were warned to ensure they did not end up blessing the umbilical cord also (useful for medicinal cures), or extraneous objects that might be used for later magical practices. Synods such as those of Cervia (1577) and Melfi (1675) suggested baptising the child naked; but in (colder) Aosta the apostolic visitor G.F. Bonomi in 1576, and Nunzios later, condemned this procedure.[37]

Betrothal and Marriage

In the Council of Trent the Church laid claim to full control over betrothals and marriages, especially in the main decree, *Tametsi*

(Chapter 2). Ludvig von Pastor saw reform of the family, and marriage in particular, as the most important conciliar programme after the reform of the clergy.[38] Subsequent conciliar and synodal legislation testified to the perceived importance of the topic, and the difficulties in persuading the laity to obey the rules.

The Council demanded, however, that a marriage be canonically validated by being witnessed by a priest (normally the parish priest of one partner), and two other witnesses, with the use of an approved formula, 'Ego vos in matrimonio coniungo, in nomine Patris et Filii et Spiritus Sancti' [I join you in marriage, in the name of the Father, Son and Holy Spirit), or similar in Latin or Italian according to provincial usage. This was preceded (unless by special episcopal dispensation), by public announcements (banns) in the parish church(es), on three previous feast days to ensure no impediments existed. Those contracting clandestine marriages, or evading these procedures, committed mortal sins, and were subject to ecclesiastical punishments. The couple might be sacramentally wed in the eyes of God, but the Church could put them asunder until due canonical process was fulfilled. The sacramental bond could not be annulled, so while the couple might never come together again, they could not marry another until the original partner was dead. The Church did not demand parental or guardian consent to a marriage of minors, though advised it should be sought; but some secular rulers, from Duke Emmanuele Filiberto of Savoy in 1566 to Grand Duke Peter Leopold of Tuscany in the later eighteenth century, made it a civil offence to marry without such consent.

How quickly the new rules were enforced, and records of marriages kept is not clear, given the patchiness of suitable Church documents. Records for the southern area of Cilento (dioceses of Capaccio, Vallo di Lucania and Policastro), suggest a persistence of clandestine and irregular marriages through the period, even an increase in the eighteenth century.[39] The Church in Italy turned marriage into a Church matter, confining notaries to a secular role for dowries, and removing them as marriage makers. Ecclesiastical courts became the arbiters of valid marriages. The Church did not produce a formal marital liturgy. Gabriele Paleotti for his Bolognese parish priests provided a guide on what should or could be involved, with comments on the importance of marriage. He emphasised the need for banns, and a check on impediments to forestall later complications; the desirability of parental consent. He wanted priests to check the couple knew the Pater Noster, Ave Maria and Ten Commandments. The wedding ceremony should not be a fashion display, but conducted in a seemly manner; no dance music or 'ridiculous spectacles' on the way to or from the church, or excessive feasting – but he was not banishing suitable hilarity. The wedding itself should consist of the Mass, the blessing of the ring, a sermon, and the final linking of the couple under a veil. A final blessing on the couple as they left the church was desirable; but only for those of the parish, and only for the first marriage, not for widows or widowers. The blessing was to be delayed if the wedding was in a closed season – from the first Sunday in Advent to Epiphany, and from the beginning of Lent until the Easter octave. How common such helpful guides were elsewhere in Italy is not clear.[40]

The constant repetition of *Tametsi*, or similar decrees, in synodal legislation, as well as warnings to parish priests from vicars to announce the rules from the pulpit, and enforce them, suggest a long uphill struggle to get the laity and clergy, to conform fully. It had to be emphasised that a valid betrothal (*de futuro*), was no longer turned into a valid marriage by consummation; new witnessed promises were needed. We know from court records that in dioceses like Padua and Feltre people long believed that 'consent makes a marriage' without benefit of clergy. Courts themselves could be confused over differences between future and present promises, and were quite free with dispensations to 'regularise' irregular 'marriages', presumably in the interest of social harmony.[41] In some supplementary interpretations, even if vows *de presenti* were properly exchanged, the couple was not to consummate until receiving a nuptial blessing at a solemn Mass; and that might be delayed, as Paleotti indicated. In the southern diocese of Capaccio (under Salerno), couples were excommunicated for cohabiting before receiving such a nuptial blessing to complete the process. The same records suggest that it was there reasonably easy to obtain a licence from a vicar general to have a wedding celebrated in a church other than the parish(es) of the couple, and even in a private house.[42]

A priest had to be present to make a wedding canonically valid; but he need not explicitly consent, nor even speak to validate it. The Congregation of the Council ruled in 1581 that a marriage was still legal even if the priest was present under some compulsion, provided two other witnesses were involved. In Manzoni's famous nineteenth-century historical novel (set in seventeenth-century Lombardy), *I Promessi Sposi* (*The Betrothed*), the ploy attempted by the lovers – trying to complete their marriage by exchanging vows *de presenti* when their priest was under pressure from a local baron to stop it – could have been judged successful in reality had the couple managed to say the magic words while the priest was still present in the room. Pope Benedict XIV indicated that such ploys to evade clerical and parental approval were a menace still in the eighteenth century.[43]

In contrast to lovers wanting to marry against opposition, parents or guardians tried to force marriages against the wishes of one or both in a putative marriage, as of old. Tridentine legislation trying to ensure genuine consent by the couple did not prevent pressures continuing. However, some partners were able to secure annulments or legal separations because they had been forced into marriage, as Joanne Ferraro's recent study of the Patriarch of Venice's court records has shown.[44] Cases were made that a woman out of 'grave fear' (not just 'reverential fear') of parents and other relatives had been forced to agree to a marriage promise, that she had been similarly forced to consummate it, without love or consent. The court could then annul the marriage (so the couple could marry chosen partners), or at least order a separation, significantly meaning the return of the dowry to the woman. Real fear nullified the sacrament; and consummation, if under fear, would not inhibit a new marriage. A husband might even consent and not contest the woman's plea, when he realised she would never willingly be a wife, and her family had frightened her into it; as in the case of Lorenzo Comelli and Paolina Pirron in 1629 (though it took 15 years to reach this agreement). Ferraro's study suggests that forced marriages were quite common, and that people from all levels of society, at least in Venice, could secure a remedy. Camilla Belloto, daughter of a silk weaver and a prostitute, in 1617 initiated a case for formal separation alleging her husband, textile worker from Palmanova in Friuli, had married her to exploit her as a prostitute, so he was not a true husband. When this claim failed, she was successful in 1620 with a different claim for annulment, that her tyrannical father had forced her into the marriage, had 'sold' her to the husband for prostitution.[45]

Annulment, effectively 'divorce' even if the Church did not admit that word, and separation could come for other reasons than fear-forced original contracts and forced consummation. 'Divorce' might be used when a court officially ordered or ratified a permanent separation of a couple, who could not marry again. Original deceptions, failure to understand what was happening as an 'innocent', cruelty during the marriage, abandonment and other factors could all be involved, though a failure by one of the partners to consummate the marriage was a common claim – whether or not the 'true' cause.

Oscar Di Simplicio's study of Sienese cases shows that courts accepted not only adultery, but physical violence as grounds for a separation order, especially when a wife indicated she would rather be imprisoned than return to a cruel husband. Husbands secured separations following the wife's immorality, desertion or scolding.[46] Many witnesses might be called, and much prurient evidence offered, before a decision was reached. Theatricality and fictionalisation to assist a case was evident, as well as human tragedies and miseries. Many petitioners were mature and acting long after the initial contract. In entertaining such cases, and granting significant numbers of separations, and even annulments, the Church was recognising that Tridentine procedures to guarantee voluntary consensual marriages were not that successful, and that subsequent marital breakdown could be recognised.

Many popular practices and beliefs surrounding marriage came under synodal attack. Condemnations may reflect just one case, or a prevalent habit. Various synods told priests to ensure engaged couples attended church when banns were read; according to the 1577 Rimini synod, some feared they would go deaf on hearing the announcement. Many condemned those who consummated the relationship between betrothal and banns 'on the pretext of avoiding witchcraft which will impede copulation' (Rimini 1624); they should be kept apart and surveyed until all ceremonies were completed (Perugia 1575). Alternatively, the couple might avoid sex for some time after the blessing, to deceive witches and demons who might attempt to harm conception – 'The Nights of Tobias', as this was called. The condemnation of drinking at church weddings (as from Milan 1565 or Anagni 1596), along with attacks on old habits of toasting, then breaking glasses and plates on the church floor, throwing grains, distributing foods, making a pie with live birds in it (with sexual implications, Viterbo 1584), muttering obscenities in the groom's ear may eventually have produced more sober church scenes. But it was probably harder to eliminate the jokes, horse-play, obscenities and rough music accompanying the couple to and from church, as discouraged by Paleotti, and condemned by Perugian bishops in 1600 and 1632. Widows might be deprived by church leaders of a second blessing on remarriage, but bishops tried to curb public animosities against second marriages, condemning the practices of 'scampanate': the loud ringing of bells and other noises as they went to church (alleviated or stopped if she paid a fine, or distributed wine). Sometimes such activities were organised by local youth societies, youth abbeys, as in

Piedmont, which led a number of popular religious practices, entertainments, and social-inversion critiques of society. Such procedures against remarrying widows (punished for making life difficult for younger unweds), persisted in such varied parts of Italy as Basilicata, Montefeltro and the Valtellina until the early twentieth century – reflecting limits to episcopal control and legislatory fulminations.[47]

In a more positive vein, bishops and parish priests offered comments and guidance on Christian marriage. While Carlo Borromeo followed the traditional teaching that marriage was an inferior status to celibacy, and a remedy against fornication and sin, he was ready to stress, as in his 1584 homily, that a good Christian marriage was the foundation of a stable society, and the way to bring up moral children; marriages planned for status and money created disorder. Paleotti appended to his earlier mentioned guide for curates 24 sermons, in different styles, they might use, or adapt. For him marriage gave three benefits – faith, offspring and a sacrament (sermons 1 and 10). A voluntary matrimonial union was of a divine and human nature, like Christ's union with his Church (3, 10 and 12). He used the Old Testament story of Tobias (a standard text in the Vulgate, if banished to the Apocrypha in King James' Anglican Bible), to stress the desirability of a suitable preparation for marriage, (sermons 2 and 7). The parish priest might still pick a sermon about marriage being a remedy against illicit sex and sin (sermons 3 and 6).[48]

Confession

The relationship between parishioner and priest was likely to be closest, most fraught or most satisfying through the process of confession, penance and absolution. As already indicated reforming bishops were intent on priming parish priests, as well as specialist confessors, to conduct confessions effectively, and to discuss general problems arising in meetings of clergy. The place of confession in early modern religion and society has been, and remains, hotly contested.[49] Some have seen the Reformation as partly caused by unease about the tyranny of the fifteenth century confessional procedure (as notably attacked in the north by Oecolampadius), as manuals encouraged a greater intrusion into the lives of the public. Possibly in light of this, Bartolomeo Fumo's well recommended *Summa* (1554), warned confessors not to be interrogators, not seek too many details about other people, and just encourage the penitent to speak willingly; to pressurise only when the penitent was excessively reticent. Neapolitan archbishops warned that excessive questioning might incite to sin, and the 1614 Roman Ritual cautioned that confessors risked putting ideas into young persons' heads through direct questioning.[50] However some modern scholars argue that post-Tridentine reformers led by Borromeo and his admirers created an intrusive confessional society, with the parishioners pressurised by parish priest, specialist confessors, and the inquisitors.[51] However, some eagerly sought confession, as clearly not onerous. Borromeo, and later Roberto Bellarmine themselves complained that absolution was too easily granted by most priests and confessors.

Confession became more common, and more private. The long running campaign for more frequent communion for the laity, by confraternities, Jesuits, lay reformers like Buonsignore Cacciaguerra, bishops like Agostino Valier, necessarily meant more frequent confession as prelude; though one suspects that confessions other than before Easter Communion might be brief and perfunctory, if it was a private individual act at all. The introduction of the 'secret' confessional box has been noted as a significant post-Tridentine innovation, fostered most by Borromeo, even if he was not the inventor (but possibly Gian Matteo Giberti in Verona), and later described in his *Instructiones* on architecture.[52] The wooden confessional was to have a chair for the confessor, and a kneeling place for the penitent, with a partition and grill to separate them; all basically within an enclosed box. It was designed to give specific place within the church for private confession; and to inhibit physical contact between confessor and penitent. Contrary to later discussion, and practice, it was not designed to hide the priest, introduce anonymity between confessor and penitent, or shield from the rest of the church that a confession was taking place. It was to prevent overhearing the confession, but especially to limit the chance of unseemly contact, especially with female penitents. From 1565 a number of dioceses besides Milan recommended the construction of partitioned confessionals, including in Bologna, Brescia and Fiesole. Later they could become elaborate structures incorporated into new architectural designs – as in San Fedele, Milan or San Paolo, Bologna. By the early seventeenth century, Visitors were regularly checking on their installation in humbler parish churches.

The confessional structure may have encouraged greater voluntary confession, with some physical separation, and avoidance of direct eye contact. Lawrence Stone argued that Catholic private confession, in contrast to Protestant practices, provided for many a safety valve, relief from guilt, especially over sexual matters; provided the confessor was not too inquisitorial. Lay enthusiasm for confession may be adduced from seventeenth-century printed literature and illustrations popularising techniques of self-examination and confession. Many women, up to the mid-sixteenth century often reluctant to attend confession, may have been attracted to frequent confession, as a socially acceptable way of leaving the house, meeting other women in church, and as a chance to discuss personal, including sexual, and family matters outside the household, and with more or less guaranteed secrecy. Giovanni Romeo suggests the development of female confession as a mass movement, encouraged by Jesuits. Neapolitan women developed strong bonds with particular confessors, preferably parochial or regular Regulars, rather than a less known itinerant confessor. The confessor might be carefully selected, to avoid excessive sexual control or condemnation. Confession could be a healing and comforting process, as well as punitive and threatening.[53]

The threatening nature of the confessional process, for some, cannot be denied. Borromeo's system undoubtedly tried to use the confessional to unmask heresy, if not sexual misdemeanours. He took full advantage of the authority given by Trent to bishops to vet and licence confessors from the Orders, and to build them into a network of confessional control.[54] As serious Protestant heresy diminished, intrusions went deeper into undesirable social behaviour. In dealing with heresy Borromeo organised his confessors to use penance and absolution to bring about conversion; he almost bullied his confessors to prevent them being too lax in absolving before the penitent showed contrition, and recognition of errors of belief and ways. Confession could readily become a trial procedure. Absolution could be delayed to establish genuine recantation. Non-parochial regular confessors were urged to cooperate with parish priests to secure a full picture of the penitent's record. Borromeo increased the range of cases that had to be reserved for confession and absolution by bishops, vicars general and Cathedral penitentiaries, which might add to the fear of penitents. From archbishop to parish priest the power of imposing public penances to secure absolution aided a strong disciplining process and fear mechanism. The confession was meant to be secret, the confessor not meant to reveal what was confessed, even if to a murder, rape, or serious heretical beliefs. The public penance could partly reveal the sins at issue and add to shame. Borromeo led the way in following a 1559 Bull and subsequent Inquisition order that confessors should question penitents whether they knew heretics and what they did or said, and whether they had prohibited books. If they gave a positive reply they had to be made to report to an Inquisition tribunal, without absolution. Inquisition records do not indicate that priests and confessors broke the confessional seal to tell the Inquisition what the penitent had confessed; but many supposedly 'voluntary' appearances and self-denunciations must have been under such pressure. This transferral of investigation could lead to naming others and causing them trouble (avoided in a normal confession), as Vienna Bertapaia uncomfortably realised in having to denounce her son-in-law to the Venetian tribunal in 1576, to avoid her own excommunication.[55] (See Chapter 9.)

The confessional seal of secrecy worried many, priests and laity. Lombard congregations of clergy at least, and Jesuits, debated whether dire changing circumstances meant it could sometimes be broken; or broken after the penitent's death to do right for heirs or neighbours. Trent had insisted that secrecy was a social necessity even if not divinely ordained. Bassiano Staurengo, addressing fellow priests in the *pieve* of Incino insisted on it, on both sacred and efficacious grounds. He noted that parishioners were fearful of confessing all sins 'to the greatest detriment of their soul, because the devil tells them to be cautious', and:

> As for myself, even if the penitent were firmly committed to killing his own confessor or had assassinated my relatives, this would not allow me to accuse him, nor to use it as an excuse of anger, nor to show him any sign of this. The holy Mother Church wills all this, so that nobody will remain contaminated and all sinners will feel safe to confess.[56]

The fear of the indiscreet confessor and of gossip was an obvious factor, and might lead to continuing protests against the sacrament of confession, as among Venetian Arsenal workers in 1562.[57]

Peacemaking

Some reformers campaigned to counteract the social tensions, feuds and vendettas in villages, parishes and urban neighbourhoods. Reconciliation between neighbours was a target of confessional priests, and major preachers. Confessors could require penitents to make peace with their neighbours, or offended parties, before granting absolution. Carlo Borromeo in a 1581 Lenten address said that before the Easter sacrament people 'should abandon all hatred and enmity, and arrange for peace with everybody'. On Visitations he exercised personal influence to bring disputants to reconcile themselves. Cardinal Federico Borromeo followed a similar campaign in his preaching and Visitations. Paleotti himself went into mountain fastnesses to persuade hiding unconfesseds to return home to make peace, be absolved and receive communion. Peacemaking could be a sizable problem for the parish; in 1567 the chaplain of San Vittore in Varese reported that 46 apt for communion had failed to confess; 16 of these involved social conflicts, such as vendettas, legal suits, conflicts over honour. Priests quite often reported that parishioners adamantly refused to reconcile themselves over disputes, but Lombard correspondence shows priests battling against serious threats and abuse to achieve some reconciliations, with the increasing backing of the Religious Orders.[58]

Preaching peacemaking, practiced by Capuchins and Jesuits most notably, had an honourable tradition. Most famously it had been promoted in the early fifteenth century by San Bernardino da Siena. He had emphasised that peace was not only disturbed by physical violence, but also by verbal abuse, or backbiting (*chiaccheria*), which could be equally dangerous. He used the proverb 'La lingua non ha osso, e fassi rompere il dosso': 'the tongue has no bone but breaks the back'.[59] The Jesuits, recognising that public words could also heal, developed their peacemaking in the seventeenth century into 'the spectacle of universal forgiveness', in which they got those involved in vendettas and family feuds to reconcile themselves in public church ceremonies, after a forceful sermon, with well-rehearsed speeches by the main persons involved. They also returned to the medieval practice of an *arbitrato,* where the settlement of the dispute was ratified by a judge, agreed by the parties involved.[60]

Priest–Parishioner Relations and Immorality

Two aspects of clerical immorality – concubinage and sexual abuse of the confessional relationship – increasingly worried reforming bishops, and in the latter case, the Inquisition. Clerical celibacy had been imposed on the western Church in the eleventh and twelfth centuries, with some long-term resistance. Popular anticlericalism might suggest this was as much honoured in the breach; and the sexual immorality, real or imagined, of priests, monks, friars and nuns fuelled Protestantism. The choice of clerical marriage won converts alongside theological attractions. The reforming Catholic Church adamantly preserved the idea of clerical celibacy, and reformers attempted to impose it more rigorously, punishing more severely. A major Bull of 30 August 1568 highlighted the campaign against 'incontinent' priests. German Catholics in 1565 had asked for priests to be allowed to marry, or make married men priests; and been rebuffed. Strong attacks on the insistence on clerical celibacy emerged in the late eighteenth century, with notably Archbishop Giuseppe Capecelatro of Taranto publishing anonymously a Discourse, in which he claimed:

> It cannot be denied that the law of celibacy began to prepare the ruin of this [clerical] power; perhaps the principal consideration. Which suggested in these obscure times the enactment of a law contrary to the laws of nature, opposed to the morality of Jesus Christ, and destructive of the advantage of Religion and the State, was the spirit of the interests and greed of usurping the legacy {*spoglio*} of clerics.[61]

This generated much debate.

In reality distinctions were made between casual relations, and more permanent concubinage. The diocesan and apostolic Visitors were likely to question parishioners about sexual misdemeanours of the priests and curates, and whether they had concubines. Parishioners might condemn – or obfuscate the situation. It was expected that a priest needed female assistance, a housekeeper; bishops wanted her to be a close relative (mother, sister, aunt), or if unrelated – old; usually over 50, though the Bologna archbishop Girolamo Colonna in 1598 suggested 40, but she had to be licenced as being of good conduct by the *vicario foraneo* or archpriest.[62] Cleric and parish might connive in not noticing that the housekeeper was younger, a sexual partner (concubine), and that his bastards might be around. Sienese records suggest that such a partner, whether from another acceptable parish family or an outsider, might be judged an asset in securing access to the priest, and persuading him to understand family problems. But if she were indiscreet or bossy, she and the priest would be denounced. Parts of southern Italy may have remained tolerant of the concubine because of long-standing Greek rite communities that had allowed married clergy. Toleration could be eroded by an overweaning attitude. The Neapolitan priest Giovanni Battista Ferone had taken in Teresa Tommaso as a servant, aged 36, with the consent of her husband who could not maintain their four children, but when processed in 1778 neighbours described her as mistress of the house ('padrona di casa'). Her main accuser, Rosa Cina, called her a disturber of the peace ('inquietratrice dell'altrui quiete'), litigious, spending time outdoors with men, foul-mouthing other women; and Teresa had thrown dirty water over Rosa, and struck her daughter. The priest looked after Teresa's children, some of whom may have in fact been his. Enforcement of celibacy was harder in the south than centre and north Italy, because there were many more clerics in minor orders who could marry.[63]

In human terms it should be recognised that the life of the parish priest, and even more so the itinerant confessors and preachers, could be lonely and frustrating in many senses. A seminary education in strict boarding school conditions, following by benefices in alien territory cut the cleric from family, kin and friendship, especially when bishops discouraged socialising with parishioners. Social conditions and even pastoral care might encourage breaching rigorous segregation, and lead to dubious relations with women. The pressures to avoid female company could push the celibate cleric towards young male company, and a different abuse. Socially a cleric could more readily be seen with boys and young men; who might genuinely be running errands and being of assistance as a 'page'. The lonely Milanese Priest Francesco Finetti, in Bologna and of no fixed abode, ended up being accused of picking up a ten-year-old boy (of German origin), caring for him, maybe giving him a role as helper, but sodomising him over several days in an inn. Shocking – but not surprising, given clerical isolation? He was incidentally brought before the city's main secular court, not an ecclesiastical tribunal; but in a city and province where civic and ecclesiastical police worked together.[64]

The reforming church discouraged social contact between priests or curates, and their parishioners; and issued constant admonitions not to go to inns and bars, to drink, dice or play other games. Such was seen as leading to casual sexual relations with loose women, or less frequently young boys. Secular and ecclesiastical police, *sbirri*, were liable to raid such establishments, or even arrest a priest wandering about at night, as in Bologna. Cardinal Archbishop Girolamo Colonna, after a 1633 congregation of archpriests and *vicari foranei* issued various orders, including that curates attending feasts and funeral anniversaries, should behave modestly, and after blessing the meal should sit with another cleric or acolyte and read a spiritual book; and not attend the subsequent dancing.[65]

The confessional box, as indicated above, was designed to reduce immoral conduct between clerics – whether parish priests or separately licensed confessors – but the authorities in the seventeenth century became worried about the continuing abuse of the sacrament of penance. The Inquisition took up cases of clerical 'solicitation'; the sexual abuse in the confessional and penitential process of women, and occasionally males. As an abuse of a sacrament the offence was within its remit, and at least in the Venetian and Friuli tribunals the number of denunciations for this alleged offence increased through the period. (See Chapter 9, Table 9.1.) Such accusations could also come before other ecclesiastical courts, and these are harder to track. Some were made to the Venetian Patriarch, who was also on the Inquisition tribunal. Not all cases were full investigations or taken to full trial; and they have not had the detailed study accorded to the same crime in Spain.[66] Offences took place in and around the confessional, in convents, and in homes when parish priest or confessor went to confess a sick person. Alleged offences ranged from lewd questioning and propositions, fondling, to masturbation and full sexual acts. In some cases the females concerned might have been equally willing (with a third party complaining). In a 1623, Venice case friars of San Francesco di Paola denounced one of their number, Friar Giovanni Antonio Gervasio for soliciting several women at confession; one of them at least, Paulina, seems complicit, and her non-appearance to give evidence might have caused the case being dropped. Fra Gervasio was also accused of ignorance, including of cases of conscience and drunkenness. The confessional situation also lent itself to false accusations; as possibly with the *piovano* of San Simone in Venice in 1594, with a jealous older husband resenting his young wife's confession sessions. Here the Patriarch's court exonerated the priest when the woman withdrew her accusatory testimony.[67]

An alternative result of close relations between confessor and female penitent, was the former's fostering of a deep spirituality, asceticism, and 'living saintliness' on the part of some devout girls and women. It was usually the unattached confessors, from the Orders, rather than a confessing parish priest who became enamoured of such living saints, whose saintly cause they might subsequently promote for beatification – as with the Dominican confessor

Roberti Vittori, promoting the young Francesca Vacchini of Viterbo (1589–1609). Francesca's mother and uncle threatened the confessor with death, accusing him of undue influences over her; and rival Franciscans (whom the Vacchini family favoured), challenged Vittori's attempt to have the ascetic Francesca, who had a local cult following, beatified through the Congregations in Rome. The Inquisition squashed early attempts, to Vittori's frustration. Such females and their confessors might be charged, unofficially or officially, with sexual relations as well as fraudulent activities; though a few were recognised as living saints, supported by genuinely admiring and helpful confessors. Parish priests were likely to discourage living saints and cult support, as in Cecilia Ferrazzi's case in Venice (see also Chapters 8 and 9).[68]

Parish organisation had become more consolidated, though without the desired coherence advocated by Trent. The financial restraints on coherent reform and best parochial practice were considerable. Clerical poverty persisted, encouraging the pursuit of non-parochial incomes and immorality. Parish churches, generally better maintained, were more the focus of lay religious life. Relationships between parish clergy, curates and confessors and their lay flock were complex, sometimes tense, but alternatively too cosy for good discipline and moral behaviour. Despite the scandals, parishioners were mainly better served by priests and curates, better educated, and pushed more towards an orthodox Christian life. The way the clergy was educated, and how this was passed on to the flock is our next concern.

6 *Religious Education*

This chapter will cover aspects of the education of the clergy, primarily those going out into society as parish priests and curates, and the basic education of the faithful through pulpit, Christian Doctrine teaching, and some printed literature, as on spiritual exercises. Visual aspects of religious teaching and inspiration are discussed in Chapter 10.

Catholic reformers before Trent had recognised that many priests were profoundly ignorant, illiterate in Latin and often in the vernacular. With little doctrinal knowledge they could hardly help their flock. Moves were under way from the 1530s to improve cathedral instruction for clerics, and to provide parochial Christian Doctrine teaching for all. Venice developed church schools, organised on a district (*sestiere*) basis, funded by parishes and monasteries; they combined teaching basic doctrine through catechisms with a humanist curriculum. Little distinction was made between those intending to become priests, and those remaining secular. This remained one method, not very focused, of educating those who became priests, even when more specialist seminaries were eventually started.[1] Milan led the way with Christian Doctrine or catechism Sunday schools for children, which inspired Trent reformers. Trent also decided that diocesan seminaries would be the method for improving the knowledge and skills of potential parish priests. Additionally, the Religious Orders set about enhancing religious (and wider) education for potential clergy and those who would remain laymen in secular activities, through their own schools, colleges and universities. They also aimed to stimulate the spirituality of all, including women, through spiritual exercises – conducted with the guidance of clerics, or undertaken personally (if literate), through manuals like Loyola's *Spiritual*

Exercises and Scupoli's *Spiritual Combat.* Religious music and visual artists were stressed as aids to spiritual development.

Seminaries and Clerical Education

The Council of Trent recognised that the faithful would not follow true doctrine and moral Christian ways, unless well led and controlled by educated clergy. Visitation records starkly revealed the basic clerical illiteracy. Most clergy were trained on the job; serving as altar boys in minor orders, and then becoming priests after a little theological instruction in a local monastery. While some parish priests had had a university education, they were inclined to accept more lucrative activities, with a low-paid and less-educated substitute serving the flock (if at all). One of the claimed successful reform recommendations of the Council was the diocesan seminary. It was ordered that in those dioceses that did not already have a university or college providing a suitable number of ordinands, the bishop should institute his own seminary or *collegium*, which would train poor boys over 12 years old for the priesthood. These would be residential institutions, with strict discipline, so that the boys could concentrate on study and prayer, free from family pressures and secular temptations.[2]

The establishment of the seminaries proved difficult for many reasons. Despite a wave of enthusiasm leading to some successful creations, only about half the Italian dioceses had a seminary in operation by 1630 (and the plague and financial crises of that period saw several cease) (see Appendix).[3] Money was often lacking to create suitable accommodation for a seminary, which was a boarding institution as well as a teaching one. Some could start quickly thanks to donations of buildings by leading nobles, or the wealth of the bishop himself. Otherwise attempts to raise money by suppressing benefices and reallocating funds, or securing donations from religious houses, were strenuously opposed by the victims. Geographically, foundations appeared in odd patterns; the provinces of Lombardy, Umbria, Reggio Calabria, Ravenna were soon quite well provided, but Tuscany, the Roman and suburbican (Cardinalate) dioceses, and much of the Kingdom of Naples were poorly served. The Roman area might be seen as well provided from the many universities and colleges within Rome itself, but Cardinal Paleotti clearly did not perceive it so, and finally got one started at Magliano, for his Sabina see, in 1593, to supplement that at Velletri. Southern Italy did see a flowering in the 1580s to 1600s. The Reggio Calabria seminary and the local Jesuit college, which had a fruitful partnership (and with the Dominican Collegio del Rosario), were both destroyed in the disastrous Turkish raid in 1594, but commendably revived.[4]

The Naples seminary was quickly launched in 1568, when Archbishop Mario Carafa donated 6000 ducats to buy land and build it, but he and successive archbishops had to battle to get money from the richest monasteries (Certosini of San Martino and the Olivetans), and the Cathedral canons. Archbishop Carafa was overruled by Rome in dealing with the chapter, but had not helped his cause by using force against obstreperous canons and their agents. Archbishop Gesualdo's parish reorganisation eventually redirected money to the seminary from discontinued richly endowed parishes. The history of the Pozzuoli seminary (in Campania) exemplifies the chequered history of several. It started in 1587 with 12 pupils, but soon collapsed when taxes could not be collected for it, and not enough pupils were forthcoming. It reopened from 1624 to 1625, but failed again when its reforming Fra Martino de Leon y Cardinas moved to Palermo in 1650. It operated briefly, 1708–11, and then from 1740.[5]

The delay in creating a seminary in some cases might seem strange. Venice did not have a seminary until 1580–81, and this first was a state promoted ducal seminary, which seemingly pushed the Patriarch to start a diocesan one. However Somaschi, Jesuits and Canons had been helping train priests. Florence did not have a seminary until the early eighteenth century, though one was being planned in 1569, and other parts of Tuscany were also late in developing them. Whether the University of Pisa, and traditional training in cathedrals and monasteries, were adequate substitutes (an excuse for the non-creation), is doubted.[6]

Once started many problems arose to frustrate continuity and maintaining standards. Securing a balance between fee-paying recruits (who might become parish priests), and the poor taught freely was difficult financially; and could cause disorder. Retaining suitable staff was also problematic. Interconnections with Religious Orders – notably the Jesuits, Barnabites and Scolopians – and teaching institutions and personnel, probably led to the best results, certainly at higher levels of clerical education.

Debates continue about the real effectiveness of seminaries, especially as our knowledge of what was taught, and how many went on to be parish priests, is patchy. Thomas Deutscher, who studied the fairly successful Novara seminary system, has contrasted two recent books. Kathleen Comerford emphasises the mediocre quality of the seminary in Fiesole (theoretically founded in 1575, but not actively teaching until 1635), while Simona Negruzzo provides a more upbeat interpretation of the seminary provisions in the state of Milan/Lombardy. Milan itself had two seminaries, and five others in the diocese; Negruzzo calculates about 300 clerics were in seminary training in 1639. Novara had a main city seminary, but also small offshoots in other towns in the vast and heterogeneous diocese, which helped make it one of the most successful. Because Pavia had a university its episcopal seminary only had about 20 pupils at a time. The other dioceses in the State were small institutions – in Alessandria, Como, Cremona, Lodi, Tortona and Vigevano, though the evidence on their operation and throughput is often meagre.[7] Up to 50 per cent of Novara priests might be seminary trained; but only 10 per cent of Como ones. However, significant colleges contributed – run by the Religious Orders, from the large Brera Jesuit College in Milan, to smaller institutions of Jesuits, Barnabites and Somaschi and others in various cities, including Como, Novara and Pavia's Collegio Ghislieri (founded by Pius V). These could train potential priests independently and supplement with higher studies the basic practical education in the smaller diocesan seminaries. In Fiesole 1013 priests were ordained between 1635 and 1675; Comerford finds that 416 of these had spent some time in the seminary. Comerford notes elsewhere that none of the leading Fiesole hierarchy, including bishops, had any seminary education. Local families provided local priests who could rise to the top in the area (presumably by networking and patronage), without necessarily Tridentine-approved training. Fiesole's pupils did not become bishops or leading church figures elsewhere.[8] Deutscher expresses a more optimistic view of the seminaries' contributions, given their variety, different interactions with other education, and the diverse roles played by seminarians in later life.

The numbers of pupils in seminaries varied, but few were large. The Roman seminary opened in 1565 with 63 free pupils, and 14–15 fee-payers (*convittori*); by the early sixteenth century it settled to 40 of each. Piacenza, despite Bishop Paolo Burali's enthusiasm – or because of his rigour – could only report 10 pupils in 1579, though by 1633 it had 36 (twelve each 'free', 'half-rate' and 'full fee'), having changed its admission policy (see later). The *ad limina* reports for southern dioceses in the 1590s to 1630s indicate most operated with

10–15 pupils; the revived Reggio Calabria seminary from 1600–1630 fluctuated between 8 and 16 free places, and 6 to 27 fee-paying.[9]

What proportion of pupils became priests is seldom clear. Perugia, one of the pioneer diocesan seminaries, opened in 1564, took in 161 tonsured seminarists by 1600; and 57 of these were ordained. The number of ordinations in the diocese in those years was 181 (with 539 tonsurings).[10] Ordination could be restricted by the lack of available and acceptable benefices. Priests also came from the University or (after 1582), the Collegio Oradini, designed to train men for the priesthood after age 18. A low production rate of priests from seminaries, as suggested by Perugia, is not necessarily a sign of 'failure'. The seminaries sent out men from a poor background, with some education to serve the church on non-priestly functions, or in a full secular life. We know that the Perugian diocesan seminary provided in this period a wide-ranging education. Novara was not far behind, Fiesole clearly far meagre, with a poor library (where Perugia's was impressive); but then it was a smaller and poorer city, in the intellectual shadow of Florence and Pisa.

Attitudes to how seminaries should be run, and what taught, varied considerably. The austere Theatine Paolo Burali wanted seminaries as almost monastic institutions, with young boys strictly separated from the world and its temptations; day pupils, accepted in some places, should not be allowed. The Piacenza seminary he created thus had a very strict regime, which proved hard to enforce, especially once he moved to Naples. The Rector controlled all reading. Their vacation in September (if the family wanted them), was also to be austere. His boarding fee-payers obeyed the same rules; though they could leave (for good) at will without penalty – unlike the poor scholars. Silence was stressed in many seminaries, as in Perugia; with meals eaten in silence, as in monasteries, except for somebody reading aloud the Bible or other appropriate literature. For Milan Borromeo insisted that all talking be in Latin, including during leisure time. The Bergamo pupils were not allowed to receive or send letters without special permission; and were banned from singing 'Neapolitan' and similar lascivious songs. Attendance at Mass was daily, and students were expected to confess monthly or for major feasts, though the Roman seminary wanted weekly or fortnightly confessions. Some seminary promoters favoured having paying pupils, *convittori*, not intending to be priests, not just for financial reasons, but because – as Paleotti argued, it was a way of instructing a wider community in letters with a fear of God, which would encourage a better government of families and households.[11]

The educational content of most seminaries remains unclear, but it could range from simple training to university level higher education. The basic training (assuming entrants arrived with some Christian Doctrine knowledge, vernacular literacy, and possibly some elementary Latin) would be in grammar (Latin for reading and some composition), music and preparation for performing the sacraments and liturgy. They might be instructed in prayer, and self-examination, as the Roman seminary recommended. The Milanese seminaries instructed in preparing sermons and preaching effectively. Piacenza pupils were given in-training experience by teaching catechism in the parish churches, probably unusually. Roman seminarists could show off their intellectual attainments in public disputations. Music was deemed important, at least as linked to liturgical performance, 'so that they might securely sing their part, and make counterparts to be able then to reach another higher perfection', as the Ravenna rules stated.[12] Latin was increasingly given high priority, as a key to understanding the local 'national' vernacular language, and for access to texts on all other subjects; theological, philosophical and historical. This emphasis was fostered by the Jesuits, with their 1599 *Ratio Studiorum* guiding educational procedures and attitudes everywhere.[13] A by-product of this was that priests might be both better presenters of the Latin Mass, and more readily receive guidance and exemplification from texts in their ministry than their predecessors. The downside might be adjusting to presenting what they had learned to their average parishioners, in the local vernacular.

Attitudes towards higher studies in seminaries varied. In 1580 the Jesuit Provincial of Rome, Claudio Acquaviva, argued that Roman seminarists should not normally study dogmatic theology and philosophy, since – as apostolic Visitors in 1586 argued explicitly – this might lead them away from taking a parish benefice, and towards higher careers, defeating the key purpose of a seminary. Roberto Bellarmino and two other lecturers took a different Jesuit attitude; if such studies were ignored Italy would remain with puerile priests, in a country lamentably ignorant of theology, long neglected in university education, 'from which it arises that no country has bishops and parish priests more ignorant than Italy'.[14] He had comparative experience of the Netherlands and northern France. He did not win the day in Rome. The Milanese seminaries in the north, and more remote Santa Severina in the south, demonstrated a greater fondness for higher seminary education. In Lombardy, with or without the contributions of the Orders, seminarists judged able enough, could end up studying Grammar and Humanity through the great authors such as Cicero, Vergil, Sallust, Caesar, Horace and Ovid, along with some Greek; and move to the Jesuit Brera College for Rhetoric, Theology and Philosophy. A 1589 report on Santa Severina declared the seminary had four masters teaching Greek, Music, Rhetoric, Philosophy and Logic. Perugia seems as broad and high in its aims as Milan: basic Christian Doctrine, the Sacraments, the major Biblical texts (to be known by heart), Church History, basic Theology and Philosophy (following Aquinas and Aristotle), Latin Grammar and Rhetoric. Some knowledge of Hebrew and Greek was available and recommended. A high level in reality, as well as intention, seems probable given the long influence there of Marcantonio Bonciari senior (1553–1616), a leading humanist, teaching rhetoric and eloquence, publishing internationally successful works.[15]

The seminary system did not produce enough suitable parish priests. Simona Negruzzo has concluded that even the best dioceses fell short in both quantity and quality.[16] As already indicated the seminaries were assisted by members of Religious Orders and interconnected with the schools and colleges run separately by such as the Jesuits, Barnabites, Somascans and Scolopians. All these made a considerable difference to religious and humanities education from the later sixteenth century.

In the Lombard archdiocese, Jesuits significantly helped educate priests in Alessandria, Como, Milan, Novara and Pavia; the Somascans in Alessandria, Como, Cremona, Lodi, Pavia, Tortona and Vigevano; while the Barnabites were involved in all nine dioceses except Como. They provided their own small colleges in lesser places: the Jesuits in Bormio, Ponte and Castelnuovo; the Barnabites at Casalmaggiore. The Dominicans had their theological *Studium* at Bosco Marengo, and various other 'minor seminaries', that provided theological, liturgical and pastoral training. Where those training for the priesthood did not come through a long seminary training, they might be involved in moving about securing instruction in a variety of institutions over the years. Negruzzo stresses the positive value for a mountain curate going afar briefly to a college, or to hear theological and penitentiary canons in a cathedral or Dominican house; giving an enriching experience before ordination and promotion, and providing potential network links for a wider career. The *visita ad limina* reports provide valuable evidence of learned ecclesiasts within chapters, rich in theological knowledge, canon law and ceremonial procedures. In 1592 Milan Cathedral had 17 doctoral canons, with five teaching theology. The collegiate church of San Stefano in Vimercate had a theological provost, while its parish priest had a doctorate in theology. Such people helped train young clerics in confessional procedures.[17]

Not all were happy that clerics should be trained for secular pastoral roles by Orders like the Jesuits. The Jesuit College started in Milan in late 1564 became respected, but the diocesan clergy from the start opposed it being directly responsible for the seminary (started September 1565), as it was till 1579, when taken over by the Oblates. Milan gossip held the Jesuits to be 'ignorant and inexpert in humanist letters, unknown, wandering (*vagi*) and barbarian'. Vicar General Ormaneto squashed the secular clergy's opposition. In Rome at the same time Bishop Ascanio Cesarini opposed the idea of Jesuits running a seminary: 'it was intolerable that the education of Roman youth be entrusted to Germans and Spaniards, thus to heretics and Jewish converts (*marranos*).'[18] Fortunately, not too many shared this ignorant prejudice against Jesuits.

However trained, many clergy were still found deficient through the seventeenth century, though standards of performance – from liturgy, pastoral care to morality – had almost certainly improved, as judged by Visitations. But Archbishop D.G. Caraccioli condemned his Bari clergy in the early seventeenth century: 'with little spirituality, badly disciplined and without letters, which instead of pursuing the path of virtue, heads for that of vices; whence is maintained a seminary of persons, delinquent and totally contrary to the clerical profession, from which derives the unquiet and scandalous life of the city.'[19]

Education in the Parish and Christian Doctrine Schools

The foundations of religious education were supposedly given through catechism or Christian Doctrine schools.[20] Increasingly, from the mid-sixteenth century catechism teaching was seen as a prime duty for the parish priest or curate, and Visitors checked the regularity of its provision. Confraternities of Christian Doctrine were developed to assist; Religious Orders provided helpers.

Bologna in the first half of the fifteenth century had fostered parochial catechism teaching, with the confraternity of San Girolamo (founded 1433), providing continuity till the eighteenth century. However, the most significant impetus came from the Como priest Castellino da Castello who started catechism teaching in Milan from

1536, recruiting clerical and lay supporters. They were formally recognised as the Company of Christian Doctrine in 1546. Other cities imitated. This exemplary teaching inspired the Tridentine decree of November 1563, ordering parish priests to organise Sunday catechism teaching. They might be the only teacher; or bring in Capuchins, Jesuits or lay confraternity members to assist. In 1560 an Archconfraternity of Christian Doctrine was created to stimulate work in Rome, but it later became an Italian-wide coordinating organisation, which under Cardinal Roberto Bellarmino's inspiration spread catechism books throughout the land. The specialist Companies of Christian Doctrine proliferated at least in north-central Italy, both as a way of organising the teaching, and to provide the men and women teachers with a corporate body for their own spiritual development. In the absence of such a dedicated confraternity, members of other parish confraternities, such as Holy Sacrament ones, might help the clergy in teaching the children.

The schools varied considerably in levels of education and approaches; and seventeenth-century Visitations recorded many lapses and inefficiencies. Leaving the teaching to the parish priest alone might be deemed inadequate; the Archbishop of Ravenna in 1607 ordered a sodality to be established in every parish to assist, if nothing already existed.[21] The basic teaching was of the Creed, Our Father, Hail Mary, Ten Commandments, and possibly a selection of prayers, with some instruction on prayer. Much was rote learning. The teachers drew on various catechisms and manuals to assist the instruction, and in the better schools older children and adults might learn to read such literature themselves. The Milan schools, for example, had a *Sommario,* the basic work for the above listed items, but also with sections on virtues and sins, a stress on the seven acts of mercy as the basis of 'good works', baptismal vows. Rule books showed how the school and its work should be organised. A more advanced *Interrogatorio,* a question and answer form of Catechism, took the pupils into greater analysis of beliefs and behaviour – but largely avoiding more problematic theological issues, including purgatory and the sacraments. The main emphasis was on the efficacy of prayer, and on good works. The various types of parish and confraternity schools could use a variety of catechisms and manuals. The two major Catechisms were the Roman Catechism and Peter Canisius' Jesuit one for the benefit of the more educated teachers; while simpler catechisms were available for less able or educated teachers, and pupils who could read. Roberto Bellarmino's *Dottrina Cristiana Breve* became a key work for school use from 1597, being distributed by the Archconfraternity of Christian Doctrine throughout Italy, and to Dalmatia. Gregorio da Napoli's *Compendio della Dottrina Christiana*, for Capuchin-led teachers was another significant work.[22]

Promoting the catechism schools involved carrots and sticks. In Bologna, parts of Rome and other places, children were rounded up and compelled to attend by local parochial or confraternity officials. Corporal punishment might be used to control pupils, and punish laxity; but banned in other areas. Alternatively, schools were made more stimulating and adventurous. Some Christian doctrine schools taught children to read; notably parochial ones in major areas of Lombardy, Piedmont, Venice and Rome – and schools run by Jesuits and Capuchins; Gregorio da Napoli's text fostered this. A few schools taught writing; in this period reading and writing were treated as separate skills, not normally taught together. Singing was a significant aspect in some schools. The Jesuits from the 1560s were active in encouraging the use of *laude* to put across religious ideas and sentiments (partly borrowing from a Savonarola tradition, and reflecting Ignatius Loyola's early experience as catechist teacher). They sponsored the production of Christian Doctrine booklets, incorporating a selection of *laude*, hymns and musical examples. An influential work – *Lodi e Canzoni Spirituale per cantar insieme con la Dottrina Christiana* (Milan, 1576, under the Archbishop's licence), included 35 songs. The preface to a Venetian collection sponsored by the Venerabile Congregatione dell'Humiltà for use by the Christian Doctrine schools (*Lodi Spirituali*, 1580), stated it was designed to distract youth from singing less suitable profane songs in public and private. Printing of such works in lesser cities, like Como and Turin (still small in 1574), suggests widespread interest in this teaching approach. Roberto Bellarmino also proved an enthusiastic promoter of *laude*[23] (see also Chapter 10).

The larger schools had several classes, for different ages, and separated boys and girls. For the top stream debating competitions with prizes acted as stimuli, as in some Roman and Bologna schools. A higher level could lead pupils to become ordinands; as from that in S. Nicola a Toledo in Naples. While Trent indicated that each parish should have its own Sunday school, some important urban areas like Bologna and Rome itself (under the Archconfraternity of Christian Doctrine), assembled the children of several parishes meeting together in one larger parish church; or left the boys in their own parish, but sent girls (possibly fewer), to a combined parochial centre, or convent such as S. Ludovica, Bologna – probably for better security.[24] How far girls were involved is not that clear; Strongoli Cathedral's Christian Doctrine school certainly limited itself to boys. According to the Milan diarist Casale, that city in 1578 had more schools for females (58), than males (52).[25] The involvement of girls in the Roman Doctrine schools, as well as using women to teach the girls, has been noted for its considerable impact on female education and literacy there.[26] Some parents opposed sending their girls to socially mixed public schools. Those attending, female or male, could be subjected to abuse by non-attenders. In many cases noble women came forward to act as teachers as a way of expressing their charitable attitudes; in Brescia, Mantua, Milan, Naples, Parma, Piacenza and Venice, for example. The Duchess Leonora of Mantua created an institute to train 90 girls as teachers in the catechism schools, visited the schools and encouraged elite women to help, in teaching or funding.[27]

Within the church tensions existed over who should run the catechism teaching. Parish priests could resent a take over by the confraternity schools, such as those under the Archconfraternity of Christian Doctrine in Rome. In Lombardy Carlo Borromeo came to resent lay teaching in the Christian Doctrine schools, despite his establishing an extensive network originally with lay help. Ironically, we have the revealing diary of one of Milan's most enthusiastic lay promoters of Christian doctrine schools, the carpenter Ioan Batista Caxal (or Giambattisa Casale), catechism teacher, prior of one school, then founder and inspector of them from 1575 – till his death about 1629. Casale taught reading, writing and doctrine, 'for the honour of God and the salvation of souls and the common good'. He and other such teachers, can more ambiguously be seen as surveyors of morality, and social controllers, combating (as another Milanese Christian Doctrine member, Francesco Rinaldi, did), gambling and monkey entertainment that kept people from Mass and schooling.[28] He was influenced by the ideas of Castellino (his confessor), and was a great admirer of Carlo and Federico Borromeo. But Carlo Borromeo imposed his own rules over Castellino's, and his hagiographers tried to write out Castellino's pioneering role and inspiration, as too lay centred. The professional hierarchy must rule.[29]

The penetration of catechism teaching outside the major cities is hard to gauge; schooling was probably often very intermittent, whether taught by confraternity members, by a lone parish priest or Capuchin. Visitation records indicate that priests were asked what was available or done, but reveal little on frequency or standards. The

Roman Archconfraternity in 1609 claimed to be running 53 schools in 1609, up to 79 in 1611, with 5800 boys and 5090 girls taught by 529 brothers and 519 sisters from the confraternities. It also outreached to places like Albano and Civitavecchia. From the 1630s such enthusiasm and dynamism lessened; but some revival came under Innocent XI's pressure in 1676–77. Bologna from 1576 under Gabriele Paleotti had 40 schools run by his Congregation Della Perseverenza, supposedly teaching three or four thousand children, as well as some adults; though some parishes may have had their own schools – as they did later. Borromean Milan boasted 740 schools through the archdiocese in 1584; and the city itself had 20 504 children enrolled in 1599; but frequency of attendance is untested. It was also possible for a small diocese such as Comacchio to have good catechism teaching, from 1574. Poor communities outside Naples had Christian Doctrine schools under Jesuit inspiration in the seventeenth century.

Other religion-centred schools could provide wider educational coverage. In the 1550s the Jesuits, particularly under Antonio Possevino's youthful impetus, opened several schools for boys, starting in Naples, where they would teach Italian literature, Latin and Greek, but also Christian Doctrine on Fridays and Sundays. From 1586 the Oratorians joined them in Naples, but in poor districts such as the Mercato. The Scolopians (or Piarists), led by Giuseppe Calasanzio, in a similar spirit started a school first in Rome in the poor parish of S. Dorotea in Trastevere for 100 pupils; later moving to S. Andrea della Valle, they had 1000 pupils. In 1626 they opened their first Naples school, in the Duchessa area, notorious for its prostitutes and their offspring. These schools made available to poorer children a combination of Christian knowledge and elementary education for better job prospects. The Scolopian Scuole Pie spread quite widely with foundations in such diverse places as Narni (1617) and Norcia in Umbria, Savona (1623) in Liguria, Genoa (1624), Messina (1625), Florence (1630) and Cosenza (1631). But Calasanzio and several other teachers (especially those connected with Florence), then had their troubles with the Inquisition, for upholding Galileo's ideas, especially on atomism, which could affect Eucharist doctrine. The Scolopian Order was suppressed (from 1646 to 1656, following a hushed-up paedophile scandal), but individuals continued to maintain several schools for the children, including that in Rome, and the revival was rapid.[30]

For general schooling, the reforming bishops tried to guarantee an orthodox religious influence, by having teachers in secular schools, grammar or abacus ones, attest to their orthodox Catholic beliefs. Pius IV in his 1564 Bull, *In sacrosancta beati Petri* had ordered all teachers to take a profession of faith before their bishop or his deputed official. The survival of some of these records in Venice are both illuminating about the process, and schools involved, but also a warning that these professions were only intermittently demanded.[31]

Italian reformers thus sought to provide a range of religious teaching, under clerical leadership, but – more controversially – with lay assistance of men and women, preferably under some corporate supervision in confraternities. Though Protestants have often been praised for fostering the family religious life, and home biblical education, and Catholics attacked for neglecting this, the contrast can be misleading. On the Protestant side the Bible might often be symbol and icon, and not a perused text. On the Italian Catholic side, while the use of the vernacular Bible was first discouraged, and then essentially banned, Italian families did have access to spiritual texts, to catechisms and guides to spiritual development. Paleotti argued that if at least one member of the family improved religious knowledge through the catechism schools, and learned to pray, all in the family could benefit. Carlo Borromeo did not ignore the importance of family prayers. Some of the confraternity brothers visiting the housebound poor might check on their beliefs and praying. The Jesuits came to recommend the use of the *Spiritual Exercises* by the individual on his or her own – preferably after some lengthy instruction by a Jesuit. Lorenzo Scupoli's nearly as significant, and possibly more enticing, *Spiritual Combat*, was likewise promoted by Theatines for private contemplation and self-analysis. Much cheap, simple and illustrated religious literature was published through the period, with the key topics being the Virgin and Child, the Crucifixion, the Martyrdom of Saints. Many publications were, all or in part, in verse, (314 of the 412 catalogued by Lorenzo Baldacchini). While Venice printed the most, surviving editions appeared from a good array of cities in north-central Italy. The combination of story-telling, simple didacticism, memorable verses and illustrations could feed any adult appetite for religious self-instruction fostered by earlier schooling. These were leaflets or booklets, not the ponderous tomes of the great scholars, though the named authors included the Theatine Bishop Giambattista Del Tufo (on Christ's Incarnation, Death and Resurrection), and Bishop G.B. Castelli of Rimini (prayers against plague, 1576).[32]

Preaching

Preaching was reinforced by Catholic reformers as a prime method of educating the populace.[33] Preaching was one of the chief episcopal duties, whether addressing a normal congregation in his Cathedral, a synod of bishops, or a parish gathering during a Visitation. Several celebrated preachers became bishops – like Panigarola or Ercolani – partly for that skill, and their sermons were printed as models for other bishops and lesser clergy. As in the middle ages the old Orders continued to produce star preachers, and new Orders, notably the Jesuits and Capuchins, added to the range of preachers, preaching styles and content. Much of the preaching could be florid, and elaborate, as aimed at the papal court, and intellectual audiences; and this was often what went into print. Panigarola was a star in this baroque style, but Borromeo when hearing him as they conducted a Visitation in 1583, warned him to adjust his style for simpler folk, with something 'easy and devout'.[34] The Franciscan Cornelio Musso (1511–74) was one of the most influential preachers through the sixteenth century, in action and in print (with his first printed sermon appearing in 1530). Many preachers would follow his advice to consider several levels of audience in one sermon, from learned to less so. As a southern bishop in the 1540s, and advisor at Trent, and later to Cardinals, he was a key all-round influence. In 1554 Bernardino Tomitano wrote a book praising Musso's sermonising. He was:

> A master and model of ornament, who with both beautiful arrangement and infinite abundance of examples, knows how to explain the mysteries of God, the secrets of nature, and the precepts of religion.

He appealed to the senses and painted word pictures comparable with great contemporary paintings:

> I do not know speaking truthfully, what Titian or what Michelangelo could do with the brush and colours on the canvasses to better depict bodies than he, who by the sublime spirits of his ingenuity makes appear to us with the senses the glory of that invisible life of heaven, which here through shadows and similitudes alone we judge.[35]

Such sermonising could have wide appeal.

Gabriele Inchino's sermon guide, *Vie del Paradiso* (1607), very specifically distinguished what was suitable for parish preaching, and what for the monastic context. Gabriele Paleotti preached simply and extemporaneously round the parishes, and his published sermons designed as exemplars (as noted before for weddings) showed a flexible approach.

A leading preacher who also provided a short guide was the Capuchin Girolamo da Narni (1563–1632), much admired around Rome and the papal court, though unafraid to attack court luxury and praise the poor. His carefully edited printed versions could be used in less erudite contexts. His guide advised on sermon technique, involving careful voice control, gestures, with a high emphasis on the biblical Word. But he warned against using sermons to induce excessive fear and despair: 'Never induce sinners to desperation ... because you close the heart and it won't admit the reign of grace; but give them hope.'[36]

Analysis of sermon developments through our period suggests they covered considerable variety of topics, reducing the social criticism found in the fifteenth century, being more concerned with doctrine, backing up Christian Doctrine teaching, using the Lord's Prayer and the Creed as structural bases. Jesuits sometimes used their *Spiritual Exercises* as a trigger for sermons. Strong preaching against vices led to an emphasis on confession and communion, both in Lenten cycles, and in sermons linked to the Forty-Hour Devotion (see Chapter 10). Biblical references were heavily used as 'proof' of the main themes, but it is hard to judge how much was fully quoted in the live performance. Reformers like Borromeo wanted the New Testament, especially the Gospels, to be the heart of sermonising – but did not want the laity to read them directly in Italian.[37] Even the Gospel had to be mediated through clerical instruction. Short quotations and biblical examples were to be used to induce a Christ-like morality in the audience; to move listeners, through emotive words and word pictures, to a better life, in contemplation of a holy reward.

Encouraging social improvement, peace and reconciliation in local society was one topic for the mission preachers, as with Jesuits and Capuchins, and for bishops entering their diocese, as promoted by Musso. In the fifteenth-century Bernardino of Siena provided a model for this aspect of social education, and one might detect a line of influence into the breakaway Capuchin Order in the later sixteenth century.[38] While the sixteenth century reformers tended to encourage sermonising within the church rather than in the public square, to avoid unseemly distractions, the Bernardino-type mass public sermonising remained a feature of missionary work. This sermon would have basic messages, would be a call to repentance to a better moral life, to social harmony. The Jesuit and Capuchin missionaries, whether in remoter rural 'Indies of Italy', or in city slum districts, reckoned to create confraternities or foster schools of Christian Doctrine that would follow up with more specific doctrinal education.

Mission Work within Italy

Mission activity led by the mendicant orders had been a feature of late medieval Italian reform movements. Star missionary preachers of the fifteenth century, such as Bernardino da Siena and Giovanni da Capestrano, were models for later Catholic reformers. But as Giuseppe Orlandi has argued the mission work of our period differed in structure, methods, means and ends for the European Christian context – leaving aside the additional dimensions of mission work overseas in the Americas and the East.[39] The new missionaries in Italy were more preoccupied with remedying ignorance (whether to forestall 'Protestant' allures and errors, or counteract popular superstitions), encouraging religious education more positively, emphasising the sacraments, especially the Eucharist, and fostering post-mission follow-up through parish priests and/or confraternities. Ignatius Loyola encouraged his followers to treat their lives as a continuous mission, and the Capuchins developed a similar mentality. Where the late medieval missionary preachers tended to be lone stars (with acolytes), the post-Tridentine missionary work became increasingly a matter of team work, targeted at the populace of whole regions, rather than single cities. Generals of the Jesuits such as Claudio Acquaviva (from 1581 to 1615), and Vincenzo Carafa (1646–49) led campaigns for such controlled and coordinated mission work. They had difficulties securing enough full-time missionary Jesuits, when the Order was trying to fulfil multifarious roles, some far more attractive than popular missionary work in remote, poor, areas.[40]

The Religious Orders, most significantly the Jesuits and Capuchins, conducted major 'missions' to educate those they considered hardly Christian, whether in remote rural areas, or the poorest slum areas of large cities. The Jesuits treated much of southern Italy as 'the Indies of Italy', in need of missionary activity like the pagans of the New World, or Buddhists and Confucianists of the East.[41] Some of this thinking derived from the campaigns against the Waldensians in Calabria and Puglia, and against Calvinists in the Piedmontese mountains in the 1560s, and from an awareness that education would be better than repression. While targeting those with heretical Christian beliefs Jesuits became cognizant of a general ignorance of basic Christian belief, especially in the South. The missionary challenge was also taken up by Capuchins, as in central Italy, and then these Orders from the turn of the century were joined by others like the Theatines, Scolopians, Redemptionists and Pii Operai in missionising slum areas of the great cities of Rome, Naples and Genoa. The Pii Operai, a common-life group founded in 1600 by ex-Jesuit Carlo Carafa (1561–1633) was dedicated to popular mission work in both rural areas, and in city slums, first in Naples, then in Taranto and other parts of the Kingdom. To educational preaching was added all-round care for plague victims in 1656.[42]

The missions outside the large cities tended to focus on a major sermon, or series of sermons, often outdoors, followed by penitential processions, with intense flagellation encouraged by Capuchins, and the singing of *laude* or other religious texts (as in Jesuit processions). The display of the Sacrament might be a major aspect of processions; or the kissing of the *pax*, a peace instrument promoted especially by Carlo Borromeo. For a prolonged mission through a city, as in Lecce in 1639 under Jesuits, children were gathered in the parishes for afternoon sessions on the basics of Christian Doctrine, leading to their First Communion; instruction of adults followed Vespers. The Jesuits in particular tried to ensure that the mission was not a passing event, soon to be forgotten, by seeking to create confraternities, Christian Doctrine schools and charitable institutions that would have a more lasting impact. The missions might campaign to bring greater peace to the community, whether when dealing with the bandit infested southern areas in the 1570s to 1590s, or in the aftermath of the 1647 Masaniello Naples Revolt through much of the Kingdom of Naples. The reinvigorated Jesuit mission activity for the second half of the seventeenth century, added campaigns – with the aid of confraternities – for fuller catechising, learning of doctrines, more frequent confession and communion for the laity. Tension could exist in missionary campaigning between those wanting an emphasis on religious education, and those still concentrating on penitential attitudes and exercises. The Jesuit Paolo Segneri, a great organiser (*c.*1665–92) of missions across whole dioceses combined both aspects in intense day–night missions. The missionary impact was rendered more long-lasting by the provision of booklets on doctrine, and cheap illustrative materials, especially fostering the Marian cult. In such missionary work the Jesuits had been joined by the Lazzaristi or Fathers of the Missions, as in the Papal State in the 1640s and rural Piedmont in the 1650s, influenced by successes in France. They kept notaries busy writing out peace contracts.[43]

Considerable efforts were made through our period to educate and re-educate the Italian people in the basics of Christian Doctrine, and in a moral life. It was a combined effort of bishops, parish clergy, members of Orders and clerical associations, and lay volunteers in confraternities. Where some constituent elements were defective or absent, there was some chance that others would fill gaps, as with the missionary preachers. Other elements in the educational process included the Inquisitors, with some positive re-education as well as repression, the book censors, and the visual arts and music; all of which will be discussed in subsequent chapters.

7 *Confraternities, Hospitals and Philanthropy*

Against Protestant criticisms and theological claims Catholic authorities and individuals were challenged to emphasise the importance of good works, whose performance might assist the salvation of the performer or donor's soul, and that of the recipient of good works. Catholic reformers increased the number and range of philanthropic activities by individuals and institutions, notably from the 1490s in north-central Italy. The activities involved helping the sick, dying and dead; the poor and hungry; travellers and pilgrims; the vulnerable from abandoned babies to poor virgins needing dowries, fallen women and battered wives. Physical and spiritual needs were involved, as 'good works' could also involve prayer for others, improving religious education, encouraging frequent confession and communion, and peacemaking. Sometimes loving kindness might seem absent, and a punitive attitude prevalent; punish to redeem. Curbing sin in this world, reducing temptations, might help save the soul from perdition. Policies of care under supervision, and with the threat of punishment for those not conforming, coincided with some social control attitudes fostered by secular authorities afraid of criminal and riotous behaviour by the less deserving and dangerous poor. The philanthropy came from individuals, from the Religious Orders and civic administrations, but the lay confraternities were the chief vehicles of activity, and the organisations to which the needy would most likely turn.[1]

Confraternities

Confraternities have been mentioned already in various contexts. The word 'confraternity' covers a wide variety of religious organisations, but the terminology in English, Latin and Italian can be confusingly diverse. For pre-Reformation English historians the equivalents are often known as religious gilds or guilds; but English speaking historians mostly use (con)fraternity, brotherhood, company and congregation. The Italian words – to be noted because they appear in titles of the named institutions – are usually *confraternita, società, compagnia, fraterna, congregatione* and *scuola.* This last name, though found in various north Italian places, is mostly used for the Venetian confraternities such as the most notable Scuola Grande di San Rocco, famous for Tintoretto paintings, and still a confraternity. For such organisations, *scuola* should not be translated as 'school', as some guidebooks, like old history books, still do; though *scuola* is the normal word for an educational school. In general we are dealing with lay men – less frequently women and youths – who associate together under basic rules to pursue a part of their religious life together, and to prepare for death. We can find in our period confraternities of priests, and even confraternities of a few nuns within a convent, but our chief concern is with organisations for lay people. Some such confraternities allowed clergy as members, while others employed clerics as needed for Masses, funerals and confessions.

Confraternities were predominantly lay. As Ronald Weissman wrote, such confraternities provided 'vital forms of social insurance in life and in death'.[2] They might be seen, as Nicholas Terpstra perceptively argues, as 'modes of spiritual community', with their own 'cultural form', as expressions of early modern fraternalism, paralleled by organisations within the Lutheran, Calvinist and Orthodox churches, and by Jewish fraternities – with mutual charitable assistance as a key element. They linked spiritual expression and worldly needs, existing close to the official churches, but still seeking to distance themselves from clerical control.[3] Allowing the Catholic confraternities to remain semi-autonomous, preserving their 'cultural form', was a challenging threat to dogmatic hardline clergy. Some confraternities or individual officers in them, like Milan diarist Giambattista Casale, were caught in struggles between autonomy and dictatorial, puritanical control.[4]

Lay Confraternities in Italy have been documented from the end of the first millennium, emerging from clerical societies. The numbers expanded considerably from the thirteenth century under impulses from flagellant movements, Marian cults, the growth of hospices and hospitals, the development of trade guilds with religious and philanthropic dimensions added, evolutions in concepts of purgatory which encouraged praying in common for the souls of the departed and their early release from purgatory. Particularly under the influence of the Mendicant Orders in the fourteenth century, another type of lay confraternity emerged, the Laudesi, noted for public processions singing religious songs (*laude*) in honour of Christ, the Virgin or local saints. Some also produced religious plays and sacred representations or tableaux (see Chapter 10). As pertinently influential religious sociologists like Gabriel Le Bras have argued confraternities became the most significant forms of medieval community outside kinship groups.

Italian confraternities further evolved and were invigorated from the later fifteenth century, and became key elements in the Catholic Reform movements. A new wave of philanthropic activity built up from the 1490s, led by the Genoese Company of Divine Love of 1497. Influential offshoots soon emerged in Rome, Naples and Venice, developing hospital institutions, and responding to the crisis of the spread of syphilis after the French armies marched to Naples and back in 1494–95. Further diversification came from the Dominican inspired cult of the Rosary, taken up by a Florentine Rosary confraternity of San Marco (from 1481), and the Venetian San Domenico in Castello (aided by immigrant Germans), and from a variety of campaigns stressing Eucharist devotion. Confraternities joined in enhancing the veneration of the displayed Host, and in arguing for more frequent confession and communion by the laity.

The disasters of war after the French invasion of the peninsula in 1494 challenged many to respond charitably, and assist orphans, war widows, those sick from war wounds, plagues and epidemics. Existing and new lay confraternities, clerical congregations (some eventually evolving into full Orders like the Theatines, Oratorians, Angelics and Ursulines), and more informal groups of women as well as men, were part of the response. Following Lutheran attacks on salvation through 'good works', the Catholic response was to enhance philanthropic activity. Guidance on such activity was given by the corporal Seven Acts of Mercy, based on Matthew's Gospel, ch. 25: caring for the hungry, thirsty, naked, sick, imprisoned, strangers, and (in a seventh Act added in the middle ages), burying the dead. Such programmed activities, doing for neighbours as for Christ, in his words, were fostered by confraternity statutes and Jesuit advocacy. Sometimes they were visually programmed in paintings, as in Santi di Tito's separate panels illustrating each Act, for the currently active Florentine confraternity Della Misericordia (assisting with ambulance services); and now most famously Caravaggio's complex all-in-one altarpiece for a noble Neapolitan confraternity, the Pio Monte della Misericordia[5] (Chapter 10).

Attitudes towards lay confraternities by church and state leaders in the sixteenth century were ambivalent. They could be seen as subversive, especially if their statutes enjoined secrecy on members, as many did. Confraternities in various cities had discussed ideas thrown up by the Reformers, and allegedly harboured heretics. Rulers in Florence or Naples saw confraternities as havens for political opponents, or economically subversive artisans. However, well supervised confraternities might be political assets (as Duke Cosimo I de'Medici sought in Tuscany), and promoters of a new religious enthusiasm and beneficial philanthropy. Hence came hierarchical support for Oratories of Divine Love, for early Christian Doctrine societies. For the pioneering bishop G.M. Giberti of Verona, parochial Corpus Christi fraternities fostered Eucharist devotion in the 1540s.[6] In 1562 the Council of Trent debated the roles of confraternities, and then claimed that they, along with most hospitals and other pious places, should be subject to episcopal control. Specifically bishops had the right to visit such institutions and check their records to ensure that all pious dispositions from wills were properly executed (since such affected the salvation of souls); confraternities were to report annually on their activities relating to such aspects (though not their strictly devotional life and work).[7] Henceforth bishops demanded to see old fraternity statutes and reform them (if existing), and supervise the imposition of new ones. Fraternities, hospitals, orphanages were to be subject to episcopal visitations. Following several central rulings culminating in the 1604 Bull *Quaecumque*, new confraternity foundations had essentially to be under diocesan control and potential veto; limiting lay initiatives, and eradicating lay independence. A significant exception to this episcopal control came with the agreement that Jesuit lay Marian congregations would be subject to control by the Order not the diocese, as part of a European and worldwide network.[8] Strict constructionists have consequently removed these lay congregations from the category of 'confraternity', though for most purposes we can treat them as part of the same family. Rulers and civic governments could add levels of control and supervision, notably the Venetian Council of Ten and other committees over their Scuole.

Reforming bishops and the new Orders considerably increased the number of confraternities, and their work, while trying to ensure clerical control. Ideally they should be based in a parish church, with the parish priest or a parochial curate serving the confraternity's needs. The result was the expansion of confraternities of the Holy Sacrament and Rosary, which reformers like Paleotti and Borromeo wanted in virtually every parish. The Sacrament or other Eucharist-focused fraternities under various names (such as Scuola Venerabile, in Venice), not only existed to ensure due respect for the Host, but often acted as vestry or fabric committee, helping to finance the church, and sometimes represented a godly elite within the parish, setting moral standards and being the eyes of the hierarchy. Local parochial Rosary companies were often female focused and sometimes were women-only sororities, providing a solidarity group outside the family. However, other Rosary confraternities persisted under Dominican influence, in large Dominican churches, as in Perugia and Bologna, greater in numbers and mixed sex.[9] Other parochial confraternities developed from the later sixteenth century were the previously discussed Christian Doctrine societies, and Name of God (Nome di Dio) fraternities, which were designed to combat blasphemy, and act as peacemakers in society.

While church leaders wanted close cooperation between parish clergy and the confraternities based there, and with the latter as aids and agents to the clergy in the promotion of spirituality and pastoral well-being, the actual relationships were obviously mixed.[10] The priests might appreciate confraternal assistance, whether in teaching catechism, maintaining the fabric, providing accoutrements, paying for the organ, even repairing his house; but then be beholden, and so have problems of disciplining the fraternity or members. Many parish churches were essentially paid for fully by confraternities – whether in cities like Milan, Brescia and Venice, in the Tuscan *contado*, and in most *chiese ricettizie* in the South. If several fraternities were based in the one church, tensions could exist all round; as shown in the report of an external commission dealing in 1605 with the parish church of Crevalcore (Bologna Archdiocese). The Rosary confraternity was granted, seemingly contrary to the wishes of the parish priest, the right to extend the church so it could have its own chapel and sacristy, with public access from outside; but this must not impede access to and from the Sacrament oratory, and the latter must be allowed an iron grate so they can also hear Mass in the body of the church. Parish priests might resent the way fraternities took over altars, chapels and dictated conditions, as in Pisa.[11]

Parish-based fraternities could resent clerical intrusion, and any obligation to have a clerical chairman. Conflicts over being allowed meeting rooms in the church complex as well as an altar or chapel in the body of the church, fuelled bids for total independence in their own premises. Some new confraternities in the seventeenth century successfully resisted episcopal pressure to be placed in parochial or monastic buildings, as in Prato, where however parish-based ones still flourished. Grand Duke Peter Leopold of Tuscany and others by this stage judged that confraternities had become detrimental to parish-based religion; either drawing people away from the parish to other oratories, or disrupting the parish if based in its church. One aspect of post-Tridentine reform was thus judged a failure.[12]

To promote parish–confraternity cooperation sometimes elaborate contracts had been drawn up between parish clergy and the confraternities, as Ronald Weissman had studied for Florence. Complex divisions of responsibility and duties can be illustrated from a contract in 1648 between the Rectors of the *pieve* church of S. Michele in Bagnacavallo (Emilia), and the Sacrament confraternity, which had an altar there, plus its own separate oratory of San Bernardino.[13] The contract (arising from recent Visitation's evidence), clarified that the fraternity was responsible for the tabernacle on the high altar, and what was needed to honour the Sacrament, but not the Choir around it, or certain necessities for all altars; it should maintain its own side altar, but need not pay for a chaplain for it. For a monthly exposure of the Sacrament the company must provide lighting, but also other decorations (*addobbi*). The contract also stipulated what altar decorations, cupboards and other matter they could move to their own oratory, and what must stay in S. Michele. The company needed to spend considerably on the main altar to bring it up to (episcopal) standard; but the costs should be spread over some years, so that they need not reduce spending on the poor; in a penurious year.

Membership of confraternities was widespread, and increasing through our period, voluntarily or under parochial pressure. Few motivations for joining are clearly articulated in surviving material; Giambattista Casale's diary comments on his enthusiasm for catechistic teaching is a rare insight (Chapter 6). But we can deduce many motives from the statutory nature of confraternities, their declarations and practices. The main religious concerns were preparing for the afterlife through prayer and moral conduct, ensuring a suitable funeral and burial for self and fellow members, praying for the souls of the departed fraternity brothers, sisters and close relatives. Many called for the intercession of saints, and in particular of the Virgin. Saying or singing Offices of the Virgin, and *laude* in her honour, had been more common than the Mass, though the sixteenth century saw an increase in confession, receiving communion and adoring the Host. Group penitential exercises, notably flagellation or 'discipline', by whipping bare backs with cords, had been a special activity of one group of confraternities from the thirteenth century, though other types of fraternities such as Laudesi and Marian ones, might also practice the discipline. This could take place in darkened confraternity rooms, or in public processions. As a group activity it was largely confined to males, though women might privately flagellate. If the fifteenth century saw some decline in discipline, or a move from metal-barbed whips to softer silken cords, a return to harsher whipping was encouraged from the mid-sixteenth century, by Capuchins and Jesuits.

Processions could be a major part of confraternity life, ranging from short activities around their church interior, to major processions, joyful or doleful. Processions might celebrate the patronal saint, the Virgin, Corpus Christi, a good harvest, or be planned to placate God's wrath in the face of drought, excessive rain, or plagues. Processions would be formed to bury members, or those they were helping; they could be composed of a few brethren and sisters taking their turn; or by virtually the whole company; while a notable person might have several fraternities escorting his body. For other occasions confraternities might process on their own, or be involved in joint processional parades, linking with other fraternities, with secular and regular clergy, and civic dignitaries; as part of civic or princely celebrations (such as the birth of an heir in the Medici family), or for a major ecclesiastical occasion, such as the moving of relics, the beatification of sanctification of a local holy person. Celebratory processions could involve the parading of statues of the Madonna and Crucified Christ, favourite altarpieces, banners; the carrying of candles and torches, accompanied by music from choirs and instruments. Wine and food might refresh the participants, as when relics of local saints in Perugia were relocated in 1609, with numerous confraternities putting on displays, or marshalling tens of thousands attending.[14] Some confraternities put on religious plays (though these were frowned on by some post-Tridentine reformers), or mounted religious scenes or tableaux on decorated carts showing lavishly dressed actors, without speech or song (see Chapter 10).

Confraternities were organised corporate bodies; their statutes devoted more space to how officials and committees should be elected, and their functions, how members should be inducted and disciplined, than to liturgical procedures and social activity. Election and appointment procedures could be as elaborate as for city councils and guild officials; many posts could rotate quickly. Socially therefore membership provided opportunities for role playing, networking, influencing people and activities. Some brothers tried to evade councils or administrative posts (affecting their secular roles and employment); others were clearly happy with playing a role. As philanthropic activities expanded (discussed later), some brothers and sisters had a more active role in good works, helping the poor and needy – which they might think as helping their souls as well as those of recipients. Most work was done by small committees and officials (priors, sindics, treasurers, *festaioli* to organise processions, decorations etc., visitors to the sick), but general congregations were held annually, or occasionally more frequently, often associated with a patronal saint, or major church feast. This generally involved a major Mass, the business meeting to ratify elections and change statutes, and sometimes a feast – though this was heavily discouraged (but not successfully eradicated), by the more puritanical bishops after Trent. Feasts happily persisted in Piedmont among Pentecostal fraternities, with some knock-on charitable help for the poor.[15]

A significant incentive for membership was earning indulgences and privileges. Some enrolled as long-distance members to be part of a prayer network, and enjoy the attached indulgences. Indulgences were linked with key confraternity liturgical events; special ones added for those participating in pilgrimages, especially to distant sites such as Assisi, the Virgin's House in Loreto, and Rome for the great Jubilees (see Chapter 10). Indulgence-earning was fostered by the archconfraternity system. Some confraternities were elevated to this status by papal Bull, to be a centralising headquarters organisation; such as for Christian Doctrine, or Dell'Orazione e Morte (Prayer and Death, preparing for a good death), or Pietà dei Carcerati (helping in prisons), S. Spirito in Sassia (running a major Roman hospital complex). Their approved statutes would then be the model for any associated fraternity, thus facilitating episcopal standardisation. The Pope allocated indulgences, which could be enjoyed by affiliated brotherhoods (always providing individuals were in a fit penitent state to earn them, with God's grace). Most archconfraternities were in Rome (with affiliates all across Europe, amounting to a thousand or so by the eighteenth century with the Orazione e Morte), but a few were promoted in other cities, such as Bologna (the Della Vita in

1585, with the rival Della Morte and four others to follow),[16] and Bari (S. Antonio da Padova, in mid-seventeenth century). Cosenza which had five archconfraternities by the early seventeenth century, established a network in the southern hinterland. The importance of such indulgences is evidenced by the scattered survival, in confraternity archives, of printed notices about them, and the way they could be earned.

Philanthropy provided an increasing motivation for confraternity membership, from the late fifteenth century, as indicated earlier. The encouragement to perform good works was widespread, and not confined to confraternities, congregations and Orders, but such lay organisations were facilitators, for both donors and recipients. Confraternities and hospitals were institutions through which charitable bequests were distributed to the needy, when family members might be less diligent; and post-Tridentine bishops were more intent on seeing bequests fulfilled properly. People had previously joined fraternities to secure some assistance when sick and old, and maybe help with a dowry for a daughter. Hospices had been available both for sick members, women in labour without other support, poor travellers and pilgrims who were not members.[17] All such expectations increased through our period; and other aspects were added under the Seven Acts rubrics. The rhetoric of poverty and philanthropy encouraged confraternities, and others, to consider outsiders more, as 'neighbours'.

Philanthropy was a two-way street; trying to save the soul of the recipient, and that of the donor involved. For the recipient, in the mindset of the period, his or her soul was more important than any physical short-term assistance. Giulio Folco, in his powerful *Marvellous Effects of Almsgiving* in 1581 – as part of his long campaign to raise dowry money for poor girls – stressed that giving was particularly good for the donor's soul. He indicated that his confraternity, Vergini Miserabili (Poor Virgins) of Santa Caterina della Rosa, was more concerned with their souls as well as bodies, than some other such institutions.[18] Later the Sicilian Abbot Paolo De Angelis argued that giving alms was like depositing in heaven, for one's future profit, while Bishop Alessandro Sperelli of Gubbio, in 1666, claimed that the rich giving to the poor not only helped the donor escape the pains of hell, but brought the donor closer to God by imitating his gift-giving. So donor and recipient were both pleased.[19]

Counting actual numbers involved is hard; and cited figures may not accurately reflect active participants. The records of Visitation *ad limina* reports and apostolic Visitations, of religious Orders such as Jesuits and Capuchins, show an increase in the numbers of confraternities, notably linked to parishes and parochial work (Christian Doctrine and social welfare). Ongoing research in southern Italy, notably in Puglia, where Catholic Reform was slower to take off, documents new foundations through to the eighteenth century, though whether from a popular base rather than being imposed episcopally from above is unclear, in a kinship-focused society wary of corporate institutions.[20] The southern diocese of Benevento in 1590 had 94 confraternities for a population of 136 000, expanding to 352 for 124 924 persons in 1737. In Venice the *scuole* numbered about 120 in the early sixteenth century, and Richard Mackenney's tally has reached 387 for the eighteenth. Perugia had about 40 confraternities in the city in the early seventeenth century (for about 19 722 people in 1618), with 128 confraternities in another 88 towns and localities in its diocese/ *contado* (33 129). In Rome a 1601 guide by Camillo Fanucci to its pious institutions counted 11 confraternities associated with hospitals, 49 primarily for guild members and immigrant or visiting 'national' groups, and 52 he judged 'universal'.[21]

The numbers within confraternities varied considerably. Possibly the largest was the Neapolitan Dei Bianchi Dello Spirito Santo, claiming 6000 members in 1562; this ran a number of charitable institutions, helping abandoned girls, widows, daughters of prostitutes, and the homeless, and had the backing of top Neapolitan noble families. At the low end we find a Lombard sorority (S. Orsola in Canegrate) in 1583 with a mere four members. Many rural rosary and sacrament confraternities probably had numbers under 20; but numerous city companies of all kinds would have had 100s. The top group of Venetian Scuole, the five (six from 1552) Scuole Grandi, directly controlled by the Council of Ten, had ceilings set at 500–600 members each, though as Brian Pullan showed these limits could be exceeded – surreptitiously or with permission, to increase entrance incomes.[22] Some members could be active regularly for many years, serving on councils and as officials, and attending Masses; others might be very intermittent, but still remain on the books, since most societies seemed reluctant to expel people once accepted, except for dire misconduct.

Lay men and women, children and clergy could all be involved in confraternities as members; and be recipients of assistance. Most members were adult males and lay. While misogynist attitudes and fears of 'gossip', or a concentration on penitential group flagellation, might lead to explicit exclusion of women from fraternities, mixed-sex confraternities existed, though in most cases the women played a limited role in confraternity organisation, seldom having an equal voice. Perugia had a mixed Nome di Dio confraternity which counted at least 824 brothers and sisters (roughly equal).[23] As often the numbers of women involved in confraternities may have been underestimated though, recognising that others mighty have followed two Venetian *scuole* in saying: 'we are not naming the *sorelle,* along with the *fratelli,* so as not to multiply the words.'[24] Female membership and importance becomes clear when they were allowed their own officials, as in hospital work, visiting the sick at home, or teaching catechisms. A few female sororities are found, covering both elite noble women (the Neapolitan Devote di Gesù from 1554, or the Roman S. Anna per le Donne from 1640), furthering welfare activities, and peasant women in S. Orsola and Rosary groups, probably with prayer as the chief focus. Children and youths (a flexible terminology), could be involved, as novices awaiting full membership of an adult fraternity, or in independent youth confraternities. These are most famous from the fifteenth century in Florence, playing notable roles in religious musical and dramatic activities; though as they developed from the mid-sixteenth-century amateur youthfulness was often replaced by more professional adult domination[25] (see Chapter 10).

Confraternities could be socially exclusive or inclusive.[26] One trend was to restrict a fraternity or sorority to a particular select group; of nobles, students, a guild or group of guilds, even the blind or maim (as authorised beggars). The larger cities had 'national' confraternities for immigrants from other parts of Italy, or further afield; these provided religious activity and social welfare, and a networking system for survival in a city. They also helped travellers and temporary students (as in Bologna, Perugia and Rome). The 'nation' could be as narrow as Norcians (specialists in butchery, and sometimes castration of singers), in Rome, Bergamaschi in various cities like Venice and Rome, or as broad as 'German' (embracing Magyars and Poles) as in Perugia. Venetian *scuole* for Greeks and Slavs preserved certain special religious features.

Alternatively, some confraternities fostered inclusiveness, seeking social integration through the social orders, and combining rich and poor. The Venetian Scuole Grandi had a wide social spread, though dominated by the middling orders in their offices, with a few nobles at one end, and poor artisans at the other (hoping for almshouses, dowries and other perks). The parish-based fraternities were also meant to cover all levels of local society. Danilo Zardin stresses this inclusivity through Lombardy with its sacrament societies, though some other sacrament confraternities like those in Budrio and Bagnacavallo in the Bologna Archdioces appear socially narrow and elitist by mid-seventeenth century. In Bologna itself the parochial sacrament confraternity in SS. Vitale e Agricola started as all-inclusive, but by the early seventeenth century was essentially a narrow elite organisation, even if the Forty Hour devotions or the poor relief it organised benefited the wider parish membership.[27] In socially mixed fraternities leadership was likely to come from the wealthier orders, with members having more time to serve as officials; but lists of officials often suggest there was still room for more lowly committee members; and Vicenza's Crocefisso specifically ruled in 1602 that offices should not be reserved for nobles but spread through the ranks. A social spread for officials was especially desirable in inclusive fraternities if a fair spread of philanthropy through the membership was to be ensured.

Philanthropy

Organised philanthropy increased through our period, via confraternities and other agents of welfare. Across Europe from the early sixteenth century poverty was perceived to be increasing, and the poor – especially in cities – judged dangerous to social stability. The idle and potentially criminal poor should be disciplined, while welfare provisions and the products of loving alms-giving should be more efficiently, less corruptly, distributed to the deserving. 'Deserving' was variably defined, but was likely to include aged and infirm, especially female, orphans and poor clergy. State and city governments tended to concentrate on controlling food supplies to cope with periods of dearth (Venice being a leading example from the 1520s), then on controlling the dangerous and undeserving: sturdy beggars, conmen, prostitutes – by expelling them (as early on from Bruges, Ypres and Venice), or later institutionalising them in mendicant 'hospitals' and 'poor houses', with Bologna provided a model by the 1560s. The deserving poor were assisted through parish relief systems (as later developed in England), through guilds, confraternities, and less punitive hospitals, orphanages, conservatories, run by civic authorities or religious institutions such as confraternities.[28]

Italy generally had a mixed philanthropic system, with interaction between civic authorities, confraternities, Religious Orders, and private initiatives. Motivations and prejudices combined fear of social disorder and, sometimes, of women's sexuality, positive concern for loving one's neighbour, and saving souls of recipients and donors. Some religious leaders challenged the harsher discriminatory secular attitudes. Alessandro Sperelli argued that it was for God to discriminate between deserving and undeserving, not humans, who should assist without 'examinations and inquisitions'.[29] Increasingly Italian philanthropists sought to redeem prostitutes and their offspring, rather than purely reject them; though the redemption could lead to near monastic enclosure in conservatories, or Case delle Convertite (Houses for the (female) Converted – from immorality!), despite warnings against this by the famous Venetian courtesan-poet Veronica Franco when trying to assist other prostitutes and their daughters. However, discrimination and strict social control tended to govern activities.

Philanthropic work can best be discussed under some general prioritised headings, though institutions and individuals might be involved in several. Concern for female honour and respectability meant that many confraternities and hospitals awarded dowries for marriage or convent-entry (usually cheaper), in most cases just a few a year. Competition might be open just to relatives of the membership, or widened. Poverty, moral quality and sometimes good (or not ugly) looks came into the assessments. A few confraternities specialised in this work, most notably Rome's Santa Annunziata alla Minerva, which by the early seventeenth century was the major contributor to the 3000 dowries offered in Rome annually. Spectacular processions involving the lucky recipients drew large crowds, and comments from foreign visitors such as the English Jesuit Gregory Martin, and the French writer Montaigne (in 1581). This institution received much papal support, moral and financial, as from Pius V and Urban VII (1590).

Redeeming and assisting vulnerable girls and women were the concerns of many philanthropists. The casualties of warfare, orphaned homeless children, especially girls, widowed and raped women, and women forced into prostitution, led people like Countess Laura Gambara, Bartolomeo Stella, Girolamo Miani to start conservatories to protect them (see Chapter 1). Gambara's Conservatorio delle Convertite della Carità in Brescia was one model; initially to protect young girls after the 1512 sack of the city, it later admitted older vulnerable women, and repentant prostitutes. Miani opened an orphanage in the city in 1532. Stella helped these two spread ideas about orphanages and conservatories across northern-central Italy. The Capuchin Bernardino Ochino, before his flight, inspired through a sermon the foundation of Casa Delle Derelitte in Perugia in 1539, run by the confraternity of St Thomas Aquinas. The early Jesuits, led by Ignatius Loyola himself, were concerned with vulnerable women. He instituted in Rome the Casa di Santa Marta (1542) for ex-prostitutes and battered women; followed by the Conservatorio di Santa Caterina delle povere miserabili for prostitutes' daughters and other young girls seen as in moral and physical peril.[30] Other cities introduced conservatories for such abandoned girls, reformed prostitutes, and battered wives. Some were run by confraternities, others by civic institutions with confraternity members and Regulars assisting. The Perugian Derelitte house held about 40 girls in 1544; confraternity members raised money for its maintenance, food, clothing and dowries. They secured the backing of the leading noble families, and the city's major bibliophile and founder of a library, G.B. Pontani. Bishop Comitoli in 1622 transferred control of the House to the Barnabites, judging them better teachers for the girls.[31] These institutions could only help a limited percentage of possible users; so applications outweighed places, with the almost inevitable consequence that Perugian, Florentine and Bolognese institutions, for example, increasingly preferred girls from a less vulnerable and poor background, to avoid those who might prove troublesome incumbents.[32]

Some of these conservatories and orphanages were attached to great hospital complexes, such as Naples' S. Spirito hospital (which had about 400 abandoned orphaned girls in 1587). 'Hospitals' (*Ospedali*) in our period could range from such a large hospital complex, to a simple room serving as a hospice or restroom. Records are often vague on the nature and size of '*ospedali*' named. Many small hospices had existed in the middle ages, with a few notable larger institutions with medical facilities, such as Prato's Misericordia and Florence's Santa Maria Nuova. Through the fifteenth century secular governments in northern Italy had developed a policy of amalgamating the facilities and financial resources of small hospitals, to create major centralised city hospital complexes, such as Milan's Ca'Granda from 1459 – treated as a model centralised creation, designed and started (1456–65) by the great architect Filarete. Some such rationalisation procedures were dictated by anticlerical opposition to confraternities and priests, seen as inefficient, corrupt and betrayers of welfare principles. This was true of Duke Cosimo de' Medici's hospital policy from the 1540s. Bishops and other religious reformers were challenged to ensure that those hospitals and hospices remaining under ecclesiastical linkages should be properly administered, serve the sick and vulnerable of all kinds.

Members of fraternities, congregations and Religious Orders were also inspired to offer themselves as hospital assistants from the 1530s, to help with nursing, feeding, teaching, providing spiritual comfort. Filippo Neri tested the dedication of those wishing to join his Oratory organisation by sending them to one of the Roman hospitals to clean wounds and sores. Other great names in Catholic Reform, Bartolomeo Stella, Carlo Borromeo, Cesare Baronio, Camillo de Lellis, Luigi Gonzaga followed in promoting Christian focused hospital policies. Jesuits, Oratorians, Theatines, Capuchins all became involved in the spiritual side of hospital work, whether for those who would recover, and those on the brink of death (see Chapter 3).

Rome developed a complex of hospitals which the late sixteenth century fed propaganda that the city led the world in spiritual and physical health.[33] Modernisation of medieval hospital structures, followed by new creations, had begun in otherwise inauspicious circumstances in the early sixteenth century, and continued with input from several confraternities, from the Oratory of Divine Love, Oratorians, local artisan guilds, popes such as Clement VIII and Gregory XIII, and in the 1580s Cardinal Antonio Maria Salviati, named Protector of Hospitals from 1583. Camillo Fanucci's 1601 survey claimed 40 hospitals for Rome: 17 general-specialist ones, 19 'national' and 4 guild hospitals.[34] The star complex was S. Spirito in Sassia (originating officially back in 1201), which by 1601 had 150 beds for the wounded and fevered, but could cope with 400 during summer epidemics, men and women. It was also the leading foundling hospital, dealing with about 500 abandoned babies a year, providing education for those who survived that experience and a dangerous period of wetnursing. Its own church, built by Antonio Sangallo 1538–45, celebrated many Masses daily, and provided organ music. The archconfraternity fluctuated in the level of its assistance for paid staff, but it helped turn the hospital into one of the richest church institutions, with an income double that of St Peter's by 1624, thanks to testaments, and efficient estate management of properties in city and the Roman Campagna. Its prestige led to an aggregation of 334 confraternities worldwide by the end of the seventeenth century. The archconfraternity-hospital's wealth spawned the major bank of Santo Spirito from 1605. Its splendid buildings 'served as a beacon of charity, *hospitalum nostrum* (our hospital) of the papacy, visible to every pilgrim', in the Vatican Borgo.[35]

S. Spirito's chief rival was S. Giacomo degli Incurabili, developed by the Oratory of Divine Love, initially to alleviate the syphilis scourge (for which it developed a famous holy wood, *legno santo*, potion), but soon coping with many other incurable and curable illnesses.[36] Cardinal Salviati's expansionist work 1580–93 produced a capacity of 120 beds, served by doctor, surgeon, chemist, paid nurses, who also treated outpatients. Several confraternities added nursing, spiritual and financial assistance. Other notable Roman hospitals included S. Maria della Consolazione, fostered primarily by and for the artisans of the Trastevere district, and involving numerous confraternities; major rebuilding and expansion from 1650 gave it a wide reputation. Another Trastevere-based confraternity hospital, S. Maria dell'Orto, boasted the best pharmacy in Rome, and a richly provided church that was the centre of numerous festivals. S. Maria della Pietà dei Pazzarelli broke new ground as a hospital for the insane that started by rejecting chains, straight-jackets and other restraints, in favour of loving care. If the Spanish Ferrante Ruiz, and his 1548 Company of Poor Foreigners (*Poveri Forestieri*), were the prime movers, they had the considerable support of Carlo Borromeo, Filippo Neri, Diego Lainez. Sadly it witnessed major difficulties in the 1590s, never gained a solid financial base, returned to constraint policies under Cardinal Francesco Barberini's reform attempts in 1635.

Many lesser hospitals and hospices catered for the foreign immigrants and visitors (short and long term), and for pilgrims. The fullest propaganda success was probably the archconfraternity of SS. Trinità for pilgrims and convalescents. Promoted by Filippo Neri in the 1540s it made its first impact catering for pilgrims during the 1550 Holy Year. Its noble brother members developed an institution that assisted pilgrims and convalescents in normal years, but also nurtured 175 000 persons in the 1575 Jubilee, and 200 000 in 1600. Pilgrims were sheltered and fed usually for three days (while those from a great distance such as German states, Bohemia or Portugal could stay longer), their feet washed, entertained by music, helped visit the great basilicas to earn their indulgences (see Chapter 10).

Thus the image of Holy Rome (*Roma Sancta*), was well cultivated, as the Jesuit Gregory Martin recorded, hearing of this 'glorious' SS. Trinità work and that of many confraternities and hospitals during his 1576–78 stay in Rome.[37]

Outside Rome, hospitals and hospices were very variable. Criticisms of the confraternity hospitals continued through our period, by bishops, vicars general, and secular governments; though an anticlerical prejudice might colour the campaign, as with Duke Cosimo in Tuscany. He attempted to centralise the hospital system through the state-controlled Bigallo office, but encountered much resistance in localities. Local hospices, though poorly managed could sustain poor priests and poor widows (as superintendents), and be acceptable locally provided no family involved became too greedy (as in Buggiano), and benefits were shared around (as in Ponolano).[38]

Confraternities continued to offer alms to petitioners, but with more vetting of needs than before. In food, and thus also employment, crises giving might be 'indiscriminate', but otherwise fraternities used officials to visit homes and make other checks, and recorded those to whom they gave money, food, clothing, blankets, mattresses and medicines. Licences might be given to cover a defined period for assistance. Some help was given through specialist institutions. Confraternities, especially in the centre-south (Abruzzi, Basilicata and Molise), and Piedmont, took up the fifteenth-century Franciscan idea of providing loans through Christian pawn-broking institutions (Monti di Pietà, or dei Poveri), to avoid Jewish moneylenders. In southern areas Monti were created to help the poor invest for marriage dowries, and Monti di Frumentari lent seed and capital to poor farmers so they could sow again after a harvest disaster or family crisis. This last activity, sometimes also encouraged by Observant Franciscans – and by Paul V – increased in popularity until the nineteenth century.

Some confraternities invested in almshouses, which would be offered for the love of God (*Amore Dio*). The Venetian Scuole Grandi are best known for this; offering between 40 and 70 houses or rooms. Such establishments were eagerly sought, and sometimes were corruptly allocated to less than poor relatives of officials. Others gained their house by fairer vetting, and subsequent immoral conduct could lose it. In the case of a *scuola piccola*, SS. Trinità, it advertised to the general public a vacancy in its 10 or so almshouses on the Rialto and in St Mark's square.[39]

Much philanthropy was conducted through these specialist confraternities and institution. However, some systems of poor relief were developed, somewhat like the evolving English Poor Law parochial solutions. Parish priests were pressed to list the needy parishioners to guide the other institutions and societies, but parish-church-based fraternities designed to help the poor at home were also created. Venice provides a key example, though the evidence is fullest for the eighteenth century.[40] Under the pressure of food crises of 1544–47, parishes were instructed to establish committees under the *pievano* to identify the poor needing assistance at home (rather than being institutionalised), and organise relief. In 1563 a group of devout parishioners from SS. Apostoli ceated a Congregation of the Poor, as a kind of confraternity to fulfil this task, for their own religious benefit as well as the home-based poor. Precedents existed under Bishop Giberti of Verona from 1539, and Bishop Michele Priuli of Vicenza in 1569. Other Venetian parishes slowly followed in forming their own Fraterna for the poor, until all 69 parishes had them in the eighteenth century. Such fraternities mixed clergy and laity. The visitors to the poor rotated through the membership, ensuring a diversity of parochial supervision, and avoiding an elitist 'professionalism' that might be too prejudiced for or against families. The visitors were to ensure that the home-based sick had bread, meat, money, medicines and fire wood, but also to seek to create a Christian atmosphere in the family, even some teaching of the faith to children. Clergy and lay brothers sought funds by begging and petitioning. The parish of S. Sofia in 1602 initiated helping those 'in great misery' (as through unemployment), though not sick. In 1608 the patriarch himself pressed parish fraternities to assist those suffering from economic crisis. But ultimately the government health committee, the Provveditori della Sanità, controlled, and expanded this philanthropic coverage, which included bringing in doctors and surgeons. By the 1700s the combination of church and state leadership, and neighbourhood philanthropy had provided a basic welfare service for the poor across most of Venice. Meanwhile in one of the poorest parishes, S. Lio, the Sacrament *scuola* struggled to maintain its own poor relief work, alongside the *piovano*, based on a 'poor box' collecting system.[41]

Other philanthropic developments associated in part with changing religious attitudes include treatment of prisoners (*carcerati*), advocated by one of the Acts of Mercy. Jesuits and Capuchins joined confraternities in bringing food, drink and clothing to poor prisoners who had no help from family or alleged creditors. Increasingly they introduced some religious education, and books for spiritual comfort. In cities such as Bologna, Florence, Lecce, Milan, Naples, Rome and Venice confraternities additionally helped indebted and other prisoners secure release, by paying debts and fines, or making accommodation with complainants or creditors. Some, like Lecce's Jesuit influenced SS. Annunziata, recognised that many were in prison through ignorance more than innate criminality, and economic circumstances beyond their control, so deserving of educational assistance, and the means to start earning again for their families.

In Rome the Pietà dei Carcerati confraternity essentially ran several prisons, and assisted the priests (notably Jesuits), with religious education; in 1592 Clement VIII officially made this and other confraternities like the Gonfalone, as guardians of the prisons. Archbishop Alfonso Paleotti in 1595 similarly made a company within the S. Maria della Morte responsible for Bolognese prison welfare. Several specialist confraternities previously had acted as comforters of condemned prisoners, sought to secure their contrite confession, escorted them in processions to execution, arranged burials and help for the family. This work continued through our period, but in some cities like Bologna and Rome elite groups within certain fraternities became well-trained 'Comforters', to encourage contrition, reconciliation with victims, with the hope that their soul might go straight to heaven, like the Good Thief's at Christ's crucifixion. Some condemned to execution or the galleys could be pardoned through papal privileges granted to certain confraternities, and Roman guilds, provided they had made peace with the victim's family. Other confraternities, notably in Chioggia, Genoa, Naples and Rome, worked for the release of Christians captured and enslaved by the Turks, while the Roman Pietà dei Carcerati extended its charity to securing the release by their Italian owners of north African Muslim slaves, preferably being baptised as well.[42]

Through our period welfare activity thus expanded, building on some medieval precedents, but diversifying in methods and moving into new geographical areas. Whatever the mixed motivations, hard to unravel, more philanthropy was evident. Even if the physical awards were meagre and the offerings to a relatively few left the needs of many unsatisfied, there remains the impressions of a more christian caring society. The welfare society can be judged, as it was at the time, as good for the prestige of Catholicism and its Roman leadership by the seventeenth century.

Confraternities shared in this prestige. However philanthropy was only one aspect of their considerations. Joining the spiritual community could also satisfy selfish spiritual motives, allow women and men to exercise influence in local society, foster social and political networks, and maintain some lay autonomy from clerical domination.

8 *Nunneries and Religious Women*

The Tridentine attempt to enclose strictly all women who had taken full vows as nuns had wide implications for society, and produced many headaches for the male church leaders seeking to enforce it. Success would deprive women of the opportunity to play a religious role in open society outside the control of male family members. We have seen already how attempts to have nuns and tertiaries operating unenclosed were severely frustrated, as with the Angelicals (Chapter 3). Many women avoided both marriage and the convent, but that stark choice was often presented, especially to girls in upper society, and most realised, soon after Trent, that once in a convent it was hard to move freely in and out, as had been quite easy before.

'Aut virum, aut murum', either a man or a wall, was a fifteenth-century Latin proverb; it encapsulates what some reformers wanted more forcefully in the sixteenth century.[1] Fortunately, not all reformers were as rigidly hostile to female activity outside home and convent. Some bishops still promoted the Orsoline Company, founding new institutions in Ferrara (1587), Bologna (1608), Modena (1620), with specific attitudes encoded that they should promote a 'third state', for celibate women to serve God in the world and remain honoured at home, and that this could and should be promoted by fathers of families.[2]

The wide social implications of strict enclosure (*clausura*), were considerable. Much interesting literature has been produced recently in English and Italian on the topic, as on religious minded women who gained notoriety – as living saints, or frauds. The literature has covered the 'tyranny' of forcing females into nunneries, and the resulting miseries and scandals; the attempts of nuns and outside family or admirers to breach the walls; but also lively cultural lives in some convents, with music, theatre, letter-writing and painting. Some nuns could have a true and lasting religious vocation, and others (less devout), find a convent a base for social and political influence.

Nunneries and Female Enclosure

Many young females over the centuries were pushed by families into the religious life at an immature age without realising the implications and without great dedication; often when families were unable or unwilling to provide a suitable marriage dowry. While few nunneries were totally 'free', the costs to the family of monacisation and maintenance in nunnery was much less than for marriage. Commitment through vows to the religious life without spiritual enthusiasm and satisfaction could later on become very burdensome, especially if superiors attempted to ensure the vows were obeyed. The problem of nunneries was seen by some during the Council, such as Francesco Palmio, as central to the spirit of Tridentine reform.[3] Much dispute and tension ensued.

The numbers of females involved were significant. Estimates suggest that from 3 per cent to 6 per cent of the female urban population were in convents, with some cities having much higher ratios. Gabriella Zarri suggested between 9.8 per cent and 13.8 per cent for Bologna, which in 1570 had officially 2198 nuns in its 61 742 population; in 1633 there were 2128 *religiose* in 29 houses (1636 choir nuns, 492 *converse* (see later), with 264 *educande* to be taught. Florence had about 2826 women in 45 convents out of 26 267 inhabitants in 1552, and 4200 out of 76 000 inhabitants in 1622. In Venice in 1581, 2508 were recorded as inhabiting nunneries (out of a population of 134 877); in 1642 officials counted 1991 choral nuns, 599 *converse* and 315 *putte educande* (girls subject to *clausura* rules, while being educated within nunneries), in its central nunneries, excluding some on remoter islands. The city population had probably fallen to about 120 000 as the result of the 1629–33 plagues. Rome in the period 1600–19 averaged 6300 nuns, maybe 5.8 per cent of Rome's female population; this expanded to 8323, or 7.2 per cent for the period 1660–79. Nuns were more numerous than friars or priests in the first period, though friars overtook them in the second half. A smaller area like Prato had 1200 nuns in 10 convents in 1591, for a city and *contado* population of 13 994, (maybe just under 6000 people in the city itself). Naples in 1585 had 22 female convents with 1754 nuns, while in 1630 Lecce (population over 10 000) had 593 nuns in 8 convents. The presence or absence of nunneries in the *contado* varied; at the end of the sixteenth century the duchy of Montefeltro had a nunnery in nearly every *castello*, but Bologna, Parma and Pisa dioceses had virtually none outside the cities.[4]

A disproportionate number of choir nuns came from the upper levels of society, since most nunneries required a 'dowry', and continuing contributions to expenses. A few convents in major cities, mostly Franciscan, and more in poorer parts of the country catered for females from lower sectors of society. Some confraternities offered dowries for poor honest females that could be used either for marriage or convent entry. The preponderance of elite nuns made it harder for the authorities to implement full enclosure. The patrician imbalance was most notable in Venice, where 70–80 per cent of the choir nuns were from patrician families; and the resistance to full enclosure consequently very strong. In Venice, S. Zaccaria was essentially a noble house for generations past, with some very elaborate rituals (especially for the election of the abbess), encouraged by the doge as well as patriarch. By the seventeenth century convents such as S. Alvise, S. Caterina, S. Andrea and S. Spirito had almost become as noble. S. Chiara was, however one for lesser ranked families.[5] Females from humbler backgrounds could however lead convents; in 1599 Benedetta Carlini was sent, aged nine, from a fairly humble family in a Tuscan village, to join a rising community of Theatine females in Pescia. She was the first prioress when it became a fully enclosed convent in 1619. The Theatine Order here would accept women from humble backgrounds. Benedetta gained a reputation as mystic, visionary, prophet, marked by the stigmata. She however ended a prisoner condemned as a false saint, and active lesbian (though which was the worse sin is not clarified by the surviving records).[6]

The decree concerning nunneries and their enclosure was one of the last to be approved in December 1563, after a hurried discussion at the end of November. It claimed to be renovating *clausura* (it being part of canon law since 1298), and boldly ordered that females, once they had professed their vows, should not leave the monastery, even for illness.[7] The Trent discussions pretended that enclosure had been the norm, though sometimes breached. That some Orders had never had strict enclosure made subsequent imposition, contrary to rule and tradition, harder to enforce. While the Trent fathers argued strongly that enclosure was necessary to avoid scandals, they admitted a crucial problem: 'The large majority of nuns enter religion because they are compelled to by threats or reverential fear of parents or relatives.' This happened 'so that they will renounce the inheritances due to them in order to favour their brothers and sisters'.[8] They recognised that consequentially some convents were 'Sacred brothels'.

The Tridentine remedy sought to ensure that their monacisation was freely conducted, and after the age of 16. But the post-Tridentine reformers seemed more intent on the enforcement of enclosure, and less on checking that vows were freely made. Yet bishops a century later were prepared to admit, as the Bishop of Mantua did in 1661 that 'I know the *suore* are women and women who very unwillingly see themselves restrained.'[9] After Trent a few women managed to get their vows annulled, and become free to leave, and even marry, if they could prove gross coercion into taking vows. For example, Caterina Angelica Frosciante, a Dominican nun in S. Andrea in Spoleto in 1682 was released by the Sacred Congregation of the Council, on the grounds that her brothers had forced her to enter the convent in 1655 under death threats, and then her sister, already a nun, had beaten her until she had agreed to take the vows. However, the decision seemed to rest more on her being under age, only 14, when it happened, than on the violence involved. The Council produced a printed text of this case.[10]

What was being demanded was a major change, to be met with considerable opposition from within convents, and from outside, by the secular families, but also some clerical leaders who spotted difficulties. Various states such as Tuscany and Venice established their own magistracies to supervise convents, and those dealing with them; these could both assist and impede the bishops and Congregations.[11] While fathers and brothers might want the females in a convent to save on marital dowries, many still desired access to them, whether from affection, family solidarity, or in recognition that their nuns could still exercise power and influence, through networking with other families.

The sudden imposition of full *clausura* shocked those women who had entered expecting to be able to take visits out of the convent, as with the Udine nun who in 1601 reflected: 'I was told by my relatives: "Do become a nun, but then you will come home often to see us".'[12] Understandably, resistance was offered by nuns caught in the changing policy. Roman nuns and nunneries faced intense pressures, leading to escapes, suicides and revolts, as Niccolò Ormaneto tried to execute his master Carlo Borromeo's rigorous policy in a Visitation of Rome from 1566. Convents vigorously contested, legally and physically, those trying to build more secure structures, as in Florence (S. Maria Annunziata, called Le Murate) and Prato (S. Vicenzo).[13] In southern Italy battles to close nunneries that could not be made secure, redistributing the nuns to other convents (new and old), interference in the hitherto fairly free lives of aristocratic nuns, led some nuns having their vows annulled. Two from the most aristocratic S. Patrizia, Naples, were allowed to marry.[14]

Feverish activity followed Trent to ensure strict enclosure: new walls built, windows giving views of the outside world bricked up, doors blocked that might give too ready access to any church or chapel attached to the convent which would allow contact with the general public. Grilles were created so nuns could observe services, even sing and be heard, but not seen. The parlour, needed for some contact with priests and confessors, or necessary visitors, was supposedly to be secure, so that the nuns could talk through grilles, but not be touched or fully seen. However nuns, their relatives, admirers found ways to evade some of these restrictions and break through barriers. Patriarchs of Venice, archbishops of Bologna and Florence and their Visitors, were particularly intent on ensuring the physical environment implemented enclosure. Laity, and nuns, certainly in Venice, were as intent to limit physical impediments to reasonable communication. In 1594 the Nunzio in Venice reported that the nuns of two Franciscan convents had struck against the physical restrictions, and 'tore down the wall of the cloister, entered the exterior churches, opened the doors, and stayed there for a whole day, walking about the church, and returned to their seclusion after the government threatened them'. Secular policing powers were brought in to control the situation, and the abbesses and vicars of the two convents were imprisoned in other monasteries.[15]

After the Tridentine enclosure spree, clerics occasionally admitted that they needed to show sympathy towards reluctant nuns. The Bishop of Mantua in 1661 told the Congregation of Bishops and Regulars that 'I know well that the nuns are women, and for that matter women who unwillingly see themselves constrained', and Cardinal Giovanni Battista De Luca, a member of the same Congregation in his 1675 *Il vescovo pratico,* declared that while pastoral care required some rigour and austerity for the nuns' protection, 'one needs a considerable degree of leniency, since we must feel pity for these women imprisoned for life and deprived of all the satisfactions which lay women of comparable rank enjoy.'[16]

Nuns could not be isolated, for practical reasons and because of the different kinds of inhabitants. Many convents had three or four kinds of inhabitants: the fully professed choir nuns, the *converse*, some older women not under vows (sometimes called *professe*) such as widows or others seeking refuge and *educande*. *Converse* were women who took simple vows and were not fully consecrated choir nuns. In the more prestigious nunneries the *converse* were often of lower social status, unable to afford a full convent dowry, and acted as servants for the elite nuns, so also called *servigiali* in Tuscany.[17] The *educande* were girls, normally aged from about eight to early 20s, who were educated within a convent, whether in preparation for marriage or for life as a nun. They were supposedly boarders, observing enclosure rules while there; but naturally many families wanted to retain contact, by having the girly home for a time, or visiting them. Milan's San Paolo had its *educande* moving fairly freely.[18] The *converse* and *professe* (if mature and deemed not to be sexually in danger), provided links with the outside world, and brought in gossip. Since endowments and incomes for many nunneries were much less than for male houses, and nuns could no longer seek alms as they had done, the *converse* and *professe* filled such roles. While this could solve financial problems, scandals arose when such *converse* misbehaved with their freedom, as Venetian Patriarchs complained in the 1590s of some from San Sepolcro, Santa Maria Maggiore and Santa Maria di Miracoli.[19]

Males had to have access. The convent inhabitants regularly needed confessors and priests and occasionally doctors. Venetian records show such visitors delayed and gossiped long beyond professional need, to be courted by nuns who had made sweetmeats, cakes and delicacies for them. Workmen needed access to build, and repair, while others brought supplies. While small supplies were handed over via the *ruota*, or rotating platform, which allowed such to be received without provider or conventual recipient seeing each other, we know from clerical orders in Venice and Bologna, and actual Venetian cases, that nuns readily conversed with workmen, or female and male retailers. In 1599 the patriarch expressed concern that the *professe* in the Venetian nunnery of S. Maria di Miracoli were carrying correspondence in and out for the nuns; this must be vetted by the abbess.[20] Despite the high walls, and problems of canals, Venetian youths were caught – and punished – for being too close to convents, for serenading or insulting, with the assumption that nuns and *educande* might hear and see. Others entered the churches close to the nuns' grilled chapel, or into the conventual parlour and similarly showed-off, or exposed themselves, like the musician Pasqualin in 1611 in various nunneries, for which he was sentenced to ten years in the galleys.[21] That such persons were punished, indicates that policing was at least intermittently active, and that a neighbourhood watch readily reported. In Venice again nuns in some convents had close contact with prostitutes, who desired conventual churches for spiritual refuge, or the nuns for gossipy friendship and off-duty female companionship. In the case of prostitute Malipiera Malipiero in 1612, close physical and improper contact with nuns was alleged. In the Roman nunnery of S. Maria di Campo Marzia a mid-seventeenth century nun, Costanza Theodili had as a servant a public prostitute who produced two children to the scandal of the monastery, and fear for the impact on the young *educande* there.[22] Whore – nun friendship could add to the worldly wisdom of the latter.

Stricter enclosure raised financial difficulties. Conventual 'dowries' and payments for living expenses covered some costs; but convents needed endowments providing steady incomes, and in most cases probably alms. Some nunneries were richly endowed, such as S. Zaccaria in Venice, Le Murate in Florence, S. Vitale e Agricola in Bologna, S. Maria in Stella, Milan, and many in Naples, like S. Patrizia. In such places leading families might build and fund substantial cells, to house their female relatives, often in successive generations. Attempts were made to curb this 'ownership' of cells, as in Bologna by Archbishop Lodovico Ludovisi from 1621,[23] Nuns found other sources of income; educating boarding girls might be the most lucrative, or housing rich widows. They might earn by taking in clerical laundry, selling lace work or medicines. The S. Chiara Franciscans of Pistoia sold vestments, altar cloths, wine and pigeons; S. Girolamo just outside Florence lent money to other convents and monasteries, having income from commercial investments in the Mercato Vecchio. Bologna convents sold liqueurs they distilled, along with medicines and ungents. By the seventeenth century many convents had attracted donations, invested them wisely, and as in Verona, lent money at low interest rates to secular families.[24]

Supposedly, enclosure would safeguard virginity.[25] However, enough people reported scandals to indicate that walls were not protective, that nuns were assaulted by, or had willing sexual relations with, authorised visiting confessors, sundry other clergy, and lay visitors who secured entry. If the men were kept out, lesbianism might be an alternative threat or comfort. Venetian court records show that Patriarchal decrees and fulminations against sexual sins, excessive contact with workmen and sellers, bawdy jibes and so forth were based on realities or forceful accusations of namable persons. In Venice city officials were proactive policemen, looking for offenders, in city and on the mainland. But such policing did not stop nuns getting pregnant by male intruders, or in 1623 emerging from the walls for gondola journeys and parties. Francesco Capello's nun lover brazenly wore a purple overcoat and green stockings.[26] Venetian secular authorities threatened the molesters of nuns with heavy penalties, including death sentences from 1605 – though Mary Laven failed to find such being carried out in her survey up to 1650. The relevant magistracy of the Provveditori sopra monasteri was however active against those either too friendly or too hostile to nuns, holding trials of men eating inappropriately with nuns, or shouting abuse at them, visiting the parlours without any legitimate reason, or dressing 'lasciviously' in their presence. A significant number of 'criminal and disciplinary' trials under this magistracy involved priests and friars – 58 out of 263 between 1550 and 1650. They of course had legitimate access to nuns and *converse*, and more opportunity to abuse that access than lay men and women.[27] However, very serious crimes could be unmasked, including rape, as in a multi-person case in 1608 – 1609 involving up to 15 noblemen – masquerading, penetrating space and some bodies – at a convent that surviving documents kept anonymous, but which was identified by the famous English ambassador, Sir Henry Wotton, as Sant'Anna – later to be Arcangela Tarabotti's abode. Several nobles were banished, others lost their status, but none was executed for carnal knowledge of a nun.[28]

All this suggests an exciting life, for some. Conventual life for nuns could be boring, frustrating, poverty-stricken – or busy, stimulating, fulfilling in religiously appropriate, or in immoral, ways, and with many comforts, especially in urban convents. Patrician nuns in the richer convents of Venice, Naples, Rome or Bologna could have comfortable cells, with *converse* at their service. But for all the daily life of nuns, *converse* and *professe* would have been a routine of communal services and solitary prayer and meditation; it varied whether meals were taken communally or solitarily in the cell. Arangela Tarabotti voices the classic complaints:

> Oh how wearing it is to find oneself always sitting at the same table with the same food. How tormenting to retire every night to the

> same bed, always to breathe the same air, always to conduct the same conversations and to see the same faces![29]

In well-endowed convents some nuns would be employed on business affairs, with official posts rotating between the older nuns, with or without politicking. For some, opportunities for power and responsibility within the convent would be more fulfilling than in a secular family life. Some convents were part of parochial life, with additional roles to be played in dealing with male clergy. By the seventeenth century many convents had accumulated property to be managed; incomes received, expenditures on properties agreed, decisions to be made about legal suits, over properties, or the fulfilment of wills. The considerable archival material on Bologna convents brought this home, when hunting for evidence on more spiritual and cultural matters. Whatever outside male assistance they received, some nuns thus had active and responsible secular roles.

Abbesses, prioresses and other nuns who dominated the chapters of wealthy nunneries, could be powerful within the house, the Order, and in the outside world. Renée Baernstein has well shown this with a Sfondrati dynasty of women (relatives of Pope Gregory XIV) dominating in and from San Paolo, Milan; cultured, talented and ruthless.[30] By the seventeenth century the world of Roman nunneries was heavily influenced by matrons of the Roman aristocracy, old and new; from the major papal families such as the Aldobrandini, Barberini, Borghese, Ludovisi, or other older Roman oligarchs such as the Altieri, Cesi, Colonna, Massimi, Orsini and Savelli. They provided financial support, and dictated artistic patronage within the walls of chapels and living quarters; and they could dominate the internal politics of the convent as and when they took vows, and retired to a convent as a widow. Some offered exemplary spirituality as well as patronage, such as (another) Vittoria Colonna (1610–75), who became the Carmelite Chiara Maria della Passione. She joined a poor nunnery, Sant'Egidio in Trastevere in 1628, but was later to help her sister Anna Colonna (wife of Taddeo Barberini), found and finance the Regina Coeli. She also appeared to lead a small circle of devout mystically inclined men and women. These Roman matrons extended their monastic patronage and leadership to nunneries founded or expanded in localities outside Rome, such as Albano and Palestrina.[31]

For those with limited dedication, with little skill or interest in reading, or without access to books, the daily life would have been very tedious and frustrating, with any break in the routine welcomed. The smaller and poorer convents would have been worse for the indifferent, while the large rich houses often provided a varied and stimulating life. Personality clashes tearing communities apart are revealed when they led to trials, or were unearthed by a Visitation. In the convent of S. Vito on the island of Burano in the Venetian Lagoon, the long-standing hostility between Sisters Anna Marchi and Colombina gave rise to three trials between 1607 and 1621, centring on accusations against Sister Colombina's alleged love relations and sexual exploits.[32]

Highlight moments existed to break the monotony. The vesting (*vestizione*), of a new nun could be a splendid occasion, as could the *professione*, taking the final vows. It could involve family and friends bringing the girl to the convent, processions, lengthy ceremonies and rituals; nuns would have prepared special foods and delicacies for the lay visitors and clergy, which would not have passed their mouths untasted. When a girl educated in the nunnery left instead to be married, equally elaborate and enjoyable ceremonies were offered, at least in Venice. Nuns' own sisters visited on the eve of their wedding, showing off their finery – as Venetian Patriarch Giovan Trevisan lamented, and sought to control. The nuns through their grilles watched and appreciated entertainments put on in the convent parlour, where the laity assembled. The election of an abbess was often a splendid affair, attracting church dignitaries, leading nobles, and requiring food-giving.[33] The Visitation to a nunnery offered opportunities for diversion, often in practice with little serious inquisition into the state of affairs (as opposed to the quality and seemliness of the altars, accoutrements and decorations).[34] Gifts were showered on the nuns at ceremonial occasions. While the nun's habit might seem lacking in interest, the inventories and the patriarch's monitory orders indicate that nuns had fun in creating tiny variations in their garments, their veils, cuffs, collars, headbands, and ruffs, in head pins and pectoral crosses; competing over fashionable handkerchiefs, and in how much thinly veiled breast they could expose – as they greeted visitors at the grilles. The Venetian Patriarch Giovan Trevisan in 1579 banned nuns from having 'blond and curly hair', platform shoes, 'pleated and elaborate shirts in the fashion of secular women, and fine handkerchiefs'; but he and his successors went on banning variations of such stylish competitiveness, suggesting limited effectiveness. Behind the parlour, many clearly still wore coloured dresses, earrings, broaches, as condemned by Patriarch Francesco Vendramin.[35]

In some nunneries food was grown in gardens, and animals were kept. Gardens were important for food, recreation and contacts. Chickens were treated as pets (in dormitories sometimes), as well as providers of eggs. Authorities tried to stop nuns having chickens, dogs, and parrots as pets, with limited success. The 1622–23 Visitation to S. Cristina, Bologna (Camaldolese), revealed tensions over dogs, chickens, even a cat in the choir, and two nuns keeping sheep, cows and asses – for gratification, and costing the convent money. *Converse* looked after dogs for some nuns, to the resentment of others. It is not clarified whether such issues led to one *conversa* being attacked by a nun, drawing blood from her head![36]

The general quality of food within nunneries would have varied considerably, as did the attitude of nuns. Some nuns deliberately fasted to excess, living largely off stale bread and water, which might have contributed to hallucinations and mystical experiences. While for the normal nuns, and monks, rules of fasting curtailed eating, it should not be assumed that they were necessarily malnourished. A recent study of the food supplies for a good selection of southern Italian monasteries, male and female, indicates that their inhabitants had plentiful and varied supplies of food, especially fish and vegetables, and that they were probably better fed than most of the secular neighbours.[37]

The *parlatorio* played a significant role in the more relaxed nunneries: as public space where nuns and *professe* met outsiders, supposedly speaking through grilles, but where also they might move more freely when outsiders were not present. Here they met family visitors clergy, or doctors; celebrated before postulants took full vows, received former *educande* and their families returning for prenuptial parades and blessings. But it was the location for more dubious activities: plays, music and dancing, cards and gambling. Prostitutes would come in and entertain the nuns with music and dance, as in San Vito on Burano in 1627. By the eighteenth century the paintings of Pietro Longhi, Franceso Guardi and some anonymous painters indicate much jovial activity, puppet shows, dalliances and fancy dress parades.[38]

While major sexual scandals attract the attention, their prevalence can be exaggerated. Laven argues that while there was much intercourse between nuns and others – offensive to the authorities, if a relief from their boredom – most of this was social rather than fully sexual. The priorities were talk and gossip, attention-paying to be boasted about among friends once separated; it might involve some touching in the parlour through the grilles, but also gift-giving both ways. Nuns cooked and sewed for distinguished or influential visitors and clergy; they were also sometimes accused of passing out surplus food from their own farm supplies, in-convent chickens, and kitchen production, to feed artisan families nearby.[39]

Some nunneries taught young girls within their confines; and even brought up infants in their midst, as was revealed in Cividale in the 1590s. Such concerns gave the nuns activity, stimulus, maybe a vocation. It also posed problems, and created temptations; so some nuns (as in S. Cristina, Bologna), declined to teach.[40] In 1592, Patriarch Lorenzo Priuli addressed orders to 11 nunneries which were teaching girls for money (*a spese*); while accepting that they should continue, he was relaying the worries from the Congregation for the Regulars in Rome that rules were ignored. The Patriarch had to licence those admitted, aged between 7 and 25 and virgins. They could only leave for grave medical reasons. They should observe the *clausura* as if nuns; dress plainly (*positivamente*) without gold ornaments, jewelry, blonde-died hair. They could not bring in a servant, or have a *professa* allocated to them personally. They could not have profane pictures, musical instruments, dogs to walk or parrots. They must not enter nuns' cells. They would be assigned teachers who would teach them to read 'good and devout books, and principally the book of Christian Doctrine, and make them learn it by heart (*a mente*)'. Rome itself continued to have such problems. In the later seventeenth century the authorities were involved in many disputes over which girls might be taught within Rome's convents, with what freedom of movement, and at what charge.[41]

Understanding the spiritual and psychological position of a fairly dedicated nun, one neither over-zealous nor troublesome, is clearly difficult, given the kind of documentation usually available. Illumination comes from correspondence of Don Alfonso Lupari to his niece, Antonia Ludovica, in the Benedictine nunnery of SS. Vitale e Agricola in Bologna.[42] They were from a noble Bolognese Senatorial family. Alfonso, son and heir, became a Theatine. Don Alfonso was based in Piacenza during the period of surviving letters, 1622–30 (but mostly 1628–30). He was a kindly spiritual comforter to Antonia, advising on suitable and varied reading (which should involve intellectual play as well as devotion), warning against being too ascetic and penitential, consoling her when her 'best friend' sister left for another nunnery. He consulted her about his sermons, and commented on what she composed herself; one for a vesting ceremony was beautiful, but too long for the occasion, and better for Good Friday.[43] Such an epistolary relationship, with a few visits from him, was obviously helpful. How frequent?

Convent Culture

Recent research has emphasised cultural activities and vitality within some nunneries. Nuns could have a lively musical life, as singers, instrument players and composers; they performed and wrote plays; they painted pictures; they could contribute to religious debates.[44] Given the noble intake into many convents, that girls were taught in convents, and often stayed to become nuns themselves, the literacy level was likely to be high, and literary production potentially learned in many city convents, if not rural ones.

Nunneries had not been immune to the religious debates of the mid-sixteenth century. Pier Paolo Vergerio (Chapter 1) had a sister Coletta, as a Clarissa nun in S. Francesco, Udine, where she instructed others in the new faith; revealed when Nicola da Treviso penetrated the cloisters to convert them to Anabaptism. In the late 1550s, a Neapolitan Calvinist, Pietro Gelido, helped organise a group in Venice, and infiltrated the nunnery of S. Girolamo. A nun there, Prudenza Corona confessed to having received various books from a Neapolitan notary, including a Genevan Catechism, with which she had re-educated herself (in the Calvinist faith), and several other nuns. In 1590 coadjutor Bishop Francesco Barbaro prosecuted Clarisse nuns in Udine for heresy, and was sniffing for heresy in his 1601 Visitation.[45] To what extent many nuns retained secret heretical thoughts further into the post-Tridentine period is unclear, but some authorities wanted to ensure they did not have access to prohibited books – whether vernacular Bibles, religious tracts, or unseemly secular literature.[46] The intense book-hunt after the 1596 Index (Chapter 9), included investigating convent libraries.

The convent libraries, and nuns' holdings in their cells, only marginally studied, were variable. The Benedictine house of S. Marta in Genoa had a library of 263 printed volumes; while a selection of convents in L'Aquila recorded between 7 and 36 titles at the end of the sixteenth century. The Observant Franciscans in Umbria documented their holdings; their 19 Clarisse houses in the Province had over 1100 printed volumes (and uncounted manuscripts), ranging from 8 in Assisi's Della Benedetta to 169 in S. Maria di Monteluce, outside Perugia. The earlier mentioned Genoese convent's list contained only three suspect titles, including the Spaniard Antonio de Guevara's *Monte Calvario* (a 1555 Venetian translation). Four Perugian convents (according to lists sent to Rome 1599–1600), had 70 titles to be expurgated or banned, including Guevara again, works by Dante and Petrarch, vernacular translations of New Testament texts, and Nicolò Malerbi's Italian translation of the whole Bible. They were potentially reading dangerously and excitingly.[47] A collection of inventories of possessions in cells in S. Margherita, Bologna (Benedictine), in 1613 reveals a number of books (seldom clearly specified), in Italian and Latin, some utilitarian such as breviaries and Offices of the Virgin, others spiritual. Suor Pantasilia had 12 unspecified spiritual books, while among her varied collection Suor Monacha Felice Ariosti had (Scupoli's) *Combattimento Spirituale*. Some nuns had their own music books in this convent noted for singing.[48]

Literary contributions were made by convent inhabitants. Focus has moved on from the major spiritual writings of the saintly figures such as Caterina de Ricci, Maria Maddalena de'Pazzi or Teresa of Avila (whose *Vita* was well known and influential in Italy), to lesser writings and conventual correspondence.[49] Some nuns became historians of their own convents, and were ready to interweave outside worldly events, as in Giustina Niccolini's history of Benedictine Le Murate, Florence. Fiammetta Frescobaldi, of S. Giacopo di Ripoli in Florence, not only wrote the history of her own Order, but produced a digest of Francesco Guicciardini's great *Storia d'Italia*, a study of the Venetian Patriarchate, and also histories of Persian kings, of the east and west Indies. Arcangela Tarabotti, besides railing at the suppression of nuns in convents against their wills, and entering the debate on the status of women, and Eve's equality, or superiority to Adam, was ready to attack Venetian sumptuary laws against secular women.[50]

Letter-writing was seemingly an increasing conventual activity; whether for mundane, spiritual private consideration, or for a wider public impact. Some nuns' correspondence was published to inspire and console others. Saints Caterina de' Ricci (1522–90) and Maria Maddalena de'Pazzi (1566–1607) provided two models of conventual letter writer. Pazzi (a Carmelite nun in Florence's S. Maria degli Angeli from 1583), wrote rarer letters primarily to edify and encourage other Sisters in Christ, and also to respond to the tribulations of other nuns doubting their vocation and worthiness. Ricci was more in the tradition of 'divine mothers' who addressed a wider variety of correspondents, mainly in the outside world, to encourage wider reform and moral behaviour. Caterina de'Ricci's letter-writing, from S. Vincenzo in Prato, was on a daily basis (aided by amanuenses); an excess criticised by the Dominican Bishop Vincenzo Ercolani (though himself a prolific letter-writer), as detracting from a calm life of prayer. But her letters comforted lay figures such as Filippo Salviati, a long-term friend – after she apparently miraculously cured his wife in 1543.[51] Battistina Vernazza (1497–1587), daughter of the Genoese Oratory's co-founder, and Mother Superior of Lateran canonesses in Genoa, became famous for her mystical writings based on Scripture, religious poems, and devotional tracts. Her partially published correspondence with a Lateran canon in Piacenza, Gasparo Scotto, became a valuable public guide to the spiritual life and a conventual life of contemplation.[52]

Other correspondence was more practical and less intense – exemplified by the letters of Suor Maria Celeste (1600–34) to her father Galileo. This correspondence (covering 1623–33), has been much highlighted, and made available in English, by Dava Sobel, notably for insights into Galileo's period of investigation and house-arrest in Siena and Arcetri. Her chatty, non-literary correspondence, provides interesting glimpses of the more mundane life of a poorish convent and 'average' nun, lacking privacy, sometimes food, adequate books to read or to instruct her – even on letter-writing.[53] She was clearly kept busy, and writing business letters for the abbess took precedence over writing to her father.[54] Galileo in happier times in the 1620s had helped his daughter and her convent of S. Matteo; in her last years her gifts (delicacies or medicines) to him and her expressed worries about his health, may have eased his pains.

Theatre was a significant activity in nunneries in many cities, expanding from Renaissance precedents. Elissa Weaver has carefully studied plays from Tuscan convents (and bringing in Bologna and Amelia). But convent theatre is mentioned in Sacred Congregation and visitation records throughout Italy from Genoa and Venice to Ancona, Naples and Messina.[55] Some reformers had qualms about its continuation, especially if it involved secular themes, dressing-up, with cross-dressing in male roles, and especially if performed for outsiders rather than for self-instruction and internal entertainment. Patriarch Priuli in 1595 tried to curb the dressing-up, if not the plays; while he had in 1593 generally ordered plays be confined to illustrating biblical and saints' stories.[56] Some productions had elaborate scenery and musical effects, as well as costuming; and would have involved cooperation from outsider suppliers and builders. A production gave many nuns in a convent plenty to do. Some convent plays were provided by famous writers, notably Giovan Maria Cecchi (possibly the leading religious dramatist of his day), and Michelangelo Buonarroti the Younger, who wrote for his nieces in S. Agata, Florence, including a surviving play about one of that Saint's miracles. Galileo Galilei wrote one play at least (not traced), for his illegitimate daughter. Nunneries used printed plays, borrowed manuscript texts from other convents, but some plays were written by nuns in house, especially the *maestra* teaching girls.

Some convent plays were built on the Sacred Representation tradition (of confraternity fame in Tuscany and Umbria in particular), and on *Laude*, hymn singing and practices – hence the musical dimensions. Just as the secular court theatre developed *intermezzi* – musical interludes between acts of plays often with elaborate scene settings involving machinery and dancing – so some mid-sixteenth century and later plays produced by convents added them; as for *The Play of Saint Catherine of Cologne* (by an anonymous nun), used by a number of convents. Convent plays dealt with ethereal or saintly themes, but also the thoroughly worldly, and even dangerously erotic, as with as a David and Bathsheba play, written by the confessor to the nuns of S. Silvestro di Pisa in Genoa. Beatrice del Sera in mid-century, in her *Amor di Virtu*, showed, like others, good knowledge of secular literature (whether Boccaccio, Petrarch or Ariosto). She (in a convent from age 2), and others reflected the frustrations and loneliness of the convent life, but also conveyed effective spiritual messages. Plays brought out humour, notably in scenes involving lower-order characters or the old. Issues of dowries and marriages featured, aimed at the *educande*, and their having to choose. A nun like Annalena Odaldi, from S. Chiara in Pistoia, in her *Commedio di Nannuccio e quindici figliastre* (Nannucio and fifteen step-daughters), focused on marriage themes, provided a very positive view of convent life; and of the education available for the *educande* which make them good wives.[57] Moderata Fonte (or Modesta Pozzo, d.1592), now celebrated for her impressive dialogue *Il merito della donne* as a contribution to the debate on the merits and equality of women, was educated in the convent of Santa Marta – before marriage. There plays were part of her educational background, and through them she became star reciter to visiting lay women. Whether or not she helped write for the convent, she wrote a secular play later for production before the Doge.[58]

Exciting recent writing has highlighted the range and variety of music produced in convents. The singing of *Laude* persisted, but in the post-Tridentine period nuns' choirs became well recognised in cities like Bologna, Milan, Genoa, Siena and then Venice for refined – ethereal – singing of high quality, notably in a modern style of motet singing.[59] Members of the public would come to certain convent churches to hear the 'disembodied voices' singing behind the grilles of the church galleries. Controversially, males helped train the singing nuns, and provided compositions, most notably by the later seventeenth-century in Venice, the 'red-priest' Vivaldi, composing for orphanage institutions such as the Pietà, which combined girls and professed nuns. However, some nuns became notable composers, and had their works published for use beyond their own convent walls. For the early post-Trent period the notable convents for music were in Bologna. The musical developments were against a background of conflicts with Archbishops Gabriele and Alfonso Paleotti, and the Sacred Congregations in Rome, over if and when organs could be used (and where), and other instruments to accompany voices; and whether male musicians could help. Negative attitudes to male helpers led to greater opportunities for nuns, such as Maria Isabella Trombetta with her trombone in S. Gervasio e Protasio in the 1570s; Laura Bovia developed a nuns' group of singers in S. Lorenzo in the 1580s, and fostered one in Florence. Bolognese convents like S. Pietro Martire and S. Caterina in Strada from the 1590s were reputed for solo singers, as part of the Mass. S. Cristina then became praised for elaborate *concerti*, by a major composer, Suor Lucretia Orsina Vizzana. Her motet collection for grand convent celebrations was published: *Componimenti Musicali* in 1623. An aunt, the convent organist, probably taught her. Sadly the divine music was composed by an increasingly sick and then unstable Lucrezia, her condition worsened by conflicts between the nuns, and even physical battles with the archbishop's officials following publication. Theologically several motets stress the real presence of Christ in the Host, and the importance of the musical art in response to Jesus' own inspiring voice.[60]

Milan in the seventeenth century also developed a strong convent music tradition, partly thanks to the enthusiasm of Cardinal Archbishop Federico Borromeo, and his personal commitment to both church music, and the well-being of nuns. He welcomed lutes and violins being played inside convents and donated instruments. He accepted complicated polyphony, as well as solo singing. Chiara Cozzolani (1602–*c*.77), in the convent of S. Radegonda became the most notable nun composer, and her works were also published in several volumes from 1640 to 1650. Suor Chiara's music, as in the

Concerti sacri of 1642 and Psalms of 1650, ranged from solo motets, duos and trios to a four-part Mass. Motets in dialogue form, as saints conversed, gave full opportunities for angelic female voices. Her 1650 Vespers collection had some elaborate concerto composition, possibly originally for the visit of Maria Anna of Austria, Philip IV's fiancée. Later, especially as abbess, 1660–73, Chiara faced a hostile attitude to music, and stricter enclosure, from Archbishop Alfonso Litta. Her composing was curtailed or at least it remained unpublished.[61] Sienese nunneries were allowed to put on full-scale operas by this late period, attracting public attention; sponsored by the Chigi family, which placed many talented daughters in convents.[62]

Some nuns have been revealed and studied as significant painters, as well as scene decorators. Some naturally came from painting families. The Roman painter Domenico Fetti's sister Lucrina having traveled with him to Mantua became a nun in Sant'Orsola, where she painted female saints, and portraits of females in the ruling Gonzaga family in the period *c.*1614–29. The leading mid-sixteenth century woman court portraitist Sofonisba Anguissola, from Cremona, taught her sisters to paint, including Elena who became a nun in Cremona. Giorgio Vasari in his Lives of the Artists noted one seemingly more prolific nun-painter, Plautilla Nelli (d.1587), in the Florentine convent of S. Caterina da Siena where a *Last Supper* is still to be found. She was apparently one of several painting nuns there. Several painting nuns have recently been identified in Roman convents in the seventeenth century, such as the Carmelite Maria Eufrasia della Croce (d.1676), in S. Giuseppe a Capo.[63]

The policy of strictly enclosing nuns was not fully effective in policing terms, security could be breached, immoralities continue, family contacts remain. Both nuns and some authorities recognised that the inhabitants could feel like prisoners, even if they were originally willing entrants. Others, however were clearly fulfilled in a religious vocation, while even for the less dedicated convent life need not have been tedious and deadening, but have some stimulus and satisfaction.

Some Other Religious Women

The enclosure policy clearly frustrated female religious expression outside the convent, though some remained possible through confraternities and surviving congregations like the Ursulines. We have already noted dominant and influential women in the early reform period and part of philanthropic movements. This continued. For example, in Venice a major institution to protect vulnerable girls, the *Zitelle*, was founded in 1559 – 60 largely by patrician women (influenced by the Barnabites), who had already got involved with the hospital of the *Derelitte* (abandoned girls); led by women from noble clans, like Andriana Contarini, Isabella Grimani and Soprana Corner. In 1574 Chiara Contarini left half her estate for the building of a new hospital-conservatory for girls.[64] Women could show their religious inclinations and preferences in bequeathing large sums of money to favourite churches, confraternities and nunneries. Some, as from the Sienese nobility, merely paid for a large number of Masses of the dead, which might indirectly help fund the chosen institution. Others directly contributed to philanthropic acts, buildings and decorations. Somebody like Baronessa Caterina Cerbone, clearly took her time over deciding what charities should be the beneficiaries in her will.[65] Olwen Hufton's work shows the importance of female funding for early modern Catholicism Europe-wide, especially as backers of the new Religious Orders like the Jesuits.[66]

A few women tried precariously to express deep religious feelings on the fringes of society. Viewed as 'living saints' by some, they risked condemnation by church courts as heretical 'pretend saints' and false prophetesses. Fascinating recent work on the topic has been dominated by Gabriella Zarri and Anne Jacobson Schutte.[67] In outlining some fairly unusual individual cases I hope to hint at possibly more common practices and attitudes.

Cecilia Ferrazzi is probably best known. Investigated by the Venetian Inquisition tribunal in 1664, she was unusually given permission to record her own story, as part of a long investigation, before conviction of pretence of sanctity (September 1665). Anne Jacobsen Schutte has translated this part as an 'Autobiography'.[68] Uneducated, orphaned young during the 1630–33 plague, Cecilia abhorred the idea of marriage, but was too poor to enter a suitable convent. She had serious medical problems, was clearly often in pain – before dropping gall-stones near the altar. She had many visions, and earned a local reputation as a saintly figure, supported by laity and some clergy, including to some extent initially a leading exorcist, Father Giorgio Polacco (confessor to Benedictine nuns, and Patriarch's vicar governing female religious). Her main work was however looking after vulnerable children and young women, and she came to run refuges (Sant'Antonio di Castello and elsewhere) – involving about

300 females aged 5 to late 20s, when she was arrested in 1664. While conservatories for vulnerable girls and women were quite fashionable, Cecilia was unusual in being a dominant organiser without much benefit from males, such as confraternity officials. Her denunciation was triggered by a relative of some girls, and a former protégée, accusing her of mistreating and virtually imprisoning them; in her eyes she was protecting them from relatives who probably wanted them back on the streets as prostitutes. Cecilia could express her dedication through charitable works, living on the fringes of the convent world, staying in some, but not committed. She changed confessors and spiritual advisers very rapidly; some were supportive, some hostile. While Anne Schutte stresses 'obedience' in Cecilia's autobiographical language, Cecilia seems to be seeking a male supporter both to back her philanthropy, and assure her that her visions of saints and the Virgin were genuine, not devilish deceit. Some of her 'girls' seemingly confessed to her, as if in a sacramental confession. This alleged conduct contributed to her condemnation as 'lightly suspect' of heresy, and a sentence of 7 years in prison. In practice she was released in under 2 years to a house arrest under Cardinal Gregorio Barbarigo in Padua, who with the backing of the Venetian government secured her full release in January 1669; dying in Venice in 1684. Cardinal Barbarigo (1625–97, beatified 1761, canonised 1960), had in the 1650s been influenced by Ferrazzi's religious reputation, among other Venetian spirituals, male and female, leading to his own ordination and episcopal career. As Bishop of Bergamo (1657–64) he met the couple to be discussed next (see Chapter 11).[69]

The views about Cecilia were doubtless affected by another case, that of Maria Janis, condemned a couple of years before 1662 – for pretending to live off the Eucharist alone.[70] She was very closely attached to one priest (Pietro Morali) who traveled with her. They were reported by a nosey neighbour in a Venetian building, spying through a chink in the partition between rooms, suspicious of their relationship. Maria believed the Virgin had instructed her to feed on the holy wafer alone, and Pietro Morali admiring her sanctity provided her with the consecrated host (for which he was condemned). They had come originally from a Bresciano village (Zorzone). Their friendship had developed through working together in the Confraternity of Mary Virgin of Consolation of the Holy Belt. Maria had helped the priest teach Christian Doctrine; the leather belt, which confraternity members wore, allegedly helped people fulfil their dreams, so many flocked from other villages. Maria for a while retreated to a hermit's existence, accompanied by eating problems, and visions of the Virgin. Eventually, the priest seemingly stabilized her condition with the host as food; he tutored her about the saints, in reading and in mental prayer. She then looked after him. Facing excessive interest in her miraculous living off the Host, but also suspicions of their close spiritual relationship, they traveled together to Rome, then to Venice – and were arrested. Maria was eventually judged a fraud over her host-alone eating. Some decades before, however, Angela Maria Pasqualigo, a patrician rejecting family marriage plans, had been judged a living saint for this feat, and a 'great heroine' according to her Theatine biographer. She, like Cecilia, helped poor girls though not so systematically. Eventually, Pasqualigo had got permission to start a Theatine affiliated nunnery – and became strictly enclosed in 1647. Her genuineness had been attested by the previously mentioned father Giorgio Polacco. The more plebeian and non-Venetian Maria had her similar request to be 'tested' rejected; and when Polacco asked the learned Pasqualigo what she thought of Cecilia Ferrazzi's religious credentials, she was hostile. Sisterly support was lacking.[71]

Maria Janis had learned from her priest about mental, silent prayer. This was seen as dangerous ground by authorities in the seventeenth century, and sometimes later associated with Quietism. One movement focusing on silent prayer was generated from the Church of S. Pelagia in Milan, initially under a Giacomo Filippo Casolo. From there disciples, Pelagini, took ideas and practices up into the Bresciano, and then across northern Italy by the 1680s. Inquisitors showed concern from 1655 in the Valcamonica. Silent prayer might seem an innocuous activity; but the advocates were believed to encourage group sessions in which lay men and women also discussed the Gospel, and preached – including the women. They were informal confraternities undermining parochial authority. Silent prayer was more significant than the Eucharist. While much is opaque about the Pelagini, seemingly in the diocese of Brescia and Bergamo many women were involved. Some of the high-class women, especially at St Pelagia itself, also concerned themselves in charitable work, including seeking to save prostitutes. Some brothers and sisters in the fraternities had ecstatic experiences and prophesied. Married Pelagini were encouraged to abstain from sex, but their attackers claimed they indulged in indecencies where priests solicited the female penitents. Here we are dealing with many more women (and men), in a number of places, than in the more isolated cases of Ferrazzi, Janis or Pasqualigo.[72]

The female Pelagini probably largely followed male leadership, as maybe did Pasqualigo. In my view, if not Anne Schutte's, Cecilia Ferrazzi was a dominant initiator of religious practices, as was Maria Janis. Cecilia was probably not much liked or loved by male supporters. But some of the living saints had priests adoring and loving them, whether chastely or not. Antonia Pesenti, an illiterate Venetian in the 1660s, saw visions of the Virgin in front of a Byzantine painting and had the priest Francesco Vincenzi fall in love with her. Pesenti got other young women to gather around the picture, and Vincenzi choreographed ceremonies; then sold 'Relics' to those visiting Santa Ternita: bits of cloth soaked in sweat of the entranced females.[73] A Bologna seamstress Angela Mellini in the 1690s, who was able to write a short diary, had ecstatic religious experiences with visions of Christ (sometimes triggered by silent prayer): 'my Jesus exposed my breast and opened my ribs and took my heart and in place of it he put all the instruments of the sacred passion'. She seemed able to predict the future, and was devoted to ejaculatory prayer. Eventually, Angela was treated as a spiritual mother and confessor by one admiring Franciscan priest, Giovanni Battista Ruggieri. This inversion of roles was too much for higher authority, who charged her with 'affected sanctity'. She was released after penances, and the most affected priest sent away from Bologna – for discussing problems of his own chastity with a woman. Ruggieri had given her a biography of another heart-suffering holy woman, Cecilia Nobili, lay sister of Nocera Umbra to read. Angela produced a diagram of her suffering heart, with a commentary – this matched fairly well the post-mortem description of Cecilia Nobili's heart, with burn and nail marks on it.[74]

For the Inquisitors, bishops and Roman Congregations, these were difficult women, presenting delicate cases. Women who undermined, or ignored, male clerical control, who appeared to act like female priests, had to be controlled, but authorities had to be wary of offending popular enthusiasm. We can now turn to a wider consideration of the Inquisition, its control and re-education.

9 *Repression and Control*

Control over society and religious life took many forms, and we have already encountered facets of this in considering the powers of bishops and their vicars, in the increased influence of parish priests, with charitable institutions that could restrict as well as comfort, and in the educational policies and practices of Sunday schools. However, the Inquisition is most associated with Catholic repression, and judged the chief weapon of the 'Counter Reformation'. The Inquisition tribunals could be brutally repressive, but some of their procedures can be positively interpreted as re-education towards a better Christian life, eradicating superstitions and attempts at magical practices that few would welcome continuing. The first trial of the miller Menocchio (Domenico Scandella), and the early trials of the Friulian *benandanti*, night-battlers, can be seen both as learning processes for inquisitors, and re-education exercises to induce right thinking in the accused.[1] Some activities of the early Inquisition featured in Chapter 1, while Chapter 3 outlined the basic structures of the Roman Inquisition. This chapter will look more closely at procedures, targets, effects and interactions with society.

Much of the activity of the Inquisitions has been misunderstood, partly through the institutional secrecy surrounding them, partly from the long history of counter-propaganda – Catholic and Protestant – since their foundations. The nastier results of Inquisition activity – which undoubtedly existed – must be seen in a certain context. Other ecclesiastical courts and secular institutions often had a much more brutal record of executions, torture and lesser punishments. Many writers fail to distinguish between medieval Inquisitions operating in localised situations and early modern (or modern) Inquisitions as centralised and institutionalised in Spain, Portugal and then in Rome; between the state governed Iberian Inquisitions and the Holy Office in Rome; between Inquisitions and inquisitorial investigatory and trial procedures. Inquisitorial legal procedures by the sixteenth century had been adopted and adapted from ecclesiastical usage by courts in much of Europe. In the hands of untrained or poorly trained judges and magistrates, influenced by local hysteria, using torture to excess, and lacking a central monitoring control such courts could and did perpetrate much injustice and cruelty, especially in the pursuit of 'witches'.[2] But such should not be used to distort the record and roles of the Holy Office in Rome, or even the Iberian tribunals. What follows seeks to provide a balanced view of the Inquisition tribunals within Italy.

The Holy Office of the Inquisition was developed as a permanent bureaucratic and executive body following the Bull *Licet ab initio* of 21 July 1542 (Chapter 3). It was not a monolithic organisation, and conditions varied over time and place within Italy. While a fairly impressive central organisation developed in Rome, this did not have a uniform network of tribunals, inquisitors and helpers throughout Italy, but had to deal with local state realities and power struggles. Even within Rome power struggles between Cardinals were played out within the Holy Office. The creation of the Congregation of the Index of Prohibited Books (1571), though dependent on that of the Holy Office, soon set up personality conflicts and rival policies – to the benefit of those wishing to avoid strict controls, but embarassing for a censor like the great Roberto Bellarmino being censored and opposed.[3] In terms of punishment for heretical offenses, hawks and doves, or retributionists and educationalists, operated throughout the period, on most issues. Such differences appear in the known correspondences between the centre and the periphery; as is being revealed, following the opening of Holy Office archive in Rome in 1998.[4] Bishops, abbots, prioresses as well as the secular powers – while ultimately liable to Inquisition control – were ready to frustrate inquisitorial operations, and defend some accused or some book collections.

The number of local tribunals and branch offices of the Inquisition is not clear. Gigliola Fragnito through her penetrating studies of book censorship, using correspondence from the central archive, has so far produced the following list for those operating by the early seventeenth century or added later: Adria, Alessandria, Ancona, Aquileia, Asti,

Bergamo, Bologna, Brescia, Capodistria, Casale Monferrato, Ceneda, Cividale, Como, Crema (1614), Cremona, Faenza, Fermo (1631), Ferrara, Florence, Genoa, Gubbio (1631), Mantua, Milan, Modena (started 1598), Mondovì, Novara, Padua, Parma, Pavia, Perugia, Pisa, Reggio Emilia (1598), Rimini, Saluzzo, Siena, Spoleto (1685), Tortona, Treviso, Turin, Venice, Vercelli, Verona, Vicenza and Zara.[5]

The Kingdom of Naples is excluded from this list – since tribunals as such could not be created, by order of the King of Spain; though the Archbishop of Naples could unofficially operate inquisition-like investigations with other bishops. Beyond such tribunals or local offices, the scant cases surviving from the Florentine records suggest that the Florence inquisitor used a variety of local clerics to act as inquisitorial agents.[6] The staffing of the Inquisition, centrally and regionally was limited, which restricted what denunciations and accusations could be pursued. While most investigations started from neighbours' denunciations, or parish priests and confessors pressurising penitents to report themselves 'voluntarily', the Italian Inquisitions lacked the proactive public support found with the 'familiars' of the Spanish Inquisition. Italian Inquisition officials could spend little time on spying out troublesome behaviour and beliefs, though they might keep track of known troublesome families or individuals, and make enquiries of other tribunals. Vicenza and Venice linked up over Bernardin Barbano of Vicenza in 1573; first noted for Anabaptism some time before, he had not recanted. In 1586 the Venetian tribunal, the Patriarch's court and others cooperated in tracking the continuing Lutheran interest of the Cerdoni family from Dignano.[7] The contact between centre and periphery could be very variable. Correspondence between Rome and Bologna or Venice might be very regular, but that with remoter areas meagre. In 1611 Cardinal Pompeo Arrigoni wrote to the Udine Inquisitor, complaining of not having heard from him for months, 'as if in that city and diocese there were no inquisitor, nor any causes and business happening to be dealt with'.[8]

We know most about the Venetian tribunal, because – given its bilateral operation between church and state – its archives became part of the state archive on the fall of the Republic and Inquisition after 1797. These archives are very full and a mine of information on Venetian society as well as the operation of the Inquisition.[9] Many files were opened with a denunciation; some received no further recorded attention; some were followed up with interviewing of witnesses and then dropped. Only a minority of 'cases' became a full inquisitorial investigation, leading to formal charges, a full trial (with sometimes a defence response), leading to a result. Cases were dropped or frozen probably because judged to be inspired by malice, too trivial, or there was little chance of finding corroboration and witnesses. Inquisitors might leave the file as pending, in case another accusation arrived against the named person(s). The tribunal might pursue an investigation a little, to test validity and seriousness. Witnesses might be questioned, some confirming an original accusation, and no apparent attempt to question the accused be recorded. A denounced person, as over magical practices or derogatory remarks against fasting, the saints or the Pope, might be then questioned, and warned against repetition rather than formally tried; as with the flour porter Domenico Longino, caught in 1573 singing a lewd song against the Pope being buggered by a Cardinal Colonna.[10]

Once the Roman Inquisition was well formalised (after the paranoia of the Paul IV period), Inquisition procedures were generally legalistic, conducted with professionalism by well-trained church lawyers and notaries, with theological advisors to hand if necessary. Notaries recorded the proceedings fully (though translation from dialect, and some editing, must sometimes have been involved), and copies could be made to circulate to other tribunals, to Rome's Holy Office, for a defence lawyer who might plead mitigation, or even bring in defence witnesses. Once a case was deemed serious, the procedure through inquisitorial questioning to formal trial and sentencing, could be lengthy. The court wanted to be meticulous and avoid mistakes, it might take time to find witnesses, while slowness gave the accused the chance to contemplate in prison, convent or under house control – and reappear with a helpful confession. While Italian accused probably had a clearer and quicker idea of what was alleged against them than in the Iberian Inquisitions, they might decide while waiting to second-guess, and prepare a pre-emptive admission that would mitigate any punishment. In contrast with secular courts and other ecclesiastical courts, the Inquisition tribunals were ready to tarry over cases, as Giordano Bruno found as he sweated it out in the Holy Office prisons for years, (1593–1600, in Venice, then Rome). 'Prison' conditions were very variable; a special Inquisition prison (probably better physically than many civic ones), a local secular prison, or a monastic cell. Length of time in prison, not knowing when the next formal questioning would come, was probably the main fear mechanism, a psychological torture rather than physical.

Physical torture (usually the *strappato*, being strung up by wrists tied behind the back, and then dropped to wrench the shoulders), was used on accused and intransigent witnesses; but less frequently than in secular courts.[11] Inquisition rules limited the time for any torture period (usually 30 minutes), and frequency or any repetition. The central Holy Office tightened control over its use, essentially making local tribunals get its permission for use.[12] From the evidence of the Venetian cases, torture was rarely imposed even if more often threatened. What was said under torture was recorded by a notary (even the calls on the Virgin and cries of anguish – Oihme!); to be confirmed in substance later, free of the torture chamber. Some accused made admissions and confessions merely under the threat of torture; but significant others survived without making a true, or fearfully false, admission, and so were dismissed or escaped serious charges and punishments. From notarial transcripts of what supposedly transpired under Inquisition investigation atmosphere and nuances are hard to detect; and we do not know what informal tortures or deals were perpetrated off the record down in prison. However, surviving records give no hint of unofficial torture, no accusations of such are made by those who remained intransigent. Some records show accused willing to argue with the inquisitors, and not appear too fearful, as with the miller Menocchio (at least in his first trial), Cecilia Ferrazzi in Venice, or the *benandanti* in Friuli, men and women who supposedly left their bodies at night to do battle with evil forces and witches, threatening their crops.[13]

Evidence from within the Inquisition records indicate that some accused learned to dissimulate and manipulate to secure a quick release; to confess just enough, and of whatever validity to satisfy the tribunal. In 1580 Alvise Capuano's wife said that her husband had wished to teach all the imprisoned how to get out quickly, and said he who risked a death sentence 'needs to know how to feign and simulate to escape such forces, but once out of prison was able to believe and do what he pleased and appeared to him'. Giovanni Paese in 1577 had claimed that a previous confession had been produced by this very tactic. We need to read the responses in that light.[14]

Sentencing

By contemporary standards Inquisition sentences were in reality mild. Death sentences were few, a life sentence declared in the first formal sentencing, might soon be followed by a milder punishment, recognising contrition. Release to house arrest might follow, as noted with female pretend saints, and as happened to Galileo in 1633. He was first released into the care of the Archbishop of Siena, (who favoured some of his work and opened his library to him), then house confinement at his villa Arcetri, outside Florence. We cannot have a full record of death sentences, or actual executions. Critics seize on the famous executions – of Pietro Carnesecchi (1567), or Giordano Bruno (1600). But the execution rate was low in comparison with capital sentences from secular courts across Europe. Rome's tribunal executed (with some public show usually), about 135 people from 1553 to 1601, a number of those were called from other tribunals because the case deemed so serious. The Venetian tribunal executed (by quiet drowning) about 25 in the century, and only 2 were executed from 1587 to the early eighteenth century. The Friulian tribunals of Aquileia and Concordia between 1544 and 1599 sentenced 15 to death, of which only 5, including Domenico Scandella, were actually executed, though 2 more, initially tried in Udine, were condemned and executed in Rome. The Republic's Council of Ten and other civilian courts executed 168 people in the sixteenth century. 'Martyrs' under the Inquisitions were fewer than in England under Catholic Mary (about 300, 1553–58), or Anglican Elizabeth; and 308 were executed for treason against the English crown, 1542–50.[15]

Humiliation in a public sentencing, sometimes called an *auto,* was in the 1550s to the 1560s a significant feature in sentencing, especially in Rome. While influenced, through Gian Pietro Carafa probably, by the Spanish auto-da-fé (which also featured in Sicily), the mainland Italian *auto* was a sentencing phenomenon (usually in a church), and not accompanied by executions or burning in effigy, as in the Iberian system. Public humiliation on a lesser scale remained one aspect to deter others, as with post-confessional penances from a bishop or confessor.

Physical punishments, such as being flogged through the streets or outside a major church, with placards indicating the offences, were part of the public punishment and education process. A Genoese who had made a Faustian pact selling his soul to the Devil and erecting an altar to him, featured at an *auto* in St Peter's Rome in 1577, but was only flogged.[16] Sentences to the galleys, useful for the Papal and Neapolitan navies, were appropriate for the healthier heretics, as for two lay Neapolitans and a priest Scipione Messita from Bianco (in Campania?), condemned at the 1595 Roman *auto,* for having books to help practice diabolic magic, or dealing with a necromancer. Messita survived that experience, to have his file reopened in 1622.[17] Penitential punishments, in public or private, as the main sentence were apparently more common from the later sixteenth century. This was partly because by then few charges were brought concerning Lutheran or Calvinist beliefs, or major attacks on central Catholic Doctrines. The charges were more concerned with magical practices, superstitions, the misuse of sacraments (rather than total denial of their validity), and traffic in or reading of prohibited books (but not the most dangerous). For such, penitential punishments were deemed appropriate, following a re-education process through the investigation proceedings.

Those artisans and merchants who benefited from Inquisition 'leniency' might, however suffer serious economic difficulties, encouraging compromises. For example, Zuan Donato (alias Donà) della Colombina was a wealthy pharmacist when he was investigated in Vicenza in 1547; in 1564 he appears in another trial in Venice, now as 'a poor man who makes rosary beads from agate', who relied on wealthier supporters to invite him to dinner. What religious compromises were involved are not clarified.[18]

Indicative both of sentencing policies, and interaction of centre and periphery is a Bologna case. The local inquisitor sentenced Giovanni Paolo Delle Agocchie in 1589 to abjuration and three years in prison for hitting an image of the Madonna, and heretical swearing. 'Prison' turned into house arrest; but when he escaped, with a woman convicted of sorcery, the inquisitor ordered the confiscation of his property, and a death sentence for contumacy and being a relapsed, impenitent heretic. After going to Geneva, Delle Agocchie reappeared in 1593, as a prisoner of the Roman Holy Office. There however, Cardinal Santoro called for copies of the full papers from Bologna, and with his fellow Inquisition Cardinals ruled that the second sentence had been irregular and contrary to a canonical decree, because it was declared before Delle Agocchie had been absent a year; and flight from 'prison' did not mean he was 'relapsed'. So the property had to be restored to his relatives, with any lost profits; Delle Agocchie was sentenced to the galleys for five years, as if he had received no other sentence. The Bologna inquisitor was reprimanded for illegitimate harshness, and not observing due process. Rome annulled other death sentences given in Bologna; possibly because the local inquisitors were going beyond the manuals and guidelines, and showing anger when the accused were thwarting their authority (as with prison escapes), rather than over the heretical offences.[19]

Public Condemnation and Controlling Major Heresy

Italian inquisitions did have some well-publicised sentencing ceremonies in what was called an *autodafè*; with executions coming later. The papacy was not unaware of the impact of 'public humiliation';[20] but other rulers could be more dubious, whether the Dukes of Mantua or the Venetian Republic. Most well-publicised *autos* came in the 1550s and 1560s, with Pope Pius V notably seeing publicity value from exemplary public condemnations in Rome, which would be reported further afield, through ambassadors who attended, and printed news-sheets. Indulgences were offered to those attending. The Roman *autos* usually took place inside S. Maria sopra Minerva, given its close links with the Dominicans who provided most inquisitors. Executions might follow some time later, with less spectacle. The Roman *autos* mostly paraded between ten and fifteen persons at a time. Through the period till 1600 about one in ten was executed soon after. Some *autos* had no death sentences, and some condemned were executed without appearing publicly; normally if unrepentant, and showing defiance. The Church wanted suitable publicity for its efforts to maintain orthodoxy, punish the really serious offenders, but show some mercy to the truly repentant.

The first recorded *autodafè* was on 6 June 1552, when seven Lutherans (two friars, plus secular priests), were paraded, wearing yellow tunics, and reconciled (*rebenedire*), before a great crowd. Seemingly none was executed, but from eleven Lutherans paraded on 21 March 1553, one was hanged and burned on the 4 September: Giovanni Buzio da Montalcino, who had preached heresy in Naples. His heretical books were burned five days later. His death rang alarm bells in the North and made him a Protestant martyr.[21] Some major *autos* after the closure of the Council (starting in December 1564), constituted similar warning marker points, hitting at Valdesians and Waldensians as well as Lutherans and hybrid heretics.

The most significant *auto* involved Pietro Carnesecchi on 21 September 1567, attracting a large throng, many cardinals and prelates. A sick man after a very long and gruelling investigation, his final condemnation was a notable occasion. He can be seen as a great survivor, having first been tried (and cleared himself), in 1546. On his own admission (at his third trial in 1566) 'it was in Naples in 1540 that I began to have doubts about purgatory and confession', and he then avidly read books by Bucer and Luther. To the Roman inquisitors in December 1566 he said: 'We were of the opinion that [Luther] was a great man because of his wisdom and eloquence, and we also held that he acted sincerely in his own way, namely that he did not deceive others if he was not first deceived by his own opinions.'[22] His intellectual acumen and courage, and the protection of powerful princes had enabled him to argue his way out of trouble, until on the death of Countess Giulia Gonzaga the Inquisition seized correspondence fully incriminating Carnesecchi as a convinced heretical believer rather than one showing sympathetic interest. At the *auto* the master of ceremonies Firmano admired his beautiful aspect and nobility, as he listened to the two-hour reading of the sentence against him. Carnesecchi and another friar were burned on 1 October.

Carnesecchi's public condemnation probably carried several different messages. It warned intellectuals that arguing their way out of trouble with the Inquisition, claiming they read and talked from a spirit of enquiry, would no longer succeed; few would attempt brazenly to take on the Inquisition. Political protection of high-profile heresy was unlikely to be forthcoming. Thereafter however, the Inquisition tribunals became less concerned with deep challenging beliefs of salvation by faith alone, the Trinity, Sacraments, and intellectual arguments about them, and became more interested in less worrying, vaguer, challenges by less influential persons.

Interestingly, Mario Galeota, abjuring at an *auto* in Rome before Carnesecchi's on 22 June, had been more leniently treated. He had provided Countess Giulia Gonzaga with manuscript copies of his friend Valdes' works; he had also translated some, and organised their printing. In 1566 he abjured ideas derived from them and from the *Beneficio di Cristo*; notably that 'faith alone justifies and saves man'. He had denied that good works gave merit, denied purgatory and the intercession of saints, the validity of monastic vows, and so forth. But he was not judged as dangerous as Carnesecchi. He was sentenced to 5 years in prison, away from Naples. Inquisitor Giulio Santoro in the context of religious troubles in Naples (1559–64), had noted Galeota as 'one of the authors of tumult, previously investigated, disciple of Valdes', and pushed Rome, and especially Cardinal Ghislieri to pursue him.[23] In May 1571 Galeota was apparently leading a normal life in Naples, and died in 1586, probably accepting the Valdesian cause was misguided as well as defeated. When the *Beneficio* and Valdesian works had been banned he had said: 'It matters very little to me, because they are in my head, and no one can erase them from there, and even if they can prevent me reading them, they cannot take them from my mind.'[24] The Congregation of the Index set out to ensure that the next generation would not read these works in the first place.

The Roman *autos* involved heretics sent from all over Italy. *Autos* and executions took place elsewhere. While the Holy Office liked to handle severe heresy cases centrally, it valued as propaganda public warnings and shows of authority in other states and cities. Some condemned might appear at an *auto* in Rome, and then be sent home to be executed or otherwise publicly punished, as in various cases from Faenza in the 1560s. Faenza provided several heretics for Roman condemnation, from conventicles of Lutheran and Calvinist persuasions. In 1569, it had its own *autodafè*, notable for the subsequent gruesome execution of a gentlewoman, Camilla Caccianemici (wife of Camillo Regnoli who had been executed in Rome back in 1559), who was thrown from the Podestà's palace window with a rope around her neck, which pulled her head off. She was seen as coorganiser with her husband of a conventicle, and had remained very active, according to a spy, after their first trial and his execution. This spectacle probably ended the Faenza movement. In 1570, the new Legate for Romagna, Cardinal Alessandro Sforza, purged the city council, and established a special magistracy to police the city and assist the local inquisitor – as, euphemistically, the Hundred Pacifiers (*Centi Pacifici*).[25]

Another heretically troublesome city, Mantua, saw three *autos* in the city or nearby Casale in 1568–69, with Cardinal Borromeo attending that at Casale on 5 April 1568, along with members of the ruling Gonzaga family and other notables. Pius V and the Gonzagas had a bitter conflict over the nature of the abjurations and who should be publicly shown; the Duke failed to protect his closer servants from public shame. The Inquisition's unofficial position in the Kingdom of Naples inhibited *autos*, if not executions, but the Archbishop of Naples had *autos* at least in 1564 and 1571. The latter involved 12 women of Catalan origin, paraded in their yellow *abitelli*, who, according to a chronicler had 'lived secretly for many years like Jews (*alla giudaica*) and committed many excesses'. Two remaining obstinate were sent to Rome, for public execution. In remoter Squillace (Calabria) the non-resident bishop and inquisitorial Cardinal, Guglielmo Sirleto, had his vicar and nephew Marcello

Sirleto conduct *processi*; one person at least was publicly sentenced in the Cathedral, before a large crowd enticed by indulgences. A relapsed heretic, Cesare di Stalati, was executed a few days later by the secular arm, fully contrite, and a soul saved, according to Marcello Sirleto; this marked the end of the Waldensian evangelicals in Calabria, driving other survivors to exile in Geneva.[26]

Papal attitudes towards heretics were clearly variable; Sixtus V, while presiding over a harsh secular regime through the Papal State, for law and order and the elimination of banditry, took a more relaxed view over any heavy punishment of religious offenders, and discouraged *autos*.[27]

Censorship

Since the full development of printing and its involvement in the religious struggles in the north in the 1520s, church and lay authorities had sought to control what was printed and circulated.[28] Though precedents for the censorship of 'lascivious' Italian vernacular literature existed in the later fifteenth century, the main censoring came by the 1530s, and 1540s, as when the *Beneficio di Cristo* was attacked. Various cities like Florence, Milan and Venice in the 1550s produced prohibitive indexes, setting precedents for broader literary censorship of the unseemly or anticlerical.[29] The Roman Inquisition took charge of ecclesiastical censorship, and maintained this supervision even after 1571, when the separate Congregation of the Index was started. Rivalry existed as well as partnership, and the full Holy Office was ready to countermand the more specialist Congregation. Clement VIII in 1600 explained to Cardinal Baronio that the Congregation of the Index controlled authors, their books, printers and readers, but not heresy, which was the Inquisition's territory – which could allow the latter to interfere with all the rest![30] Much tension existed as Peter Godman has shown. The Master of the Sacred Palace, acting for the Pope, might seek reconciliation, or add to the confusion. This could both accentuate control, and also hinder activities; impede the suppression of what already existed, delay matters for those wanting to clear their potential publications.

To resist Protestantism it was desirable to curb the flow of books and pamphlets into Italy, whether by land or sea. Probably the most vulnerable area was the Venetian Republic's territory, with so many passes carrying goods from the north. From Rome's viewpoint a significant step was the Venetian Council of Ten's order in 1569 that all imported books be inspected in the customs house, with an inquisition official present.[31] However, while this inhibited large-scale importation of obvious heretical texts, there were clearly ways of importing books and pamphlets into different parts of the mainland, and then smuggling them through to Venice itself. Venice had plenty of adept book smugglers, including Roberto Meietti, an early expert on disguising books by false, innocent-looking, frontispieces.[32]

Foreign merchants in major cities were under surveillance, and if under any suspicion their wider contacts were investigated. When four foreign merchants living in Bologna (including one from Nuremberg, another from Ravensburg), were suspected of 'lutheranisim', Cardinal Santoro instructed the Bologna Inquisitor Giovanni Antonio da Foiano to check their houses for prohibited books, investigate their contacts, their servants, any correspondence with other heretics, and whether they ever talked about the holy faith with anybody.[33]

The main guides to censorship were the Indexes of Prohibited books (*Index Librorum Prohibitorum*), of 1559 (the Pauline under Paul IV's dictating, and the most severe), 1564 (the Tridentine, supposedly softer after protests at the Council), and the 1596 Clementine Index, which governed censorship subsequently. Publications were divided into three classes; authors who were major teachers of heresy (heresiarchs), all of whose works past or to come were banned; individual works by known authors, suspect of heresy or offensive; works whose authorship was unclear (anonymous or pseudonymous), similarly suspect or offensive. The Clementine Index also provided rules for future censoring, and procedures for correcting and expurgating published works. Titles might be temporarily listed as prohibited, until a new corrected edition was passed, or until existing copies had passages and words inked out, to allow reuse and sale. Of course, suitable persons could receive licences to read prohibited books, to help decide on corrections, or to prepare attacks on their heretical views. Bishops, printers and booksellers were expected to have copies of the Index, so as to control who and what was printed, sold and read. Consultation of the printed Indexes soon showed that they were hard to use. A 1632 reprint of the 1596 Index had a lengthy adjunct (*Elenchus*) to facilitate cross-referencing; but this made it a 679-page volume.[34] To ease the burden, the Congregation and local bishops periodically issued simpler lists to assist the control system, as has become clear from the newly available volumes of correspondence – in the Holy Office archive – mainly dealing with the Clementine Index and the follow-up. Some of the local lists would go beyond the big Index, or evade some of its prohibitions; reflecting some of the arguments at the centre over what should be banned, amended or fully tolerated.[35]

Publishers, printers and booksellers were liable to persecution and loss of stock. Book and print shops were raided, even by Carlo Borromeo himself in Milan. Given the importance of Venice in publishing and international trade, the city's industry was tempted to produce illegal works, import and export others. A notorious international dealer, Pietro Longo was executed by drowning in 1588. In 1587 the Venetian tribunal executed another, Girolamo Donzellini of Brescia; he had remained involved in trafficking in Protestant books since an original denunciation to the Inquisition in the 1540s, being arraigned again in 1560 and 1574. More discreet associates such as the Valgrisi and Ziletti, however, escaped that harsh fate.[36] While the Republic showed some cooperation over censorship, its representatives increasingly argued for a liberal censorship policy (in religious and literary aspects, but not political works dangerous to the Republic), both to preserve the economic interests of their printing industry, and because leading patricians were intellectually experimental themselves. Venetian Inquisition cases through the seventeenth century reveal printing and circulation of prohibited books at several social levels.[37]

Looking briefly at the impact of post-Tridentine censorship, it is clear from Gigliola Fragnito's own particular study, and the recent collection of essays edited by her, that a major casualty was Italians' access to the vernacular Bible after 1596.[38] That Index banned all vernacular translations – and Italy has been rich in full or partial translations, though Nicolò Malerbi's (from 1471), was the front-runner – and also sought to ban outright, or subject to expurgation, books that too fully quoted from the Bible in Italian. Bartolomeo Dionigi's popular biblical compendium (*Compendio istorico del Vecchio e del Nuovo Testamento*, 1586 and later), was another casualty, and when somebody tried to publish it again in 1670, it was soon Indexed. The 1596 Index triggered an intense book hunt throughout much of Italy. While the Bible hunt was the main target, much else was caught. The Paduan inquisitor boasted to Rome that under his supervision 29 sacks of banned books had been burned, and his 'great zeal' was praised.[39] Given that true Protestant works had been largely eradicated or driven behind false bindings and frontispieces, the trawl was of popular religious literature, and detrimental to ordinary literate people not versed in Latin. The extent of the purge varied according to the strength of local opposition. The haul showed that the previous implementation of Index bans had not been that thorough, and that licences to hold prohibited books had been rather freely given, in the eyes of the new hardliners, led by Cardinal Giulio Antonio Santoro. The unexpurgated writings of controversial secular writers like Castiglione, Machiavelli, Pietro Aretino were also rounded up, confiscated or burned. In terms of religious writing and reading Ernesto Barbieri argues that old favourites dealing with the life of Christ, the Virgin, works of hagiography, collections of religious literature were preserved, reissued, and writers and printers encouraged to publish writings suitable for the new devotion of the revived church, and helping to refashion society and morality, to the approval of the majority. The Jesuit Antonio Possevino tried a counter index as it were, a recommendation of what should be read, and could be read profitably with the correct emendations, (in his *Bibliotheca Selecta*, Rome, 1593).

Some of Barbieri's colleagues in the Fragnito collection of essays, however emphasise detrimental effects not just of banning, but of expurgation, on other kinds of literature. Expurgation was very slow, and variable; sometimes pedantically hunting for names of heretics to black out, or to replace *coitus* (judged obscene), by *copula* (acceptable).[40] A large number of books were rendered inaccessible, pending decisions and actions, whether involving Jewish studies, or books on duelling – which was a particular target. Castiglione's *The Courtier* was seized by some for having comments on duelling and honour. Ugo Pozzo stresses the impact on wider literature. The works of major older writers like Dante, Boccaccio, Castiglione, Petrarch, Pulci were changed in style and content, often with the willing cooperation of scholars who thought they could improve them. Such work had been going on since the 1564 Index, but the post-1596 campaign accentuated the tendency. With more 'dangerous' authors like Machiavelli (a class-one author in 1559), some – especially in Florence and Venice – argued that some of his works, on War, Florentine history, and even the *Discourses*, should be allowed in amended form (such as removing his attacks on the Papacy). Pius V's confessor, Bishop Eustacchio Lucatelli, in 1570 claimed the Inquisition had nothing against him. Some Congregation members thought it better to licence expurgated editions, to counteract illegal unpurged editions, which were still being found – as in 1568 at the Venetian printer, Girolamo Calepin (better known for his published list of prostitutes, *Tariffa delle Putane*).

The appointed censor of the Discourses in 1587 declared: 'I admire his style. Many of the things that are fundamental to the governance of the state ... he treats so fully and eloquently that nothing could surpass him. In conclusion this book could be republished', with a few alterations. But Machiavelli in 1596 remained a fully banned author, thanks to Inquisitor Santoro who saw him as evil, defeating Baronio's more open-minded or pragmatic opinion.[41]

However intense the hunt for prohibited books could be, especially after the imposition of the 1596 Index, books were still smuggled into parts of Italy and circulated. The Venetian Republic remained the gateway, both because of its continuing widespread commercial contacts as part of the world economy, and because of its particular concern to be Catholic but different from Rome. The Interdict Crisis of 1606–07 (Chapter 3), encouraged a subversive book trade in opposition to the Papacy, and it proved hard to eradicate thereafter what had entered Venice. Nunzio Berlinghiero Gessi in 1609 warned Rome of the political and practical difficulties in seeking out prohibited books, though he indicated Rome need not be too alarmist, since the State had an interest in preventing the more subversive Protestant imports of books and ideas. He said Protestant and vernacular Bibles were available. Indicatively, a Franciscan Father-General on visiting a Venetian Conventual monastery in May 1609 found he was listening to the reading of a Protestant Bible – lacking its identifying front and end pages.[42] A book printer and distributor like Roberto Meietti was still stocking anti-Catholic works from Germany in 1621, 33 years after the Inquisition had first tried to curb him, and despite Gessi's further attempts in 1609 to curtail his trading. State authorities, including lay members of the Inquisition tribunal, were reluctant to stop such an important bookman, who had played a major role in publishing Paolo Sarpi's work in the Interdict crisis, and who could be accepted as an official of the printers' guild in 1611.[43]

As some testimony on what subversive literature remained available despite book raids, burnings and confiscations, we have the allegations of friar Fulgenzio Manfredi who, having served as a pro-Republican theological support for Venice in the Interdict crisis, turned in 1608, and informed Rome about works that Venetian nobles and others accessed. He alleged that most nobles possessed works by Machiavelli and Calvin's *Institutes* (in Latin). Many further down the social hierarchy had access to Protestant vernacular versions of the New Testament, Italian editions of the Psalms and of Calvin's Catechism produced in Geneva.[44]

An early cultural target in the immediate post-Trent campaign was Hebrew literature; and this came in the centre of Hebrew printing, Venice. The 1553 burning of the Talmud was followed by an onslaught on Hebrew books, their printers and sellers in September 1568. Possibly over 8000 folio volumes of key texts such as the *Midhrash Rabba* and the *Mahazor Sephardim* were burned; others were confiscated and sent abroad, and the Jewish publishers and sellers heavily fined. This attack, by the Esecutori contro la Bestemmia (the state body which dealt with the enforcement of press regulations as well as with cursing and blaspheming), allegedly came because the producers were not following the rules about issuing licenced expurgated editions, but also because of fears that Jews were subverting the Republic by acting as agents for the Ottoman Turks. This was a damaging onslaught on the supply of Hebrew books, and it put various publishers out of business. However, Paul Grendler suspects that the burning was not as complete as claimed; and some publishers, like Marc'Antonio Giustiniani and his family, were soon back producing Hebrew books, and moving them around the wider Venetian empire, places like Cephalonia and Zante. By the 1590s, the numbers of publishers producing Hebrew books had risen again, learning from the Giustiniani's successful ploys and evasions, and 'the Jews, with the aid of the Giustiniani family, obtained the books they needed'.[45]

So censorship and book control had successes for the authorities (especially with vernacular Bibles), but loopholes existed, and resources were inadequate for thorough control. The imponderables remain of what literature was never written because of fear of censorship; how much purging and rewriting undermined a spirit of criticism; also how much still circulated and was imported, once the late 1590s purge was over.

Changing Inquisition Targets

Once major theological heresy was deemed to be under some control, and the tide turned against 'Lutheran' and Valdesian heresies, the Inquisitions attended to the eradication of superstition, erroneous Christian practices, 'pagan' survivals, immorality, misuse of the sacraments.

The pattern of change, and some breakdown of types of concerns, can be judged from Tables 9.1 and 9.2.

Table 9.1 Accusations and denunciations before Venice and Friuli Inquisition Tribunals, 1547–1720

	Venice			*Friuli*				
Major charge	*1547–85*	*1586–1630*	*1631–1720*	*1557–95*	*1596–1636*	*1637–76*	*1676–1716*	*Major charge*
Lutheranism	717	109	77					
Anabaptism	37	0	1					
Heresy in general	68	27	6					
Judaizing	34	16	28					
Mohammedanism	10	27	42					
Calvinsim	13	18	29					
Greek orthodoxy	3	8	11					
				3	44	134	56	Apostasy from the faith: include Lutheran, Anabaptist, Calvinist, Orthodox, Muslim views
Atheism/Materialism	1	4	14					
Apostasy	15	17	12					
Heretical propositions	62	26	107	164	102	53	23	Diverse heretical propositions: include sexual moral errors, anticlericalism, lesser blasphemies
Prohibited books	93	48	40	44	48	132	11	Possessing/reading prohibited books
Prohibited meats	23	12	16	120	156	42	7	Prohibited meats
Blasphemy	17	41	61	13	22	20	3	Heretical blasphemy and swearing (*bestemmia*)
Abuse of sacraments	9	12	106	26	17	41	21	Abuse of sacraments
Bigamy	3	7	12	[1]				Bigamy (12 cases 1611–70)

Table 9.1 Continued

	Venice			*Friuli*				
Major charge	*1547–85*	*1586–1630*	*1631–1720*	*1557–95*	*1596–1636*	*1637–76*	*1676–1716*	*Major charge*
Concubinage	7	5	4	[2]				Concubinage (1 case 1596–1611)
Adultery	3	7	0					
Sodomy	5	5	5					
Solicitation	3	22	72	1	4	48	29	Solicitation
Magical arts	59	319	641	62	347	287	77	Magical arts (*magia, stregoneria*)
Offending Holy Office	10	8	6	14	18	21	4	Offending Holy Office: include prison escape; false witness; ignoring penances; abusing officials
Pseudo-sainthood	0	1	5					Pseudo sainthood (8 cases 1611–70)
False testimony	14	7	4					False testimony (2 cases 1611–70)
Illegal Mass	2	4	14					Illegal Mass (1 case 1611–70)
Miscellaneous; include irreverence, sacrilege, irreligiosity	21	66	31	43	43	40	3	Irreverence, irreligiosity, sacrilege
Total	1229	816	1344	490	801	818	234	

Sources: (Table constructed from Tedeschi and Monter's Tables in Tedeschi (ed.) *Prosecution of Heresy*, 'Toward a Statistical Profile', Appendix 1 (p. 105), for Venice; and Sarra, 'Distribuzione statistica', Table B, for Friuli. The classifications follow different categorisations. For further comparison, figures for some accusations buried in Scarra's figures, but identifiable in Monter and Tedeschi's table for Friuli, Appendix 2 (p. 106), (but using different period breakdowns), are given in brackets [...]. Note that the decade 1647–56 saw a major intensification of denunciations, providing 117 of the Prohibited Books figure, 30 of the Abuse of Sacraments, and 287 of the Magical Arts from the 1637–76 period.)

Table 9.2 Accusations and denunciations to the Neapolitan Inquisition 1564–1740; highlighting main categories only

Main Charge	*1564–90*	*1591–1620*	*1621–1700*	*1701–40*
Protestantism	19	18	26	1
Judaizing	41	8	20	0
Mohammedanism	126	67	13	0
Heretical propositions	38	86	50	6
Prohibited books	7	9	15	0
Magical arts	178	498	387	64
False testimony	98	3	8	0
Total	735	1021	1086	196

Sources: (Table taken from Tedeschi and Monter, as earlier, Appendix 3 (p. 107). Here giving only the main categories.)

The tribunals of Venice and Friuli (combining the Patriarchal diocese of Aquileia and diocese of Concordia), and Naples, provide the best countable evidence of all tribunals so far, given the nature of their archival survivals and cataloguing. The Naples figures are cited selectively, for space reasons, and because I have not sampled the archives (as I have in Venice), nor studied detailed explanations behind Tedeschi-Monter's digest (unlike for Friuli). The classifications and counting are of accusations, denunciations and self-denunciations, not completed trials, and represent the main initial charge (often as noted by old archival cataloguers); the numbers are for individuals. Secondary charges, or accusations, revealed under further investigation can become more interesting, to inquisitor or modern historian. Monter and Tedeschi have partly shown this in their intriguing Tables. Lutheranism was used vaguely in Venice (as in Naples), and 'Heresy in general' is not very helpful, especially given the numbers in Friuli in the first period; but accused, witnesses and inquisitors could be confused and vague about kinds of 'heresy'.

The range of inquisitorial targets was considerable, but much derived from local denunciations, the product of neighbourhood tensions, not just an elitist educated programme. The differences, especially in the earlier periods, between north and south were over the different 'other' groups in the key cities of Venice and Naples. The latter, with its proximity to north Africa, and with Spanish links was likely to have Muslims, and people forcibly converted from Muslim to Christian, under suspicion. Venice had its Ghettos of Jews, who in fact had significant contacts with the main city, its true Christians, and

Jews converted to Christianity, many of them originating in Iberia and victims of forced conversion.[46] The Republic took a fairly tolerant view that those forcibly converted could revert to Judaism and live with co-religionists in the Ghettos. A number of people could readily be accused of moving back and forth between the two faiths, especially if they were trading with the Ottoman Empire (notably in Salonica), since the Turks looked reasonably favourably on Jews.[47] The Venetian Mediterranean Empire was shrinking before Ottoman expansion, leading to an influx of Greek Orthodox and Catholics who had lived close to Muslims. The 'prohibited meats' category reflects not only the traditional reluctance of some to obey rules on fasting, especially through Lent, but it could be treated as a sign of Protestantism; and it was easier 'evidence' than rumour of what might have been said or read privately contrary to the Catholic faith. The significant shifts to 'magical arts' reflected a greater awareness through pastoral care of what the common beliefs of practices might be, and possibly the impact of better Christian teaching leading to neighbours reporting deviance, as well as confessors pressurising self-confession.

The Inquisition records are a fascinating mine of information on what Italians believed they or others could do or believe. Magical arts were used in attempts to forecast the future – by casting beans, throwing a rope, or looking into a glass carafe (*inghistera*) – to interfere positively or adversely in love affairs, find hidden treasure or lost property, to give protection against bullets (9 cases in Friuli, 1611–1785). More widespread and significant were the cases involving medicines and healing for humans and animals. This was the world of secondary or alternative medicine, especially for those who could not afford, or distrusted the doctors. Mixed together were the uses of herbs, ungents, talismans and blessed objects. The bishops and inquisitors were most concerned with the misuse of the sacraments and sacramentals for healing purposes: holy oil, sacramental wafers, or items surreptitiously blessed by the priest such as the umbilical cord, or papers with magic writings or symbols. Women were the main practitioners, but not exclusively so; torture and the worst punishments were for clergy allegedly cooperating in the misuse of sacraments and blessings. The 'magic' was aimed at curing ailments, helping pregnancies (or abortions), or coping with mental illnesses and 'possession', when it was in competition with the authorised church exorcists. Much of society was complicit in the use of remedies and some magic. When however the 'good' magic failed to work, in curing health or love, or was deemed to be 'evil' magic causing harm, deaths or sexual betrayals, then denunciations could follow, and a witch (*stregha*) be blamed.

The suppression of superstition and witchcraft (*stregoneria*) was part of the re-education and social control campaigning of the Inquisition and episcopal courts and legislation. Italy did not see the 'witchcraze', whether or not a women-hunting phenomenon, against group witchcraft that allegedly, and sometimes in reality, was attempted in much of Europe. From the mid-sixteenth century most accusations of superstition, sorcery, magic and witchcraft came before the inquisitors, rather than episcopal or secular courts, where inquisition tribunals fully functioned; but in the Kingdom of Naples, archbishops like Paolo Burali, bishops and their officials played a fuller role. Investigation by well-educated professionals, following due process and with some guides to suitable legal procedures, meant that social panic found elsewhere was rare. The limited use of torture militated against mass denunciations of others. As usually with the Iberian Inquisitions, inquisitors were sceptical of neighbourly denunciations and animosities (as the source of many magic accusations), and they were inclined to see females accused, and self-denunciated, as more deluded and ignorant, than dangerously in league with the Devil or devils. Many interesting denunciations were filed by the Venetian tribunal with no further recorded investigation. While ready to accept the efficacy of 'magic' (black or white), and that individuals might invoke the Devil to aid their magical practices, inquisitors and their officials in Italy were sceptical of the Sabbat, or orgiastic rites. As bishops and their vicars, as well as inquisitors became more aware of popular beliefs and practices in the post-Tridentine reform campaigns, they could be puzzled, shocked and surprised by what was believed and attempted – as with the *benandanti* night-riders of Friuli. But re-education through investigation and trial was as much a response as panic suppression.

So numerous 'cases' of magical arts were opened, as indicated by the tables given earlier. Some such inquisition files have been well utilised in accessible books by Carlo Ginzburg, Ruth Martin and Guido Ruggiero for Venice and its mainland territories. Other illuminating books by, for example, Giovanni Romeo and David Gentilcore, utilise episcopal and other sources, as well as inquisition ones, to study magical practices, elsewhere, in the South or Tuscany. The authorities seldom panicked, or acted with great aggression. This 'limited aggression of the church against witches (*streghe*) is a pre-existing given in the moderating intervention of the greatest authorities of the Inquisition ... based on a rooted tradition of scepticism'.[48] The clergy could well face panic about witches in their congregations, as the Sienese parish priests of Frosini and Abbadia Ardenga did in 1591 and 1596, largely over infant deaths.[49] While bishops and lesser clergy might be exposed to pressures from below to treat alleged witches harshly, inquisitors and top hierarchs tended to restrain – as eventually in the case (1594), of Gostanza da Libbiano, the 'witch' midwife of San Miniato, in Tuscany, when the Florence office overruled the local view of her as a harmful witch and devil worshipper. She was better seen as midwife, and alternative medicine healer, who could spin fabulous tales of the Grand Devil, appearing as 'Polletto', and his pleasure city.[50]

Inquisitors and other clergy had problems both in defining and categorising types of magic and superstition, and in standardising legal procedures against them. The main guideline from the Roman Inquisition was not published until 1624: *Instructio pro formandis processibus in causis strigum, sortilegium & maleficiorum*, though in-house versions may have circulated through some tribunals from about 1620. Detecting witchcraft and witches was not easy, and views could vary considerably on what was serious, and how the accused should be punished. When the *commissario generale* of the Holy Office, Antonio Balducci, heard in 1573 that the Bologna Inquisitor Innocenzo da Modena was investigating some women who told the priest at Mass that 'You lie through your throat' ('*Tu menti per la gola*'), he told him to diligently check whether they were *streghe*, 'because this is one of their prime principles'. But Balducci was soon worried that Innocenzo was too aggressive against these women. Such matters had to be handled carefully and quietly, to avoid public trouble. In 1589, Cardinal Santoro interfered in the Bologna Inquisitor Giovanni Antonio da Foiano's case against Maria de'Gentile, condemned as a *strega* for having learned to '*far battezzare la calamita*' (a lay woman's misuse of the baptismal rite for magical or prognostication purposes).The inquisitor wanted her executed by the secular arm, but the cardinal on receiving the court records of accusation and defence (and her confession), eventually ordered that (having been in prison 2 years awaiting this ruling), she should be banished from Bologna and its *contado* for 2 years, and the inquisitor should impose some salutary penances at his discretion. Dall'Olio suggests that Rome's delay in recommending this sentence may have reflected arguments in Rome about how to punish such on offence.[51]

Inquisitors as they penetrated remoter areas found strange beliefs and practices, and were puzzled by practitioners, including the *benandanti*, or night-battlers in Friuli, made famous by Carlo Ginzburg. Friulian men and women, supposedly selected by being born with the caul, claimed they could leave their bodies at night and fly off in spirit to battle with evil witches threatening to damage crops. According to Ginzburg, by the mid seventeenth century, inquisitors had persuaded the practitioners they were the evil witches. Ginzburg's book was criticised for not considering the number of cases involving *benandanti*, and their contexts. Franco Nardon remedies the situation.[52] He produces tables and maps showing the different kinds of cases in Friuli concerning magic, *stregoneria* etc. and *benandanti*. He gives some indication of the social origins of some of the men and women involved, and the outcomes. The investigation of *benandanti* claiming to do battle for good at night is just one aspect of investigating magical practices and popular medicines. Those accused of, or claiming, this night-battling activity could also be involved in healing processes, or making contact with dead souls. The ecstasies of the *benandanti* might be united with masquerade rituals, and processions for the dead, with the living dressed as animals. From the late sixteenth century to about 1670 women are particularly under scrutiny in these Friuli investigations. Nardon suggests that this is because of the new roles of parish priests under reforming bishops and vicars general, with new emphases on chastity and virginity. Women and men might be seen in competition with priests, and the male *benandanti* in particular as competitors with the clergy over exorcisms. Many inquisitors were fairly sceptical about *benandanti* claims. It is one inquisitor, Giulio Missini from Orvieto, operating in Aquileia and Concordia 1645–53, who was convinced that the *benandanti* were seriously evil and witches. For others far more important were the local priests accused of magic and necromancy. Also *benandanti* might be seen as useful, for being able to identify the bad witches; male and female.

Between 1574 and 1716, 82 people were denounced in the Aquileia and Concordia tribunals as *benandanti*; but in only 33 instances did this lead to a formal *processo*, and in only 16 was a formal sentence given (10 males, 6 females). Prison sentences were given to 4 (including the first puzzling 2, Battista Moducco and Paolo Gasparutto),[53] while others were merely admonished, or given *penances*. Giulio Missini, seems to have dealt with 350 accusations, of which only 12 involved *benandanti*, one more than a group involving sabbats, pacts or sex with the Devil and sacrilege. The number of his cases involved in magic and love magic divination and the abuse of sacraments (with priests involved in many) were 80; and 112 concerned owning or reading prohibited books.[54]

Franco Nardon's study shows that the Inquisition had many minds, many different priorities and biases; that there was no straight development over the period with the inquisitorial elite persuading people, who thought they were doing good, that they were the evil ones.

Exorcism was recognised as a legitimate approach to troubled or 'possessed' parishioners; and also for more physical medical illnesses. The Church linked up with orthodox medicine to battle against physical conditions deemed (in the view of the sufferer if not others), to have been caused or affected by 'cunning' men or women and their magic. But exorcism was a rite with procedures requiring careful guidelines and licenced practice. If 'the divine mirrored the diabolical', the church had to teach the differences, and control the means of true exorcism.[55] The late sixteenth century and onwards apparently shows a considerable increase in exorcist procedures. A greater fear of low-level sorcery, witchcraft and maleficious deeds (*maleficia*), among a lay public as well as clergy, was fed by pressures on people to confess more frequently, and self-denounce as well as report on others. Troubled nuns, affected by unwelcome strict enclosure, or overexcited into appearing as 'living saints', were deemed by some confessors as suitable for exorcist treatment; as by Fra Alessandro da Firenze dealing with possessed nuns in a Cortona convent. He used or misused the Eucharist, but also brought in a local astrologer. As Adriano Prosperi argued (though possibly exaggerating the extent to which Italians were 'terrorised' by evil and illnesses),[56] that lesser secular clergy and members of the Orders were stimulated to control and cure the work of those possessed by devils. They used therapeutic means and 'white magic'; with the distribution of relics, talismans, medallions with *'Agnus Dei'* images, with blessed umbilical cords, the use of Holy Oil, or with full exorcist rituals. Much was dubious in the eyes of the higher authorities, and episcopal legislation forbade or warned against certain procedures, but 'good', 'white', magic was not cast aside. Guidance on legitimate procedures was offered, notably in Girolamo Menghi's *Compendio dell'arte essorcistica, et possibilità delle mirabili et stupende operationi delli Demoni, et de'Malefici* (Bologna, 1576, and later editions). He resurrected exorcism as a nearly forgotten art, and encouraged the Church to be more active in the precarious interactions between medicine, magic and religion, when the practices of 'magic' seemed more threatening.[57]

Sexual Control

Recent historians have discussed more frankly the extent to which the post-Tridentine church attempted to control more forcibly the sexuality of the populace, lay and clerical; affected by a supposed increase in clerical misogyny, and a reaction to the greater acceptance of male homosexuality under Renaissance classical stimuli. The Church had long intruded into the sexual lives of penitents; some of the Reformers had attacked the use of fifteenth-century confessional manuals as being too tyrannical and impertinent, leading to the denial of confession as a sacrament. But the growing emphasis on frequent private confession from the mid-sixteenth century led inevitably to a greater awareness, and discussion, of sexual matters, even if some Church leaders warned confessors against being too specific, in case they put ideas into the heads of penitents. As Giovanni Romeo has emphasised,[58] a whole range of sources, under-studied, show the considerable activity of the post-Tridentine church in matters sexual; reflected in synodal and diocesan legislation, in dealing with betrothed couples and advising on marriage, in extensive consideration of matrimonial causes, in attacking concubinage of priests and laity, in attending to 'solicitation' cases (the physical molestation of penitents when confessing), and so forth. Sexual behaviour and sexual problems could feature prominently in Visitation reports or in Nunzio records. Female sexuality becomes an issue – for investigators at the time, and prominently for modern commentators – in considering cases of 'living saints', and whether they were genuine or pretend (with or without sexually motivated male confessors or priests). The stricter enclosure of convents presented greater problems of sexual frustration, and sublimation in religious activities and manifestations, and derangements calling for exorcism.

The Inquisition became increasingly involved in sexual issues. Since marriage was a sacrament, any activities that impugned that institution could be deemed heretical, and thereby within the Inquisition's remit. Most notably this meant bigamy, but it might include bestiality and sodomy, even if secular courts were more likely to try such cases. Paul IV in November 1557 ruled that the supreme inquisitors had full powers over sodomy cases; with what effect is not clear. The Imola tribunal considered a number of such offenses between 1558 and 1578. Sodomy was raised as an issue in a few Venetian cases, as the sole or main accusation, (see Table 9.1). However, in 1600 the Pope ruled that the central Holy Office tribunal should not handle this 'nefarious crime'.[59]

The previous discussion indicates that the Inquisition ranged widely in its coverage of 'heresy', both from proactive intentions to eradicate both serious theological challenges, and also sorts of 'popular' practices that deviated from good Christian belief and behaviour. The degree of harsh repression, as opposed to monitory instruction and correction, varied over time, and according to locality and the individuals involved. Space does not allow real illustration of the bizarre beliefs and practices alleged or attempted, though hinted at in discussing the *benandanti.* Neighbours were ready to denounce others when scandalised by un-Christian behaviour, as well as when the 'magic' they sought failed; when the casting of beans or a rope (the *corda*) failed to reveal what the future held, the location of lost or stolen property, or buried treasure. The 'failure' of special ointments and potions, applied to the accompaniment of incantations or distorted prayers, or the failure of illicit use of holy oil, led to some denunciations. The inquisitors took a sceptical view of such reporting, and put few to full trial.[60] Some delators were doubtless shocked and wanted their neighbours brought to correct Christian belief and behaviour, and saw the Inquisition as the path to education and correction. Thus Lugretio Cilla, 'as a good Christian, not being able to tolerate being seen as having little honour or reverence for our Lord Jesus Christ', in 1587 denounced Valeria Brugnalesco and her daughter Splandiana Mariano for 'using many sorcerous incantations and diabolic objects with a thousand conjurations of the devil' to find stolen property; and for using semen in love concoctions. They allegedly used the *inghistera* (a glass caraffe with a long neck) containing holy water for conjuring up spirits, assisted by children. More interestingly they admired the Jewish faith, and Valeria had taught Jewish girls when living in the Venetian Ghetto. In this case the two women were brought to confess, sentenced to be whipped from S. Marta through the streets to the Rialto, pilloried, and exiled for 5 years. A mitre on their heads read: 'By the Holy Inquisition for love magic, witch-craft and bean-casting.'[61]

Modern commentators need not condemn all inquisition activity as cruel and unnecessary.

10 *Churches, Cultural Enticement and Display*

The Catholic Church appealed to the senses, as well as – or instead of – the intellect. Even in using the Word, and commenting on the Word, preachers summoned up images, just as the *Spiritual Exercises* encouraged visualisation. If some early Catholic Reformers wanted simplicity, clarity and asceticism, much of the Catholic reforming effort from the later sixteenth century encouraged both spiritual uplift and education through the eyes and ears. The church environment should be fit for hearing and seeing; paintings be narratives to educate, or visual encouragement to contemplation; statues would enhance the cults of old and new Saints; music should move the soul, and accentuate the emotion of key words. Outside the churches a religious community spirit could be celebrated by colourful and noisy musical processions. The faithful were entertained and enticed by singing, theatrical action or display. This chapter will consider some aspects of the sensual and environmental enticement, education and occasionally fearful admonition. Rome in particular, under the papal leadership of especially Sixtus V, Paul V, Urban VIII and Alexander VII, was at the forefront of an expensive campaign to conquer through display and involvement. Alexander VII in particular wanted Rome to be seen as the Religious Theatre for the Catholic Church.[1]

The cultural scenes shifted from caution and puritanism – even repression and destruction – to flamboyant display and exuberant conquest of the emotions and senses. Through the Council and in some of its decrees leading reformers were intent on eliminating the lascivious (a favourite word in our period) – whether in paintings, church music, plays and carnival activities. They wanted worship and teaching to be clear, simple and uncontroversial. Strong minority groups at the Council managed to save the use of polyphonic music within churches (even if only being able to use the human voices and organs), and prevent a major whitewashing of fresco paintings and a curb on new church decoration. St Gregory's old idea of paintings providing the Bible for the illiterate buttressed the argument for having seemly didactic paintings. Soon puritanism declined, and positive campaigns developed to use the visual arts, music and theatre to both instruct, and lift eyes and emotions towards heaven. The new Religious Orders were major contributors to the cultural changes, first the Theatines, then the Oratorians and Barnabites, followed by the Jesuits. The move to display, and cultural adventurousness was aided by leading cardinals, whether dedicated reforming theorists like Gabriele Paleotti and Federico Borromeo, or less religiously committed cardinals with more wordly and aesthetic interests, who were ready to pay for art and music in public as well as private places, and to back experimental artists such as the Carracci, Caravaggio and Guido Reni.

The cultural shifts contributed strikingly to religious revival and enthusiasm, as well as to religious education. The Catholic Church may have stressed 'emotion' too much, downplayed the Word and theology, downgraded the intellectual aspects of religion, swamped the general public with colour and sound to avoid challenges to doctrine, and rethinking of the Gospels – with the vernacular Bible denied to them, and services in Latin. But this avoided the intense bickering of Protestant sects, which came to bore the less literate and intellectual, and the frigidity of Calvinist Puritanism.

Churches and Chapels

Churches and their environs, as often the major public arena or social space for a village or parochial district of a city, underwent significant changes and improvements from the mid- or later sixteenth century. Socio-religious reform, and the changing attitudes outlined above, required closer attention to be paid to the physical environment. The Renaissance period had created new splendid churches, paying lavish attention to new chapels and redecoration within old ones. They particularly honoured rich families and testified to their wealth, more readily boasted of in a new period of conspicuous consumption. But when in the spirit of Catholic reform, bishops, vicars general and apostolic visitors made their Visitation inspections, they often revealed lamentable conditions in local churches. With varying speeds, improvements were made to ensure higher standards of public space within and beside churches. They should more appropriately serve the wider public (as opposed to private donors and Mass sayers, or the memorial interests of the elite few), and enhance the religious and social teaching of the church and secular backers.

The inequities of the parochial systems meant many redundant or underused churches or chapels in some areas, a shortage in others. The former, particularly in large cities like Rome and Naples, were sometimes reallocated to new Orders or the confraternities. Gradually through the late sixteenth to eighteenth centuries new churches were produced for new areas, and the old dilapidated churches redeveloped or repaired. As the new Orders gained support and wealthy patrons they erected new major churches, notably in Rome, Naples and Milan, to be at the centre of their manifold operations. These churches and their increasingly elaborate interior decorations set standards for lesser churches.

Visitation records show that churches in the late sixteenth century were generally in poor condition; dilapidated, windowless and leaky, and their altars, frescoes and pictures in need of repair or replacement. The situation revealed lack of care or shortage of suitable resources. Bishop Domenico Bollani's orders after his 1566 Visitation of Brescia diocese exemplify some of the problems: at Ostiano he wanted the walls whitewashed where not frescoed, a new window with more light, three altars properly equipped and decorated; at Canneto the choir and high altar were to be altered for the priest to celebrate more fittingly – and the local nobles be given a place in the choir; at Malpaga di Calvisano he ordered roof and vault repairs, and a new floor with no more burials allowed inside the church. Bollani ordered significant repairs for about 20 per cent of churches visited. When Monsignor A. Peruzzi visited the Turin Archdiocese (1584–85) he was equally critical. Turin Cathedral had defective wooden altars, broken statues, with ill-lit and airless chapels; the magnificent church at Chieri needed major wall and roof repairs, and Peruzzi ordered four confessionals to answer the new approach to secret confession; the tabernacle at San Giorgio di Castellette needed remaking, and a wooden statue of St George on horseback was to be removed and buried, because women used it improperly, for fertility reasons, in processions. Even in Rome in the seventeenth century Visitation reports noted the parlous state of various parish churches, in the midst of squalid poverty of parishioners.[2]

The reactions to such complaints were varied and haphazard. The Brescia diocese saw much parish church rebuilding in the 1570s and 1580s – such as the sizeable ones designed by G. Todeschini at Desezano, Rovato and Toscolano. Limited funds however, often inhibited quick reactions. In the Milan Diocese Carlo Borromeo and his agents were active visitors, ensured the building of churches in newly populated parishes, and Borromeo provided highly detailed – and influential – Instructions on church architecture and decoration; yet orders for the creation of proper stone altars with demonstrative tabernacles for the Host were often not fulfilled until the eighteenth century. [3] However, a priest and his flock in poorer areas could be enamoured of their church and make strenuous efforts to improve the fabric, and restore it after earthquake damage, as father Matteo Pinelli did at Cerliano in the Mugello in the early seventeenth century [4] (see Chapter 5).

Church structuring now in general required a clear nave space with a good view of the high altar, so the congregation could hear sermons clearly, observe the celebration of the Mass, and clearly see the displayed Host. Side chapels were needed for the celebration of numerous lesser Masses, as for the dead; for more private Masses, Offices of the Virgin and so forth for confraternities and guilds. In old churches such corporate bodies as well as leading local families had to be kept happy as chapel and altar patrons, for the overall financing of the church. In building new churches this financial aspect was a notable consideration for designing, and even the planning of the order of construction. For the new Theatine church in Rome, Sant'Andrea della Valle, priority was given to chapels close to the façade entrance, being allocated to sponsoring families, including the rising Barberini family. These chapels took precedence over building the crossing area and agreeing on the number of domes. The Barberini Chapel featured Gian Lorenzo Bernini's first independent sculptures (while working under his father Pietro), portraying elder Barberini family members.[5] This patron-artist association had great consequences for the splendour of St Peter's, the Barberini papacy, and the Church's image, when Maffeo Barberini was elected Pope Urban VIII and Gian Lorenzo became the Pope's favourite architect-sculptor and architect for St Peter's.

Considerations of congregational needs led to a preference for the elongated Latin cross design, with a wide nave, aisles off which side chapels could be entered with limited disturbance; and with a choir (if needed or desired), behind the main altar. As the confessional 'box' became more accepted, it might be incorporated into the structural design, in nave pillars, as strikingly in Gherardo Silvani's 'baroque' S. Gaetano, Florence (*c.*1604–49), where confessionals were emphasised by saintly statuary and coloured stonework.

Renaissance architects had responded to neoplatonic concepts of divine mathematical perfection, with ideas for more centralised churches: the Greek Cross, the circular and the oval. These were seen in the post-Tridentine period as unsuitable for normal multi-purpose churches, though Carlo Borromeo was prepared to accept such for special purpose churches, such as a plague commemoration church, S. Carlo al Lazzaretto. Notably the new basilica of St Peter's, which was developed according to a Greek Cross design by Michelangelo when envisaged as the church for Pope and hierarchy, had one of its arms extended by Della Porta and Carlo Maderno to create a vast nave for huge congregations of the faithful. The new Bologna Cathedral of S. Pietro was designed by the Barnabite Giovanni Magenta and followers from 1605, with congregational needs to the forefront.[6]

Many old churches were modified to assist hearing sermons and seeing the altar. Choirs were removed from the nave and placed behind the high altar, naves were cleared of tombs and monuments, as ordered by Pius IV in S. Maria in Aracoeli. Plinths, steps and balustrades were introduced to ensure celebrants were visible, and protected from the press of people. Most famously Giorgio Vasari, architect and painter as well as art historian, organised for Duke Cosimo I of Florence the modification of both S. Croce and S. Maria Novella, clearing monks's choirs, screens and tombs from the nave, and replacing obstructive aisle altars with a sequence of aedicules with new paintings.[7]

There was an argument when building the new Il Gesù in Rome for the Jesuits from 1568 whether audibility would be lost if the standard Roman flat-roof nave was rejected in favour of a high curved vault and high dome over the crossing. Earlier in Venice, a Franciscan, F. Zorzi, had stressed in 1535: 'But in the nave of the church, where there will be sermons, I recommend a ceiling (so that the voice of the preacher may not escape nor re-echo from the vaults).' Once Il Gesù proved that the preacher need not suffer from such a design, this kind of structure became standard. Ultimately, in the seventeenth century this structural design increased opportunities for dramatic emotional decoration in ceiling vaults, drums and domes. Architects developed techniques in basic structure and architectural decoration of focusing the eyes of the congregation on altars and celebrants, as G. Della Porta showed early on in S. Maria ai Monti, Rome (1580). Such designs made churches more user friendly for preacher, celebrant, and attentive congregations.[8]

Outside the church much was done to create impressive entry facades and doorways, with space cleared in streets and squares to facilitate the assembly of the public, and spectacular processional entries into the church. Domes, symbolising heaven, became more prevalent as beacons calling the faithful to worship.

Both facades and interiors were increasingly decorated through the seventeenth and eighteenth century, to serve the rhetoric and didactics of the Church; designed to control, stimulate, warn; to emphasise corporate beliefs, common practices, and a sense of community. A complex example of a facade is that of S. Maria presso S. Celso in Milan where G. Alessi and Martino Bassi made the two-storeyed frontage a display area for profuse didactic sculpture: free-standing figures of saints and angels; narrative relief plaques showing the Adoration of the Kings and of the Shepherds, or The Presentation in the Temple, culminating in the Resurrection scene in the apex; an enclosed courtyard with portico in front controls and encourages the beholder before this didactic stage-setting.[9] The evolution of the design of St Peter's in Rome was affected by attitudes to a frontal approach. Maderno added an extensive and elaborate façade to the nave; while this impeded the intended effect of viewing Michelangelo's drum and dome, it provided an effective backdrop for papal blessings of the crowds in the piazza. Gian Lorenzo Bernini and Alexander VII produced the now famous colonnade (adorned with illustrative statues), to embrace and corral that crowd, and focus its attention on the façade, and then a seemly entrance into the basilica. They originally intended a third section of the colonnade to create an enclosed arena, with gaps allowing processions and carriages to pass through.

Major internal sections of a church, a chapel complex within it, or a separate oratory (as for a confraternity), operated as multimedia. Besides the main paintings and sculpture, the effects were accentuated by elaborate marble altars and balustrades, marble or iron altar rails, by beautifully inlaid choirstalls, stone and wood-carved pulpits, gilded altar frames and twisted columns (as in the churches of Lecce and Naples). Stucco decoration and figurative statuary could link parts of the church or chapel, encourage the eye to move restlessly through interior space, and in a heavenly direction; and add movement to great ceiling paintings (as in Il Gesù, Rome). The lavishness may have diverted money from charity, but it could encourage new donations and patronage. It also was designed to convince the public of the spiritual splendour and wealth of the true Catholic Church, as the Theatine Del Tufo stressed when lauding the way rich Neapolitan patrons (often female) endowed and decorated the churches of this new preaching and parish-running Order.[10]

Total effect, using all the visual arts, was by the seventeenth century a goal. G.L. Bernini's first publishing biographer, Francesco Baldinucci, stressed this aspect of his achievement. Besides his contribution as mastermind of the final stages of St Peter's, Bernini was to perfect this in the architecture, sculpture and marble decoration of the Jesuit novitiate church of S. Andrea al Quirinale, and various Roman chapels, such as the Chigi Chapel in S. Maria del Popolo. More famously, the Cornaro chapel with *The Ecstasy of St Theresa of Avila*, in S. Maria della Vittoria, provided an embracing total effect of involvement for the willing believer and observer, based on the Saint's own autobiographical account of her ecstasies, and being pierced by God's love. The chapel was also a celebration of the Venetian Cornaro family's contribution to the Church.[11]

The religious sense of community for the laity was probably most potent among confraternity members; whether in chapels and rooms attached to parish and collegiate churches, or in their own independent oratories and churches. Here confraternity membership encouraged a corporate spirit, often across normal social barriers and differences. The physical environment was enclosing, with didactic paintings near at hand, and with greater personal participation in communal prayer, flagellation or music. Key examples are the Venetian Scuole of San Rocco and San Fantin, the Roman S. Giovanni Decollato and SS. Crocefisso, Perugia's S. Francesco, Florence's Archangel Raffael.[12]

Visual Arts

Tridentine legislation and subsequent episcopal activity sought to eliminate, 'lascivious', and inappropriate paintings from public churches. Theoretically, designs for new altarpieces or frescoes were subject to episcopal approval before installation. Gabriele Paleotti advised artists to submit drawings or small painted versions for approval before painting the full picture, but evidence is limited on actual practice, and even when a contract stipulated a prior vetting it was not necessarily so fulfilled. Visitation reports indicate some scrutiny of old work, though often more a matter of replacing worn frescoes and panels, than strict censorship. Bishop Pietro Camaiani of Ascoli however, following his diocesan visitations (1567), secured the destruction of several paintings; because they were damaged or inappropriate; for not being in conformity with the Gospels or recognised hagiography of a saint; and for painting cardinals and popes and religious in hell. In the Cathedral, figures of Saints Catherine and Lucy had to be altered to remove lasciviousness (presumably covering provocative breasts).[13]

In a much-misunderstood case, talked up because it apparently made the Venetian inquisitors appear philistine dunderheads, Paolo Veronese was questioned (not tried) in 1573, about a 'Last Supper', for the convent of SS. Giovanni e Paolo (now in the Accademia, Venice). Superficially, the inquisitor was concerned that the painting showed a lavish open–portico scene, with numerous extra people and animals, not consonant with the Gospel. Veronese acted as a dumb painter, just wanting to fill space in a huge canvas; he was in fact part of cultured circles, with erudite patron-friends. Almost certainly, the inquisitor was gently probing to see if two figures dressed as Germans at the edge of the picture, receiving bread and wine as guests, were deliberately painted so, to advocate communion for laymen in two kinds (as was still allowed for some Catholics in German lands, but not in the rest of Catholic Europe). Such indirect message-making was perfectly feasible in the period. Veronese made no changes; the title was altered to 'Feast in the House of Levi'.[14]

Bishops, artists and art commentators accepted the challenge to produce effective religious art, and allied visual effects, but no standardised post-Tridentine art emerged, because the purposes were many and varied, beyond the basic desire to 'delight, teach and excite (*commovere*)' in Paleotti's words. Theorists and practitioners agreed that content, style, colour effects should be fittingly matched, and showing off technique and skill for its own sake be avoided. For Paleotti, 'pictures serve like an open book the capacity of all kinds of people … and so allow them to be understood, when the painter does not wish to confuse them, by all nations and intellects, without other teaching or interpretation.' 'Pictures are silent preachers to the people.'[15] Art should be realistic so that the onlooker can believe in what is happening, and get involved in events. But emotional effects and presentation should enhance the impact of the work. For the painter–poet Romano Alberti, in his *Trattato della Nobilta della Pittura* (1585), aimed at the Roman painters' Academy of St Luke, the painter should follow processes of rhetorical composition as for literature.[16] The painter G.P. Lomazzo, who turned theorist on going blind, was followed by the great poet Giambattista Marino (who knew many artists), in stressing the rhetorical value of colour effects, and the importance of facial emotions; for Lomazzo the onlooker's emotion should be moved by expressions of anger, pathos and joy on the faces in the painting. Marino also stressed in his *Dicerie Sacre* (1615), that the viewer should be led to imaginative contemplation – 'Imagine the Virgin's tears dropping on to this Shroud', when discussing the Turin Shroud as a divine painting. Similarly, the Jesuit *Spiritual Exercises* encouraged the penitent to conjure up a physical image, a mind picture: 'Imagining Christ our Lord present before me on the Cross, to make a colloquy with him.'[17]

A vast amount of new religious painting was produced in our period. Just a few names can be mentioned while stressing some themes and characteristics of rhetorical presentation.[18] In considering roles and purposes of art as communication with the public, several approaches can be separated. The most direct didactic purposes were fulfilled – as for centuries – by narrative paintings, whether sequences of frescoes, or now oil-painted canvases and panels, around a chapel or even up in the ceiling; or a single story-telling painting. These dealt notably with the lives of Christ, the Virgin, Saints and their miracles or martyrdom. Here the stylistic or rhetorical stress was on bold clarity and a sense of action. The Venetians had been leading contributors in this category, (notably with Carpaccio's earlier work for confraternities), and remained so through our period, with Jacopo Tintoretto's famous series for the Scuola Grande of San Rocco as pre-eminent (1564–87), combining New Testament stories of the Virgin and Christ, with Old Testament prefigurations.[19] Now less known, but important for religiosity in north-central Italy was the Madonna Della Ghiara[20] pilgrimage church in Reggio Emilia, filled with stories of the Virgin's life by Bologna artists. Domenichino's frescoed narratives of the saint in the S. Cecilia Chapel in S. Luigi dei Francesi, Rome, used a clear heroic classical style to persuade the onlooker.

A second category was that of the contemplative work, to be meditated upon more peacefully; the Virgin and Child, Christ on the

Cross, a contemplating Saint. Many of these were small pieces on lesser altars, or for private devotion. However, Guido Reni's large *Crucifixion* (*c.*1616, now in Bologna Pinacoteca), invites lengthy contemplation before what seems the timeless atmosphere of its setting, along with the sad contemplation of Mary Magdalene and St John. This was a model for seventeenth century Crucifixions.

A third and contrasting type was based on overwhelming the audience with emotion and colour, notably in connection with heaven and salvation. The expanded interest in domes provided opportunities for depicting the heavenly host, Assumptions and saints in Glory; as also did nave ceilings and apses. Artists like Lanfranco and Domenichino in the early seventeenth century returned to what Correggio had created in dome painting a century before. Lanfranco's *Virgin in Glory* for the Roman Theatine S. Andrea della Valle (1625–28), and Pietro da Cortona's *Trinity in Glory* in the Oratorian Chiesa Nuova (1647–51) had a large impact, on immediate audiences and other art.[21] The Jesuit shift to full dramatic oratory was most famously marked by G.B. Gaulli ('Baciccio'), sponsored and advised by Bernini, in *The Adoration of the Name of Jesus*, for the nave ceiling of Il Gesù (1674–79), with illusions of movement through to heaven. Even more theatrically illusionist was their S. Ignazio ceiling celebrating the world missionary work of the Jesuits (by Andrea Pozzo, 1691–94), where nave pillars seem to continue into the heavens.[22]

Individual paintings helped teach important doctrines. The centrality of the Eucharist was obviously stressed in the considerable number of Last Supper paintings, but all sorts of other teaching pictures were added: saints, like St Jerome, receiving communion, spectacular presentation of *The Mass of St Gregory* (e.g. Il Cerano's in Varese, 1616–17), emphasising *The Institution of the Eucharist* (notably by Barocci in Rome), and drawing parallels in *The Supper at Emmaus* (as in Caravaggio's example in the National Gallery, London). Many works emphasised the sacrament of confession, often personalised by showing St Peter and his repentance; here Guercino, Lanfranco and Guido Reni followed the recent teaching of Panigarola and Bellarmino. Since Orders and confraternities stressed the importance of praying for the release of souls from purgatory, visual encouragement was given. The Venetian Scuola of San Fantin had a whole ceiling of panels on this theme, since it undertook to pray for anonymous, uncared for, souls.[23] The Virgin's role as intercessor in this context was emphasised, as in Federico Zuccaro's fesco in Il Gesù, and Guercino's *St Gregory and Souls in Purgatory* in S. Paolo Maggiore, Bologna.

Salvation by good works was visually advocated in many other ways. The Seven Acts of Mercy have been discussed already in this context (Chapter 7). Now most famously the Pio Monte della Misericordia, a fraternity of philanthropic nobles in Naples, encouraged their work by commissioning Caravaggio's *Seven Acts of Mercy* (where all the acts are alluded to in one complicated powerful scene), and works by other artists like G.B. Baglione, B. Caracciolo, F. Santafede encouraging separate acts of burying the dead fittingly, releasing prisoners or slaves providing hospitality. The confraternity had to fight off attempts by the Viceroy to obtain Caravaggio's work.[24] Venetian Sacrament confraternities commissioned Last Supper scenes from Tintoretto for their chapels in parish churches, which not only celebrated the Eucharist but, by the incorporation of extra figures at the side or below, encouraged the earning of salvation by feeding beggars (in S. Polo), or mothers and children (in S. Marcuola). While the message-making in Pio Monte was for the enclosed fraternity membership, the advocacy of the Tintoretto paintings was both for the commissioning confraternity, but also for all parishioners. Saints might be brought in to give leadership, as with two Neapolitan works by B. Schedoni (1578–1615; now in Capodimonte Gallery, Naples): *Almsgiving of St Elizabeth,* where the saint succours children and old men, and *St Sebastian cared for by pious women,* who successfully nurse this saint's arrow wounds. [25]

The rhetorical methods used by painters were diverse, and more elaborate than in earlier Renaissance pictures. Gestures were dynamically used not only to express dramatic reactions within the scene, but to attract the viewers' and worshippers' attention, to be participants; and side characters might make eye-contact. Many works attempted a seamless connection between the onlooker, the earthbound painted scene, and heavenly activity or blessing at the top (as in paintings of *The Resurrection of Christ,* or *Assumption of the Virgin,* by Annibale and Lodovico Carracci).[26] Altarpieces now in galleries often lose the intended effect, because hung too low; book and slide reproductions, taken straight on, similarly distort the intended impact of viewing from well below, kneeling at the altar rail, or viewing a side-panel obliquely. Many other paintings invite participation in the scene, without a heavenly superstructure. Tintoretto's Last Supper scenes could suggest the onlooker was in the room; in the San Rocco version we are being led up the steps by a dog. The rhetoric involved might be clear and simple, or highly complicated. Musical parallels were made at the time, as in Borghini's *Il Riposo*. The seventeenth century art historian G.P. Bellori wrote of Lanfranco's *Virgin in Glory*:

> Thus this painting has rightly been likened to a full choir, in which all the sounds together make up the harmony; because, at the moment of hearing, no particular voice is listened to in particular, but what is lovely is its blending and the general cadence and substance of the singing.

Lanfranco's polyphonic work might be contrasted with monodic recitative of his rival Domenichino's *Life of St Andrew* scenes in the apse of the same church, as clear narration. Lanfranco was attacked (by Domenichino supporters), for breaking the unity of time, having new saints Gaetano da Thiene and Andrea Avellino joining Peter and Andrew.[27]

A single artist could fit several of my categories and employ varied rhetorical techniques. Federico Barocci (d.1609) can be exemplary. Based in Urbino, well protected by the Duke, he was much admired by Philip Neri. Neri (according to his canonisation proceedings and early biographers), was found rapt in ecstasy or even levitating while contemplating one of Barocci's paintings, his first for the Chiesa Nuova, *The Visitation* (1583–86).[28] Barocci later painted *The Presentation of the Virgin* (1593–94) for it. A striking early work (1566–69) was *The Deposition* for Perugia Cathedral, which exemplifies the new approach to apt expressionism. The stillness of Christ's inert body contrasts with the agitated reaction of attendant women who rush to support the fainting Mary. The agitation is conveyed by expressions, gestures, the movement of colourful garments, with the yellows and reds in particular linking the figures and providing a structural unity. San Bernardino (for whose chapel the painting was commissioned), watches, and his gestures invite spectator involvement. Many of Barocci's works concern the Virgin, often in quiet scenes for contemplation, using gentle gestures to invite participation. In *Il Perdono d'Assisi* (S. Francesco, Urbino), the Virgin signifies Christ's blessing with her open-palmed left hand, while her right pushes towards the onlooker, and below St Francis, leaning almost of the picture, similarly uses his hands for display and invitation.[29] Some Holy Family scenes suggest happy domesticity; and Barocci is one of the few painters to treat the cat as benign, not evil! – as in *La Madonna del Gatto* (London NG). Barocci's *Madonna del Popolo* (1575–79. Uffizi, Florence) for an Arezzo confraternity, but in a public church, teaches that charity will earn a heavenly blessing. Help is being given to a blind musician, a begging cripple, and poor mother with child, while better-off children are caught between watching these poor and the blessing on offer from the heavenly scene at the top, encouraged by mothers. Gentlemen in the centre, possibly signifying confraternity donors, also have dual concerns between earthly philanthropy and heavenly reward. Gestures, looks and colour tones foster a helix-like movement of the observer's eye from bottom to top of the picture, earth to heaven – and back; the blessing on all. An angel invites the viewer's participation.[30]

The audiences were often, of course, limited if paintings were for a parish church in town or country, or private confraternity chapel – but not always. What was produced for the great Roman churches potentially could affect millions on pilgrimage visits over the decades. Crowds flocked to see Barocci's work unveiled in the Chiesa Nuova, or Caravaggio's controversial *Death of the Virgin*, when removed from a Roman church and sold to Mantua. Also artists, their studio, or unconnected copyists provided versions for different patrons and churches. Much more significantly, printed versions of many paintings, and scenes for *Quarantore* celebrations (see below), festivals and major funerals were circulated and sold. The Carracci and Barocci (who himself produced an etching of *St Francis Receiving the Stigmata* like his *Perdono* painting), accelerated a process of dissemination of high-quality images that had been fostered from the 1520s to the 1530s – though cheap and cruder wood-block prints had a longer history. In particular, devotional images of the Virgin would have been available for contemplation in many homes. Print shops had sophisticated selling techniques.[31]

Churches, chapels, oratories and their decorative, environment, thus at their most effective, created a more cohesive and integrated environment, inspiring a community spirit, encouraging the learning and dissemination of the teachings of the church, and also sometimes stimulating outward-looking social action.

Music

The fathers at the Council of Trent had divided views on the role of music in church services and religious celebrations.[32] The condemnation of instruments other than organs for the church services had some impact of the development of church music, and especially in Rome dampened enthusiasm for and experimentation in polyphonic music. However, even in Rome (Giovanni Luigi da) Palestrina, a favoured composer during the Tridentine discussions, soon developed acceptable and seemly polyphonic Masses. His *Missa Papae Marcelli*, written for Pope Marcellus II's Requiem in 1555, when published in 1567 became a touchstone for a modified polyphony. His Masses (which inched forward to a new polyphonic experimentation in time with the Vatican's slow pace), became standard fare in Catholic churches for centuries to come. He eventually wrote 105 Masses and over 200 motets. Music became very much an exciting, adventurous and popular aspect of revived Catholicism in Italy, under a variety of impulses, and in several locations, as Iain Fenlon has notably demonstrated.[33] The peculiar 'private' positions of the Ducal Chapel of S. Barbara in Mantua, and of the Doge's Chapel of San Marco in Venice, allowed them to ignore Tridentine restraints, and any episcopal interference. Duke Guglielmo Gonzaga, who had Santa Barbara built as the Trent Council was closing, saw it as the base for a reformed Catholic liturgy, with powerful music. He was a composer in his own right, and desirous of having Palestrina as his court religious composer.[34]

The key composer to find favour with the Tridentine reformers was Vincenzo Ruffo, who became *maestro di capella* in Milan Cathedral in 1563. His preface to a collection of Masses published in 1570 claimed:

> in accordance with the decrees of the Holy Council of Trent I was to compose some Masses that should avoid everything of a profane and ideal manner in worship ... I composed one Mass in this way: so that the numbers of the syllables and the voices and tones together should be clearly and distinctly understood by the pious listeners ... Later, imitating the example, I more readily and easily composed other Masses of the same type.[35]

Ruffo and Palestrina were joined by Marc'Antonio Ingegnero (d. 1592), in Milan, as an acceptable setter of the Mass. Other composers like his pupil Claudio Monteverdi (1567–1643), were soon to bring more experimentation on the fringes of the Mass, and on alternative forms of religious composition; and then at the heart of Masses and Vespers.

Despite the conservative warnings Italian religious music became exciting, varied, widely appealing through our period, benefiting from developments in Netherland–Italian secular music, and cross-fertilising with them. The danger was with the central part of the Mass – no great distortion of the words. But much appealing and adventurous music could be provided by the organ – played before and after the Mass, or in between the main liturgical points. Motets, voices with or without instruments, could be part of an extended Mass, or of other celebrations. Soon Vespers were treated as a path to spiritual uplift, using voices, organ and other instruments. The organ was the acceptable instrument for church use, and increasingly widespread in urban churches, but not absent from parish churches or oratories in smaller communities; as one can deduce from Matteo Pinelli's career. Some organs were small and portable. In later seventeenth-century Rome many churches used harpsichords and instrumental groups as well as, or instead of, organs. What was played is hard to tell; even in the great city churches in Rome evidently much was improvised, continuing an oral teaching tradition. Along with spectacular Toccatas at the start, various kinds of music could be played interspersed through the Mass, with instrumental music or sung motets at the elevation, organ improvisations and formal *canzone* through communion. Limited evidence suggests that secular tunes were still improvised between the main parts of the service. The amount of organ and harpsichord music published was meagre, though compositions of the great keyboard composer and performer Girolamo Frescobaldi were printed.[36]

The enticing power of music to move the spirit, and attract people to religious devotions was well recognised; and the effect could be enhanced by complex mood changes, variations in numbers of voices and instruments. If this was argued in print by a professionally interested composer like Giovanni Animuccia, we also find it noted by the English Jesuit Gregory Martin, commenting on his experiences in Rome in 1576–78, and hearing polyphonic music – 'such musike, such voices, such instruments, al ful of gravitie and majestie, al moving to devotion and ravishing a mans hart to the meditation of melodie of Angels and Saintes in heaven'. Jesuits were soon admitting, like Michele Lauretano in the German College in Rome, that Gregorian chant did not have the 'sweetness' to keep worldly men coming to church, and that instrumental and measured music should also be used. [37] Another Englishman, Thomas Coryat, visiting Venice in 1606–08, attended a night-time service in honour of San Rocco, in the Scuola Grande di San Rocco, which was dominated by music, vocal and instrumental 'so good, so delectable, so rare, so admirable, so superexcellent, that it did even ravish and stupifie all those strangers that never heard the like ... I was for the time even rapt up with Saint Paul in the third heaven.' A CD has reconstructed what might have been heard in San Rocco composed by Giovanni Gabrieli in particular.[38] This and several other Venetian Scuole benefited from composers and performers who were at the same time developing polyphonic, multi-choral, and instrumental music in St Mark's basilica. The violin was being developed to rival the viol family of instruments, seen by some as being the instrument closest to the human voice, and most 'expressive', so most acceptable.

Religious experience through music gained considerably from theoretical discussion and musical experimentation focusing on the relationship between words and music, with how musical effects could bring out the joy or pathos, anger or lamentation implied by a word, as well as by an event. The word painting could apply to secular love motets of joy or lamentation, or to religious equivalents. The Neapolitan Don Carlo, Prince of Gesualdo (*c.*1560–1613), who had to flee north to Ferrara after killing his wife and her lover (1590), composed love madrigals and religious motets, noted for wayward harmonies, excessive dissonances and very expressive musical tension, as found in his Responses for Maundy Thursday, or motets from his *Sacrarum Cantionum* (1603), which emphasise the (his?) agonised mood of guilt, and sense of sin and death.[39] His music, as from the Responses, inspired Roman Oratorian circles.

Claudio Monteverdi from Cremona first made his impact largely in secular music, with madrigals and early operatic works at the Mantuan court under the Gonzagas, but his experimentation fed into religious music, especially after he moved to Venice to be *maestro di capella* at St Mark's in 1613. The complex structure of St Mark's, especially with its numerous subdivisions and galleries lent itself to the use of many 'choirs' (which could be of voices, portable organs with viols, violins, trombones and so forth), playing off against each other, echoing, or responding as in debate. The word painting was brought out in settings of the Psalms like *Dixit Dominus* (Ps.109) or *Laetatus Sum* (Ps.121), in the *Magnificat*, or motets like *Laudate Dominum* or *O quam pulchra est.* How Monteverdi could shift from secular music to religious, using vocal polyphony, declamatory monody, and a full range of instrumental colouring was demonstrated in his 1610 Vespers, composed in Mantua when unhappy with his treatment there, probably in a bid to move to a church position in Rome or Venice. Late in his career came the glorious Mass of Thanksgiving, sung in St Mark's on 21 November 1631 on the feast of the Presentation of the Virgin, as part of the city's celebratory day for the end of the devastating plague. The Byzantine painting of the Virgin and Child, called the Madonna Nicopeia, (of Victory) was honoured in the Mass, and then paraded with trumpets and singing to the site where they were starting to build Longhena's S. Maria della Salute, as a thanksgiving plague church. The Mass, coordinated and partly composed by Monteverdi, was not printed, but has been 'reconstructed' by Andrew Parrott. Reports at the time indicate that Monteverdi used trumpets together with voices for the Credo and Gloria; probably for the first time, and hardly acceptable to the Tridentine mood.[40]

A medieval musical tradition was happily developed through the period into early modern Catholic practices; the singing of *laude*. *Laude* were spiritual songs, often in praise of the Virgin, which were sung mainly as part of processions (as by confraternities), though they could be incorporated into internal church services. The medieval *laudesi* traditions, associated most with Umbria and Tuscany, were taken into Roman heartlands in the mid-sixteenth century, by reforming Tuscans, particularly Philip Neri and his supporters, who formed the confraternity and then the Order of the Oratory. Less spectacularly, the Dominicans maintained Savonarolan enthusiasms, in the Roman Dominican Church of S. Maria sopra Minerva. They not only helped save Savonarola's works from complete condemnation in the 1559 Index (see Chapter 4), but promoted *laudesi* singing as well. As Iain Fenlon stressed, on the back of a common support for Savonarola, the Oratorians and Dominicans of the Minerva jointly promoted religious music to inspire themselves and a wide public, and shared composers like Giovani Animuccia.[41] Much of the singing in processions discussed elsewhere continued this kind of religious singing.

Oratorios, sliding into full religious operas (as acting and dancing with costumes and elaborate sets were added to stationary singing and declamation), were developed and increasingly professionalised through our period, as dramatic musical presentations of Biblical stories, lives of saints, and conflicts of vices and virtues. They were essentially organised by and for the confraternities and congregations, the Jesuit and Oratorian Orders, but with many open to the public. Some nunneries performed them. Under the Barberini family during Urban VIII's pontificate, religious operas were part of the court scene, lavishly presented.[42] Florence notably developed the dramatic Oratorio, starting with the youth confraternity of Archangel Raphael (which became more adult over the period), but the genre was taken up by several other confraternities. J.W. Hill in particular has shown the extent and popularity of sung religious drama, at all levels of society, through to the late eighteenth century. Florence and its composers like Emilio de'Cavalieri, influenced Rome and Bologna, and drew back inspiration from them in the mid-seventeenth century, as when the Oratorian house made its mark in Florence.[43] A key marker in the evolution of religious opera was Emilio de'Cavalieri's *Rapresentazione di Anima e Corpo* (Body and Soul), a moralising work performed in the Roman Oratory for the Jubilee of 1600; described as 'a sermon in dialogue interspersed with (choral) hymns', it had an influential audience led by some music loving cardinals.[44]

The Jesuits in Rome took up the oratorio and sacred opera, in Italian and Latin, especially gaining attention from compositions by Giacomo Carissimi (1605–74), choir master at the Jesuit church of S. Apolinare, with titles like *Jonas, Job* and *Balthazar*. One of the most impressive oratorio/opera composers in Rome was Luigi Rossi (1597–1653), who came from the South, with Neapolitan training, was made organist at San Luigi dei Francesi, but patronised by the Borghese then Barberini families (and especially Cardinal Antonio Barberini). He produced secular cantatas, religious cantatas or oratorios, and religious opera. Two cantatas/oratorios, 'The Penitent Sinner' (Il peccator pentito) and 'O the blindness of the miserable mortal' (O cecità del misero mortale), set penitential poems probably to be sung in Lent, using several singers, and stringed instruments like viols, violins and theorbo. Voices and instruments express deep emotions of remorse and despair, counteracted by hope derived from repentance. Rossi's 'Joseph, son of Jacob', for five soloists and orchestra, was a more interactive drama, again playing on a full range of emotions as the family meets up in Egypt, facing accusations, recriminations, calls for mercy and forgiveness.[45]

One of the most notable religious operas was *Il Sant'Alessio*, with music by Stefano Landi to a libretto by Giulio Rospigliosi (later Pope Clement IX, 1667–69), and promoted by Cardinal Francesco Barberini. Seemingly first performed in 1631 on a modest scale, an expanded version was mounted in a Barberini palace to honour the Imperial ambassador, and the fullest versions were given in seven performances during Carnival 1634 for different types of audience. The story concerned Alexis, a fifth-century Roman patrician who disappears to the East, returns as a Christian hermit to Rome where he resists temptations, including from the Devil to return to family, wealth and paganism. On his death his family testifies to his sanctity. Opportunities were presented to praise the Roman people, to laud spiritual and human love, and encourage sanctity, with much moving music, including the almost obligatory 'lament' (by the family), and Alessio's own internal conflict between love of family and spiritual harmony. Performances had elaborate machinery and scenery, some designed by Pietro da Cortona. The newsletters (*Avvisi*) praised the singing, scenery and costumes; and lasting publicity came with a printed account, also illustrating the stage settings. Prologues were adjusted to honour different foreign princes as guests of honour on the night. All this redounded to the honour of Rome, the papal family, and the ultimate joy of living a saintly life.[46]

By the mid-seventeenth century music was deeply involved in the religious scene, in public churches, confraternity oratories and chapels, private palaces, convents and monasteries. Some audiences were exclusive, but the effects could spread to much wider congregations. Only a few cities have been mentioned here, but composers and Venetian printers produced much advanced music for northern Italian parish churches, as well as cathedrals. For example, Lodovico da Viadana was a 'working' composer who, even while at Mantua Cathedral, was providing stylistically up-to-date music for limited resources in Portogruaro (Friuli) or Fano (Marches), to be published in his *Cento Concerti Ecclesiastici* of 1602 – for one to four voices and an organ. Jerome Roche points to significant composers and organists across the Veneto, including Asolo, Chioggia, Murano, Padua, Portogruaro, Treviso, Verona and Udine, with Bergamo probably the most impressive. The Duchies of Ferrara, Mantua and Parma all provided vital church music as well as secular court music; with Modena partly replacing Ferrara after 1598. Bologna and Milan dominated their areas, in the latter case to the detriment of other Lombard cities, except Novara where the Cathedral had a series of important composers. Cathedrals were not necessarily the most prominent musical centre in a city (it was not in Bergamo), and other churches or confraternity oratories (as in Parma and Bologna) might be leaders, especially when Vespers or Compline provided the motif.[47]

I have noted music's importance for spiritual uplift and aid to devotion. Some music was meant to enhance textual meaning, as well as emotions. But it was a recognised condition – danger – that people would attend Mass or Vespers for the music only, leaving after organ toccatas and other early contributions. As Nicolo Farfaro said in a *Discorso* on ancient and modern music:

> The church of S. Apollinare [Rome], which today boasts the most exquisite singing in the world, draws large congregations, but if

> they are observed closely it is obvious that they come not out of religious sentiment or for the divine office, ... but simply to hear the music: this is clearly shown by the fact that once the motet after the Magnificat is over, everyone knows there will be no more music, and they all go, leaving the church empty, without waiting for the end of Vespers.[48]

Forty-Hour Devotions (Quarantore)

The Forty-Hour Devotion became an enticing educational and spiritual event, motivated by those seeking a greater respect for and adoration of the Host, and a reminder of Christ's sacrifice. It could require scenic structures, sculptures, paintings and lighting to emphasise the displayed Host on the altar. It involved personal prayer and contemplation, but it might also be accompanied by sermons, music and singing. The fundamental concept was to have the Host on display in a monstrance, with other special effects, for a period of 40 hours, either continuously or spread over three days if the organisers did not want night-time visiting. The public came to visit, adore, pray, hear sermons and homilies, possibly watch a celebration of a Mass. The period would end with a High Mass.[49]

The Devotion, probably first developed in 1527 by a Milanese priest, was most significantly promoted by the Barnabite Antonio Maria Zaccaria, the Capuchin Giuseppe Plantanida (from 1537 in Sansepolcro), and from 1550 in Rome by Filippo Neri. Thereafter, the Devotion was encouraged by various Religious Orders and confraternities. For Jesuits and others this Devotion was to provide an alternative to or distraction from less seemly carnival activities. The Capuchins scheduled theirs as a three-day start to Holy Week. The Orders and confraternities organised groups of laity and clergy for the seemly visiting of the Host. The location might be in the cathedral, in a major monastic church, confraternity oratory, or in a sizable parish church. Bologna possibly had the fullest range and variety. A boastful report, with sketch, on the 1597 *Quarantore* organised in the chapel of the Confraternity of Santa Maria della Morte, one of Bologna's leading confraternities, indicated an altar backed by a painted apparatus of a heavenly scene, flanked by statues of the Madonna and angels, and colourful decorations everywhere. Lights from numerous candles were enhanced by mirrors. This was the proudest and richest apparatus ever seen in Bologna, while the most splendid music also provided for the occasion surpassed even that produced for Easter 1593.[50] Bishop Gabriele Paleotti organised key parish churches to take turns to putting on the Forty-Hour displays, and similar Eucharist-focused processions of shorter duration (the *Decennale Eucarista* or *Addobbi*), replacing the old city-wide Corpus Domini processions. They could now foster parochial communities and their sense of pride, (provided the rich were prepared to help fund the display). The processions might be accompanied by music, and the route brightened by tapestries and carpets hung from windows. The church and chapel interiors were similarly festooned.[51]

Rome inevitably competed to provide elaborate *Quarantore* celebrations, organised by the Jesuits, Vatican officials or confraternities. San Lorenzo in Damaso, a parish church hosting many confraternities was a major arena for Forty-Hour devotions. One in 1608 was advertised as follows:

> When all are kneeling and the doors are closed, the music will begin to elevate the souls to God. Then Father Fedele will deliver the sermon, and it will be as a mediator between the soul and God, in order to reconcile everyone with His Divine Majesty; and each will be disposed as God our Lord will inspire.[52]

In 1633 in the same church the leading painter–architect Pietro da Cortona constructed a major apparatus, lit with lamps, for a great display; and this was to be reused in later years. He and his backers were probably consciously seeking to rival an illusionary Glory of Paradise (lit by 2000 lamps) that Gian Lorenzo Bernini had designed in 1628 for the Pauline Chapel in the Vatican. Such celebrations not only were to impress those who attended, but to some extent a wider public, when prints of the settings were made for distribution.[53]

Processions, Pilgrimages and Theatricality

Processions were one of the most important aspects of religious life, often combining spirituality, entertainment, with propaganda for the Church as a whole, a city or village, and the religious and secular organisations involved.[54] Processions could be indoors around a particular church, or massive parades through a great city, with ranks of clergy, members of the Religious Orders, civic councillors, cohorts of confraternities, with crosses, paintings, banners, candelabra and candles, and musicians. We have mentioned a number of roles for processions in dealing with confraternities. The processions could be doleful – for funerals, for expressing penitential sorrow and promises for a new way of life during the missions of Capuchins and Jesuits; for invoking God's mercy in the face of afflictions of bad weather, disease, war threats, and even plague – even if some considered that such processions would only encourage the spread of plague; as argued in the great plague scares in Milan and Venice in 1575–77. Lively and enthusiastic processions were mounted to celebrate Easter, Corpus Christi, a canonisation or beatification, the feast-day of a major saint, the translation of relics from one location to another, or the dowering of poor girls. The enthusiasm for processions of all kinds is well brought out in Giambattista Casale's Milan diary.[55]

Processions had been a spectacular part of medieval religious and civic life; our period sees a continuation, but with more lavish display for the great occasions. The 1551 Tridentine decree on the Eucharist wanted the Host processed through the streets, and so boosted Corpus Christi processions and displays. The Jubilee Years every quarter-century, spectacularly from 1575 onwards (but with 1550 setting some precedents), and the canonisations of the seventeenth century, led to the most eye- and ear-catching parades in Rome; to be enjoyed by tens or hundreds of thousands of pilgrim visitors from all over Italy and further afield.

Processions were often associated with plays (with speaking actors) and scenic 'representations' (*rappresentazioni*), involving staged scenes along a processional route, or scenes mounted on carts, with characters dressed up but not acting. A long medieval tradition lay behind these activities. The play-acting aspect came under attack from puritanical reformers, because they could involve comic as well as tragic scenes, leading to bawdy. However, the theatrical aspects involving scenery, sculptures, people dressed up but not speaking, were backed by lighting and mirror effects; the use of music were developed to enhance worship and message-making.

Rome had from the 1490s a spectacular Passion play staged in the Colosseum, organised by the Gonfalone confraternity. This was preceded by a penitential procession led by the brothers, imitating Christ's path to Calvary. The plays were banned from 1539, but the confraternity continued its own penitential procession, to the Colosseum till 1545, then to St. Peter's to honour relics put on display – namely a fragment of the True Cross, Veronica's veil and Longinus' lance. These relics were to receive enhanced veneration through the next decades, to challenge the Protestant attacks on relics. These relics were eventually housed in the great pillars for the dome of the new St Peter's, with suitable statues at the Crossing to honour them – organised by Gian Lorenzo Bernini, who himself sculpted the Longinus statue. The 1550 Jubilee led to more processions and rituals expanding from this Gonfalone one, with other major confraternities joining. A processional ritual that came to dominate was the torchlit Maundy Thursday one culminating in the Vatican's Pauline Chapel. The procession started in the Gonfalone's Oratory, with a commemorative meal, the foot-washing ceremony, and feeding of the poor. Others joined as the parade moved through Rome. This public candle-lit ceremony much impressed the English Jesuit, Gregory Martin, living in Rome 1576–78, who commented on the voluntary whipping drawing blood; by then St Peter's was involved, with Veronica's veil shown to the penitents. By 1601 Camillo Fanucci in his guide to Rome's piety stressed this Maundy Thursday procession as involving most confraternities, and constituting one of Rome's greatest expressions of piety.[56]

An impression of how a Corpus Christi celebration came to be presented in Rome is shown in an anonymous painting of an event in the piazza outside the new St Peter's, about 1646. Crowds assemble under huge canopies stretching from the façade and a bell-tower on the Vatican palace side (later demolished when Bernini's colonnade was constructed), while numerous coaches are assembled in the piazza.[57]

Processions were significant both for participants and observers. The sense of social involvement of participants, with anticipations of spiritual benefits, whether suffering through self-whipping, or more joyfully singing *laude* and praising the Virgin, is easily recognised. It was a spectator experience. People watched from windows, from which they may have hung colourful cloths, tapestries and carpets to show wealth. Visitors could pay for window and balcony space. Some paid a costly 2–3 *scudi* to observe the procession of the heart-relic of the newly sanctified Carlo Borromeo being processed through Rome on 22 June 1614. The procession, featuring numerous confraternities carrying 1500 torches, was led by twenty-five cardinals.[58]

A post-Tridentine development was what David Gentilcore has called 'the Christianisation of the carnivalesque'. The Jesuits, Redemptionists, and others turned penitential processions into gruesome carnivalesque displays. In a 1646 procession in Squinzano members from all levels of society joined a flagellant procession. Covered in ashes, linked together with chains and cords like a prison chain-gang they wound their way through the city. A repentant prostitute was dressed in sack-cloth as Mary Magdalene, and beat her breast with a stone, while a local noble had his young son help him beat himself with a stone. Farm workers used farm implements as well as chains to mortify themselves, cutting through the flesh to the bones. While women were meant to avoid such scenes, they could be found watching, weeping and lamenting, imploring the mercy of God. Fervour for such penance could lead adulterers to make public penance for society's benefit (as in Torre Paduli in Terra d'Otranto in 1655), the voluntary surrender and burning of playing cards, offensive books or images. Much of this must be treated as genuine fervour, promoted by dynamic preaching, and not a matter of coercion; ultimately constituting personal and public relief and release. Naturally the forsaking of adultery or gambling might be only short-lived. More pleasantly Jesuits organised masked children's processions before First Communion; boys as angels, girls as virgin saints and martyrs.[59]

Pilgrimage remained in our period a significant aspect of religious life and the bid for personal salvation, as in the middle ages. It might be undertaken as a lonely personal act of contrition, or part of a communal adventure to earn indulgences, with some entertainment as when organised by confraternities. The pilgrimage might be a reasonably short distance to a regional shrine, as in Assisi, Bari, Reggio Emilia, Impruneta or Loreto. The two long-distance pilgrimage targets were the Virgin's House in Loreto, and Rome. Sixtus V had made strenuous efforts to make Loreto (in the Marches) a major pilgrimage centre. His statue blesses those who enter the main baroque domed church. Within elaborate sculptured marble encased the little brick house that had supposedly been the Virgin's house, and which had miraculously been moved to Dalmatia, and then flown by angels to Loreto for safety. Revitalisation of Marian cults ensured it stayed a major pilgrimage point in central Italy, along with Assisi. We have encountered Father Matteo Pinelli, parish priest of Cerliano in the Mugello (Tuscany). In 1608 he went with five of his parishioners to Loreto on pilgrimage, early on in his ministry, possibly as a prelude to encouraging work on the Holy Sacrament company and oratory. He copied Latin inscriptions placed in the church, for later study and inspiration if he could not return on pilgrimage.[60]

Rome was very deliberately built up as an enticing pilgrimage target, so that those coming from far or near would return home with an image of the Eternal City, as fit to lead the universal Catholic Church. The increasingly splendourful Holy Year Jubilees were the high points, but pilgrims coming in others years were also catered for by clerics and confraternities. Estimates suggest that about 175 000 pilgrims visited Rome for the 1575 Jubilee, over 200 000 for 1600 and 1625. The archconfraternity of SS.Trinità (one of Filippo Neri's early creations in the 1540s), was the chief organiser of hospitality for pilgrims (claiming to help 169 000 or so in 1575), but it was backed by other confraternities and monasteries. They provided shelter, food, feet-washing, sometimes musical entertainment and religious celebrations in their own premises. Confraternity groups were assisted in visiting the major Roman basilicas, and St Peter's, for more services, blessings from cardinals, bishops and maybe the Pope. So the pilgrims earned indulgences, and hopefully were impressed by the majesty and charity of the Mother Church in the Eternal City. The pilgrimage as an appealing event was highlighted by a long account by a Perugian canon, which I summarised elsewhere, of the Perugian Company of Death (Della Morte) pilgrimage to Rome for the 1600 Jubilee.[61] The main participants were the wealthy, with servants; and they were right royally entertained, spiritually and gastronomically there and back; and while in Rome by their host archconfraternity Della Morte. Besides food and wine, there was more interest in frequent communion, relics, and music (singing and string playing), than in new architecture – possibly because they did process demurely heads-down, thereby earning papal praise. In practice much redevelopment of Roman churches, and decoration of the Roman religious scene, was generated by Popes and cardinals in preparation for Jubilees.[62]

Rome through the year offered resident or visitor a considerable range of processions, celebrations outside or inside, and in combination. The Roman diarist Giacinto Gigli chronicled much from 1608 to 1657; he was involved in civic government, and had access to papal circles.[63] He noted and described fairly regular processions, such as those by the Rosary Company, based in S. Maria sopra Minerva. But he dwelt on more special events, such as the highly musical procession, organised by the blacksmith's company, of a recently arrived relic of Sant'Eligio (or St Louis), his arm, from France, because their fraternity church was dedicated to him. The Florentine confraternity of S. Giovanni in 1622 at Pentecost paraded relics of the newly canonised San Filippo Neri (beard hairs and tooth), given his Florentine origins. This was a way of calling together – with music – those in Rome with Florentine connections. In 1625, as part of the Jubilee celebrations the Rosary company in October bid to outdo other celebrations, with a commemoration of the Rosary and its particular association with the 1571 Battle of Lepanto, defeating the Turks. The processional route was lined with silks and tapestries. The vast procession of clergy, friars, confraternity members, and other laity was accompanied by many choirs, and candles, while some carried large paintings of the naval battle, and representations of the Mysteries of the Rosary. The Pope's daughter-in-law led female confraternity officials escorting 31 poor maidens to whom the company was providing dowries for marriage or a nunnery. At the end was an architectural construct carried to show off an Image of the Virgin, adored by many Dominican saints.

Gigli was exuberant about the 1650 Jubilee, and many processions with music, paintings, constructs. One highlight was a procession and display to and in the Piazza Navona, organised by the Spanish 'national' confraternity of the Holy Resurrection at S. Giacomo, celebrating the Holy Sacrament, the Rosary, and Spanish–Iberian 'unity' (then being challenged by a Portuguese revolt). Various display structures were built around two complete fountain structures in the Piazza, and the Bernini's incomplete Four Fountains one. Every year this Spanish confraternity took over the Piazza Navona; on the feast of the Immaculate Conception they paraded those girls and women to whom they were offering dowries; and on Easter Sunday they had a dawn procession to the church, accompanied by music, religious or political theatrical displays. Fireworks celebrated the Host reaching the church.

The Piazza Navona had become a theatre for the World in Rome. It was used for celebrating a papal succession (the *Possesso*), for carnival and secular occasions, when were organised scenes of the Resurrection, jousts, sea battles (since it could be conveniently flooded), wine fountains and firework displays. Paintings, prints, literary accounts ensured that a wider public had a spun version of what took place, whether for the honour of the Church, a cardinal or princely family, confraternity – or all together. This was the counteraction against Protestant complaints, and the other side of the coin from repression.

11 *Conclusions: Successes and Failures*

Re-forming the Church in Italy and creating a more respectable Christian society, as desired by reformers from, say, Girolamo Savonarola, G.M. Giberti, Angela Merici and Girolamo Miani to Gregorio Barbarigo and Paolo Segneri, was daunting, and none would have been too complaisant about 'success' by the time of the great Jesuit preacher Segneri's death in 1694. Most would have concurred that the Church was more effectively structured than in Savonarola's day, with greater value attached to Christian morality, possibly a more caring society, and not threatened by a theological revolution. Barbarigo, Segneri and a Pope like Innocent XI, knew they must continue reforming, combat human frailty; they had the enthusiasm to cajole others to continue campaigning.

By way of conclusion I offer some summaries of what had changed, and what challenges remained for these reformers. The overall picture from the late seventeenth or early eighteenth century might appear gloomy, but some bright aspects can be highlighted.

Serious theological challenges to orthodox Catholicism existed throughout Italy in the first half of the sixteenth century; competitive, often hybrid, sceptically tentative rather than dogmatically certain enough to conquer, and overthrow Petrine Rome's control. By the 1570s the Papacy could be reasonably content that the serious threat of high theological heresy had been eliminated, by repression, fear tactics, a few exemplary executions, and the retreat of the more adamant into exile. Knowledge of, interest in, Protestant theology remained to be spotted by Inquisitors or denouncing neighbours, but this was confinable. The Inquisition and bishops could concentrate more on campaigning against worrying, but overall less damaging, superstitions, magical practices, pagan rites and immorality. Such issues kept them busy; individuals might be successfully re-educated, but the practices and superstitious beliefs recurred from generation to generation – as with the *benandanti*, or throwers of the *corda*. Church leaders, lesser clerics and exorcists into the eighteenth century faced the problem that 'Divine mirrored diabolic'; 'rapturous flights to paradise resemble witches' flights to the sabbath', and so they struggled to distinguish the living saint from a woman witch.[1]

Trent, developing earlier precedents, fostered reconstruction of church and society, with very mixed and variable results. Standardisation was not achieved in the diocesan and parochial structures, in refinancing the church's operations, in the seminary, in the use of Provincial Councils or synods. My Appendix data was designed to cover to about 1630. It can reveal many gaps, showing that Provincial Councils and synods had not been held, or only rarely, seminaries not founded. My partial recording of later operations or creations emphasises the continuing omissions; or a date of new reform enthusiasm. Some areas were not getting their first seminary, Provincial Council, or even synod until the eighteenth century, or even after the Restoration. Standardisation and equalisation of the diocesan and parochial territories and population had hardly been attempted. However, many dioceses had a much more effective organisational network from bishop to parishioner, whether to suppress the deviant, or help the faithful. Parochial organisation and control was basically strengthened, physical churches better kept by the seventeenth century, and a lot was done in the eighteenth. Whatever the vagaries of the educational institutions, and limitations of the seminaries, the clergy was better educated, and the parishioners more fully instructed, whether by parish clergy, confraternities, Religious Orders, or self-help printed material. Continuing or improving lay religious enthusiasm might be judged favourably, given the way churches and chapels were built or rebuilt in more lavish decorative ways in many parts of Italy, and the considerable number of new fraternity creations up to the Revolution, whether in Venice or Puglia. However, critics complained that the confraternity activity was detrimental to a cohesive parochial society, and was one reason that Grand Duke Peter Leopold of Tuscany abolished most of them in his Duchy in 1785.[2]

A more caring church and society emerged from late fifteenth century changes, seen in the outward-looking activities of lay confraternities, the work of Religious Orders, of parish poor relief policies, of hospitals and institutions for the vulnerable. These may count as success stories, even if punitive aspects (to save souls more than bodies), are not to modern taste. Some historical research indicates tendencies to divert much charity to the moderate poor rather than those in serious need, especially in conservatory institutions. Enlightenment critics attacked the religiously successful short-term charity of fraternities and hospitals, for being economically detrimental, by encouraging idleness; just as they saw the large monastic population as unproductive. The Grand Duke and his advisers again acted on this view.

Conflict between sixteenth century and modern mentalities particularly affect assessments of the Church's treatment of women and their religiosity. I view the comparatively successful (for Borromeo or Burali) strict enclosure of nuns, and the suppression of a 'third way', as ultimately detrimental to the Church as well as individuals. A wave of enthusiasm for an active Christian life for women was largely repressed. For some though, convent life could be rewarding, culturally exciting, spiritually moving, and socially fulfilling; but purgatory for many.

We talk of 'the Church', implying a coherent if not monolithic organisation with a clear doctrine. While a Pope like Paul IV might have desired that, it was never achieved. In the complex geography, socio-economic diversity, and political disunity of the Italian peninsula we encounter many 'churches' and societies. Some steps might have been made towards Paolo Prodi's new monarchy of the Papal Sovereign, based on the Inquisition, other Congregations, the centralising force of Jesuit discipline, and the common book of Tridentine legislation, to be interpreted by the Pope not a Council. In reality the papal monarchy, political and spiritual, could not be monolithic. Political monarchism, or absolutism, could hardly be enforced within the Papal State, let alone into other state areas, as the Venetian Interdict crisis showed. It was not just a matter centre against periphery, of getting papal Roman writs to run in Turin or Squillace. The 'Church' itself was made up of competing institutions and individuals, following different ideal 'models', or selfish interests. We have shifting conflicts, and changing alliances, between the episcopacy, Congregations, the Religious Orders at the higher levels; between parish priests, confraternities, monasteries, local hospitals at the lower. We are, therefore, as Simon Ditchfield stressed, 'in search of local knowledge'. We can pick a selection of local knowledges (in one sense of the phrase), and decide that Italy had produced an authoritarian confessional, disciplining society (in parts of Lombardy) – or a hardly changed violent, superstitious and chaotic one (as in areas of Friuli, Puglia or Calabria). That we know a certain amount about the latter implies, though, improved knowledge and concern from church leaders who investigate problems. It also makes Ditchfield's point about a 'reciprocal relationship with the centre', whether that centre was Rome, the archbishop in Naples, or the Inquisitor in Udine.[3]

Two more flavours of local history, from the mid- and late seventeenth century can illustrate some points above: from women on the streets (or canals), allegedly challenging ideas and speaking fearlessly; and an episcopal seat.

First in Venice. In June 1646 a certain Anzola Civrana was denounced; Venetian, aged about 50, living a dishonest life, possibly married to a second-hand clothes dealer, (*strazzarol*). She went about denying the immortality of the soul, the soul was a 'sporchezzo' (bit of dirt); and she claimed that learned and literate men agreed with her. One companion, Maddalena, refused to take sacraments, and was heard to attack St Francis who, she said, kept a prostitute from the age of 15. The case was not pursued by the tribunal.[4] In 1652 a certain Elisabetta was denounced. She was called a German, and probably came from Trieste. She ran a kind of hostelry, *locanda,* in S. Moise parish, to which many undesirable people came, foreigners but also more long-settled Venetians. She talked fluent Italian as well as German – could write at least in German. She did not observe fast days, and clearly encouraged others not to observe Lent; used magical practices, such as throwing the *cordella* for love magic, and suspiciously played around with statues, especially of St Anthony. In December 1652 a German prostitute called Julia was denounced, after a discussion about the Blessed Caietano. Drunk, but also when sober, she was the centre of lively discussions within the house and across balconies. She made fun of the saints, attacked the idea that pieces of canvas or wood could produce miracles. One should only approach God, not saints. One witness reported Julia discussing religious matters with her and other women, and citing Holy Scripture – Julia saying 'you others don't know what Sacred Scripture says the way I do'. Another witness declared she was ready to have Julia as godmother to her child – provided she reduced the drinking. The record, with a number of witnesses questioned, indicates several people were involved in the discussions – all women. Foreigners might be blamed for such evils – but Julia was fluent in Venetian and talking to a mixed group. The witnesses tend to suggest that they treat her as a mad drunk, and she only said the heretical things then – but one wonders! Again the Inquisition record indicates no follow-up after a few witness reports.[5]

Second we have a new 'model' bishop: Cardinal Gregorio Barbarigo. His devout Venetian father had been noted for charitable works, but initially as a fine civil law student he entered into diplomacy. Meeting in Münster the papal ambassador Fabio Chigi, who gave him a copy of Francis de Sales' *Introduction to the Devout Life*, he moved towards a religious career. Back in Venice he was influenced by several male and female 'spirituals', including Cecilia Ferrazzi. His parish priest urged him to become a secular priest rather than retreat into an Order, and thus he became (under the favour of Fabio Chigi, now Alexander VII), Bishop of Bergamo (1657–64), and Padua (1664–97). Synods, Visitations, correspondence with parish clergy, showed him as a very caring pastoral bishop; he maintained considerable scholarly interests, fostering Padua University and a seminary. He was involved in the printing of a translation of the Koran, was sympathetically concerned about relations with Jews, and with the problems, as noted before, of putative female 'living saints' like Cecilia Ferrazzi and Maria Janis. More than sixteenth-century 'models' like Borromeo, he seemed better aware of the highs and lows of female spirituality. His own very ascetic and moral private life was well noted at the time.[6]

The conflicts and tensions within the church system prevented the creation of an overweening church, left room for some dissent (if discreet), and debate. The diversity of forces within the church, clerical and lay, meant that when some cooperated, education was improved, philanthropy spread more widely, and religious culture became more exciting, varied and enticing. While Tridentine puritans, worried about lasciviousness, or lack of clarity in liturgy and teaching, would have been shocked by much seventeenth-century religious culture (as with paintings of St Agatha's martyrdom),[7] average parishioners might have been enthralled.

In the eighteenth century enlightened intellectuals attacked the role of the Church in state and society, helped get the Jesuits disbanded in 1773 (though the pressures for this were largely from outside Italy), undermined institutional expressions of Christian charity, and railed against the intellectual suffocation of censorship. But till their fall Jesuits were highly significant educators, including in training enlightened critics like Cesare Beccaria. Local congregations as well as Orders and bishops, embellished churches, promoted altars honouring saints, founded new confraternities. The Churches were still healthily popular in diverse ways, even if critics could rightly point to defects of organisation, corruption and immorality. Positive and negative verdicts, naturally, depended on who you were, and where.

Appendix: Italian Bishoprics[1]

(Continued)

Dioceses	*Status*[2]*: Independent (I), or Archdiocese (named)*	*State*[3]	*Bishops 1560–1630*	*Seminary founded*[4]	*Prov. Councils (PC); Synods*[5]
Acerenza and Matera	Acerenza and Matera	Naples	9	1673	1607
Acerno	Salerno	Naples	8		
Acerra	Naples	Naples	8	1652/54	1619
Acqui	Turin; or Milan?	Piedmont	4	1580	1624
Adria	Ravenna (seat at Rovigo)	Venice	5	1592	1564, 67, 69, 71, 75, 78, 83, 92, 94, 1627
Agrigento	Palermo	Sicily–Spain	12	1611	1589, 1610, 30
Ajaccio or Mariana	(in theory Pisa)	Genoa (Corsica)	5	1575	1569, 1617, 18, 57
Alatri	I	Papacy	7	1588	1585, 86, 1602, 08
Alba/Albi	Milan	Piedmont	10	1566	1562, 94
Albano	Cardinalate See	Papacy	32	1628	1590, 1641
Albenga	Genoa	Genoa	7		1571, 83, 1613, 18, 23, 29
Aleria	(in theory Pisa?)	Genoa (Corsica)	7		1571
Ales and Terralba	Oristano	Sardinia	10		1564, 66
Alessandria	Milan	Piedmont	7	1566	1602, 05, 06, 07, 08, 13, 17
Alessano	Otranto	Naples	10		1587
Alghero	Sassari	Sardinia	9	1603	1567–70(1), 72, 81, 85
Alife	Benevento	Naples	8	1651	

Amalfi	Amalfi	Naples	9	1635–48	1594 PC 1597
Amelia or Amerino	I	Papacy	8	1788	1595
Anagni	I	Papacy	6		1596
Ancona	I	Papacy	5	1556?	1654
Andria	Trani	Naples	7		1582
Anglona and Tursi	Acerenza-Matera	Naples	8		1656
Aosta	Tarantaise (French Archbishopric)	Piedmont	8	1565	1835
Aquileia[6]	Aquileia	Venice	9	1604	PC 1596 1565, 95, 1600, 02, 05
Aquino	I	Naples	5		1581
Arezzo	I	Tuscany	4	1641	1597, 1714
Ariano	Benevento	Naples	7	1565	1714
Ascoli Piceno	I	Papacy	5	1568	1568, 71, 72, 91, 96, 1626
Ascoli (Sariano)	Benevento	Naples	7		1692
Assisi	I	Papacy	6	1574	1565
Asti	Milan	Piedmont	7		1565, 78, 84, 88, 91, 93, 97, 1601, 05, 06, 20, 27, 28
Avellino	Benevento	Naples	6	1567	1654, 1748
Aversa	I	Papacy	6	1566	1594, 1619
Bagnoregio	I	Papacy	8	1636	1573, 99, 1615, 29
Bari	Bari	Naples	7	1612	1594, 1607, 24
Belcastro	Santa Severina	Naples	12		
Belluno	Aquileia	Venice	4	1568	1629
Benevento	Benevento	Papacy[7]	4	1567	PC 1567, 71, 99 1567, 94

(Continued)

Dioceses	*Status*[2]*: Independent (I), or Archdiocese (named)*	*State*[3]	*Bishops 1560–1630*	*Seminary founded*[4]	*Prov. Councils (PC); Synods*[5]
Bergamo	Milan	Venice	7	1567	1564, 68, 74, 83, 1603, 13, 28
Bertinoro	Ravenna	Papacy	6	1708	1750
Bisceglie	Trani	Naples	8		1692
Bisignano	Rossano	Naples	14	Pre 1594	1571, 89, 1604, 16, 27, 30
Bitetto	Bari	Naples	7		
Bitonto	Bari	Naples	6		
Bobbio	Genoa	Piedmont	6	1603	1565, 74, 1603, 06, 09, 10, 21, 25
Boiano and Campobasso	Benevento	Naples	6	Pre 1627; 1690	1784
Borgo San Sepolcro	Florence	Tuscany	5		1641
Bologna	I, 1518–82; then metropolitan	Papacy	7	1567	Annually 1566–91 (except 67, 86), 94?, 95, 1620, 23, 30 PC: 1586
Bosa	Sassari	Sardinia	14		1591
Bova	Reggio Calabria	Naples	7	1622/65	
Bovino	Benevento	Naples	5		1578, 1838
Brescia	Milan	Venice	4	1568	1564, 74/75, 83, 1603, 13, 28
Bressanone[8]	Salzburg	Empire		1609	1603
Brindisi	Brindisi	Naples	6	1608	1605–14(2), 13, 14, 15, 16, 17, 18, 19, 21, 22
Brugnato	Genoa	Genoa	8		1581, 1625

Cagli	Urbino	Papacy	7	1654	1708
Cagliari	Cagliari	Sardinia	8	1576; 1622	1576, 1628
Caiazzo	Capua	Naples	5	1564	1681
Calvi	Capua	Naples	8		1588
Camerino	I	Papacy	9	1564–65 1597	1571, 87, 97, 98, 1630
Campagna and Satriano	Conza	Naples	7		1827
Caorle	Venice	Venice	7		
Capaccio	Salerno	Naples	6	?, 1586–90?	1 pre 1574, 83, 93, 1617, 29
Capo d'Istria (Koper)	Aquileia	Venice	6		1637
Capri	Amalfi	Naples	5		
Capua	Capua	Naples	7	1567	PC 1569, 77, 1603, 1726
Cariati and Cerenza	Santa Severina	Naples	11	*c.*1621 Verzino; to Cariati 1635	1594, 1621?, 1641, 1652
Carinola	Capua	Naples	9	1627	1726
Casale Monferrato	Milan	Piedmont	10	1566	1597, 1622
Caserta	Capua	Naples	6	1580	1560–63(1), 1745
Cassano all'Ionio	Reggio Calabria. I, from 1597	Naples	9	1588	1581, 89, 1604, 12
Castellamare	Sorrento	Naples	8		

(Continued)

Dioceses	*Status*[2]: *Independent (I), or Archdiocese (named)*	*State*[3]	*Bishops 1560–1630*	*Seminary founded*[4]	*Prov. Councils (PC); Synods*[5]
Castellaneta	Taranto	Naples	5		1590, 95, 1600
Castro	Otranto	Naples	9		1656
Castro	I, Suppressed 1649 (Aquapendente now)	Papacy Umbria	9		1632?
Cattaro (Kotor)	Bari	Venice Dalmatia	8		
Catania	I, From 1609 Monreale	Sicily	10	1572	1564, 90, 1609, 15, 22, 23
Catanzaro	Reggio Calabria	Naples	7	?; failed by 1592;	1587–1617 annually?, 1634/36, 1677
Cava dei Terreni	I, or Benedictine Order	Naples	7	1592	1638
Cefalù	Messina	Sicily–Spain	9	1590	1584, 1618, 27
Ceneda (now Vittorio Veneto)	Aquileia	Venice	5	1587	1565, 70, 1628, 42
Cephalonia-Zante	I, and Venice contesting	Venice	6		
Cervia	Ravenna, but Bologna 1582–1604	Papacy	8	*c.*1590;[9] 1827	1577?

Cesena	I; 1623 under Ravenna	Papacy	6	1569	1564.66, 73, 74, 82, 90
Chieti	Chieti	Naples	12	1568	1635, 1616
Chioggia	Venice	Venice	12	1580	1603, 16
Chiusi and Pienza	I; under Siena by 1620	Tuscany	6	1656	1583
Città delle Pieve.	I; created 1600 out of Chiusi	Papacy	3	1605	1654
Città di Castello	I	Papacy	8	1638	1674
Città Ducale	I	Naples	7	1658	
Città Nova	Aquileia	Venice Istria	7	1644	
Civita Castellana and Orte	I	Papacy	5		1626, 29
Colle di Val d'Elsa	Florence Created 1592	Tuscany	2	1615	1594
Comacchio	Ravenna	Venice	6	1779	1579
Como	Aquileia	Venice	6	?; 1646	1564, 79, 98, 1618, 33
Concordia	Aquileia	Venice	4	1603	1587
Conversano	Bari	Naples	7		1660
Conza	Conza	Naples	9		1584, 97, 1647
Corfu	I	Venice Island	6		
Cortona	I	Tuscany	9	1573	1588, 1615, 24
Corzola[10] Korčula	Durazzo; then Ragusa	Venice Dalmatia	6		
Cosenza	Cosenza	Naples	11	1566; 1590	1603, 12 PC 1579, 96[11]

(Continued)

Dioceses	*Status[2]: Independent (I), or Archdiocese (named)*	*State[3]*	*Bishops 1560–1630*	*Seminary founded[4]*	*Prov. Councils (PC); Synods[5]*
Crema	Created 1580 under Milan; 1612 Bologna	Lombardy	4	1583	1583, 86, 90, 91/95, 96, 1600, 03, 08, 19, 26
Cremona	Milan	Lombardy	6	1565	1564, 99, 1603
Crotone	Reggio Calabria	Naples	12		
Faenza	I	Papacy	9	1576	1565, 69–80(10, incl.69, 74), 1615, 20, 29
Fano	I	Papacy	6	1569	1593, 1613
Feltre	Aquileia	Venice	4	1594?	1668
Ferentino	I	Papacy	6	1677	1605
Fermo	I Metropolitan 1589	Papacy	8	?1564, but by 1574	1628, 50 PC 1590
Ferrara	I	Papacy[12]	6	1584	1592
Fidenza (Borgo S.Donnino) Created 1601	I, later Bologna control?	Parma-Piacenza	4	1624	1584, 1608, 15, 24
Fiesole	Florence	Tuscany	7	1636	1564, 85, 1612, 22
Florence	Florence	Tuscany	4	Early 1700s	1569, 89, 1603, 10, 19, 23, 27, 29
Foligno	I	Papacy	10	1648/49	1571
Fondi	I	Naples	6	1596	1605

Forlì	I	Papacy	8	1659	1564, 1610, 28
Fossano	Turin. Created 1592	Piedmont	5	1608	1595
Fossombrone	Urbino	Papacy	7	1581	1629
Frascati and Tuscolo	Cardinalate See	Papacy	31	1652	1669
Gaeta	I	Naples	5	1563; 1613	1779
Gallese	I, 1563–69. Added to Città di Castello	Papacy	2		
Gallipoli	Otranto	Naples	5	1624	1661
Genoa	Genoa	Genoa	7	1657	1586, 88, 96, 1603, 04, 19 PC *c.*1574
Gerace-Locri	Reggio Calabria	Naples	8	1565	1593, 1651
Giovinazzo	Bari	Naples	6		1679
Gravina	Acerenza-Matera	Naples	10		
Grosseto	I	Papacy	6		
Guardalfiera	Benevento	Naples	10		1692
Gubbio	I	Papacy	5	1601	1632
Iesi	I	Papacy	6	1564	1600, 26
Imola	Ravenna; but Bologna 1582–04	Papacy	8	1567	1572, 74, 77, 79, 84, 92, 99, 1604, 22, 24, 28
Ischia	Naples	Naples	3	1756	1599
Isola	Santa Severina	Naples	8		
Isernia	Capua	Naples	7	?, closed by early 1600s	1693

(Continued)

Dioceses	*Status*[2]*: Independent (I), or Archdiocese (named)*	*State*[3]	*Bishops 1560–1630*	*Seminary founded*[4]	*Prov. Councils (PC); Synods*[5]
Ivrea	Turin	Piedmont	4	1565	1584, 88, 89, 90, 92, 98, 1601, 02, 05, 18,22
Lacedogna	Conza	Naples	7		
Lanciano	I	Naples	8	1610	1878
L'Aquila	I	Papacy	8	1567; 1601	1581
Larino	Benevento	Naples	5	1564/66; 1694	1663
Lavello	Bari	Naples	11		
Lecce	Otranto	Naples	3		1663
Lesina	Benevento. Suppressed 1567	Naples	1		
Lessina (Hvar)	Spalato	Venice Dalmatia	3		
Lettere	Amalfi	Naples	10		
Lipari	Messina	Sicily–Spain Island	9		
Lodi	Milan	Lombardy	6	1574	1574, 91, 1619
Lucca	I	Lucca	2	1574; 1637	1564, 66, 70, 71, 74, 79, 90, 93, 1625
Lucera	Benevento	Naples	7		1875

Luni-Sarzana	I	Genoa	5	1591	1568, 82, 91, 95, 1616
Macerata United with Recanati 1571[13]	I; under Fermo 1589	Papacy	3	1615	1651
Mantua	Aquileia	Mantua	8	1594	1564, 67, 77, 85, 88, 91, 94, 95, 98, 1600, 04 ,07, 10, 12, 16
Marsi	I	Naples	6	1563, and *c.*1590 in Pescina	1612, 25, 53
Marsico Nuovo		Naples			1643
Martorano	Cosenza	Naples	8		
Massalubrese	Sorrento	Naples	7		1627
Massa Marittima	Pisa	Tuscany	9		1586
Mazara del Vallo	Palermo	Sicily–Spain	9	1579	1575, 84, 1609, 23
Melfi and Rapallo	I	Naples	9	Early 1600s; 1665	1574–90(1), 98, 1624
Messina	Messina	Sicily–Spain	10	1573	1588, 1621
Milan	Milan	Lombardy	3	Four: 1564, 68, 79, 1630	PC 1565, 69, 73, 76, 82, 1609 24 Synods 1564–1611
Mileto	I	Naples	7	1592; 1640	1587, 91, 94
Minervino	Bari	Naples	4		
Modena	Ravenna	Modena	8	1566	1565, 72, 75, 94, 12, 15, 17, 24
Molfetta	I	Naples	5		1726

(Continued)

Dioceses	*Status*[2]: *Independent (I), or Archdiocese (named)*	*State*[3]	*Bishops 1560–1630*	*Seminary founded*[4]	*Prov. Councils (PC); Synods*[5]
Mondovì	Turin	Piedmont	5	1573	1573, 92, and 1 other 90/1601
Monopoli	I	Naples	7	1668	1585
Monreale	Monreale	Sicily–Spain	5	1590	1554, 69, 75, 93, 97, 1622
Montalcino	I; separated from Pienza 1599	Tuscany	3		1613, 18, 48
Montalto	Created 1586. Fermo	Papacy	3	1652	1630
Montefeltro	Urbino	Papacy	5	1570	1592, 1601/05(1), 02/6(1), 08, 11, 14
Montefiascone	I	Papacy	8	1666	1591, 1622
Montemarrano	Benevento	Naples	5		1727
Montepeloso	Trani	Naples	12		
Montepulciano	I	Tuscany	6	1561	1642
Motula	Taranto	Naples	8		
Muro Lucano	Conza	Naples	9	1565	1728
Naples	Naples	Naples	8	1568	1564, 65, 67, 71, 95, 07 PC 1576
Nardò	I	Naples	7	1674	1583–95(1), 1619, 74
Naxos and Paros	Naxos and Paros Greek islands[14]	Venice	8		
Nebbio	Genoa	Genoa Corsica	19		1614
Nepi and Sutri	I	Papacy	11		

Narni	I	Papacy	5	1660	1567, 1625
Nicastro	Reggio Calabria	Naples	8	*c.*1570	1858
Nicotera	Reggio Calabria	Naples	5	1655	1578–82(1), 82–88(2), 90–92(1), 1705
Nocera de'Pagani	Salerno	Naples	6	1694	1608
Nocera Umbra	I	Papacy	3	1569	1606, 5 more before 1630
Nola	Naples	Naples	4	1568	1588, 94
Noli	Genoa	Genoa	4		1692
Nona	Spalato	Venice Dalmatia	6		1598
Novara	Milan	Lombardy	12	3:1565/66; 1573; 81	1568, 76, 90
Nusco	Salerno	Naples	7		1748
Oppido Mamertina	Reggio Calabria	Naples	8	1699	1671, 99
Oria	Taranto. Separated from Brindisi 1591	Naples	3		1641
Oristano	Oristano	Sardinia	8		PC 1566 1646
Ortona Created 1570	Chieti. Campli added 1588[15]	Naples	3		1878
Orvieto	I	Papacy	5	1566–71; 1614–21[16]	1564, 68, 90, 92, 1627
Osimo	I	Papacy	5	1564	1564, 66, 76, 93, 94
Ossero	Zara	Venice Dalmatia	4		1660
Ostuni	Brindisi	Naples	6		1586
Otranto	Otranto	Naples	5		PC 1567 1641

(Continued)

Dioceses	*Status[2]: Independent (I), or Archdiocese (named)*	*State[3]*	*Bishops 1560–1630*	*Seminary founded[4]*	*Prov. Councils (PC); Synods[5]*
Padua	Aquileia	Venice	7	1570/71; 1670	1564, 66, 79, 1624
Palermo	Palermo	Sicily–Spain	7	1583–91	1555, 60, 64, 86, 1615, 22, 34
Palestrina	Cardinalate see	Papacy	34	1616	1592
Parenzo	Aquileia	Venice	4		1650
Parma	Ravenna	Parma-Piacenza	6	1564/66	1564, 75, 81, 83, 1602, 21
Patti	Messina	Sicily–Spain	6	1610	1567, 84
Pavia	I	Lombardy	7	1564	1566, 71, 1612
Pedena or Piben	Aquileia	Venice Istria	5		
Penne-Atri	I	Naples	7	? till 1570; early 1600s[17]	1681
Perugia	I	Papacy	8	1559[18]	1564, 67, 75, 82, 1606, 15, 18, 21, 32
Pesaro	Urbino	Papacy	6	1575	1560/76, 80
Piacenza	I, claimed by Milan; Bologna after 1582	Parma-Piacenza	7	1568/69	1570, 74, 89, 99, 1610, 22

Pienza and Montalcino	I, joint 1563–99	Tuscany	1 joint. ? Pienza		
Pisa	Pisa	Tuscany	12	1552;[19] 1627	1582, 1615, 16, 24
Pistoia	I; 1599 under Florence. Prato joins as co-bishopric 1653 with Cathedral status	Tuscany	7	1682 Prato; 1693 Pistoia	1565, 86, 1604, 25
Pola	Aquileia	Venice Istria	8		
Policastro	Salerno	Naples	7	1625	1582/05(1+?), 1610/29(1), 1632
Polignano	Bari	Naples	8		
Pontecorvo, 1565	Separated from Sora 1565	Naples		(1565, in Sora); 1625	1632
Porto	Cardinalate See	Papacy	28		
Potenza	Acerenza-Matera	Naples	7		1581, 1606
Pozzuoli	Naples	Naples	4	1587–1624–50; 1708–11; 1740–	1602.04
Ragusa[20]	Ragusa Modern Dubrovnik	Ragusa	10	Pre 1616	
Ravello	I	Naples	7		

(Continued)

Dioceses	*Status*[2]*: Independent (I), or Archdiocese (named)*	*State*[3]	*Bishops 1560–1630*	*Seminary founded*[4]	*Prov. Councils (PC); Synods*[5]
Ravenna	Ravenna	Papacy	5	1567	PC 1568, 82 1564, 67, 70, 71, 80, 83, 93, 99, 1607, 09,13, 17, 27, 40
Recanati-Loreto[21]	I, united with Macerata 1571	Papacy	4	1571	1572, 83, 88, 92, 1609, 23, 26
Reggio Calabria	Reggio Calabria	Naples	2	1567	1565–92 annually; 1595–1636 (17), 1663 PC 1565, 74, 80, 1602
Reggio Emilia	Ravenna	Modena	9	1614–48[22]	1581, 89, 95, 97, 1613, 14, 27
Rieti	I	Papacy	10	1564	1645
Rimini	I; Ravenna from 1604	Papacy	7	1568	1577, 78, 80, 93, 96, 1602, 24, 30
Ripatransone	Created 1571. Fermo	Papacy	8	Post 1623	1576, 84
Rome	Pope as Bishop	Papacy	12	1565	
Rossano	Rossano	Naples	11	1563; 1594	1574, 94
Ruvo	Bari	Naples	5		
Sabina	Cardinalate See	Papacy	40	1593	1590, 92, 93, 94, 97

Sagona	I. (in theory Pisa?)	Genoa Corsica	7		1574, 1585–1606 (exact nos. unclear)
Salerno	Salerno	Naples	9	1564/65	1557, 64, 65, 67, 79, 88, 1615, 30 PC 1566, 79, 96, 1615
Saluzzo	I	Piedmont		?; 1629	1585
S. Angelo dei Lombardi and Bisaccia	Conza	Naples	8		1623
San Leone	San Severina. Suppressed 1571	Naples	2		
San Marco	Rossano	Naples	19	1580	1723
San Severi, Sanseverino	1586–89 and 1646– under Fermo; in between part of Fermo	Papacy	3		
San Miniato	Florence. Created 1622 out of Lucca	Tuscany	1	1650	1638
San Severo	Benevento; seat moved here from Civita 1572, changing name	Naples	9	1678	1681
Sant'Agata dei Goti	Benevento	Naples	8	1566–70	1585, 87, 1621
Santa Severina	Santa Severina	Naples	5	1566/72; 1581	1566–72 (several), 73, 76, 1688 PC 1597
Sarno	Salerno	Naples	7		1677
Sarsina	Ravenna	Papacy	3	1643	1575, 86?

(Continued)

Dioceses	*Status*[2]*: Independent (I), or Archdiocese (named)*	*State*[3]	*Bishops 1560–1630*	*Seminary founded*[4]	*Prov. Councils (PC); Synods*[5]
Sassari	Sassari	Sardinia	8	1568	PC 1606 1555, 1625
Savona	Genoa/Milan contested	Genoa	7	1568	1586, 89, 92, 97, 1603, 21, 27
Sebenico (Šibenik)	Spalato	Venice Dalmatia	6		1564, 1602, 04, 11, 14, 18, 23, 26
Segni	I	Papacy	6		1710
Senigallia	Urbino	Papacy	7	1574/77	1591, 1627
Sessa Aurunca	Capua	Naples	6	*c.*1606	
Siena	Siena	Tuscany	7	?1614	PC 1599 1705
Siponto	Siponto-Manfredonia	Naples	10		PC 1567
Sora	I	Naples	9	1565	1611
Sorrento	Sorrento	Naples	7	1681	1585, 1627 PC 1567, 72, 84
Sovana	I; ? then Siena	Tuscany	4		1626
Spalato	Spalato modern Split	Venice Dalmatia	5		1688
Spoleto	I	Papacy	7	1604	1564, 83, 84, 1621
Squillace	Reggio Calabria	Naples	6	1565	1600, 74
Strongoli	Santa Severina	Naples	12		1593, 95, 97

Suda	Naxos and Paros (see earlier)	Venice	6		
Syracuse	Monreale	Sicily–Spain	8	1567?	1553, 67, 87, 94, 1623, 32
Taranto	Taranto	Naples	10	1568	1614
Teano	Capua	Naples	9	1576	1588, 1690
Telese or Cerreto	Benevento	Naples	10	1593	1687
Tempio and Ampurias	Sassari	Sardinia	8		1695
Teramo	I	Naples	4	?; 1674	1681
Termoli	Benevento	Naples	10	Early 1600s	
Terni	I	Papacy	9	1653	1567, 92/09(1)
Terracina (later Sezze)	I	Papacy	7	1650	1784
Tivoli	I	Papacy	6	?1635	1636
Todi	I	Papacy	4	1608	1568, 76
Torcello	Venice	Venice	7		1582, 92, 94, 1628
Tortona	Milan	Piedmont	4	1565	1595, 1614, 23
Trani	Trani	Naples	7	1627	1589
Trau/Tragir	Spalato	Venice	6		
Trento	Aquileia	Empire	4	1593	1593
Trevico	Benevento	Naples	8		1703
Treviso	Aquileia	Venice	5	?1564	1565, 70, 81, 92, 1604, 19
Tricarico	Acerenza-Matera	Naples	7		1800
Trieste	Aquileia	Venice	8		
Trivento	Benevento	Naples	6	1575	1721
Troia	I	Naples	8		1735

(Continued)

Dioceses	*Status*[2]*: Independent (I), or Archdiocese (named)*	*State*[3]	*Bishops 1560–1630*	*Seminary founded*[4]	*Prov. Councils (PC); Synods*[5]
Tropea	Reggio Calabria	Naples	6	1593/94; 1615	1586/87, 92, 94, 98, 1618
Turin	Turin	Piedmont	6	1566	1547, 65, 75, 96, 1606, 10, 14, 24
Ugento	Otranto	Naples	7		1720
Umbriatico	Santa Severina	Naples	8	1609	1590s–1610s[23], 1597, 1618, 30
Urbino	Metropolitan from 1563	Urbino; Papacy	6	1574	1570, 1628 PC 1590
Valva and Sulmona	I	Papacy	5	1629	1603, 29
Velletri and Ostia	Titular Cardinal	Papacy	18	1570	1673
Venafro	Capua	Naples	4		1634
Venice	Venice	Venice	5	1581	1564, 68, 70–71, 78, 92, 93, 94, 1612
Venosa	Acerenza-Matera	Naples	12		1589, 1614
Ventimiglia	Milan	Piedmont	10		1608

Vercelli	Milan	Piedmont	8	1566	1572, 73–84 annually, 1600
Verona	Aquileia	1567	5	1567	1566, 1629
Veroli	I	Papacy	8	1611	1568–92(2), 1595–98(2), 1626–28(1), 1665
Vicenza	Aquileia	Venice	8	1566	1565, 66, 73, 83, 87, 91, 97, 99, 1611, 23
Vico Equense	Sorrento	Naples	7		
Viesti	Siponto-Manfredonia	Naples	9		1699
Vigevano	Milan	Piedmont	7		1572, 78, 87, 1608
Viterbo	I	Papacy	6	1637	1564, 68, 73, 84, 1614, 24
Volterra	I	Tuscany	7	1590	1590, 1624
Volturara and Montecorvino	Benevento	Naples	10		1631
Zara	Zara; but some Verona influence	Venice Dalmatia	10		

Notes

1 Religious Crises and Challenges in Early Sixteenth Century Italy

1. My *Early Modern Italy*, ch. 1 for an overview; Hay and Law, *Italy… 1380–1530.*
2. Setton, *Papacy and the Levant,* III, 404 (quote), 554–6; IV, 581–4. Setton's massively documented work highlights the interaction of the religious and the imperial power struggles.
3. Chastel, *Sack of Rome.*
4. Fletcher and Shaw (eds) *World of Savonarola.*
5. Caponetto, *The Protestant Reformation*; the translators started with the original 1992 edition, but (possibly rather hurriedly) sought then to incorporate additions from the 1997 second Italian edition. Silvana Seidel Menchi's 'Italy', and John Martin's 'Religion, Renewal', provide very valuable clear surveys; David Peterson, 'Out of the Margins', full bibliography. The classic work of Delio Cantimori (1939/67), *Eretici Italiani del Cinquecento,* concentrated most on the impact of those who went into exile.
6. Silvana Seidel Menchi, 'Italy', esp. 181–4.
7. Caponetto, *Protestant Reformation,* esp. 52.
8. John Martin, *Venice's Hidden Enemies.*
9. Fragnito, *La Bibbia al rogo.*
10. Seidel Menchi, 'Italy', 193; Carlo Ginzburg, *Nicodemismo.*
11. Caponetto, *Protestant Reformation,* quoted at 66; for a list of those Italians seen by him as most influenced by Valdes, 67; Massimo Firpo, 'Italian Reformation … Valdes'.
12. Mayer, *Reginald Pole,* esp. 79, 105, 190, 450–1.
13. Seidel Menchi, 'Italy', 186.
14. Setton, *The Papacy and the Levant.*
15. Seidel Menchi, 'Italy', 187.
16. Caponetto, *Protestant Reformation*, 23.
17. Caponetto, *Protestant Reformation,* 19.

18. Grendler, 'Religious Restlessness', and 'Utopia'; on Aretino's less-known religious writings, Cairns, *Pietro Aretino*; Ugo Rozzo, 'Italian Literature on the Index', 216–18.
19. Caponetto, *Protestant Reformation*, 70–3, 76–93. 'The "Beneficio di Cristo" ', translated, with an introduction by Ruth Prelowski, in Tedeschi (ed.), *Italian Reformation Studies*, 21–102 .
20. Prosperi, *Tribunali*, 22–3.
21. Caponetto, *Protestant Reformation*, 67–9, 348–9.
22. Caponetto, *Protestant Reformation*, 96–100 on the 'Ecclesia Viterbiensis' and its impact. See Dermot Fenlon, *Heresy and Obedience*, ch. 6; Thomas Mayer, *Reginald Pole*, ch. 3.
23. Caponetto, *Protestant Reformation*, 100–3, 109, 45 (quote), 49–50, 142–56.
24. Caponetto, *Protestant Reformation*, 275–87; Berengo, *Nobili e mercanti*, esp. 359ff; Prosperi, *Tribunali della coscienza*, 551–3, 573–4.
25. Hewlett, 'A Republic in Jeopardy', 14–19, quote p. 16.
26. Caponetto, *Protestant Reformation*, 56–7.
27. Caponetto, *Protestant Reformation*, 208–12, quotations from 211, 239–40 (on Siculo); Carlo Ginzburg, *Il nicodemismo*, 170–81; Delio Cantimori, *Eretici Italiani*, 53–6.
28. Seidel Menchi, 'Italy', 187; John Martin, *Venice's Hidden Enemies*, esp. 150–1, 235–43.
29. Seidel Menchi, 'Italy', 191–2.
30. Del Col, 'La confessione', with the confession pp. 128–35; see also Del Col *L'Inquisizione nel Patriarchato*, esp. LXXXVII–CIX on range of investigations in diocese of Feltre, CIV–CV on Strigno visit.
31. Del Col, 'La confessione', 127.
32. Kuntz, 'Voices from a Venetian prison', and 'Profezia e politica'.
33. Kuntz, 'Dionisio Gallo', 173. Caponetto, *Protestant Reformation*, 178–9 on Ugoni.

2 The Council of Trent and Bases for Continuing Reform

1. Modern edition of published decrees: Alberigo, J. (Giuseppe) *et al. Conciliorum Oecumenicorum Decreta* (1973 edn used; cited as *COD*); much more documentation behind this council work in *Concilium Tridentinum* (1901–38) (cited as *CT*); translations from *Canons and Decrees*, ed. Schroeder. The chief modern historian has been Hubert Jedin; his massive *Das Konzil von Trient* (4 vols, Rome, 1948) had only its first two volumes translated, *A History of the Council of Trent* (1957–61); for our purposes much more relevant, and readable is his *Crisis and Closure* (1967). Quicker digests include: Marc Venard's 'Trent, Council of', in P. Levillain (ed.) *The Papacy*, 1517–23; H. Jedin (ed.) *History of the Church*, vol. V, chs 35 and 37; Mullett, *Catholic Reformation*, ch. 2.
2. Jedin (ed.) *History of the Church*, vol. V, 465–6, 476–7, 496 (for attendance); same, *Closure*, 80–1.

3. Jedin, *Crisis and Closure*, 173.
4. Duval, 'L'Extrême-onction', and 'Confession'. Jedin, 'Confession'.
5. Jedin (ed.), *History of the Church*, V, ch. 37; Jedin, *Closure*, 90–1, 110–11; Alberigo in *Il Concilio* (1965), 491, 522; Cozzi, 'Domenico Bollani', esp. 567–70 on divided Venetian views.
6. Alberigo, 'Potestà episcopali', 522.
7. *Canons and Decrees*, ed. Schroeder, 34–5; Mullett, *Catholic Reformation*, 44.
8. Küng, *The Council and Reunion*, 112.
9. *Canons and Decrees*, ed. Schroeder, 75; Mullett, *Catholic Reform*, 48.
10. Jedin, *Crisis and Closure*, is best single study both of the final stage, and digesting his overall views.
11. Mullett, *Catholic Reformation*, 55.
12. Mullett, *Catholic Reformation*, 60 quoting Trent texts.
13. Zarri, 'Il Matrimonio tridentino', esp. 444–51.
14. *Canons and Decrees*, ed. Schroeder, 180–90.
15. Zarri, 'Il matrimonio', esp. 481–3; Mullett, *Catholic Reformation*, 65; my *Early Modern Italy*, 111–15, 177–9.
16. Alberigo, 'Potestà episcopali'; CT IX, 49, 147, 179, 218, 588, 620–2 for main debating points; *Canons and Decrees*, ed. Schroeder, 161–3, for Session 23, Cap. IV, esp. canons 6–7, as anathemas.
17. Paolo Sarpi, *Istoria del Concilio Tridentino*, ed. C. Vivanti.
18. Jedin, *Chiesa della fede*, 288–9.
19. *Canons and Decrees*, ed. Schroeder, 192–3.
20. De Boer, *The Conquest*, 66–7; CT 9, 795–879 (discussion), 982 (article), 1100–1 (Ragazzoni).
21. Barletta , *Aspetti della Riforma*, 140; Rasi, 'L'applicazione.', 236–7.
22. Trisco, 'Borromeo ... and Trent', 63.
23. 'Diary of Giambattista Casale', in Cochrane and Kirshner (eds) *Readings*, 412–13.
24. Hufton, 'The Widow's Mite', and The Wiles Lectures, Queen's University, Belfast, May 1999.
25. Black, 'Perugia and church reform'.
26. Küng, *Council*, 114.
27. Caponetto, *Protestant Reformation*, 258–9; *Il Sommario*, ed. Bianco, Figs 7 and 8 which reproduce admissions from Tamburino and Maranello's *processi.*

3 Centre and Peripheries: The Papacy, Congregations, Religious Orders

1. Wright, *The Early Modern Papacy* is an indispensable guide; Kelly, *Oxford Dictionary of the Popes* for succinct biographies; Hudon, 'The Papacy in the Age of Reform'.
2. My 'Perugia and Papal Absolutism'.
3. Prodi, *Il sovrano*, and translation *The Papal Prince*; Prodi, 'Il "sovrano pontefice" '; Prosperi, *Il Tribunale*; A.D. Wright *The Early Modern Papacy*,

esp. 1–14, 271–2 summaries of rival views, and his. Krautheimer, *Rome of Alexander VII.*

4. L.von Pastor's monumental *History of the Popes* devoted much space to conclaves.
5. Wright, *Papacy*, 48; Pullapilly, *Caesar Baronius.*
6. Wright, *Papacy*, 53.
7. Hudon, *Marcello Cervini*, esp. 172–3, and his 'The Papacy', 53–6.
8. Wright, *Papacy*, 68–81; uses: Broderick, 'The Sacred College'.
9. Po-Chia Hsia (1998), *Catholic Renewal*, 98.
10. Reinhardt, *Kardinal Scipione Borghese.*
11. Hammond, *Music and Spectacle.*
12. Reinhardt, *Scipione Borghese*, 97–8.
13. Duffy, *Saints and Sinners*, 188.
14. Prodi, *Paleotti*, vol. 2, 425–526; see Wright, *Papacy*, 72–5.
15. Prodi, *Il sovrano pontefice*, 186 (my translation from Latin).
16. Tomaro, 'Implementation', 75–6; Agostino Borromeo, 'Vescovi Italiani', 30–31.
17. Niccoli. *Vita Religiosa*, 128–9, for 1605.
18. Wright, *Papacy*, 235; see also Peter Partner, 'Papal Financial Policy'.
19. Antonovicz, 'Counter-Reformation Cardinals'; Evennett, *Spirit of the Counter-Reformation.*
20. Wright, *Papacy*, 81–3.
21. Wright, *Papacy*, 68–9.
22. Molinari, *Card. Teatino Beato Paolo Burali, and Epistolario del Beato Paolo Burali.*
23. Mullett, *Catholic Reformation*, 143–4.
24. Parisella, ' "Liber Litterarum" '.
25. Tomaro, 'Implementation', 76–7, and 83, n. 47 (my trans.).
26. Lefevbre, 'Congregation du Concile'. See *Canons and Decrees*, ed. Schroeder, 183–5.
27. A. Stella, *Chiesa e Stato*; Chambers and Pullan (eds) *Venice*, translates extracts from Bolognetti's reports, 206–8, 223–4, 236–7; Paul Grendler, *Roman Inquisition*, 269–70.
28. Fragnito, 'Vescovi e Ordini Religiosi', 14; Borromeo, 'Vescovi italiani', 33–4.
29. AdS Perugia, Editti e Bandi 8 fols. 292–3; my 'Papal Absolutism', 521, 535.
30. Chambers and Pullan (eds), *Venice*, 225–7, extracts from case made to Cardinals for Interdict. See William Bouwsma, *Venice and the Defense of Republican Liberty*, 342–50.
31. Bouwsma's *Venice* digests much of the debate.
32. Cited Wills, *Venice: Lion City*, 348, from 341–55 on crisis.
33. Hillerbrand (ed.), *Oxford Encyclopedia*, vol. 2. 'Inquisition', 317–19, and 'Index of Prohibited Books', 313–14; Grendler, *Roman Inquisition*, esp. ch. II, in Venetian context; *L'Inquisizione Romana in Italia nell'età moderna* has various valuable essays; R. Canosa, *Storia dell'inquisizione*, vol. V, 209–46 on procedures.
34. Prosperi, *Tribunali*, 38; his chs ii and iii, as a key study of foundation and spread of tribunals.
35. Setton, *Papacy and the Levant*, 627.

36. Grendler, *Roman Inquisition,* 35–42; Del Col, *L'Inquisizione nel patriarchato,* esp. XXII–XXVII.
37. Davidson, 'Rome and the Venetian Inquisition'.
38. Eliseo Masini, *Sacro arsenale, overo prattica dell'Officio della Santa Inquisizione,* Genoa 1621; modern edition *Il manuale degli inquisitori,* Milan, 1990. See Tedeschi, *Prosecution of Heresy,* esp. Essay 6, 'The Organization and Procedures', and 7, 'The Roman Inquisition and witchcraft ... an "Instruction" on correct trial procedure'.
39. Dall'Olio, 'I Rapporti'.
40. Ginzburg, *Cheese and Worms,* esp. 127–9; A. Del Col, *Domenico Scandella,* 156–65, quoting 165.
41. Dall'Olio, 'I Rapporti', esp. 258–60.
42. Dall'Olio, 'I Rapporti', 249–50. Evidence from Ermenegildo Todeschini *Cathologus inquisitorum* (1723), and his ms in Archivio di San Domenico, Bologna ms I.17500, based on what districts reported to the Holy Office in 1707.
43. Dall'Olio, 'I Rapporti', 255 n. 24; AAF, S. Uffizio, Filze 2–3 (1608–1775).
44. Mullett, *Catholic Reformation,* ch. 3, Po-Chia Hsia, *Catholic Renewal,* ch. 3, and Robert Bireley, *Refashioning,* ch. 2 all provide valuable guides on new Orders, in a European context. Richard DeMolen (ed.) *Religious Orders* has fuller studies of each; Gigliola Fragnito, 'Ordini religiosi' for fuller Italian consideration.
45. Lewis, 'Recovering the Apostolic Way of Life', 282.
46. Kenneth J. Jorgensen 'The Theatines', in DeMolen (ed.) *Religious Orders*; von Pastor, *History of the Popes,* 10: 418; Giovanni Battista Del Tufo, *Historia della Religione de'Padri Chierici Regolari* (Rome, 1609). Marcocchi, *Riforma Cattolica,* 2: 444–51. *Il Combattimento Sprituale* was first published anonymously (Venice, 1589), but under Scupoli's name a few days after he died (Bologna, 1610). Rosa, 'La Chiesa meridionale', 338–40, including 1650 figures.
47. Bearnstein, *A Convent Tale* (quoting 66 and 69), well covers Negri's story, and the transition of San Paolo from an open convent to aristocratic power base behind closed doors and grilles.
48. Zarri, *Le Sante Vive;* Schutte, *Aspiring Saints.*
49. O'Malley, *The First Jesuits,* stands out from the vast literature as the best lengthy all-round study by a judicious Jesuit scholar.
50. Mullett, *Catholic Reformation,* 91–2.
51. Irving Lavin, 'Bernini's Death'.
52. Mullett, *Catholic Reformation,* 92.
53. O'Malley, *First Jesuits,* 182–5, and see below Chapter 7.
54. Jedin (ed.), *Atlas* (1990), 78 Map.
55. Donnelly, 'The Congregation of the Oratory', in DeMolen (ed.) *Religious Orders* is a good introduction (by a Jesuit). Ponnelle and Bordet, *St Philip Neri* (1932–79), remains a good contextual study. Pullapilly, *Caesar Baronius,* deals with some of the Order's tensions as well as Baronio's historical contributions.
56. Grendler, 'The Piarists', in DeMolen (ed.), *Religious Orders,* 263. See now Karen Liebreich, *Fallen Order,* for a paedophile scandal leading to the suppression of the Order in 1646, though most schools continued to function.

57. Black, *Italian Confraternities*, 190–1; Camillo Fanucci, *Trattato*, 68–71; Rosa, 'La Chiesa meridionale', 342–3.
58. Gleason, 'The Capuchin Order', in DeMolen (ed.), *Religious Orders*; Jedin (ed.), *Atlas* (1990), 79; Jedin (ed.), *History of the Church*, 569; Norman, 'Social History of Preaching', esp. 139, 142.
59. Fragnito, 'Ordini religiosi', 140.

4 Episcopal Leadership

1. Bergin, 'Counter-Reformation Church', 34.
2. CT, V, 984; VIII, 378; XIII, 1, 607–12, 655; IX, 6, 226–41; Jedin, *Chiesa della fede*, 464, 565–7, 590; Alberigo, in *Il Concilio di Trento* (1965), 73, and 471–523 on episcopal power more fully.
3. Wright, 'The significance', 357.
4. Black, 'Perugia and Reform'. See also Cesareo, 'The Episcopacy'; Agostino Borromeo, 'I vescovi italiani'; Donati, 'Vescovi e diocesi'. Sources for the Appendix on Italian Bishoprics are given there, and apply to much given below.
5. Grosso and Mellano, *La Controriforma ... Torino*, I: 250.
6. Eubel, *Hierarchia*, IV, 71.
7. Donati, 'Vescovi e diocesi', 335–7, also exemplifying misappropriations of episcopal incomes.
8. Nanni and Regoli, *San Miniato*, 30–2.
9. Black, 'Perugia and Reform', 433–4.
10. Black 'Perugia and Reform', 435.
11. Eubel, *Hierarchia* III, 337; IV, 374.
12. Logan, *Venetian Upper Clergy*, 456–71.
13. Eubel, *Hierarchia*, III, 304–5; IV, 323; n. 13: 'Dr. theol., sed ad docendum non idoneus; qui denuo tenetur emittere profess. Fidei.'
14. Bouwsma, *Venice*, 358–61.
15. Hillerbrand (ed.), *Encyclopedia*, 1: 203–5 (Robert Trisco); Headley and Tomaro (eds), *San Carlo Borromeo*, wide-ranging collection of essays, partial substitute for a suitable biography in English; Prodi, 'San Carlo Borromeo e il Cardinale Gabriele Paleotti', on comparison of two 'models'; Prodi, 'Charles Borromée, archevêque de Milan'.
16. Tomaro, 'Borrromeo and Implementation', 75.
17. *Storia di Milano* X, Parte I.
18. 'Diary of Giambattista Casale', extracts cited in Cochrane and Kirshner (eds) *Readings*, 418–20 (from *Diario*, 237–8, 243–4); later, Chapter 6, on Casale's roles.
19. Alberigo, 'Carlo Borromeo come modello'.
20. Carlo Bascapé, *Vita e Opere*, 840.
21. Prodi, 'San Carlo Borromeo e ... Paleotti', 138–9. My translation from Italian, with altered punctuation.
22. Hillerbrand (ed.) *Encyclopedia*, 3: 197–8 (Paolo Prodi); Paolo Prodi, *Il Cardinale Gabriele Paleotti* is a densely informative life and works; Prodi, 'Lineamenti', digests some of his organisational work.
23. Prodi, *Paleotti*, 563–6.

24. *Discorso intorno alle imagini sacre et profane* (Bologna, 1582), with modern edition in Paola Barocchi *Trattati d'arte del Cinquecento,* 2 (Bari, 1961), 117–510, discussed by Prodi, *Paleotti,* 2, ch. XVIII, and his 'Ricerche sulla teorica delle arti figurative'.
25. Quoted by Prodi, *Paleotti,* 478; his ch. XVII discusses the treatise *De Sacri Consistorii Consultationibus.*
26. Prodi's approach to Paleotti's disappointments with Rome have been linked to the disillusion of Prodi's own group of Christian Democrats in the 1950s; see Ditchfield, ' "In search of local knowledge" ', 277.
27. Black, 'Perugia and Reform', esp. 433–4; letters to and from Ercolani, and nephew Timoteo Bottonio, in BCP MS 135 (mainly 1568–86, with Bottonio's life of his uncle, fols. 243–5), and MS 479 (mainly 1546–69).
28. Fragnito, 'Ecclesiastical Censorship', 92–3, 97; Iain Fenlon, 'Music and Reform', 244.
29. BCP MS 479 (G. 68), 26 December 1562.
30. Sonnino, 'Le anime dei romani', 349, Table 5.
31. Borromeo, 'Vescovi italiani', 41.
32. The collected legislation of Borromeo's six provincial councils and eleven synods were first published as *Acta Ecclesiae Mediolanensis* in 1582.
33. Borromeo, 'Vescovi italiani', 52–3.
34. Da Nadro, *Sinodi diocesani italiani* (1960) was a valuable foundation.
35. *Ravennatensia* I (1969), 143–53; Black, 'Perugia and Reform', 436 n. 28, 435, 437; *Decreta et Monita synodalia Ecclesiae Perusinae ... Napoleonis Comitoli* (Perugia, 1600).
36. AABol Visite Pastorali vol. 144 contains various "Ordini et avvertimenti", before and after Colonna's second and third synods, 1636, 1637.
37. Black, 'Perugia and Church Reform', 437; *Statuta et Constitutiones Synodi Diocesis Perusine* (Perugia, 1566); *Statuta et Constitutiones Synodalis lecte et publicatae in Secunda Dicesana Synodo Perusina* (Perugia, 1587), held 15–16 October 1567; *Decreta et Monita edita et promulgata in Synodo Diocesana Perusina ... 1582* (Perugia, 1584); *Istitutioni et Avvertimenti per il Buon Regimento del Clero Diocesano ...*, made in various congregations and reprinted according to Bishop Comitoli's orders in 1600 (Perugia, 1602).
38. Nubola and Turchini (eds), *Visite pastorali; Archiva Ecclesiae* vol. 22–3 (1979–80), devoted to studies of Visitations; Mazzoni and Turchini (eds), *Le visite pastorali,* more analyses.
39. Borromeo, 'Vescovi italiani', 96 n. 143.
40. Chambers and Pullan (eds), *Venice,* 224 (quotes), 206–8.
41. Scaduto 'Le "Visite" di Possevino'.
42. Villani, 'Visita ... Orfini', quoting 17. Places visited from Naples onwards: Anagni, Arriano, Avellino, Bari, Barletta, Bisceglie, Bitetto, Bitonto, Brindisi, Conversano, Ferentino, Foggia, Giovenazzo, Misagne, Molfetta, Monopoli, Naples, Nola, Ostuni, Polignano, Rutigliano, Ruvo, San Germano, Trani and Troia; Mario Rosa, 'La Chiesa meridionale'. 295–6.
43. Grosso and Mellano, *La Controriforma ... Torino,* I, 247–50.
44. For example, Donvito and Pellegrino, *L'Organizzazione Ecclsiastica,* for southern Italy.
45. Gentilcore, 'Methods and approaches', 77; Ditchfield, ' "In search of knowledge" ', 281–2.

46. Personally sampled examples: AAF Visite Pastorali 26, Archbishop Pietro Niccolini's Visitation in Florentine countryside, 1635–40 (very full), and AArchBol Visite Pastorali vol. 123, Fasc. 4, Rev. Rodolfo Paleotti's city Visitation, 1598 (crisper).
47. AAF VP26, fols. 130–4.
48. Nubola, *Conoscere per governare.*
49. Cesareo, 'The episcopacy', 78.
50. Borromeo, 'Vescovi italiani', 60 and 96, nn. 150–1, quoting G.P. Guissani, *Vita di S. Carlo Borromeo* (Rome, 1610), 81–2.
51. Wietze de Boer, *The Conquest of the Soul.*
52. Wietze de Boer, *Conquest of the Soul,* esp. ch. 2, quoting from 62. Borromeo's *Avvertenze ... ai confessori nella città et diocese sua* are included in *AEM* vol. 2, cols. 1870–93.
53. ASB Corporazioni Religiose: S. Sacramento di Bagnacavallo vol. 424 (29 August 1649 entry for veto), and Rosario di Bangnacavallo vol. 394.
54. Greco, 'I giuspatronati laicali', 534, 538.
55. Davidson, 'The Clergy of Venice'; see below Chapter 5.
56. Greco, 'I giuspatronati', 547–9, 560–2 is best digest.
57. Carla Russo, 'Parrocchie, fabbricerie'; Greco, *La parrocchia a Pisa,* 25–37, 43–4, 58–61, 64–5; Rosa, *Religione e Società,* 67–8; Donvito and Pellegrino *L'Organizzzazione Ecclesiastica,* 8, 11.
58. Donati, 'Vescovi e diocesi', 352–4.

5 Parish Priests and Parishioners

1. This chapter draws from my *Early Modern Italy,* ch. 10, and my 'Confraternities and the parish', providing much more detailed referencing.
2. *COD* (1973), cols. 767–68: trans. from *Canons and Decrees,* ed. Schroeder, 204.
3. See Kümin, 'The English parish in a European perspective'. On Italy key works: Hay, *The Church in Italy,* esp. 20–5; Mario Rosa, 'Le parrocchie italiane'; Salimbeni, 'La parocchia nel Mezzogiorno'; sources cited in Black, 'Confraternities and the parish', n. 2–7.
4. Gentilcore, *Bishop to Witch,* 37; Carroll, *Madonnas that Maim,* 96–104.
5. Greco, *La Parocchia a Pisa,* 39; on persistence of the *pieve* systems, Rogger, 'Diocesi di Trento', esp. 199–200.
6. Davidson, 'The clergy of Venice'.
7. Sources in Black, 'Perugia and Reform', n. 43–7.
8. Deutscher, 'The growth of secular clergy', 386.
9. Black, 'Perugia and Reform', 448; Chiacchella, 'Storia della parrocchia'. A.S. Pietro, Perugia, Libro dei Contratti 32, fols. 22–8 on San Costanzo issues, and Diverse vols. 38 and 89, passim, on the battles between Perugian bishops and the abbots.
10. Black, *Early Modern Italy,* 171; F. Russo, *Storia dell'Arcidiocesi di Reggio Calabria;* Deutscher, 'The growth of secular clergy', esp. Table 1; Toscani, 'Il reclutamento', esp. 577–85.

11. Nubola, *Conoscere per Governare*, ch. 7.
12. Toscani, 'Il reclutamento', 586.
13. Mezzadri, 'Il Seminario', 39.
14. William Barcham, *Grand in Design*, 73–8.
15. Davidson, 'Clergy of Venice'; Greco, *La Parrocchia a Pisa*, 25–37, 43–4, 58–61, 64–5.
16. De Boer, *Conquest of the Soul*, 23, 31, n. 56.
17. Masetti Zannini, 'Richerche sulla cultura'.
18. Gordini, *Ravennatensia* vol. 3, 171–5; Samaritani, *Ravennatensia*, 3, 467–9, 483–4.
19. Nubola, *Conoscere per Governare*, 254–5.
20. Preto, 'Benefici parrocchiali'; Castagnetti, 'Le decime'.
21. Preto, 'Benefici parrocchiali', 804–5, 808–9; Villari, *La Rivolta Antispagnuola* (1976 edn), 62–7; Lopez, *Riforma Cattolica*, esp. 34–5, 44–5; Volpe, *La Parrocchia Cilentina*, 10, 17.
22. Toscani, 'Il reclutamento', 602.
23. Fanti, *Una Pieve ... Lizzano*, and 'Il fondo delle 'Visite Pastorali'.
24. My, *Early Modern Italy*, 169–70, and n. 5–7.
25. *Institutioni et Avvertimenti per il Buon Regimento del Clero Diocesano di Perugia ...* (1600, and reprinted 1652).
26. Gordini, 'Sinodi diocesani', *Ravennatensia*, 2, 260, and 'Formazione del clero', *Ravennatensia* 3, 173–4; Carlo Borromeo, *Constitutiones et Decreta condita in Provinciale Synodo* (Brescia 1569); G. Paleotti, *Ordinationi ... MDLXVI. Armilla* = Bartolomeo Fumo, *Summa casuum conscientiae, aurea armilla dicta* (1550), by Dominican Inquisitor at Piacenza; *Antonina* = St. Antoninus of Florence (1389–1459), *Summa Theologica* (printed first 1477). *New Catholic Encyclopedia* 6 (1967), 221, and vols 1: 646–7 and 9: 1121. The vernacular version might have been *Antonina vulgar* (Venice, 1500: British Library: IA 23521), which is also called his *Confessionale.*
27. Masetti Zannini, 'Ricerche sulla cultura', 65–7; Sposato, *Aspetti ... Calabria*, 198 (Costanzo).
28. 'La Libreria di un parroco di Città in Padua.'
29. My, 'Perugia and Reform', 443–4.
30. De Boer, 'The curate of Malgrate', and *The Conquest of the Soul*, 64, 186, 258–9.
31. Lapucci and Pacciani (eds) *Zibaldone ... Pinelli.*
32. John Bossy, 'The Mass'; Jean Delumeau, *Catholicism*, 197–9; on sexual segregation, *Institutioni et Avvertimenti per il Buon Reggimento del Clero Diocesano di Perugia rinovati 1600* (Perugia, 1612), 23–4, 27; Cardinal A. Ludovisi, *Rinovationi di alcuni ordini* (Bologna, 1620), ch. VII on synodal legislation on Masses; some examples in *Ravennatensia*, 2, 524–7, 535–6, 541–2, and P. Lopez, *Riforma Cattolica Napoli*, 14–15.
33. De Boer, *Conquest*, 246–48, with his translations.
34. Corrain and Zampini, *Documenti:Emilia-Romagna*, 4, 11–12, *Umbria* 21, *Marche*, 11–12, *Piemonte e Ligurie*, 19, 21, 43, *Italia Meridionale*, 10–11, 20, 22; Lopez, *Riforma Cattolica Napoli*, 10–12.
35. Sposato, *Aspetti Calabria*, 195; Scaduto, 'Le "Visite" di Possevino', 381.

36. Jedin, 'Le origini dei registri parrocchiali'; Ebner, 'I libri parrocchiali di Vallo della Lucania', and 'I libri parrochiali di Novi Velia'.
37. Corrain and Zampini, esp. *Documenti ... Marche*, 4, 17, 27–8, *Emilia-Romagna*, 20, *Italia Meridionale* 3, 28, *Venezia*, 5; Ferraris and Frutaz, 'Visita apostolica ... Bonomi', 45–6, 54–5, 57, 69–71.
38. COD (1973), 753–59; von Pastor, *History of the Popes*, vol. 15: 355–6, 376; *New Catholic Encyclopedia*, vol 9, 'Marriage', 258–94, and vol. 13 'Tametsi', 929; *Dictionnaire de Théologie Catholique*, 9.ii (1927), 'Mariage', cols. 2196–207 (sacrament), 2232–61 (Trent and aftermath); Nino Tamassia, *La famiglia*, 150–95; Jedin, *Crisis and Closure*, 140–4.
39. Volpe, *La parrocchia Cilentina*, 5–6, 70–83.
40. Gabriele Paleotti, *Del Sacramento del matrimonio. Avvertimenti alli reverendi curati* (Bologna, 1577, and Venice 1607 (marginally revised), consulted; Vatican Library); Prodi, *Paleotti*, 2: 126–8.
41. Rasi, 'L'applicazione delle norme'.
42. Ebner 'I libri parrocchiali' (1973 and 1974).
43. Alessandro Manzoni, *The Betrothed* and *I Promessi Sposi*, ch. 8; Brandileone, *La celebrazione*, 29–35.; *DTC*, 9. ii col. 2248.
44. Ferraro, *Marriage Wars*. She sampled 118 cases for annulment for 29 randomly chosen years between 1565 and 1624, of which 75 per cent had female petitioners (28).
45. Ferraro, *Marriage Wars*, 45–9, 33–8.
46. Di Simplicio, *Peccato Penitenza*, ch. 8.
47. Corrain and Zampini, *Documenti etnografici*, esp. *Emilia Romagna*, 16–18, *Lombardia*, 11–12, *Marche, Umbria e Lazio*, 23–4, 30; Corrain and Zampini, 'Costumanze', 61 for 'Notte di Tobia' *Bandi dell'Illustre et Rmo. Monsignore Francesco Bossi. Vescovo di Perugia* (Perugia, 1575). On 'scampanate' see also N. Zemon Davis, 'The reasons of misrule'.
48. Carlo Borromeo, *Le piu belle pagine delle omilie*, ed. C. Gorla (1926), 117–21; Paleotti, *Del Sacramento del matrimonio.*
49. Bossy, 'Social history of Confession'; Lea, *A History of Auricular Confession* (1896) remains valuable, esp. vol. 2: 412–60.
50. B. Fumo, *Summa* (1554), 95v–101r, 'Confessio Sacramentalis', 101r–3r, 'Confessor'; Lopez, *Riforma Cattolica*, 17; H.C. Lea, *Confession*, 1: 373–4.
51. Notably Prosperi, especially in his *Tribunale*; De Boer, *The Conquest*; T. Tentler, 'The Summa ... Social Control'.
52. De Boer, *The Conquest*, ch. 3, with Fig. 2 sketch based on Borromeo's description in *Instructiones.*
53. L. Stone, *Family, Sex, and Marriage*, 142, 499, 527; Naselli, 'L'esame di coscienza'; Sodano, 'Donne e pratiche religiose'; G. Romeo, *Esorcisti, confessori*, 149, 170–3, 196.
54. De Boer, *The Conquest*, 33–5 on Trent and impact of control of confession, and ch. 2 on the coercive approach.
55. Prosperi, *Tribunali*, 230–2; W. De Boer, *The Conquest*, 62–3; John Martin, *Venice's Hidden Enemies*, 187.
56. De Boer, *The Conquest*, 277–83, quoting from 278–9, his translations. (Precise date not given, but *c.*1568–72?)
57. Martin, *Venice's Hidden Enemies*, 185–7.

58. De Boer, *The Conquest*, 198–206; John Bossy, *Peace*, ch. 1 ('Italy'), esp. 8–11, 25–6.
59. Polecritti, *Preaching Peace*, 125, 142.
60. Gentilcore, 'Adapt Yourselves', 280.
61. Valerio, Donne', with quote from 67. See Sposato, *Aspetti Calabria*, 66–7, 142–5; S. Tramontin, 'Visita apostolica Venezia'; Black, *Early Modern Italy*, 174–6.
62. ASBol Visite Pastorali vol. 144, 'Ordini e Avertimenti ... 1598', no. 11.
63. Di Simplicio, 'Perpetuas', and *Peccato, Penitenza*, ch. 6; Valerio, 'Donne', esp. 83–6 (on Teresa).
64. ASB Tribunale del Torrone vol. 5743 (1628–30), fols. 126r–204v.
65. My, *Early Modern Italy*, 175–6; AABol Visite Pastorali 44 (1632–43), 'Ordini et avvertimenti', fols. i–vii.
66. My, *Early Modern Italy*, 175, 180–1, 201 (Table); Mariangela Sarra, 'Distribuzione ... inquisizione in Friuli', Appendice Tavola A.
67. ASV S.U. Busta 80 'Gervasio/Gervatio'; APVen, 'Criminalia S. Inquisitionis 1586–99', fols. 85–102 'S. Simone'.
68. Gotor, *I beati del papa*, ch. 5.

6 Religious Education

1. Comerford, 'Clerical Education'; Grendler, *Schooling*, 60–1.
2. Black, 'Perugia', esp. 441–2.
3. Comerford, 'Italian Tridentine Diocesan Seminaries', has a valuable Table, used in my Appendix. Also: Guasco, 'La formazione del clero: I seminari' for major coverage and bibliography; Negruzzo, *Collegij*, esp. 11–39 as general introduction.
4. Prodi, *Paleotti*, 2: 566; F. Russo, *Storia di Reggio Calabria* 2: 125–9; Sposato, *Aspetti, Calabria*, 39–40, 100.
5. De Maio, *Le origini del Seminario*, esp. 76–81, 88–90, 126–41; Lopez, *Riforma cattolica Napoli*, 118–24.
6. Tramontin, 'Due seminari'; D'Addario, *Aspetti*, 206–7.
7. Deutscher, Review of Kathleen M. Comerford, *Ordaining the Catholic Reformation* (2001), and Negruzzo, *Collegij*.
8. Comerford, 'Clerical Education', 252.
9. Pellicia, *Preparazione*, 291–2, 302; Sposato, *Aspetti*, 150 (Table), 39–43, 190, 203–7.
10. Gabriejelcic, 'Alle origini'; my, 'Perugia and church reform', esp. 441–2.
11. Molinari, 'Il seminario di Piacenza', esp. Appendix giving rules, 51–65, and Molinari (ed.) *Il Seminario di Piacenza*; Guasco, 'La formazione', 657; Rimoldi, 'Istituzione'; Paschini, 'Le origini del Seminario Romano'; A.G. Roncalli, *Gli Inizi del Seminario di Bergamo*; P. Prodi, *Paleotti*, 2: 144–6.
12. Duranti, 'Il seminario di Ravenna', 150.
13. Negruzzo, *Collegij*, 27–8; more widely, Waquet, *Latin or the empire of a sign*, esp. ch. 2
14. Pellicia, *La preparazione*, 296–8.

15. Rimoldi, 'Istituzioni', 431–6; Sposato, *Aspetti*, 43–4; Gabriejelcic, 'Alle origini', 82–92, 120–41; *Diz. Bio. Ital* 11 (1969), 676–78, 'Bonciari Marcantonio'.
16. Negruzzo, *Collegij*, 21–2.
17. Negruzzo, *Collegij*, 26, 30, 41–2, 44–5.
18. Negruzzo, *Collegij*, 56.
19. Masi, *Organizzazione ecclesiasatica Puglia*, 93.
20. Following based on my, *Italian Confraternities*, 223–8, *Early Modern Italy*, 183–6, and 'Confraternities and the parish', 13–15, all citing many Italian sources. Grendler's contributions, in his *Schooling*, esp. ch. 12, 'The Schools', 'Borromeo', and 'The Piarists' are very helpful. *COD*, 763, for relevant Trent decree.
21. *Decreta Diocesanae Synodi Ravennatis primae a Pietro Aldobrandino* (Venice, 1607), fols. 8v-10v, 'De Doctrina Christiana'.
22. Grendler, 'Borromeo' and 'The Schools'; Franza, *Il Catechismo a Roma*, esp. 59–67, 95–6, 219–32; Arsenio D'Ascoli, *La Predicazione*, 268–70 (on Gregorio da Napoli).
23. Rostirolla, 'Laudi e canti religiosi', esp. 700–17, 755–61; Kennedy, 'Unusual Genres'.
24. AABol, Visite Pastorali, vol. 123, Fasc 4. City Visitation of Rodolfo Paleotti, 1598, esp. 18–19.
25. Casale, *Diario*, 329–33.
26. ASVR, Arciconfraternita della Dottrina Cristiana, palchetto 168, vol. 417, Congregationi 1599–1608; Franza, *Il Catechismo*; Pellicia, 'Scuole di Catechismo'; Black, 'Confraternities and the Parish', 13–15.
27. Grendler, 'Borromeo', 166.
28. *Diario* fully printed in *Memorie storiche della diocesi di Milano* 12 (1969), 209–437, with translated extracts in Cochrane and Kirshner (eds) *Readings*, 411–26, quote 411 (*Diario*, 224–5). See also Zardin, 'Relaunching Confraternities', 206–7.
29. Carlo Borromeo, *Decreta condita in Concilio Provinciali Mediolanoni Secondo* (Brescia, 1575), 4.
30. My *Italian Confraternities*, 226–7, with sources; Grendler, 'The Piarists'; Leibreich, *Fallen Order*.
31. Grendler, *Schooling*, 42–4.
32. Baldacchini, *Bibliografia delle stampe popolari religiose*, esp. 10–11, 20.
33. Norman now provides a splendid readable coverage in her 'Social History of Preaching', with bibliography, highlighting Roberto Rusconi's vital contributions; see esp. his 'Predicatori e predicazione'.
34. Norman, 'Social History of Preaching', 136.
35. Cited by Norman, 151–2; Marcocchi, *Riforma Cattolica*, 713–17.
36. Cited by Norman, p. 178
37. Rusconi, 'Predicatori', 95.
38. Polecritti, *Preaching Peace* on Bernardino of Siena.
39. Orlandi, 'La missione popolare', esp. 420–1.
40. Orlandi, 'La missione popolare', 423–7.
41. Rusconi, 'Gli Ordini religiosi maschili', esp. 242–52; Scaduto, 'Tra Inquisitori e Riformati'.
42. Orlando, 'La missione popolare', 428–9.

43. Gentilcore, ' "Adapt Yourselves" ',, esp. 275 for Lecce example; Rusconi, 'Gli Ordini religiosi', 246–52; Orlandi, 'La missione popolare', 432–4; Rienzo, 'Il processo di cristianizzazione'; Bossy, *Peace*, 8–11, 14, 27–9.

7 Confraternities, Hospitals and Philanthropy

1. Black, *Italian Confraternities*, esp. chs 7–10 indicate both attitudes to poverty, and studies on philanthropic activities through confraternities, and linked hospitals or other institutions. This work documents much that follows through this chapter. For an update see my 'The development of confraternity studies', in Terpstra (ed.), *Ritual Kinship*, with other articles therein, and our composite bibliography. My 'Confraternities' (1996), for brief European-wide context. Fundamental on attitudes in a European context are Pullan's articles: 'The old Catholicism, the new Catholicism', 'Support and Redeem'.
2. Weissman, *Ritual Botherhood*, ix.
3. Terpstra, 'Ignatius, Confratello: confraternities as modes of spiritual community', esp. 176–7.
4. Zardin, 'Relaunching confraternities', 206–7.
5. Black, *Italian Confraternities*, 3, 258–61; illustrations in: *La Comunità Cristiana*, Figs 13–14 and opposite p. 241 (Santi di Tito); *Painting in Naples*, colour pl. p. 65; Hibbard, *Caravaggio*, Figs 138–43, Langdon, *Caravaggio*, pl. 32; *Age of Caravaggio*, Fig. 13.
6. Prosperi, *Tra evangelismo e controriforma*, 272.
7. *COD*, 740, Session XXII, Canons VIII and IX; Black, *Italian Confraternities*, 63.
8. Châtellier, *Europe of the Devout*, on network through Europe.
9. On the fascinating background history of the Rosary cult: Winston-Allen, *Stories of the Rose*.
10. Black, 'Confraternities and the parish'.
11. ASBol, Corporazioni Religiose, Compagnia del Ssmo Rosario in Crevalcore, vol. 1/7813, Miscellanea, 5 May 1605; Greco, *La parrocchia a Pisa*, 77–80.
12. Fasano Guarini, *Prato storia di un città*, 2: 540–1; D'Addario, *Aspetti della Controriforma*, 319–20.
13. Weissman, *Ritual Brotherhood*, 201–12; ASBol, Corporazioni Religiose, S. Sacramento di Bagnacavalo. Vol. 424, Decreti, 22 Nov. 1648.
14. Black, *Italian Confraternities*, 111–12, based on A. Giovio, *Descrittione de sei Apparati et pompe fatte in Perugia* (Perugia, 1610).
15. Torre, 'Faith's boundaries', 248–53.
16. Terpstra, *Lay Confraternities*, 219–20, updating my *Italian Confraternities*, 74.
17. Henderson, *Piety and Charity*, is an excellent study of the range of activities, for Florence.
18. Giulio Folco, *Effetti mirabili de la Limosina et sentenze degne di memoria* (Rome, 1581), but with Preface dated 24 dec. 1573; my *Italian Confraternities*, 171, 179–80, and Lance Lazar's forthcoming book, *Working in the Vineyard of the Lord* for a Jesuit context.

19. Paolo De Angelis, *Della limosina overo opere che si assicurano nel giorno del final giuditio* (Rome, 1615); Alessandro Sperelli, *Della pretiosita della limosina* (Venice, 1666), esp. 16, 107–13, 116; see my, *Italian Confraternities*, 17 (quoting De Angelis), 145–7.
20. Many articles in Bertoldi Lenoci, (ed.) *Le Confraternite pugliese*, and her ed. *Confraternite, Chiese Società;* with her own survey, 'La sociabilità religiosa pugliese'.
21. My *Italian Confraternities*, 49–57 and Appendix 1, my, *Early Modern Italy*, 160–1; Mackenney, 'Public and Private', and 'The Scuole Piccole'; Camillo Fanucci, *Trattato di tutte le opere pie dell'alma città di Roma* (Rome, 1601).
22. Pullan, *Rich and Poor* (1971) was the pioneering work, see esp. 33–4, 86–98. See also his collected essays, *Poverty and Charity* (1994). Scuole Grandi: S. Marco, S. Rocco, Della Misericordia Della Carità, S. Giovanni Evangelista, and from 1552 S. Teodoro.
23. AdiSP, Religiose Soppresse, S. Domenico, Miscellanea 77. Some names are repeated.
24. Mackenney, 'The Guilds of Venice', 40, and my, 'The Development', 15.
25. Eisenbichler, *The Boys of the Archangel Raphael*; See now also, Polizzotto, *Children of the Promise: The confraternity of the Purification and the socialization of youths in Florence, 1427–1785.*
26. Black, 'Early Modern Confraternities' , focused on this.
27. Zardin, 'Relaunching', 195–6; ASBol, Corporazioni Religiose, S. Sacramento di Bagnacavallo, vol. 424 (1635–1734), and Ssmo di Budrio, vol. 4/7852, vol. 4 (1647–90); Fanti, 'La parrocchia dei SS.Vitale e Agricola', 225–31.
28. Pullan, 'The Old Catholicism', and ' "Support and Redeem" '; Cavallo, *Charity and Power*, on varied benefactor attitudes and policies.
29. Alessandro Sperelli, *Della Pretiosita*, 297; see my, *Italian Confraternities*, 146 for a fuller translated quotation.
30. Lance Lazar's forthcoming book *Working in the Vineyard* covers these in some detail; meanwhile see his 'The First Jesuit Confraternities', and 'Daughters of Prostitutes'.
31. My, *Italian Confraternities*, 209.
32. Terpstra, ' "In loco parentis" ', 115–17, and 'Mothers, sisters, and daughters', ... ; my, *Italian Confraternities*, 209–10.
33. My, *Italian Confraternities*, 184–200 for basis of what follows.
34. Camillo Fanucci, *Trattato*, but esp. for key hospitals praised below, 15, 17, 34–53, 56–58; my *Italian Confraternities*, 191–6 for modern sources.
35. Howe, 'Appropriating Space'. 235.
36. Arrizabalaga and others, *The Great Pox*, esp. chs 7 and 8.
37. Gregory Martin, *Roma Sancta*, esp. 188, 205, 232–7.
38. Terpstra, 'Competing Visions'.
39. Pullan, *Rich and Poor*, esp. 77–8, 185, 347–9, 353–4. and *Poverty and Charity*, no. X; ASV Scuole Piccole e Suffragi, Busta 706, SS. Trinita alla Salute, Libro 3, 'Notariato' 1649–1710.
40. Vianello, 'I 'Fiscali delle miserie'.
41. APV Parrochia di S. Lio: Amminstrazione vol. 6; 'Accordi fra il capitolo di S. Lio e la scuola del SS. Sacramento', 23 April 1695; Registri

degli Infermi vol. 1 included a list of sick in 1630, and some help offered.

42. My, *Italian Confraternities*, 217–23, with many sources and examples; Terpstra, 'Piety and punishment', and 'Confraternal prison charity', on Bologna; Paglia '*La Pietà dei Carcerati*', and *La morte confortata*, the key studies of Roman practices and attitudes, emphasising the new religious impacts.

8 Nunneries and Religious Women

1. Medioli, 'The enforcement of *clausura*', 143.
2. Zarri, 'Monasteri femminili', esp. 402–3, and 'Dalla profezia', 210–15.
3. Andretta, 'Il governo dell'osservanza', 401–2.
4. Weaver, *Convent Theatre*, 12–13, esp. n. 6; Zarri, 'Monasteri femminili e città', 402, 421–2; Laven, 'Venetian Nunneries', ch. II; Laven, *Virgins of Venice*, 202, n. 10; Black, *Early Modern Italy*, Appendix on Population (218–20); Fragnito, 'Gli Ordini Religiosi', 126, nn. 10, 11; Sonnino, 'Le anime dei romani', 348–50; Lowe, *Nuns' Chronicles and Convent Culture*, 144–54 (her splendid book appeared too late for full consideration here).
5. Laven, *Virgins of Venice*, 48, 211–12, n. 12; Sperling, Convents, 26–9. For pre-Trent circumstances of San Zaccaria: Primhak, 'Benedictine Communities', 92–104.
6. Judith Brown, *Immodest Acts*.
7. Medioli, 'The enforcement'; Creytens, 'La riforma dei monasteri femminili' (1965); CT IX 1044–69, for decree and discussions; Zarri, 'Monasteri femminili', 398–411
8. Medioli, 'The enforcement', 149–50, quoting anonymous contributors.
9. Medioli, 'Lo spazio del chiostro', 356.
10. Medioli, 'To take or not to take', esp. 128.
11. Weaver, *Convent Theatre*, 21–2.
12. Medioli 'Enforcement', 152; cf. Weaver, *Convent Theatre*, 19–20 for fuller quotation; Zarri, 'Monasteri femminili', 386.
13. Andretta, 'Il governo dell'osservanza', 403–4; Weaver, *Convent Theatre*, 23, n. 30; cf. Lowe, *Nuns' Chronicles*, 123–6, 260–3.
14. Novi Chavarria, *Monache e Gentildonne*, 70–90; Miele, 'Monache e monasteri', 102–4.
15. Sperling, *Convents*, 129, 327 n. 65.
16. Medioli, 'Dimensions', 166–7.
17. Weaver, *Convent Theatre*, 24.
18. Baernstein, *Convent Tale*, 94–7.
19. See Laven, *Virgins of Venice*, 8, 48, 84, 119–21; APV: Atti Patriarcale riguardanti le monache, 'Decretorum et mandatorum monialium', vol. for 1591–9, ff. 115r–6r, 24 April 1599 Patriarch to S. Maria di Miracoli, showing concern with their staying overnight away from their quarters next to the monastery.
20. APV. 'Decretorum et mandatorum monialium', 1591–9, fols. 115r–6r.

21. Laven, *Virgins of Venice*, 96.
22. Laven, *Virgins of Venice*, 130; Andretta, 'Il governo dell'osservanza', 423, n. 116.
23. Zarri, 'Monasteri femminili', 388–92; Novi Chavarria, *Monache e Gentildonne*, 120–7.
24. Weaver, *Convent Theatre*, 26–9; Zarri, 'Monasteri femminili', 393, 424.
25. Medioli, 'Enforcement', 151.
26. Sperling, *Convents*, 156–7.
27. Laven, *Virgins of Venice*, 149 and 233, n. 25, with 150–53 exemplifying trial cases 1625–6, and 165–6 on priests and friars.
28. Laven, *Virgins of Venice*, 156–9.
29. Laven, V*irgins of Venice*, 99, translating Arcangela Tarabotti, *L' 'Inferno monacale'*, edit. Francesca Medioli (Turin, 1990), 101.
30. Bearnstein, *Convent Tale*, chs 4, 5.
31. Andretta, 'Il governo dell'osservanza', 405–13.
32. Sperling, *Convents*, 152–3.
33. Lowe, 'Elections of abbesses'; and now her *Nuns' Chronicles*, esp. ch. 6 on a variety of ceremonies.
34. Sperling, *Convents*, 137–41, 167–9, 176–7; Laven, *Virgins of Venice*, 107–8.
35. Sperling, *Convents*, 121–4. cf. Laven, *Virgins of Venice*, 1–5, 102–203.
36. ASB Demaniale, S. Cristina, vol. 48/2909, 1622–23, Visitation, 15r–17r, 26r–29r.
37. D'Ambrosio and Spedicato, *Cibo e Clausura* , esp. 54–61, 77–9; APV, 'Decretorum et mandatorum monialium', vol. for 1591–9, vol. for 1620–30; Black, *Early Modern Italy*, 30; Laven, 'Venetian Nunneries', ch. V, and her *Virgins of Venice*, ch. 10, 'Between Celibates'.
38. Sperling, *Convents*, 158–69; Laven, *Virgins of Venice*, Figs 14, 16, 17, and index under 'parlours', 'prostitutes'.
39. Laven, *Virgins of Venice*, esp. 123–4, 153–4, 171–2, 177; APV: 'Decretorum et mandatorum monialium', vol. for 1591–99, ff. 111v–15r, Instructions in March and April 1599 on the administration of the Convertite (a monastic institution mainly for repentant prostitutes), threatened prison conditions on those who gave away food or goods, even to relatives.
40. ASB Demaniale, S. Cristina, vol. 48/2909, 1622–3 Visitation, 11v, 19v.
41. Zarri, 'Monasteri femminili', 396; APV. 'Decretorum et mandatorum monialium', 1591–9, fols. 33v–35v, 2 Nov. 1592. The nunneries named: S. Servolo, S. Mattio de Mazorbo, S. Anna, S. Iseppo, S. Zuanne Laterano, S. Rocco et Margarita, S. Girolamo, S. Latia, Ogni Santi, S. Marta, Spirito Santo. For Rome: Andretta, 'Il governo dell'osservanza', 423–4.
42. ASB Corporazioni Soppresse. SS.Vitale e Agricola, vol. 93/3242, folder of 'Lettere Diverse'; some transcribed in Zarri, 'Il monastero dei Santi Vitale e Agricola' see also Fanti, 'La parrochia dei Santi Vitale e Agricola', esp. 225, 230–1.
43. ASB ... vol. 93/3242, 'Lettere Diverse', 25 Feb. 1630 (sister), 12 Dec. 1622 (sermon).
44. Weaver, *Convent Theatre*, ch. 1.

45. Caponetto, *The Protestant Reformation*, 192–3, 216, 224; Zarri, 'Dalla profezia', 209–10.
46. Rusconi, 'Le biblioteche degli ordini religiosi', 73–7.
47. Rusconi, 'Le biblioteche', 64–6, 74–7; Compare, 'Biblioteche monastiche'; on Guevara and Malerbi, see Fragnito (ed.), *Church, Censorship*, 196–7, 125 and 129; and on Malerbi, Fragnito *La Bibbia al rogo*, esp. 25–43.
48. ASB Demaniale, S. Margherita, vol. 51/3198, Carte Diverse; Monson, *Disembodied Voices*, esp. 29–30, 60–61.
49. Zarri (ed.), *Per lettera*, esp. Scattigno, 'Lettere dal convento', 313–57, and Belardini, ' "Piace molto a Giesù" ', 359–83.
50. Lowe, 'History writing', and *Nuns' Chronicles*; De Bellis, 'Attacking sumptuary laws'.
51. Scattigno, 'Lettere dal convento', esp. 323–4; Riccardi, 'Mystic Humanism … Pazzi'.
52. Solfaroli Camillocci 'La monaca esemplare'.
53. Scattigno, 'Lettere dal convento', esp. 329–35; Sobel, *To Father*, with English translations opposite the Italian text, unindexed; see her *Galileo's Daughter* for the commentary on the letters and contexts.
54. Letter of 14 March 1629, *To Father*, 106–111.
55. Weaver, *Convent Theatre*, for much of what follows (56 n. 20 for geographical range); and her 'The Convent Wall in Tuscan Convent Drama', for most of what follows.
56. Laven, *Virgins of Venice*, 134–5.
57. Weaver, *Convent Theatre*, 113–18 (St Catherine), 71 (David), 151–69 and passim (Beatrice and her play), 170–8 (Annalena Odaldi), 204–6.
58. Laven, *Virgins of Venice*, 134–8; Weaver, *Convent Theatre*, 64. cf. Moderata Fonte, *The Worth of Women*, translated by Virginia Cox.
59. Weaver, *Convent Theatre*, 46–7; Monson (ed.), *The Crannied Wall*, esp. his 'Disembodied Voices', 191–209, and Kendrick, 'Traditions of Milanese Convent Music', 211–33; Bowers, 'The emergence of women composers in Italy, 1566–1700'.
60. Monson, 'Disembodied Voices', 201. The *Componimenti*, sung by Catherine King and others in 'Musica Secreta', on CD (CKD 071) by Linn Products, Glasgow; with comments by Craig Monson; Monson, 'The making of … Vizzani's *Componimenti Musicali*'.
61. Kendrick, 'Traditions', 216–26. Cozzolani's 'Dialogues with Heaven' motets, also Musica Secreta, CKD 113.
62. Reardon, *Holy Concord*, esp. ch. 4.
63. Weaver, *Convent Theatre*, 37–9, with Fig. 3 for Nelli's *Last Supper;* Trinchieri Camiz, ' "Virgo non sterilis" … Nuns as Artists'.
64. Black, *Italian Confraternities*, 207; Aikema & Meijers, *Nel Regno dei Poveri*, 225–8.
65. Cohn *Death and Property in Siena*, ch. 11.
66. Hufton, 'The Widow's Mite'.
67. Zarri, 'Living Saints', *Le Sante vive*, and *'Il "terzo stato"* ',; Zarri (ed.), *Finzione e santità;* Schutte, *Aspiring Saints.*
68. *Cecilia Ferrazzi. Autobiography of an Aspiring Saint*; analysed by Schutte, *Aspiring Saints*, esp. 13–15, 125–31, 164–6, 190–2, 207–11, 225–6; also her 'Inquisition and Female Autobiography', and 'Failed Saints'.

69. Schutte, *Aspiring Saints*, 121–31 (Polacco), 92–3, 260–1 (Barbarigo); Zardin, 'Gregorio Barbarigo'.
70. Tomizza, *Heavenly Supper. The Story of Maria Janis*, by a famous novelist, but using the archival records.
71. Schutte, *Aspiring Saints*, esp. 12–13, 162–4, 192–3; and her 'Santità femminile "simulata" e "vera" ', 297–9.
72. Signorotto, *Inquisitori e mistici*; see my Review in *Journal of Modern History* 63 (1991), 588–90.
73. Schutte, 'Failed Saints', 191–2; according to Schutte, 'Santita femminile', 292–3.
74. Ciammitti, 'One Saint Less', explaining her diagram, 151–3.

9 Repression and Control

1. Ginzburg, *The Cheese and the Worms* and *Night Battles*; Del Col, *Domenico Scandella*.
2. Levack, *The Witch-Hunt*, esp. ch. 3 on 'The legal foundations' most relevant to this point.
3. Shown in Godman, *The Saint as Censor. Robert Bellarmine Inquisition and Index*.
4. Fragnito (ed.), *Church, Censorship and Culture*.
5. Fragnito, 'Central and Peripheral Organization', 22, n. 23, and ' … La censura ecclesiastica', 5 n. 9 (adding later tribunals).
6. AAF S. Uffizio, Filze 2–3.
7. ASV SU, busta 33, folder 'Denuncie 1572–3'; APV, Criminalia S. Inquisitionis 1586–99, fols. 12–15.
8. Tedeschi, 'Il caso di un falso inquisitore', 137.
9. Key introductions: Grendler, *Roman Inquisition and the Venetian Press*, ch. II, 'The Inquisition'; Schutte, *Aspiring Saints*, ch. 2 'The Roman Inquisition in Venice'; Del Col, *Domenico Scandella*, Introduction, esp. xxvii–xlix. I have sampled denunciations and cases from ASV SU, Buste 13, 33, 61, 66, 80, 103, 106; AAF S. Uffizio, Filze 2–3; AABol Miscellanea Vecchie, vol. 774, L'Inquisizione; these buttress my generalisations, though only a few specific examples can be cited later.
10. ASV SU 33, 14 Nov. 1573, 'Domenico Longinus portator Farina': 'Volta carta, e varda su'l messal, che trovar il Papa, che buzera / Il Gardenal, il Garndenal da ca colonna / Che cazza in culo il Papa ghe perdona.'
11. John Martin, *Venice's Hidden Enemies*, 180 reproduces Domenico Beccafumi's drawing of such a scene.
12. Romeo, *L'Inquisizione*, 42.
13. Ginzburg, *The Night Battles*, with Appendix transcribing an early trial. Nardon, *Benandanti e inquisitori*, for wider context.
14. Davidson, 'The Inquisition in Venice', 128, citing ASV, SU Busta 44, 'Felino Giuseppe', 29 Oct. 1580.
15. Grendler, *Roman Inquisition*, 57–9; Del Col (ed.) *L'Inquisizione in Friuli*, 33; Schutte, *Aspiring Saints*, 40.
16. De Frede, *Religiosità*, 335; Pastor *History of Popes*, XIX, 302.
17. De Frede, *Religiosità*, 339–40.

18. Seidel Menchi, 'Italy', 199 n. 44.
19. Dall'Olio, 'I Rapporti', 274–7.
20. Prosperi, *Tribunali*, 170.
21. De Frede, *Religiosità e Cultura*, esp. 347–50 ('Ancora sugli Autodafè'), and 300–1, 307 ('Autodafè'); M. Firpo and D. Marcatto (eds), *I Processi ... Carnesecchi*, records his lengthy investigations.
22. Caponetto, *Protestant Reformation*, *passim*, 57 and 39 for quotes.
23. Ricci, *Il Sommo Inquisitore*, 136 (quote), 55–8, 136–8, 169–72.
24. Caponetto, *Protestant Reformation*, 69–70; De Frede, *Religiosità*, 324–6.
25. De Frede, *Religiosità*, esp. 355–7; Caponetto, *Protestant Reformation*, 246–8 (Faenza).
26. Prosperi, *Tribunali*, 170–72; De Frede, *Religiosità*, 358–60, (quote 360); Caponetto, *Protestant Reformation*, 335–36; Déjob, *De l'influence de Concile*, Appendix F, 385–91, Marcello Sirleto's letters to uncle.
27. De Frede, *Religiosità*, 337.
28. Bujanda, J.M. de (ed.), *Index des livres interdits* reproduces a whole range from Europe, in 10 volumes; vol. 8 for 1557, 1559, 1564 Indexes, vol. 9 for 1590, 1593, 1596. Well illustrated for original format.
29. Rozzo, 'Italian literature on the Index', 199.
30. Godman, *The Saint as Censor*, 20–1.
31. Grendler, 'Books for Sarpi'.
32. Balsamo, 'How to doctor a bibliography', 72.
33. Dall'Olio, 'I Rapporti', 264–5.
34. *Index Librorum Prohibitorum* ... (Rome, Camera Apostolica, 1596 ... 1632), copy in Biblioteca Comunale, Perugia, I.O.1360.
35. Brought out in many essays in Fragnito (ed.), *Church, Censorship*, which is basis of much above, and what follows. See my Review in *Renaissance Studies*, 17 (2003), 122–5.
36. Grendler, *Roman Inquisition*, 190–93.
37. ASV SU Busta 80, 'De Domo Marco, Gemma Aurora', 29 April 1625; Busta 103, 'Antonio Rocco', 27 Feb. 1635 and 3 Nov. 1648; Busta 103 'Pro Francesco Valvasense', 15 Feb. 1648, (a leading printer, including of Arcangela Tarabotti's books).
38. Fragnito, *La Bibbia al rogo*; Fragnito (ed.), *Church, Censorship*, with her own article, and Edoardo Barbieri's 'Tradition and change in the spiritual literature'.
39. Fragnito (ed.), *Church, Censorship*, 35 n. 70.
40. Fragnito (ed.), *Church, Censorship*, 66.
41. Godman, *From Poliziano to Machiavelli*, Appendix, 'Machiavelli, the Inquisition and the Index', esp. 325–8 (quoting 326); Bujanda, *Index*, vol. 9, 350. Ricci, *Il Sommo Inquisitore*, 350, 355, 385.
42. Grendler, 'Books for Sarpi', 111–12.
43. Grendler, 'Books for Sarpi', esp. 111–12.
44. Grendler, 'Books for Sarpi', 110–11.
45. Grendler, 'The destruction of Hebrew books', quoting 130.
46. Ioly Zorattini (ed.), *Processi di S. Uffizio di Venezia*, transcribes denunications and trials; his 'Jews, Crypt-Jews and the Inquisition', is his recent analysis, in R.C. Davis and B. Ravid *The Jews of Early Modern Venice*, which has many other helpful articles; see also Brian Pullan, *The Jews*.

47. Pullan, ' "A Ship with Two Rudders": Righetto Marrano'.
48. Romeo, *Inquisitori, esorcisti,* 271; see also his *Esorcisti, Confessori e Sessualità.* See bibliography for other authors mentioned.
49. Di Simplicio, *Inquisizione Stregoneria Medicina,* 85–7.
50. Cardini (ed.), *Gostanza la strega.*
51. Dall'Olio, 'I Rapporti', 278–82, quoting from 279 and 281.
52. Nardon, *Benandanti e inquisitori nel Friuli,* and 'Benandanti "funebri" '.
53. Ginzburg, *Night Battles,* Appendix transcribed their case.
54. Nardon, *Benandanti,* 136–8, Tables.
55. Gentilcore, *Healers and Healing,* ch. 6, quoting 164; also his *Bishop and Witch,* 94–5, 107–13, 190–1; Prosperi, *Il Tribunale,* esp. 418–30; Romeo, *Inquisitori, Esorcisti.*
56. Prosperi, *Il Tribunale,* 427 and 421–2 on the Cortona case, investigated by the Bishop in 1579.
57. Romeo, *Esorcisti, Confessori,* 87–9; Gentilcore, *From Bishop to Witch,* esp. 94–5.
58. Romeo, *Esorcisti,* 13–14, with comments on source material.
59. Romeo, *Esorcisti,* 14 n. 3; Prosperi, *Tribunali,* 339–40.
60. See accessibly Ruth Martin, *Witchcraft and Inquisition*; Ruggiero, *Binding Passions.* I have seen examples of such denunciations in the Buste cited above, n. 9.
61. ASV SU Busta 59, 30 March 1587; see my *Early Modern Italy,* 156–67; Ruggiero, *Binding Passions,* 118–19, 249; Pullan, *The Jews of Europe,* 161; Ruth Martin, *Witchcraft,* 168. I am grateful to Tricia Allerston for help with this case.

10 Churches, Cultural Enticement and Display

1. See Mullett, *Catholic Reformation,* ch. 7, 'The Catholic Reformation and the arts' for another historian's useful approach to religious art, in European context, and using the concept of 'baroque' style as his key to discussion.
2. Guerrini, *Atti della Visita ... Bollani,* vol. 3 : 54–7, 72, 117–19; Montanari, *Disciplinamento,* esp. 91–103; Grosso & Mellano, *La Controriforma ... Torino,* vol. 2: 47–55, 190–2, 209; Fiorani, 'Confraternite', 120–2 (1624).
3. *Storia di Brescia,* vol. 2, *Il Dominio Veneto,* 864–82; Gatti Perer, 'Cultura e socialità'. Carlo Borromeo's *Instructionum fabricae et sepllectilis ecclesiasticae libri II* (Milan, 1577) became the standard guide to churches and their fitments; a useful commentary with extracts by E.C. Voelker, 'Borromeo's Influences'.
4. Lapucci and Pacciansi (eds), *Zibaldone ... Pinelli,* 90–2, 119–25.
5. Hibbard, 'Early History of Sant'Andrea'.
6. Wittkower, *Art and Architecture* (1999 edn), 84–5.
7. Hall, *Renovation and Counter-Reformation*; Lewine, *The Roman Church Interior*; Armellini, *Le Chiese di Roma,* 2: 668. cf. on church interiors generally; Wölfflin, *Renaissance and Baroque,* 111–23.

8. Lewine, *Roman Church Interior,* 32–40 (general effects), 86, 89, 226–31 (Il Gesù), 41–44, 97–100, 316–53 (S. Maria ai Monti); Heydenreich & Lotz, *Architecture of Italy,* 273–76, 280; Pirri, *Giovanni Tristano,* esp. ch. VII on Il Gesù. cf. Howard, *Jacopo Sansovino,* 67 for F. Zorzi, quote.
9. Heydenreich & Lotz, *Architecture of Italy,* 110, 292–94, Pl. 313.
10. G.B. Del Tufo, *Historia* (Rome, 1609).
11. Avery, *Bernini,* ch. 8 on both chapels, well illustrated; Lavin, *Bernini and Unity,* on theme; Barcham, *Grand in Design,* esp. 349–54, 364–86.
12. Black, *Italian Confraternities,* ch. 11; Eisenbichler, *The Boys.*
13. Fabiani, 'Sinodi ... Ascoli', 280.
14. ASV SU Busta 33, 18 July 1573. Translated transcript in Chambers and Pullan (eds), Venice, 232–36; see G. Fehl, 'Veronese and the Inquisition'; large sized illustration in Black *et al. Atlas of the Renaissance,* 98–99.
15. *Discorso intorno alle Imagine,* in Barocchi (ed.), *Trattati,* 2: 221, 497; and see Boschloo, *Annibale Carracci in Bologna,* 227, n. 3.
16. Barocchi (ed.), *Trattati,* 3: 195–223.
17. Prodi, 'Ricerche sulla teorica delle arti figurative', and Prodi, *Paleotti,* vol. 2, ch. xviii on Paleotti's art theories; modern text of his writings in Barocchi, *Trattati d'arte,* 117–509; Boschloo, *Annibale Carracci in Bologna,* reflects on Paleotti's theories. Shearman, *Only Connect,* illuminates many aspects of communication in the Renaissance that are more obviously developed in the 'baroque' period; see also Freedberg, *The Power of Images,* esp. ch. 12, 'Arousal by Image', and Argan, *Baroque Age,* on 'Poetics and rhetoric', 'Imagination and Illusion', 'Imagination and Feeling', for issues of artistic intentions discussed here.
18. The website www.artcyclopedia.com/ is a valuable tool for finding illustrations and data of known artists.
19. Nichols, *Tintoretto,* esp. chs 4–5, with colour plates; Fortini Brown, *Venetian Narrative Painting in the Age of Carpaccio,* for tradition.
20. Lindner, *Madonna della Ghiara* (Reggio Emilia, 1954), 80–8.
21. Beny and Gunn, *Churches of Rome* (London, 1981), 166–8, 218; Wittkower, *Art and Architecture* (1999), 1 pl. 53 (Lanfranco), 2 pl. 100 (Cortona).
22. Beny and Gunn, *Churches of Rome,* 220–1 (Pozzo, colour); Wittkower, *Art and Architecture* (1999), 2 pl. 175 (Gaulli), pl.143 (Pozzo).
23. My *Italian Confraternities,* 261 and pls. 6–7.
24. Whitfield and Martineau (eds), *Painting in Naples,* pl.16 and details; Pacelli, *Caravaggio: Le Sette Opere di Misericordia* (Salerno, 1984), with many ills for all artists involved.
25. Black, *Italian Confraternities,* ch. 11 'Confraternity buildings and their decorations'; Nichols, *Tintoretto,* pl. 20 (S. Marcuola, colour). See above Chapter 7, n. 5.
26. For the Carracci: www.pinacotecabologna.it and links. Wittkower, *Art and Architecture* (1999), 1 ch. 3.
27. Blunt, 'Gianlorenzo Bernini: illusionism and mysticism', *Art Bulletin* 1 (1978), 68.
28. *Age of Caravaggio,* no. 17 (with colour plate).
29. Emiliani (ed.), *Barocci,* fullest study, with colour pls. after p. XLVIII for *Crucifixion* and *Perdono.*
30. Freedberg, *Painting in Italy* (1975 edn, Harmondsworth), Fig. 287.

31. Bury, *The Print in Italy 1550–1620*, excellent illustrated catalogue, and analyses; no. 45 for *St Francis*.
32. Roche, *North Italian Church Music*, is a key guide to the range of church music produced, even if geographically limited, with many musical examples. Early chapters deal with the background of Trent and society.
33. Fenlon, 'Music and reform', for an initial quick guide.
34. Fenlon, *Music and Patronage in Seventeenth-Century Mantua*, vol. 1.
35. Translated by Fenlon in his 'Music and reform', 235.
36. Silbiger, 'Roman Frescobaldi tradition'; Bonta, 'Uses of the Sonata da Chiesa'.
37. Martin, *Roma Sancta*, 96; partly cited by O'Regan, *Institutional Patronage*, 2–3.
38. Thomas Coryat, *Coryat's Crudities*, 251–2; CD: *Giovanni Gabrieli. Music for San Rocco 1608*, directed by Paul McCreesh, 1996 Archiv 449, 180–2. See Arnold, 'Music ... San Rocco'.
39. CDs: *Carlo Gesualdo. Leçons de Tenebres*, directed Alfred Deller, 1970–87, HMA190220; Gesualdo. *Complete Sacred Music for Five Voices*, Jeremy Summerly, 1993. Naxos 8.550742. See Watkins, *Gesualdo*, esp. ch. 11 'The Responsoria'.
40. CDs: *Monteverdi Music Sacra*, directed Rinaldo Alessandrini, 1996, Opus 111, Paris OPS 30–150; *Monteverdi Vespro della Beata Vergine (1610)*, directed John Eliot Gardiner, 1990, Archiv 429 565-2; *Monteverdi Mass of Thanksgiving, Venice 1631*, directed Andrew Parrott, 1989, CDS 749876 2. From the huge literature on him Fabbri, *Monteverdi* is the best all-round study.
41. Fenlon, 'Music and Reform', 244–5.
42. Hammond, *Music and Spectacle*, for a very full picture of Barberini display.
43. Hill, 'Oratory Music'.
44. Kirkendale, *Emilio de' Cavalieri*, 233–94 (quoting 293), and 301–13 (libretto); he recommends as best CD: Hans-Martin Linde, EMI CMS 7 63421 2 (1990).
45. CDs: *Luigi Rossi. Oratorios*, directed William Christie. 1982 HMA 1901091; *Luigi Rossi, Giuseppe Figlio di Giacobbe*, directed Carlo Felice Cillario. 1994. SXAM 2009–2.
46. Hammond, *Music and Spectacle*, ch. 13. CD: *Landi. Il Sant'Alessio*, directed William Christie, 1990. Erato 0630-14340-2.
47. Roche, 'The Duet', and *North Italian Church Music*, ch. II and 51–58 (Viadana).
48. Quoted by Rinaldo Alessandrini, notes to his CD cited above.
49. See my 'The Public Face', expanding my *Italian Confraternities*, 99–100.
50. Biblioteca Comunale, Bologna. Fondo Ospedale 43 'Memorie riguardanti l'uffizio di Priore dell'Arciconfraternita dell'Ospedale di S. Maria della Morte', vol. 1, fols. 46–8, and 32–3.
51. Baviero and Bentini (eds), *Mistero e Immagine*, esp. Fanti, 'Per la storia del culto eucharistico', and some illustrations.
52. McGinness, *Right Thinking*, 84–5; Norman, 'Social History of Preaching', 161.
53. Weston-Lewis (ed.), *Effigies and Ecstasies*, cat. No.126 for Pietro da Cortona design, with my introductory article, ' "Exceeding" '.

54. My, *Italian Confraternities*, ch. 5 on processions, plays and pilgrimages, developed in my 'Public Face'; Bernardi, 'Il Teatro'; Fagiolo (ed.), *La Festa di Roma*, with many illustrations.
55. Casale, *Diario*, ed., Marcora; the translated extracts in Cochrane and Kirshner (eds), are less obvious on this.
56. Barbara Wisch, 'New Themes'; Gregory Martin, *Roma Sancta*, 89–91.
57. McPhee, *Bernini and the Bell Towers*, Fig. 93 (colour): *Corpus Christi Procession in the Piazza of St. Peter's*, from Museo Nazionale di Palazzo Venezia, *c.*1646.
58. Cerasoli, 'Diario di cose romane degli anni 1614, 1615, 1616', *Studi e documenti di storia e diritto* 15 (1896), 273–4.
59. Gentilcore, ' "Adapt Yourselves" ', 279, 284–7.
60. Lapucci and Pacciani (eds), *Zibaldone … Spinelli*, 87–8. My, *Italian Confraternities*, 117–21, 194–6 on pilgrimages and Jubilees; updated by my 'Public Face', for what follows.
61. My, *Italian Confraternities*, 118–21; Julia, 'L'accoglienza … pellegrini'.
62. Fagiolo and Madonna, *Roma 1300–1875*, 178–294 for Jubilees 1575–1700.
63. Giacinto Gigli, *Diario* (1994), esp. 72–5, 106, 146–50, 581–91; Fagiolo (ed.), *La Festa di Roma*, for illustrations as well as many articles; Nussdorfer, *Civic Politics*, 109–14; Dandelet, *Spanish Rome*, 110–15, 157–58, 168–70; Hammond, *Music and Spectacle*, has Appendix summarising the main Roman festivals in Urban VIII's reign, also paintings and prints of festivities.

11 Conclusions: Successes and Failures

1. Gentilcore, *Healers and Healing*, 164.
2. Black, *Early Modern Italy*, 214, with my 'Epilogue' more broadly offering my guide to the eighteenth century context, and sources; see also Chadwick, *The Popes and European Revolution*, esp. ch. 5; De Rosa, *Vescovi, popolo e magia*, for both late reform and continuing gross ignorance and superstition.
3. Ditchfield, ' "In search of local knowledge" ', 256, 259 (quote).
4. ASV SU Busta 103, Anzola Civran, 5 June 1646.
5. ASV SU Busta 106, Elisabetta Thodesca, 16 July 1652; Julia Meretrice, 3 December 1652. See now Ambrosini, 'Between heresy and free thought'.
6. Schutte, *Living Saints*, 92–3; Zardin, 'Gregorio Barbarigo', reviewing a 1996 conference about him.
7. Clifton, 'Looking at St. Agatha', esp. Figs 3 and 4, Francesco Guarino's paintings in a Solofra parish church.

Appendix Italian Bishoprics

1. The chief Sources for this Appendix (and Chapter 4 commentary on bishops and their work): Eubel (*et al.*) *Hierarchia*, vols. 111–V; Gams,

Series Episcoporum; Ughelli, *Italia Sacra*; Mansi, *Sacrorum Conciliorum*, vols 34–36ter; von Pastor, *History of the Popes*, esp. vols, XVII–XXXII ; Da Nadro, *Sinodi diocesani italiani*; Corrain and Zampini, *Documenti etnografici*, for printed synodal evidence; many articles from *Ravennatensia*, vols; Donvito and Pellegrino, *L'Organizzazione Ecclesiastica … Abruzzi, e Molise e della Basilicata*; Sposato, *Aspetti … Calabria*; F. Russo, *Storia … Reggio Calabria*; Comerford, 'Italian Tridentine Diocesan Seminaries', for most of the seminary information.

2. Many dioceses were 'Independent', that is, directly under papal control, though some bishops might cooperate with a nearby metropolitan archbishop holding Councils; and the status of some was contested, or ambiguous. Some sees around Rome were for Curia-based cardinals. Some monastic houses acted as bishoprics. Bishoprics on Sicily and Sardinia are included here, though not usually part of my main discussion in the text, because appointments could be part of the 'Italian' as well as royal 'Spanish' patronage systems. Some Dalmatian bishoprics, Ionian islands etc. are also listed as they remained part of the Venetian and/or Papal patronage, despite the Ottoman Turk threats or occupation.
3. This indicates the secular control, primarily in our early period; some dioceses were in more than one secular state, or subject ecclesiastically to a metropolitan in another state (e.g. Brescia).
4. If two separated dates are given, this suggests – unless otherwise indicated–a refoundation after the first seminary had folded.
5. To be treated as conservative minimum. The indication of synods is mainly based on surviving printed documents(which may mislead on the precise date of the synod meeting), as traced esp. by Da Nadro; evidence of some others comes patchily from Visitation records, which may be vague on precise dates, with a Bishop claiming he had two in his time, so given here as 1562–6 (2); I have added others as per chance noted in articles and monographs of particular bishopics. This can be misleading as an archdiocese like Ravenna has been better studied for manuscript records than those in the Kingdom of Naples. My concentration has been on the 1560–1630 period, and later synods are mainly indicative of how late some diocese came up with a synod of some impact on the record.
6. The Patriarchate of Aquileia was administered from Portogruaro, or Udine (suffragan), or even Venice; the ancient great city of Aquileia was largely ruined. Council and synods were held in different places. The 1602 synod, in Gorizia, was for Germanic and Slavonic nations within the Patriarchate.
7. Papal enclave within Kingdom of Naples territory.
8. Bressanone, in the Alto-Adige/Tyrol area, though suffragan under Salzburg, and part of the Holy Roman Empire, sometimes is counted as 'italian', because sometimes Italians held posts there; Christopher Madruzzo, Bishop of Trent 1539–67, also held Bressanone 1542–65, and he used an Italian suffragan B. Aliprandini 1558–71. Eubel, *Hierarchia*, III, 141 and IV 121.
9. A 'quasi-seminary' or clerical school existed in Massafiscaglia for Cervia diocese from *c.*1590: *Ravennatensia*, III, 121–8.

10. Though subject to non-Venetian ecclesiastical control, (Ragusa, modern Dubrovnik, being an independent Republic), this island remained part of the Venetian empire, and its Church influence.
11. The 1596 Cosenza PC was also attended by the bishops of Cariati and Umbriatico (suffragans of Santa Severina), and of San Marco (suffragan of Rossano): Sposato, *Aspetti … Calabria*, 31 and n. 85.
12. Effectively independent sub-infeudated state under the D'Este family till 1598.
13. Macerata, Recanati and Loreto had complex relationships, sometimes having different bishops after 1571. Eubel, *Hierarchia*, III 220, 231, 281 and IV 227, 293.
14. These islands, and the suffragan Suda, can be seen as a reasonably active part of the Venetian empire.
15. Campli was separated from Teramo in 1588 to be independent, but opposed; added to Ortona with town status by 1600, Donvito and Pellegrino, *L'organizzazione. Abruzzi*, 9.
16. The episcopal seminary is taken over by Jesuits in 1621.
17. Episcopal seminary vaguely noted at Atri, but Jesuit College probably doing the main training, Donvito and Pellegrino, 75.
18. A pioneering proto-seminary predating the Tridentine recommendations.
19. Another proto-seminary.
20. Ragusa was now an independent Republic, but with a strong Venetian influence; according to Eubel, *Hierarchia*, III 281, IV 291, its bishops up to 1616 were 'Italian' rather than local Ragusan.
21. Recanati, Loreto and Macerata had complex relationships. Loreto had a separate bishop 1586–91, but in 1592 Recanati and Loreto were re-united as co-equals ('aeques principalites') under one bishop, (Eubel, *Hierarchia*, III 220); and see Macerata earlier.
22. Closed, but Barnabites restart one 1654. From *c.*1590 had had a clerical school as 'quasi-seminary'.
23. Synods in 1597 and 1618 claimed that synods were being held annually, Sposato, *Aspetti*, 218.

A Brief Reading Guide

The literature behind the writing of this book is considerable, and the Bibliography only reflects part of it, but should be enough for scholars with overlapping interests, and postgraduates wanting to develop areas and themes, using Italian. This brief guide is for the student and general reader looking for the most helpful and stimulating 'further reading'. Gregory Hanlon's *Early Modern Italy*, 1550–1800 (Macmillan, 2000, pb), provides a good all-round study, but has a more pessimistic view of the seventeenth century than I provide in my own *Early Modern Italy. A Social History* (Routledge, 2000, pb), which starts a little earlier. John A. Marino (ed.) *Early Modern Italy* (OUP, 2002, pb) has two very relevant chapters: John Martin's 'Religion, renewal and reform', and Anne Jacobson Schutte's, 'Religion, spirituality and the Post-Tridentine Church'. My own *Italian Confraternities in the Sixteenth Century* (CUP, 1989; 2003, pb reprint – but no chance was given for corrections or update), has been frequently cited in several chapters, and it remains a major guide to religious social activity. For the wider church and religion context, my preference is for Michael Mullett's *The Catholic Reformation* (Routledge, 1999, pb). A.D. Wright's *The Early Modern Papacy* (Longman, 2000, pb), is an indispensable guide, digesting the huge literature on Popes and the Papacy. John O'Malley's *The First Jesuits* (Harvard UP), is vital, and balanced, on the crucial new Order, by a superb Jesuit scholar. Exciting work has recently been produced on religious women, in and out of convents; accessible highlights include Mary Laven's *Virgins of Venice* (Viking/ Penguin, 2002, pb), judicious and understanding on (mainly) the more unholy sides of convent life; P. Renée Baernstein, *A Convent Tale* (Routledge, 2002), on the battle for women to have a 'third state' between home and enclosed convent, then for a Milan convent to be a female power house; and Anne J. Schutte's *Aspiring Saints* (The John Hopkins Press, 2001), for saintly women and frauds, and the problem – especially for the Inquisition – in deciding which they were. Schutte's book is also a good way of looking at aspects of Inquisition procedures. Carlo Ginzburg's *The Cheese and the Worms. The Cosmos of a Sixteenth Century Miller* (1980 trans., John Hopkins, 1997, pb, or Penguin, 1992, pb), and *The Night Battles Witchcraft and Agrarian Cults* (1983 trans., John Hopkins, 1997, pb), are rightly famous studies of the interaction between inquisitors and local beliefs and behaviour. David Gentilcore's *From Bishop to Witch* (Manchester UP, 1992), though on a small area in southern Italy, is intriguing and helpful on many issues on the periphery.

Bibliography

Archives

Bologna

Archivio di Stato (ASB)

Corporazioni Religiose. S. Sacramento di Bagnacavallo, vol. 424 Decreti (1635–1734); Rosario di Bagnacavallo, vol. 394, Libro Maestro della Massaria (1633–1794); Compagnia del Ssmo Rosario in Crevalcore, vol. 1/7813, Miscellanea; Compagnia del Ssmo di Budrio, vol. 4/7852 Miscellania.

Corporazioni Soppresse. SS.Vitale e Agricola, vol. 93/3242: folder of 'Lettere Diverse'; S. Margherita di Bologna {Benedictine nuns} vol. 51/3198 Carte Diverse.

Demaniale. S.Cristina, vol. 48/2909, Visitation 1622–23 under suffragan Bishop Angelo Gozzadini.

ASB Tribunale del Torrone vol. 5743 (1628–30).

Archivio Arcivescovile (AABol)

Visite Pastorali, vol. 123 (H670), fasc.4, Visit to city of Rev. D. Rodolfo Paleotti, 1598; vol. 144 (H536) (Ab Girolamo Colonna, 1632–43). Miscellana Vecchie, vol. 744, 'L'Inquisizione'.

Biblioteca Comunale (Archiginnasio)

Fondo Ospedale 43 'Memorie riguardanti l'uffizio di Priore dell'Arciconfraternita dell'Ospedale di S. Maria della Morte', vol. 1.

Florence

Archivio Arcivescovile (AAF)
S. Uffizio, Filze 1–3 (on microfilm).
Visite Pastorali 26, Ab. Pietro Nicolini's *contado* Visitation, 1635–40.

Perugia

Archivio di Stato (AdiSP)
Editti e Bandi, vol. 8.
Religiose Soppresse, no. 5 S. Domenico, Miscellanea 77: 'Nomi dei Fratelli e delle Sorelle del SS. Nome di Dio 1601–'.
Archivio di San Pietro(A.S. Pietro): Libro dei Contratti, vol. 32; Diverse vols 38, 89.
Biblioteca Comunale (Augusta), (BCP)
MS 479 (G.68) and MS 135, Letters from and to Bishop V. Ercolani.

Rome

Archivio Storico del Vicariato (ASVR).
ASVR, Arciconfraternita della Dottrina Cristiana, palchetto 168, vol. 417, Congregationi 1599–1608.

Venice

Archivio della Curia Patriarcale (APV)
Atti Patriarcale riguardanti le monache, 'Decretorum et mandatorum monialium', vol. for 1591–99, vol for 1620–30; 'Criminalia S. Inquisitionis 1586–99' Archivi Storici della Chiesa Veneziana: Parrocchia di S. Maria Formosa, Scuola di S. Giosofat o dei Fruttaroli, 'Carte pertinenti', nos 1 and 2. Parrochia di S. Lio. (Catalogued under Parrochia di Santa Maria Formosa, Index II, pp. 90.) Amminstrazione vol. 6; 'Accordi fra il capitolo di S.Lio e la scuola del SS.Sacramento.' (Index p. 106–107), Registri degli Infermi 1 (1630–71).

Archivio di Stato (ASV)
Sant'Uffizio (SU) Buste 13, 33, 59, 61, 66, 80, 103,106.
Scuole Piccole e Suffragi, Busta 706, SS. Trinita alla Salute, Libro 3, 'Notariato' 1649–1710.

Printed Works

(The) Age of Caravaggio (New York, 1985).
Alberigo, Giuseppe, 'Studi e problemi relativi all'applicazione del Concilio di Trento in Italia (1945–1958)', *Rivista Storica Italiana*, 70 (1958), pp. 239–98.

Alberigo, Giuseppe, 'Le potestà episcopali nei debattiti tridentini', in *Concilio di Trento* (1965), pp. 471–523.
——, 'Carlo Borromeo come modello di vescovo', *Rivista Storica Italiana*, 79 (1967), pp. 1031–52.
——, 'L'episcopato nel cattolicesimo post-tridentino', *Cristianesimo nella storia*, 6 (1985), pp. 71–91.
——, 'Carlo Borromeo between two models of bishop', in *San Carlo Borromeo*, eds, Headley and Tomaro, pp. 250–63.
Alberigo, J. (Giuseppe) *et al.*, *Conciliorum Oecumenicorum Decreta* (Bologna, 1973).
Ambrosini, Federica, 'Between heresy and free thought, between the Mediterranean and the North. Heterodox women in seventeenth-century Venice', in *Mediterranean Urban Culture 1400–1700*, ed. A. Cowan (Exeter, 2000), pp. 83–94.
Andretta, Stefano, 'Il governo dell'osservanza: poteri e monache dal Sacco alla fine del Settecento', in Fiorani and Prosperi (eds), *Storia d'Italia*, pp. 396–427.
Antonovicz, Anthony V., 'Counter-reformation cardinals: 1534–90', *European Studies Review*, 2 (1972), pp. 301–28.
Antonucci, Laura, 'Scrivere la santità'. "Vite esemplari" di donne nella Roma barocca', in Fiorani and Prosperi (eds), *Storia d'Italia*, pp. 651–76.
Archiva Ecclesiae xxii–xxiii (1979–80) (Citta del Vaticano).
Argan, Giulio Cesare, *The Baroque Age* (Milan, 1989).
Armellini, M., *Le Chiese di Roma dal secolo IV al XIX*, 2 vols. (Rome, 1942).
Arnold, Denis, 'Music at the Scuola di San Rocco', *Music and Letters*, 40 (1954), 229–41.
——, *Giovanni Gabrieli and the Music of the Venetian High Renaissance* (London, 1979).
Arsenio D'Ascoli, Fra, *La predicazione dei cappuccini nel Cinquecento in Italia* (Loreto, 1956).
Avery, Charles, *Bernini. Genius of the Baroque* (London, 1997).
Baccichet, Moreno, 'Insediamento e devozione: la processione a San Daniele di Barcis', in *L'Incerto Confine*, pp. 69–91.
Baernstein, P. Renée, *A Convent Tale. A Century of Sisterhood in Spanish Milan* (New York and London, 2002).
Baldacchini, Lorenzo, *Bibliografia delle stampe popolari religiose del xvi-xvii secolo* (Florence, 1980).
Baldauf-Berdes, Jane L., *Women Musicians of Venice. Musical Foundations, 1525–1855*. Revised Edition, revised by Elsie Arnold (Oxford, 1996).
Balsamo, Luigi, 'How to doctor a bibliography', in *Church, Censorship*, ed. Fragnito, pp. 50–78.
Bambilla, Elena, 'Società ecclesiastica e società civile: aspetti della formazione del clero dal cinquecento al restaurazione', *Società e Storia* 12 (1981), pp. 299–366.
Barbieri, Edoardo, 'Tradition and change in the spiritual literature of the cinquecento', in *Church, Censorship*, ed. Fragnito, pp. 111–33.
——, 'Fra tradizione e cambiamento: note sul libro spirituale del xvi secolo', in *Libri, biblioteche*, eds, Barbieri and Zardin, pp. 3–61.

Barbieri, Edoardo and Zardin, Danilo (eds), *Libri, biblioteche e cultura nell'Italia del Cinque e Seicento* (Milan, 2002).

Barcham, William L., *Grand in Design. The Life and Career of Federico Cornaro, Prince of the Church, Patriarch of Venice and Patron of Arts* (Venice, 2001).

Barletta, E.A., *Aspetti della Riforma Cattolica e del Concilio di Trento. Mostra documentaria* (Rome, 1964).

Barocchi, Paola (ed.), *Trattati d'Arte del Cinquecento fra Manierismo e Controriforma*, 3 vols (Bari, 1960–62).

Bascapé, Carlo, *Vita e Opere di Carlo Archivescovo di Milano*, ed. E. Cattaneo (Milan, 1965).

Battistella, Antonio, *Il S.Officio e la riforma religiosa in Bologna* (1905, extract).

Baumgartner, Frederic J., *Behind Locked Doors. A History of Papal Elections* (N.Y and Basingstoke, 2003).

Belardini, Manuela, ' "Piace molto e Giesù la nostra confidanza". Suor Orsola Fontebuoni a Maria Maddalena d'Austria', in *Per lettera*, ed. Zarri, pp. 359–83.

Beneficio di Cristo: 'The "Beneficio di Cristo",' translated, with an introduction by Ruth Prelowski, in *Italian Reformation Studies*, ed. John A. Tedeschi, (Florence, 1965), pp. 21–102.

Beny, Roloff and Gunn, Peter, *The Churches of Rome* (London, 1981).

Berengo, Marino, *Nobili e mercanti nella Lucca del Cinquecento* (Turin, 1965).

Bergin, Joseph, 'The Counter-Reformation Church and its Bishops', *Past and Present*, 165 (November 1999), pp. 30–73.

Bernardi, Claudio, *La drammaturgia della settimana santa in Italia* (Milan, 1991).

——, 'Il Teatro tra Scena e Ritualità', in *I Tempi del Concilio*, eds, Mozzarelli and Zardin, pp. 439–60.

Bertoldi Lenoci, Liana, 'La sociabiltà religiosa pugliese. Le confraternite (1500–1900)' *Ricerche di storia sociale e religiosa*, 37–38 (1990), pp. 213–37.

Bertoldi Lenoci, Liana (ed.), *Le Confraternite pugliese in età moderna* 2 vols. (Fasano di Brindisi, 1989–90).

Bertoldi Lenoci, Liana (ed.), *Confraternite, Chiese e Societa. Aspetti e problemi dell'associazionismo laicale europeo in eta moderna e contemporanea* (Fasano di Brindisi, 1994).

Bireley, Robert, *The Refashioning of Catholicism, 1450–1700: A Reassessment of the Counter-Reformation* (Washington DC, 1999).

Black, Christopher F., 'Perugia and Papal Absolutisn in the sixteenth century', *English Historical Review*, 96 (1981), pp. 245–81.

——, 'Perugia and Post-Tridentine Church Reform', *Journal of Ecclesiastical History*, 25 (1984), pp. 429–51.

——, *Italian Confraternities in the Sixteenth Century* (Cambridge, 1989, 2003 reprint).

——, 'Confraternities', in *Oxford Encyclopedia of the Reformation*, ed. H. Hillerbrand, 1 (1996), pp. 406–408.

——, ' "Exceeding every expression of words": Bernini's Rome and the religious background', in *Effigies and Ecstasies*, ed. Weston-Lewis, pp. 1–11.

——, 'Confraternities and the parish in the context of Italian Catholic Reform' in *Confraternities and Catholic Reform*, eds, Donnelly and Maher (1999), pp. 1–26.

Black, Christopher F., 'The development of confraternity studies over the last thirty years', in *Ritual Kinship*, ed. Terpstra (1999), pp. 9–29.
——, *Early Modern Italy. A Social History* (London, 2001).
——, 'Early modern Italian confraternities: inclusion and exclusion', *Historein*, 2 (Athens, 2000), pp. 65–86.
——, 'The public face of post-Tridentine Italian confraternities', *Journal of Religious History*, 28 (2004), 87–101.
Blaisdell, Charmarie J., 'Angela Merici and the Ursulines', in *Religious Orders*, ed. DeMolen, pp. 99–136.
Blunt, Anthony, 'Gianlorenzo Bernini: illusionism and mysticism', *Art Bulletin*, 1 (1978), pp. 67–89.
Boccato, Carla, 'Risvolti familiari e attività di impresa intorno al "Marrano" Gaspar Ribiera', in *L'Identità Disimulata*, ed. Ioly Zorattini, pp. 311–20.
Boer, Wietse de, *The Conquest of the Soul: Confession, Discipline, and Public Order in Counter-Reformation Milan* (Leiden and Boston, 2001).
Bolgiani, Franco, 'Per un dibattito sulla storia religiosa d'Italia', *Rivista di Storia e Letterature Religiosa*, 32 (1996), pp. 333–433.
Bonta, Stephen, 'The uses of the Sonata da Chiesa', *Journal of American Musicological Society*, 22 (1969), pp. 54–84.
Borromeo, Agostino, 'I vescovi italiani e l'applicazione del Concilio di Trento', in *I Tempi*, eds, Mozzarelli and Zardin, pp. 27–105.
Borromeo, San Carlo, *Le piu belle pagine delle Omelie*, ed. C. Goria (Milan, 1926).
Boschloo, Anton, *Annibale Caracci in Bologna. Visible Reality in Art after the Council of Trent* (The Hague and NY, 1974).
Bossy, John, 'The Counter-Reformation and the people of Catholic Europe', *Past and Present*, 47 (1970), pp. 51–70.
——, 'The social history of confession in the Age of the Reformation', *Transactions of the Royal Historical Society*, 25 (1975), pp. 22–38.
——, 'The Mass as a social institution', *Past and Present*, 100 (1983), pp. 29–61.
——, *Peace in the Post-Reformation* (Cambridge, 1998).
Bouwsma, William J., *Venice and the Defense of Republican Liberty* (Berkeley and Los Angeles, 1968).
Brambilla, Elena, 'Società ecclesiastica e società civile: aspetti della formazione del clero dal Cinquecento alla Restaurazione', in *Società e Storia*, 4 (1981), pp. 299–366.
Brandileone, F, *Saggi sulla storia della celebrazione del matrimonio in Italia* (Milan, 1906).
Brezzi, Paolo, 'Storia della Storiografia', in *(Il) Concilio Tridentino* (1965), pp. 1–32.
Broderick, John, 'The Sacred College of Cardinals: size and geographical composition 1099–1986', *Archivum Historiae Pontificae*, 25 (1987), pp. 7–71.
Brown, Judith C., *Immodest Acts: the Life of a Lesbian Nun in Renaissance Italy* (New York, 1986).
Brown, Patricia Fortini, *Venetian Narrative Painting in the Age of Carpaccio* (New Haven, 1988).
Bujanda, J.M. de, *Index des livres interdits*, 10 vols. (Sherbrooke and Geneva, 1984–96): vol. 8 (*Index de Rome 1557, 1559, 1564*), vol. 9 (*Index de Rome 1590, 1593, 1596*).

Buzzi, Franco and Zardin, Danilo (eds), *Carlo Borromeo e l'opera della 'Grande Riforma'. Cultura, religione e arti del governo nella Milano del pieno Cinquecento* (Milan, 1997).

Caeremoniae Episcoporum iussu Clementis VIII. Pont, Max. (Rome, 1606).

Cairns, Christopher, *Domenico Bollani, Bishop of Brescia* (Nieuwkoop, 1976).

——, *Pietro Aretino and the Republic of Venice* (Florence, 1985).

Camiz, Franca Trinchieri, ' "Virgo non sterilis". Nuns as Artists in seventeenth-century Rome', in *Picturing Women in Renaissance and Baroque Italy*, eds, Geraldine A. Johnson and Sara F. Matthews Grieco (Cambridge, 1997) pp. 139–64.

Canons and Decrees of the Council of Trent. English Translation, trans. H.J. Schroeder (1941 with Latin text; used 1978 edn without it. Rockford, Ill).

Canosa, R., *Storia dell'Inquisizione in Italia*, 5 vols. (Rome, 1986–90).

Cantimori, Delio, *Eretici italiani del Cinquecento: Ricerche storiche* (Florence, 1939; reprinted 1967).

Caponetto, Salvatore, *Studi sulla Riforma in Italia* (Florence, 1987).

——, 'Ginevra e la Riforma in Sicilia', in his *Studi sulla Riforma* (1959–87) pp. 177–96.

——, 'Infiltrazioni Protestanti nella Garfagnana e nella Lunigiana', in his *Studi sulla Riforma* (1983–87), pp. 315–32.

——, *The Protestant Reformation in Sixteenth-Century Italy*, trans. Anne C. and John Tedeschi (Kirksville MO, 2000).

Cardini, Franco (ed.), *Gostanza la strega di San Miniato* (Rome and Bari, 1989; 2nd edn 2001).

Carroll, Michael P., *Madonnas that Maim: Popular Catholicism in Italy since the Fifteenth Century* (Baltimore, 1992).

Casale, Giambattista 'Diario', ed. Carlo Marcora, *Memorie storiche della diocesi di Milano*, 12 (1965), pp. 209–437.

Castagnetti, Andrea, 'Le decime e i laici', *Storia d'Italia. Annali*, 9 (1986) pp. 507–30.

Cavallo, Sandra, *Charity and Power in Early Modern Italy: Benefactors and their Motives in Turin, 1541–1789* (Cambridge, 1994).

Cerasoli, F., 'Diario di cose romane degli anni 1614, 1615, 1616', *Studi e documenti di storia e diritto*, 15 (1896), pp. 263–301.

Cesareo, Francesco, 'The episcopacy in sixteenth-century Italy', in *Early Modern Catholicism*, eds, Comerford and Pabel, pp. 67–83.

Chadwick, Owen, *The Popes and the European Revolution* (Oxford, 1981).

Chambers, David and Pullan, Brian (eds), *Venice. A Documentary History* (Oxford, 1992).

Châtellier, L., *Europe of the Devout: the Catholic Reformation and the Formation of a New Society* (Cambridge, 1989).

Chittolini, Giorgio and Miccoli, Giovanni (eds), *Storia d'Italia. Annali 9: La Chiesa e il potere politico dal Medioevo all'età contemporanea* (Turin, 1986).

Ciammitti, Luisa, 'One Saint Less: the Story of Angela Mellini, a Bolognese Seamstress (1667–17[?])', in *Sex and Gender*, eds, Muir and Ruggiero, pp. 141–76.

Cochrane, Eric and Kirshner, Julius (eds), *Readings in Western Civilization, 5: The Renaissance* (Chicago, 1986).

Cohn, Sam K., *Death and Property in Siena, 1205–1800* (Baltimore and London, 1988).

Comerford, Kathleen M., 'Italian Tridentine Diocesan Seminaries: A historiographical study', *Sixteenth Century Journal*, 29 (1998), pp. 999–1022.

Comerford, Kathleen M., 'Clerical Education, Catechesis, and Catholic Confessionalism: teaching religion in the sixteenth and seventeenth centuries' in *Early Modern Catholicism*, eds, Comerford and Pabel, pp. 241–65.

Comerford, Kathleen M. and Pabel, Hilma M. (eds), *Early Modern Catholicism. Essays in Honour of John W. O'Malley, S.J.* (Toronto, Buffalo and London, 2001).

Compare, C., 'Biblioteche monastiche femminili acquilane', *Rivista di Storia della Chiesa in Italia*, 54 (2000), pp. 469–516.

(La) Comunità Cristiana fiorentina e e toscana nella dialettica religiosa del Cinquecento (Exhibition catalogue, Florence, 1980).

(Il) Concilio di Trento e la Riforma Tridentina. Atti del Convegno Storico Internazionale. Trento … 1963), 2 vols (Rome and Freiburg, 1965).

Concilium Tridentium: diariorum, actorum, epistolarum, tractatuum nova collectio, 13 vols (Freiburg, 1901–38).

Corrain, Cleto and Zampini, Pierluigi, *Documenti etnografici e folkloristici nei Sinodi diocesani italiani* (Rovigo: Istituto Padano di Arti Grafiche; and Bologna, 1970). Assembled from *Palestra del Clero* (Rovigo, 1964–69).

Coryat, Thomas, *Coryat's Crudities* (London, 1611; photo reprint, London, 1978).

Cozzi, Gaetano, 'Domenico Bollani: un vescovo veneziano tra stato e chiesa', *Rivista Storica Italiana,* 89 (1977), pp. 562–89.

Creytens, Raimondo, 'La riforma dei monasteri femminili doppo I decreti tridentini', AA.VV. *Il Concilio di Trento* (1965), pp. 45–84.

D'Addario, Arnaldo, *Aspetti della Controriforma a Firenze* (Rome, 1972).

D'Ambrosio, A. and Spedicato, M., *Cibo e Clausura. Regioni alimentari e patrimoni monastici nel mezzogiorno moderno (sec.xvii–xix)* (Bari, 1998).

Dall'Olio, Guido, 'I rapporti tra la Congregazione del Sant'Ufficio e gli inquisitori locali nei carteggi bolognesi (1573–1594)', *Rivista Storica Italiana,* 105 (1993), pp. 246–86.

Da Nadro, S., *Sinodi diocesani italiani. Catalogo bibliografico degli atti a stampa* (Città del Vaticano, 1960).

Dandelet, Thomas, *Spanish Rome 1500–1700* (New Haven and London, 2001).

Davidson, Nicholas S., 'The Clergy of Venice in the sixteenth century', *Bulletin of the Society of Renaissance Studies,* 2 (October 1984), pp. 19–31.

——, 'Rome and the Venetian Inquisition in the sixteenth century', *Journal of Ecclesiastical History,* 39 (1988), pp. 16–36.

——, 'The Inquisition in Venice and its documents: some problems of method and analysis', in *L'Inquisizione Romana in Italia nell'età moderna* (Rome, 1991), pp. 117–31.

Davis, Natalie Zemon, 'The Reasons of Misrule', *Past and Present,* 50 (February 1971), pp. 41–75.

De Angelis, Paolo, *Della limosina overo opere che si assicurano nel giorno del final giuditio* (Rome, Giacomo Mascardi, 1615).

De Bellis, Daniela, 'Attacking sumptuary laws in Seicento Venice: Arcangela Tarabotti', in *Women in Italian Renaissance,* ed. L. Panizza, pp. 227–42.

De Boer, Wietse, 'The Curate of Malgrate, or the problem of clerical competence in Counter-Reformation Milan', in *The Power of Imagery. Essays on Rome, Italy and Imagination*, ed. Peter van Kessel (Rome, 1992), pp. 188–200, 310–16.

——, *The Conquest of the Soul. Confession, Discipline and Public Order in Counter-Reformation Milan* (Leiden, Boston and Köln, 2001).

De Frede, Carlo, *Cristianità e Islam tra la fine del Medio Evo e gli inizi dell'età moderna* (Naples, 1976).

——, *Religiosità e Cultura nel Cinquecento Italiano* (Bologna, 1999).

Del Col, Andrea, 'La storia religiosa del Friuli nel cinquecento. Orientamneti e fonti. Parte prima', *Metodi e ricerche* (Udine), 1 (1982) pp. 69–87.

——, *Domenico Scandella Known as Menocchio. His Trials Before the Inquisition (1583–1599)*, trans. J. and A. Tedeschi (Binghamton, NY, 1996).

——, *L'Inquisizione nel patriarchato e diocesi di Aquileia, 1557–1559* (Montereale Vallcellina, 1998).

——, 'La confessione di fede di un gruppo eterodosso in Valsugan nel 1559', in *Sotto il segno*, eds, Del Col and Paroni Bertoja (2000), pp. 123–35.

Del Col, Andrea (ed.), *Domenico Scandella, detto Menocchio: I Processi dell'Inquisizione (1583–1599)* (Pordenone, 1990).

Del Col, Andrea (ed.), *L'Inquisizione in Friuli. Mostra storica* (Trieste and Montereale Valcellina, 2000).

Del Col, Andrea and Paolin, Giovanna (eds), *L'Inquisizione romana in Italia. Archivi, problemi di metodo e nuove ricerche* (Rome, 1991).

Del Col, Andrea and Paolin, Giovanna (eds), *L'Inquisizione romana: metologia delle fonto e storia istituzionale. Atti del seminario internazionale* (Trieste, 2000).

Del Col, Andrea and Paroni Bertoja, Rosanna (eds), *Sotto il segno di Menocchio. Omaggio ad Aldo Colonello* (Montereale, 2002).

Del Tufo, Giovanni Battista, *Historia Della Religione de' Padri Cherici Regolari* (Rome, 1609).

Delumeau, Jean, *Catholicism between Luther and Voltaire* (London and Philadelphia, 1978).

De Maio, Romeo, *Le origini del Seminario di Napoli* (Naples,1957).

DeMolen, Richard L. (ed.), *Religious Orders of the Catholic Reformation* (New York, 1994).

De Rosa, Gabriele, *Vescovi, popolo e magia nel Sud: ricerche di storia socio-religiosa dal xvii al xix secolo* (Naples, 1971).

De Rosa, Gabriele and Gregory Tullio (eds), *Storia dell'Italia Religiosa 2: L:'Età Moderna* (Rome and Bari, 1994).

Deutscher, Thomas, 'Seminaries and the education of Novarese priests, 1593–1627', *Journal of Ecclesiastical History*, 32 (1981), pp. 303–19.

——, 'The growth of the secular clergy and the development of educational institutions in the diocese of Novara (1563–1772)', *Journal of Ecclesiastical History*, 40 (1989), pp. 381–98.

——, Review of Kathleen M. Comerford, *Ordaining* (2001), and Simona Negruzzo, *Collegij* (2001), in *Catholic Historical Review*, 88 (2002), pp. 594–96.

Dictionary of World Art, ed. Jane Turner, 34 vols. (London, 1996).

Di Simplicio, Oscar, *Peccato, penitenza, perdono, Siena 1575–1800* (Milan, 1994).

——, 'Perpetuas: the women who kept priests, Siena 1600–1800', in *Sex and Gender*, eds, Muir and Ruggiero, pp. 32–64.

——, *Inquisizione Stregoneria Medicina. Siena e il suo stato (1580–1721)* (Monteriggioni, 2000).

Ditchfield, Simon, *Liturgy, Sanctity and History in Tridentine Italy: Pietro Maria Campi and the Preservation of the Particular* (Cambridge, 1995).

Ditchfield, Simon, ' "In search of local knowledge". Rewriting early modern Italian religious history', *Cristianesimo nella Storia*, 19 (1998), pp. 255–96.

Donati, Claudio, 'Vescovi e diocesi d'Italia dall'età post-tridentina alla caduta dell'Antico Regime', in *Clero e Società*, ed. Mario Rosa, pp. 320–89.

Donnelly, John P. and Maher, Michael W. (eds), *Confraternities and Catholic Reform in Italy, France, and Spain* (Kirksville, 1999).

Donvito, L. and Pellegrino, B., *L'Organizzazione Ecclesiastica degli Abruzzi e Molise e della Basilicata nell'età post-tridentina 1585–1630* (Florence, 1973).

Duffy, Eamon, *Saints and Sinners. A History of the Popes* (New Haven, 1997).

Dunn, Marilynn R., 'Spiritual Philanthropists. Women as Convent Patrons in Seicento Rome', in *Women and Art in Early Modern Europe. Patrons, Collectors & Connoisseurs*, ed. Cynthia Lawrence (University Park, PA, 1997).

Duranti, A, 'Il seminario di Ravenna nel sec. xvi', *Ravennatensia*, 2 (1971), pp. 129–68.

Duval, Andrè, 'L'Extrême-onction au concile de Trente. Sacrament du mourante ou sacrement des malades?', *La Maison-Dieu*, 101 (1970), pp. 127–72.

Duval, Andrè, 'Le Concile de Trente et la confession', *La Maison-Dieu*, 118 (1974), 131–80.

Ebner, P., 'I libri parrocchiali di Vallo della Lucania dal xvi secolo al xix secolo', *Ricerche di Storia Sociale e Religiosa*, 2, no. 3 (1973), pp. 109–57.

Ebner, P., 'I libri parrochiali di Novi Velia dal xvi al xix secolo', *Ricerche di Storia Sociale e Religiosa*, 3, nos 5–6 (1974), pp. 65–140.

Eisenbichler, Konrad, *The Boys of the Archangel Raphael: a Youth Confraternity in Florence, 1411–1785* (Toronto, 1998).

Eresia e Riforma nell'Italia del Cinquecento. Miscellanea I (Florence and Chicago, 1974).

Eubel, K. (ed.), *Hierarchia Catholica* (Regensburg), vols iii–v (1910).

Evennett, H.O., *The Spirit of the Counter-Reformation* (Cambridge, 1968).

Fabbri, Paolo, *Monteverdi* (Trans. and revised, Tim Carter) (Cambridge, 1994).

Fabiani, G., 'Sinodi e visite pastorali ad Ascoli', *Rivista di Storia della Chiesa in Italia*, 6 (1952), 264–80.

Fagiolo, Marcello (ed.), *La Festa di Roma* (2 vols, Rome, 1997).

Fagiolo, Marcello and Madonna, Maria Luisa, *Roma 1300–1875: La città degli Anni Santi* (Milan, 1985).

Fanti, Mario, 'Il fondo delle "Visite pastorali" nell' Archivio Generale Arcivescovile di Bologna', *Archiva Ecclesiae*, xxii–xxiii (1979–80), pp. 151–67.

——, *Una Pieve, un Popolo Le visite pastorali nel territorio di Lizzano in Belvedere dal 1425 al 1912* (Lizzano del Belvedere, 1981).

——, 'La parrocchia dei Santi Vitale e Agricola dal Medioevo al Settecento', in *Vitale e Agricola*, ed. G. Fasoli, pp. 217–47.

——, 'Per la storia del culto eucaristico a Bologna', in Salvatore Baviero and Jadranka Bentini (eds), *Mistero e Immagine. L'eucharista nell'arte dal XVI al XVIII secolo* (Milan, 1997), pp. 63–5, 70–71.

Fanucci, Camillo, *Trattato di tutte le opere pie dell'alma città di Roma* (Rome, 1601).

Fasano Guarini, Elena (ed.), *Prato storia di una città, vol. 2: Un microcosmo in movimento (1494–1815)* (Prato, 1986).

Fasoli, Gina (ed.), *Vitale e Agricola. Il culto dei protomartiri di Bologna attraverso i secoli nel xvi centenario della traslazione* (Bologna, 1993), pp. 217–47.

Fenlon, Dermot, *Heresy and Obedience in Tridentine Italy: Cardinal Pole and the Counterreformation* (Cambridge, 1972).

Fenlon, Iain, *Music and Patronage in Seventeenth-century Mantua*, 2 vols (Cambridge, 1980–82).

——, 'Music and reform: the Savonarolan legacy', in Fletcher and Shaw (eds), pp. 233–49.

Ferraro, Joanne M., *Marriage Wars in Late Renaissance Venice* (Oxford, 2001).

Ferraris, G. and Frutaz, P., 'La visita apostolica di Mons. Giovanni Francesco Bonomi alla diocesi di Aosta nel 1576', *Rivista di Storia della Chiesa in Italia*, 12 (1958), pp. 27–80.

Fiorani, Luigi and Prosperi, Adriano (eds), *Storia d'Italia. Annali 16. Roma, la città del papa. Vita civile e religiosa dal giubileo di Bonifacio VIII al giubileo di papa Wojtyla* (Turin, 2000).

Firpo, Luigi, 'Esecuzioni capitali in Rome (1567–1671)', in *Eresia e Riforma* (1974), pp. 307–42.

Firpo, Massimo, 'The Italian Reformation and Juan de Valdés', *Sixteenth Century Journal*, 27 (1996), pp. 353–64.

——, and Marcatto, Dario, *I processi inquisitoriali di Pietro Carnesecchi (1557–1567). Edizione critica*, 2 vols (Città del Vaticano: Archivio Segreto Vaticano, 1998–2000).

Fletcher, Stella and Shaw, Christine (eds), *The World of Savonarola. Italian élites and perceptions of crisis* (Aldershot, 2000).

Folco, Giulio, *Effetti mirabili de la Limosina et sentenze degne di memoria* (Rome, 1581).

Fonte, Moderata, *The Worth of Women*, translated by Virginia Cox (Chicago, 1997).

Fragnito, Gigliola, 'Gli Ordini Religiosi tra Riforma e Controriforma', in *Clero e Società*, ed. Mario Rosa, pp. 115–205.

——, *La Bibbia al rogo. La censura ecclesiastica e i volgarizzamenti della Scrittura (1471–1605)* (Bologna, 1997).

——, 'Vescovi e Ordini Religiosi in Italia all'indomani del Concilio', in *I Tempi del Concilio*, eds, Mozzarelli and Zardin, pp. 13–25.

——, 'Ecclesiastical censorship and Girolamo Savonarola', in Fletcher and Shaw eds, pp. 90–111.

——, 'Central and Peripheral Organization', in *Church, Censorship*, ed. Fragnito pp. 13–49.

——, ' "In questo vasto mare de libri prohibiti et sospesi tra tanti scogli di varietà et controversie": la censura ecclesiastica tra la fine del Cinquecento e I primi del Seicento', in Cristina Stango ed., *Censura Eccliastica e Cultura Politica in Italia tra Cinquecento e Seicento* (Florence, 2001), pp. 1–35.

Fragnito, Gigliola (ed.), *Church, Censorship and Culture in Early Modern Italy* (Cambridge and New York, 2001).

Franza, Gerardo, *Il Catechismo a Roma dal Concilio di Trento a Pio VI* (Rome, 1958)

Freedberg, David, *The Power of Images. Studies in the History and Theory of Response* (Chicago, 1991).

Freedberg, S.J., *Painting in Italy* (Harmondsworth, 1975).
Fumo, Bartolomeo, *Summa, quae Aurea Armilla* (Venice, 1554).
Gabrijelcic, A., 'Alle origini del Seminario di Perugia (1559–1600)', *Bollettino della Deputazione di Storia Patria per l'Umbria,* 68 (1971), pp. 1–169, pp. 193–201.
Galasso, Giuseppe and Russo, Carla (eds), *Per la storia sociale e religiosa del Mezzogiorno d'Italia,* vol. 1 (Napoli, 1980), vol. 2 (1982).
Galasso, Giuseppe and Valerio, Adriana (eds), *Donne e Religione a Napoli. Secoli xvi-xviii* (Milan, 2001).
Gams, P.B., *Series episcoporum ecclesiae cattolicae* (Ratisbon, 1873).
Gatti Perer, M.L., 'Cultura e socialità delle altari barocco nell'antico Diocesi di Milano', *Arte Lombarda,* 42/43 (1975), pp. 11–66.
Gentilcore, David, *From Bishop to Witch: the system of the Sacred in early modern Terra d'Otranto* (Manchester, 1992).
——, ' "Adapt yourself to the people's capabilities": missionary strategies, methods and impact in the Kingdom of Naples, 1400–1800', *Journal of Ecclesiastical History,* 45 (1994), pp. 269–96.
——, *Healers and Healing in Early Modern Italy* (Manchester and New York, 1998).
Gigli, Giacinto, *Diario di Roma,* 2 vols (Rome, 1994).
Ginzburg, Carlo, *Il nicodemismo. Simulazione e dissimulazione religiosa nell'Europa del '500* (Turin, 1970).
Ginzburg, Carlo, *The Cheese and the Worms. The Cosmos of a Sixteenth-Century Miller,* trans. J. and A. Tedeschi (London, 1980).
Ginzburg, Carlo, *The Night Battles. Witchcraft and Agrarian Cults in the sixteenth and seventeenth centuries,* trans. J. and A. Tedeschi (London, 1983).
Giussano, G.P., *Vita di San Carlo Borromeo* (Brescia, 1613).
Godman, Peter, *From Poliziano to Machiavelli. Florentine Humanism in the High Renaissance* (Princeton, 1998).
——, *The Saint as Censor. Robert Bellarmine between Inquisition and Index* (Leiden, Boston and Köln, 2000).
Gordini, Giandomenico, 'Sinodi diocesani emiliani dal 1563 al 1648 ed il Concilio provinciale di Ravenna del 1568', in *Ravennatensia,* 2 (1971), pp. 235–73.
Gordini, Giandomenico, 'La formazione del clero Faentino secondo i sinodi dei secoli xvi e xvii', in *Ravennatensia,* 3 (1972), pp. 169–81.
Gotor, Miguel, *I beati del papa. Santità, Inquisizione e obbedienza in età moderna* (Florence, 2002).
Greco, Gaetano, *La parrocchia a Pisa nell'età moderna (secoli xvii-xviii)* (Pisa, 1984).
—— 'I giuspatronati laicali nell'età moderna', in *Storia d'Italia. Annali, 9* (1986), pp. 533–72.
Greco, Gaetano, 'Fra disciplina e sacerdozio: il clero secolare nella società italiana dal Cinquecento al Settecento', in *Clero e Società,* ed. Mario Rosa, pp. 45–113.
Grendler, Paul F., 'Utopia in Renaissance Italy: Doni's "New World",' *Journal of the History of Ideas,* 26 (1965), pp. 479–94, and in no. IV in his *Culture and Censorship,* (1981).
——, 'Religious Restlessness in Sixteenth-century Italy', no. III in his *Culture and Censorship* (1966).

——, *The Roman Inquisition and the Venetian Press, 1540–1605* (Princeton, 1977).

Grendler, Paul F., 'Books for Sarpi: the Smuggling of Prohibited Books into Venice during the Interdict of 1606–1607', no. XIII in his *Culture and Censorship* (1981).

——, 'The Destruction of Hebrew Books in Venice, 1568', no. XII in his *Culture and Censorship*.

—— *Culture and Censorship in Late Renaissance Italy and France* (London, 1981).

——, 'The Schools of Christian Doctrine in xvith-century Italy', *Church History*, 53 (1984), pp. 319–31.

——, 'Borromeo and the Schools of Christian Doctrine', in *San Carlo Borromeo*, eds, Headley and Tomaro, pp. 158–71.

——, *Schooling in Renaissance Italy. Literacy and Learning 1300–1600* (Baltimore and London, 1989).

——, 'The Piarists of the Pious Schools', in *Religious Orders*, ed. Richard DeMolen, pp. 253–78

Grosso, M. and Mellano, M.- F., *La controriforma nella arcdiocesi di Torino*, 3 vols (Rome, 1957).

Guasco, Maurilio, 'La formazione del clero: I seminari', in *Storia d'Italia*, eds, Chittolini and Miccoli, *Annali*, 9 (1986), pp. 575–633.

Guerrini, Paolo, *Atti della Visita Pastorale del vescovo Domenico Bollani alla diocesi di Brescia (1565–1567)* (1 Brescia, 1915; 2 Toscolano 1936, 3 Brescia 1940).

Hall, Marcia B., *Renovation and Counter-Reformation. Vasari and Duke Cosimo in Sta Maria Novella and Sta Croce 1565–1577* (Oxford, 1979).

Hammond, Frederick, *Music and Spectacle in Baroque Rome: Barberini Patronage under Urban VIII* (New Haven, 1994).

Hanlon, Gregory, *Early Modern Italy 1550–1800* (London, 2000).

Hay, Denys, *The Church in Italy in the Fifteenth Century* (Cambridge, 1977).

Headley, John M. and Tomaro, John B. (eds), *San Carlo Borromeo. Catholic Reform and Ecclesiastical Politics in the second half of the sixteenth century*, (Washington, London and Toronto, 1988).

Henderson, John, *Piety and Charity in Late Medieval Florence* (Oxford, 1994).

Heydenreich, L.H. and Lotz, W., *Architecture of Italy, 1400–1600* (Pelican History of Art, 1974).

Hibbard, Howard, 'The Early History of Sant'Andrea della Valle,' *Art Bulletin*, 42 (1961), pp. 289–318.

Hibbard, Howard, *Caravaggio* (London, 1983).

Hill, John W., 'Oratory Music in Florence, I-III', *Acta Musicologica*, 51 (1979), pp. 108–36, 246–67, and 58 (1986), pp. 129–79.

Hillerbrand, Hans J. (ed.), *The Oxford Encyclopedia of the Reformation*, 4 vols (New York and Oxford, 1996).

Howard, Deborah, *Jacopo Sansovino. Architecture and Patronage in Renaissance Venice* (New Haven and London, 1975).

Howe, Eunice, 'Appropriating Space. Woman's Place in Confraternal Life at Santo Spirito in Sassa, Rome', in *Confraternities*, eds, Wisch and Ahl, pp. 235–58.

Hudon, William V., *Marcello Cervini and Ecclesiastical Government in Tridentine Italy* (De Kalb, 1992).

——, 'The Papacy in the Age of Reform, 1513–1644', in *Early Modern Catholicism eds*, Comerford and Pabel, pp. 46–66.

Hufton, Olwen, 'The Widow's Mite and Other Strategies: Funding the Catholic Reformation', *Transactions of the Royal Historical Society*, 6th ser., 8 (1998), pp. 117–37.

L'*Incerto confine. Vivi e morti, incontri, luoghi e percorsi di religiosità nella montagna friulana.* (Udine, 2001).

L'*Inquisizione Romana in Italia nell'età moderna* (Rome, 1991).

Ioly Zorattini, Pier Cesare, *Processo di S.Uffizio di Venezia ...* , 14 vols (Florence, 1980–99).

Ioly Zorattini, Pier Cesare (ed.), *L'Identità Dissimulata. Giudaizzanti Iberici nell'Europa Cristiana dell' età moderna* (Florence, 2000).

Jedin, Hubert, *Crisis and Closure of the Council of Trent* (London, 1967).

——, 'La necessité de la confession privée selon le concile de Trente', *La Maison-Dieu,* 104 (1970), pp. 88–115.

——, *Chiesa della fede Chiesa della Storia* (Brescia, 1972).

Jedin, Hubert (ed.), *History of the Church. Vol. V: Reformation and Counter Reformation* (London, 1980).

Jedin, Hubert and Prodi, Paolo (eds), *Il Concilio di Trento come croceria della politica europea* (Bologna, 1979).

Jedin, Hubert *et al.* (eds), *Atlas d'Histoire de l'Eglise. Les Eglises Chretiennes Hier et Aujourd'Hui* (Brepols, 1990).

Julia, Dominique, 'L'accoglienza dei pellegrini a Roma,' in *Storia d' Italia,* eds, Fiorani and Prosperi, pp. 822–861.

Kelly, J.N.D., *The Oxford Dictionary of the Popes* (Oxford, 1986).

Kendrick, Robert, 'The traditions of Milanese Convent music and the sacred dialogues of Chiara Margarita Cozzolani', in *The Crannied Wall,* ed. Monson, pp. 211–33.

——, *Celestial Sirens: nuns and their music in early modern Milan* (Oxford, 1996).

Kennedy, T. Frank, 'Some unusual Genres of Sacred Music in the Early Modern Period: the Catechism as a musical event in the late Renaissance–Jesuits and "Our Way of Proceeding", 'in *Early Modern Catholicism,* eds, Comerford and Pabel, pp. 266–79.

King, Catherine E., *Renaissance Women Patrons* (Manchester and New York, 1998).

Kirkendale, Warren, *Emilio De'Cavalieri 'Gentilhuomo Romano'. His life and letters, his role as superintendant of all the arts at the Medici Court, and his musical compositions* (Florence, 2001).

Krautheimer, Richard, *The Rome of Alexander VII, 1655–1667* (Princeton, 1985).

Kümin, Beat, 'The English parish in a European context', in *The Parish in English Life 1400–1600,* eds, Katherine French, Gary Gibbs, Beat Kümin (Manchester and New York, 1997), pp. 15–32.

Küng, Hans, *The Council and Reunion,* trans. Cecily Hastings (London and NY, 1961).

Kuntz, Marion L., 'Voices from a Venetian prison in the Cinquecento: Francesco Spinola and Dionisio Gallo', in her *Venice, Myth and Utopian Thought in the sixteenth century* (Aldershot, 1999), ch. VII.

——, 'Profezia e politica nella Venezia del sedicesimo secolo: il caso di Dionisio Gallo', same, ch. XIII.

Langdon, Helen, *Caravaggio. A Life* (London, 1998).

Lapucci, Carlo and Paccini, Sergio (eds), *Zibaldone del P.Matteo Pinelli Priore di Cerliano* (Florence, 1997).
Laven, Mary, 'Venetian Nunneries in the Counter-Reformation, 1550–1630", (Ph.D., University of Leicester, 1997).
——, *Virgins of Venice. Enclosed Lives and Broken Vows in the Renaissance Convent* (London and New York, 2002).
Lavin, Irving, 'Bernini's Death', *The Art Bulletin*, 54 (1972), pp. 159–86.
Lavin, Irving, *Bernini and the Unity of the Visual Arts*, 2 vols (New York and London, 1980).
——, 'The First Jesuit Confraternities and Marginalized Groups in sixteenth-century Rome', in *Ritual Kinship*, ed. Tersptra, pp. 132–49.
Lazar, Lance, ' "E faucibus daemonis". Daughters of Prostitutes, the First Jesuits, and the Compagnia delle Vergini Miserabili di Santa Caterina della Rosa', in *Confraternities*, eds, Wisch and Ahl, pp. 259–79.
——, *Working in the Vineyard of the Lord: Jesuit Confraternities in Early Modern Italy* (Toronto, forthcoming 2004).
Lea, H.C., *A History of Auricular Confession*, 3 vols (1896).
Lefebvre, Charles, 'La S. Congregation du Concile et le Tribunal de la S.Rote Romaine à la fin du xvie siècle', in *(La) Sacra Congrgatione* (1964) pp. 163–77.
Levack, Brian, *The Witch-Hunt in Early Modern Europe* (London and NY, 1995).
Levillain, Philippe (ed.), *The Papacy. An Encyclopedia*, 3 vols (London, 2002).
Lewine, M.J., *The Roman Church Interior 1527–1580* (Columbia Univ. Microfilms, Ann Arbor, 1963).
Lewis, Mark A., 'Recovering the Apostolic Way of Life: the new Clerks Regular of the sixteenth century', in Comerford and Pabel, pp. 280–96.
'(La) Libreria di un parroco di Città in Padua nell'anno 1559', in *Libri e Stampatori in Padova. Miscellanea in onore di Mons. G. Bellini* (Padua, 1959), pp. 325–34.
Liebreich, Karen, *Fallen Order. A History* (London, 2004).
Lindner, Carlo, *Madonna della Ghiara* (Reggio Emilia, 1954), pp. 80–8.
Lockwood, Lewis, *The Counter-Reformation and the Masses of Vincenzo Ruffo* (Venice, 1970).
Logan, Oliver, *The Venetian Upper Clergy in the sixteenth and seventeenth centuries: A study in religious culture*, 2 vols (Salzburg, 1995).
Lopez, Pasquale, *Riforma Cattolica e vita religiosa e culturale a Napoli* (Naples and Rome, n.d., *c.*1965).
Lowe, Kate, 'History writing from within the convent in Cinquecento Italy: the nuns' version', in *Women in Italian Renaissance*, ed. L. Panizza, pp. 105–21.
——, 'Elections of Abbesses and Notions of Identity', *Renaissance Quarterly*, 59 (2001), pp. 389–429.
——, *Nun's Chronicles and Convent Culture in Renaissance and Counter-Reformation Italy* (Cambridge, 2003).
Mackenney, Richard, 'The Guilds of Venice: State and Society in the Longue Durée', *Studi Veneziani*, 37 (1997), pp. 15–43.
——, 'Public and Private in Renaissance Venice', *Renaissance Studies*, 12 (1998), pp. 109–30.

——, 'The Scuole Piccole of Venice: Formations and Transformations', in *Ritual Kinship*, ed. Terpstra, pp. 172–89.

Maher, Michael W., 'Financing Reform: the Society of Jesus, the Congregation of the Assumption, and the funding of the exposition of the Sacrament in early modern Rome', *Archiv für Reformationsgeschichte/Archive for Reformation History*, 93 (2002), pp. 126–44.

Mansi, G.D., *Sacrorum Conciliorum nova et amplissima collectio* (Paris and Leipzig, 1901–27; Graz reprint, 1961 also available).

Marcocchi, Massimo, *La Riforma Cattolica. Documenti e Testimonianze*, 2 vols. (Brescia, 1970).

Marcocchi, Massimo 'L'immagine della Chiesa in Carlo Borromeo', in Buzzi and Zardin, eds (1997), pp. 25–36; and in *San Carlo e il suo tempo,* 2 vols, (Rome: Edizioni di storia e letteratura, 1986), 1: 209–36.

Marcora, Carlo, 'Il diario di Giambattista Casale (1554- 1598)', *Memorie storiche della diocesi di Milano*, 12 (1965), pp. 209–437.

Marino, John A. (ed.), *Early Modern Italy* (Oxford, 2003).

Martin, Gregory, *Roma Sancta (1581)*, ed. G.B. Parks (Rome, 1969).

Martin, John, *Venice's Hidden Enemies: Italian Heretics in a Renaissance City* (London and Berkeley, 1993).

——, 'Religion, renewal and reform in the sixteenth-century', in *Early Modern Italy*, ed. Marino, pp. 30–47.

Martin, Ruth, *Witchcraft and Inquisition in Venice 1550–1650* (Oxford, 1989).

Masetti Zannini, G.L., 'Ricerche sulla cultura e sulla formazione del clero piceno dopo il Concilip di Trento. I: La cultura del clero secolare, (Note e documenti, 1573–85), *Studia Picena*, 43 (Fano, 1976), pp. 60–89.

Masi, G., *Organizzazione ecclesiastica e ceti rurali in Puglia nella seconda metà del Cinquecento* (Bari, 1957).

Masini, Eliseo, *Sacro arsenale, overo prattica dell'Officio della Santa Inquisizione*, originally Genoa 1621; modern edition: *Il manuale degli inquisitori* (Milan, 1990).

Matter, E. Ann and Coakley, John (eds), *Creative Women in Medieval and Early Modern Italy. A Religious and Artistic Renaissance* (Philadephia, 1994).

Mayer, Thomas F., *Reginald Pole. Prince and Prophet* (Cambridge, 2000).

Mazzone, Umberto and Turchini, Angelo (eds), *Le visite pastorali* (Bologna, 1985).

McGinness, Frederick J. *Right Thinking and Sacred Oratory in Counter-Reformation Rome* (Princeton, NJ, 1995).

McPhee, Sarah, *Bernini and the Bell Towers. Architecture and Politics at the Vatican* (New Haven and London, 2002).

Medioli, Francesca, *L' 'Inferno monachale' di Arcangela Tarabotti* (Rosenberg and Sellier, 1990).

——, 'Lo spazio del chiostro: clausura costrizione e protestazione nel XVII secolo', in *Tempi e spazi*, eds, Silvana Seidel Menchi *et al.*, pp. 353–73.

——, 'The enforcement of *clausura* before and after Trent', in *Women in Renaissance and Early Modern Europe*, ed. Christine Meek (Dublin, 2000).

——, 'To take or not to take the veil: selected Italian case histories, the Renaissance and after', in *Women in Italian Renaissance,* ed., L. Panizza, pp. 122–37.

Medioli, Francesca, 'The Dimensions of the Cloister: Enclosure, Constraint, and Protection in seventeenth-century Italy', in *Time, Space,* eds, Ann Jacobson Schutte *et al.*, pp. 165–180.

Mezzadri, L. 'Il seminario nell'epoca dell'assolutismo e dell'Illuminismo', in *Il Seminario di Piacenza,* ed., F. Molinari (1969).

Miele, Michele, 'Monache e monasteri del Cinque-Seicento tra riforme imposte e nuove esperienze', in *Donne e Religione,* eds, G. Galasso and A. Valerio, pp. 91–138.

Molinari, Franco, *Il Cardinale Teatino Paolo Burali e la riforma tridentina a Piacenza* (Rome, 1957).

Molinari, Franco, 'Il Seminario di Piacenza e il suo fondatore', in *Ravennatensia,* 3 (1972), pp. 21–64.

Molinari, Franco, *Epistolario del Beato Paolo Burali* (Brescia, 1977).

Molinari, Franco (ed.), *Il Seminario di Piacenza e il suo fondatore* (Piacenza, 1969).

Monson, Craig A., 'The Making of Lucrezia Orsina Vizzana's *Componimenti Musicali* (1623)', in *Creative Women,* eds, Matter and Coakley (1994) pp. 297–323.

——, *Disembodied Voices. Music and Culture in Early Modern Convents* (Berkeley, 1995).

Monson, Craig (ed.), *The Crannied Wall. Women Religion, and the Arts in Early Modern Europe* (Ann Arbor, 1992).

Montanari, Daniele, *Disciplinamento in terra veneta. La diocesi di Brescia nella seconda metà del xvi secolo* (Bologna, 1987).

Monticone, A., 'L'applicazione a Roma del Concilio di Trento. Le Visite del 1564–1566', *Rivista di Storia della Chiesa in Italia,* 7 (1953), pp. 225–50.

Mozzarelli, Cesare and Zardin, Danilo (eds), *I Tempi del Concilio: religione, cultura e società nell'Europa tridentina* (Rome, 1997).

Muir, Edward and Ruggiero, Guido (eds), *Sex and Gender in Historical Perpsective* (Baltimore and London, 1994).

Mullett, Michael A., *The Catholic Reformation* (London and New York, 1999).

Nanni, Giancarlo and Regoli, Ivo, *San Miniato. Guida storico artistica* (San Miniato, 2000).

Nardon, Franco, *Benandanti e inquisitori nel Friuli del seicento,* with Preface by Andrea Del Col (Trieste and Montereale Valcellina, 1999).

Nardon, Franco, 'Benandanti "funebri": le processioni dei morti nei documenti inquisitoriali', in *L'Incerto confine,* pp. 173–80.

Naselli, G., 'L'esame di coscienza e la confessione dei peccati in alcune stampe', *Studi e materiali di storia delle religioni,* 23 (1951–52), pp. 67–90.

Negruzzo, Simona, *Collegij a forma di Seminario: Il sistema di formazione teologica nello Stato di Milano in età spagnola* (Brescia, 2001).

(The) New Grove Dictionary of Music and Musicians, 20 vols (London,1980).

Niccoli, Ottavia, *La Vita Religiosa nell'Italia Moderna. Secoli xv- xviii* (Rome, 1998)

Nichols, Tom, *Tintoretto. Tradition and Identity* (London, 1999).

Norman, Corrie E., 'The Social History of Preaching: Italy', in *Preachers and People in the Reformations and Early Modern Period,* ed. Larissa Taylor (Brill, 2001), pp. 125–91.

Novi Chavarria, Elisa, *Monache e Gentildonne. Un labile confine. Poteri politici e identità religiose nei monasteri napoletani secoli xvi-xvii* (Milan, 2001).

Nubola, Cecilia, *Conoscere per governare: la diocesi di Trento nella visita pastorale di Ludovico Madruzzo (1579–1581)* (Bologna, 1993).
Nubola, Cecilia and Turchini, Angelo (eds), *Visite pastorali ed elaborazione dei dati: esperienze e metodi* (Bologna, 1993).
Nussdorfer, Laurie, *Civic Politics in the Rome of Urban VIII* (Princeton, 1992).
O'Malley, John W., 'The Society of Jesus', in *Catholicism*, ed., O'Malley (1988), pp. 138–63.
——, *The First Jesuits* (Cambridge Mass. and London, 1993).
——, *Trent and all that. Renaming Catholicism in the Early Modern Era* (Cambridge, Mass. and London, 2000).
——, *Catholicism in Early Modern History: a Guide to Research* (St. Louis: Center for Reformation Research, 1988).
O'Regan, Noel, *Institutional patronage in post-Tridentine Rome: music at Santissima Trinità dei Pellegrini 1550–1650* (London, 1995).
Orlandi, Giuseppe, La missione popolare in età moderna', in *Storia dell'Italia Religiosa*, eds, De Rosa and Gregory, pp. 419–52.
Pacelli, V., *Caravaggio: Le Sette Opere di Misericordia* (Salerno, 1984).
Paglia, Vincenzo, *La Pietà dei Carcerati: Confraternita e Società dei Carcerati a Roma in età moderna* (Rome, 1980).
——, *La morte confortata: riti della paura e mentalità religiosa a Roma nell'età moderna* (Rome, 1982).
Paleotti, Gabriele, *Del Sacramento del matrimonio. Avvertimenti alli reverendi curati* (Bologna, 1577; Venice, 1607 with revisions).
Paleotti, Gabriele, *Istruttione ... Per tutti quelli, che hauranno licenza di Predicare nelle ville, & altri luoghi della Diocesi di sua Si. Illustriss* (Bologna, 1586; and 1599 reprint).
Panizza, Letizia (ed.), *Women in Italian Renaissance Culture and Society* (Oxford, 2000).
Papa, Giovanni, *Le Cause di Canonizzazione nel primo periodo della Congregazione dei Riti (1588–1634)* (Vatican, 2001).
Parisella, A., ' "Liber Litterarum" Sacrae Congregationis Concilii', in *La Sacra Congregazione* (1964), pp. 447–76.
Paschini, Pio, 'Le Origini del Seminario Romano', in his *Cinquecento Romano e riforma Cattolica* (Rome, 1958), pp. 3–32.
Pastor, Ludvig von, *History of the Popes*, 40 vols (London, 1933–40), vols XXIII–XXXII.
Pellicia, Guerrino, *La preparazione ed ammissione dei chierici ai santi ordini nella Roma del sec. xvi* (Rome, 1946).
Peterson, David S., 'Out of the Margins: Religion and the Church in Renaissance Italy', *Renaissance Quarterly*, 53 (2000), pp. 835–79.
Pirri, Pietro, *Giovanni Tristano e i primordi della Architettura Gesuitica* (Rome, 1955).
Po-Chia Hsia, R., *The World of Catholic Renewal 1540–1770* (Cambridge, 1998).
Polecritti, Cynthia L., *Preaching Peace in Renaissance Italy* (Washington DC, 2000).
Polizzotto, Lorenzo, *Children of the Promise: The Confraternity of the Purification and the Socialization of Youths in Florence*, 1427–1785 (Cambridge, 2004).
Ponnelle, L. and Bordet, L., *St Philip Neri and the Roman Society of his Times (1515–1595)* (London, 1932).

Preto, Paolo, 'Benefici parrocchiali e altari dotari dopo il Tridentino a Padova', *Quaderni Storici*, 5 (1970), pp. 795–813.

Primhak, Victoria, 'Benedictine Communities in Venetian society: the convent of San Zaccaria', in *Women in Italian Renaissance*, ed., L. Panizza (2000), pp. 92–104.

Problemi di Vita Religiosa in Italia nel Cinquecento. Atti del Convegno di Storia della Chiesa in Italia (Bologna ... 1958) (Padua, 1960).

Prodi, Paolo, 'Lineamenti dell'organizzazione diocesana in Bologna durante l'episcopato del card. G. Paleotti, (1566–1597), in *Problemi* (1960), pp. 323–94.

——, *Il Cardinale Gabriele Paleotti*, 2 vols (Rome, 1959–67).

——, 'San Carlo Borromeo e il Cardinale Gabriele Paleotti: due vescovi della Riforma Cattolica', *Critica Storica*, 3 (1964), pp. 135–51.

——, 'Ricerche sulla teorica delle arti figurative nella riforma cattolica', *Archivio Italiano per la Storia della Pietà*, 4 (1965), pp. 123–212. Reprinted separately (Bologna, 1984).

——, 'Charles Borromée, archevêque de Milan', *Revue d'Histoire Ecclésiastique*, 62 (1967), pp. 379–41.

——, *Il sovrano pontefice, un corpo e due anime: la monarchia papale nella prima età moderna* (Bologna, 1982).

——, 'Il "sovrano pontefice" ', in Romano and Vivanti, *Storia d'Italia*, vol. 9 (1986), pp. 198–216.

——, *The Papal Prince. One Body and Two Souls* (Cambridge, 1988).

Prodi, Paolo and Reinhard, Wolfgang (eds), *Il Concilio di Trento e il moderno* (Bologna, 1996).

Prosperi, Adriano, *Tra evangelismo e controriforma: G.M. Giberti (1495–1543)* (Rome, 1969).

——, *Tribunali della coscienza. Inquisitori, confessor, missionari* (Turin, 1996).

Pullan, Brian S., *Rich and Poor in Renaissance Venice: the Social Institutions of a Renaissance State to 1620* (Oxford, 1971).

——, ' "A Ship with Two Rudders": Righetto Marrano and the Inquisition in Venice', *Historical Journal*, 20 (1977), pp. 25–58.

——, 'The Old Catholicism, the new Catholicism, and the Poor', in *Timore e carità. I poveri nell'Italia moderna*, ed., Mario Rosa (Cremona, 1982), pp. 13–25.

——, *The Jews of Europe and the Inquisition of Venice 1550–1670* (Oxford, 1983).

——, ' "Support and Redeem": Charity and Poor Relief in Italian Cities from the fourteenth to the seventeenth century', *Continuity and Change*, 3 (1988), pp. 177–208.

——, *Poverty and Charity: Europe, Italy, Venice 1400–1700* (Aldershot, 1994).

Pullapilly, Cyriac, *Caesar Baronius. Counter-Reformation Historian* (Notre Dame and London, 1975).

Radke, Gary M., 'Nuns and Their Art: the case of San Zaccaria in Renaissance Venice', *Renaissance Quarterly*, 54 (2001), pp. 430–59.

Rasi, P., 'L'applicazione delle norme del Concilio di Trento in materia matrimoniale', *Studi di Storia e Diritto in onore di Arrigo Solmi*, 2 vols (Milan, 1941) I: pp. 235–81.

Ravennatensia. Atti dei Convegni. Periodic publications. Volumes used: I–III (Cesena, 1969–72).

Reardon, Colleen, *Holy Concord within Sacred Walls. Nuns and Music in Siena, 1575–1700* (Oxord, 2002).

Reinhard, Wolfgang, 'Le carriere papali e cardinalizie. Contributo alla storia sociale del papaato', in *Storia,* eds, Fiorani and Prosperi, pp. 263–90.

Reinhardt, Volker, *Kardinal Scipione Borghese (1605–33)* (Rome,1984).

Riccardi, Antonio, 'The Mystic Humanism of Maria Maddalena de'Pazzi', in *Creative Women,* eds, Matter and Coakley, pp. 201–11.

Ricci, Saverio, *Il Sommo Inquisitore. Giulio Santori tra Autobiografico e Storia (1532–1602)* (Rome, 2002).

Rienzo, M.G., 'Il processo di cristianizzazione e le missioni popolari nel Mezzogiorno', in *Per la storia sociale,* eds, Galasso and Russo, vol I. (1980) pp. 452–66.

Rimoldi, A., 'Istituzioni di S.Carlo Borromeo per il clero diocesano Milanese', *La Scuola Cattolica,* 93 (1965), pp. 427–58.

Roche, Jerome, 'The Duet in early seventeenth-century Italian Church Music', *Proceedings of the Royal Musical Association,* 93 (1966–67), pp. 33–50.

——, *North Italian Church Music in the Age of Monteverdi* (Oxford, 1984).

Rogger, Iginio, 'Il governo spirituale della diocesi di Trento sotto i vescovi Cristoforo (1539–1567) e Ludovico Madruzzo (1567–1600)', in *Concilio di Trento,* vol. I (1965), pp. 173–213.

Romeo, Giovanni, *Inquisitori, esorcisti e streghe nell'Italia della Controriforma* (Florence, 1990).

——, *Esorcisti, confessori e sessualità femminile nell'Italia della Controriforma. A proposito du due casi modenesi del primo Seicento* (Florence, 1998).

——, *L'Inquisizione nell'Italia moderna* (Rome and Bari, 2002).

Roncalli, A.G. (Pope John XXIII), *Gli inizi del Seminario di Bergamo e S.Carlo Borromeo* (Bergamo, 1939).

Rosa, Mario, *Religione e società nel Mezzogiorno tra Cinque e Seicento* (Rome and Bari, 1976).

Rosa, Mario (ed.), *Clero e Società nell'Italia moderna* (Bari and Rome, 1997).

Rostirolla, Giancarlo, 'Laudi e canti religiosi per l'esercizio spirituale della Dottrina Cristiana al tempo di Roberto Bellarmino', in *Bellarmino e La Controriforma,* ed. R. De Maio (Sora, 1990), pp. 661–849.

Rozzo, Ugo, 'Italian literature on the Index', in *Church, Censorship,* ed. Fragnito, pp. 194–222.

Ruggiero, Guido, *Binding Passions. Tales of Magic, Marriage and Power at the End of the Renaissance* (Oxford, 1993).

Rusconi, Roberto, 'Predicatori e predicazione', in *Storia d'Italia. Annali 4: Intellettuali e Potere,* ed. C. Vivanti (Turin, 1981), pp. 995–10.

——, 'Gli Ordini religiosi maschili dalla Controriforma alle oppressioni settecentesche. Cultura, predicazione, missioni', in *Clero e Società,* ed. Mario Rosa, pp. 207–74.

——, 'Le biblioteche degli ordini religiosi in Italia intorno all'anno 1600 attraverso l'inchiesta della Congregazione dell'Indice. Problemi e prospettive di una ricerca', in *Libri, biblioteche,* eds, Barbieri and Zardin, pp. 63–84.

Russo, Carla, 'Parrocchie, fabbricerie e communità nell'area suburbana della diocesi di Napoli (xvi–xviii secolo)', in *Per la storia,* eds, Galasso and Russo, vol. 2 (1982), pp. 9–79.

Russo, F., *Storia dell'Archdiocesi di Reggio Calabria. Vol. 2: Dal Concilio di Trento al 1961* (Naples, 1963).

(La) Sacra Congregazione del Concilio di Trento. Quarto centennario della fondazione (1564–1964) (Città del Vaticano, 1964).

Samaritani, A. 'Catechismo, eucharista e tempio nella Comacchio postridentina', with 'Fonti inedite', *Ravennatensia,* 2 (1971), pp. 433–547.

San Carlo e il suo tempo. Atti del convegno internazionale nel IV centenario della morte, Milan 21–26 Maggio 1984, 2 vols (Rome, 1986).

Sarpi, Paolo, *Istoria del Concilio Tridentino,* ed. Corrado Vivanti, 2 vols (Turin, 1974).

Sarra, Mariangela, 'Distribuzione statistica dei dati processuali dell'inquisizione in Friuli dal 1557 al 1786. Tecniche di ricerca e risultati', *Metodi e ricerche* (Udine) 7 (1988), pp. 5–31.

Scaduto, Mario, 'Tra Inquisitori e Riformati. Le missioni dei Gesuiti tra i Valdesi della Calabria e delle Puglie', *Archivum Historicum Societatis Jesu,* 15 (1946), pp. 1–76.

——, 'Le "Visite" di Antonio Possevino nei domini di Gonzaga', *Archivio Storico Lombardo,* 11 (1960), pp. 336–410.

Scaraffia, Lucetta and Zarri, Gabriella (eds), *Donna e Fede. Santità e vita religiosa in Italia* (Rome and Bari, 1994).

Scattigno, Anna, 'Lettere dal convento', in *Per lettera,* ed. Zarri (1999) pp. 313–57.

Schutte, Anne Jacobson, 'Inquisition and Female Autobiography: the Case of Cecilia Ferrazzi', in *The Crannied Wall. Women,* ed. Craig A. Monson, pp. 105–8.

——, *Aspiring Saints. Pretense of Holiness, Inquisition, and Gender in the Republic of Venice,* 1618–1750 (Baltimore and London, 2001).

——, 'Religion, spirituality, and the post-tridentine Church', in *Early Modern Italy,* ed. Marino, pp. 125–42.

Schutte, Anne Jacobson, Thomas Kuehn, Silvana Seidel Menchi (eds), *Time, Space and Women's Lives in Early Modern Europe* (Kirksville, 2001).

Seidel Menchi, Silvana, 'Italy', in *The Reformation in National Context,* eds, Bob (Robert) Scribner, Roy Porter and Mikuláŝ Teich (Cambridge, 1994), pp. 181–201.

Setton, Kenneth M., *The Papacy and the Levant (1204–1571),* vols. 3–4, *The Sixteenth Century* (Philadelphia, 1984).

Shearman, John, *Only Connect. Art and the Spectator in the Italian Renaissance* (Princeton, 1992).

Signorotto, Gianvittorio, *Inquisitori e mistici nel Seicento italiano. L'eresia di Santa Pelagia* (Bologna, 1989).

Silbiger, Alexander, 'The Roman Frescobaldi tradition, *c.*1640–1670', *Journal of American Musicological Society,* 33 (1980), pp. 42–87.

Sobel, Dava, *Galileo's Daughter* (London, 1999).

Sobel, Dava, *To Father. The Letters of Sister Maria Celeste to Galileo 1623–1633,* translated and edited (London, 2001).

Solfaroli Camillocci, Daniela, 'La monaca esemplare. Lettere spirituali di madre Battistina Vernazza (1497–1587)', in *Per lettera,* ed. Zarri, pp. 235–61.

Sommario: Il Sommario della Santa Scrittura e l'ordinario dei cristiani, edit. Cesare Bianco con una introduzione di J. Trapman (Turin, 1988).

Sonnino, Eugenio, 'Le anime dei romani: fonti religiose e demografia storica', in *Storia*, eds, Fiorani and Prosperi (2000), pp. 329–64.
Sperelli, Alessandro, *Della pretiosita della limosina* (Venice, 1666).
Sperling, Jutta, *Convents and the Body Politic in Late Renaissance Venice* (Chicago, 1999).
Sposato, P., *Aspetti e figure della Riforma Cattolico-Tridentino in Calabria* (Naples, n.d., [*c.*1965]).
Stella, Aldo, *Chiesa e Stato nelle relazioni dei nunzi pontifici a Venezia* (Vatican City, 1964).
——, *Dall'anabattismo al socianismo nel Cinquecento veneto* (Padua, 1967).
——, *Anabattismo e antitrinitarismo in Italia nel sedicesimo secolo* (Padua, 1969).
Stone, Lawrence, *Family, Sex and Marriage in England 1500–1800* (London, 1977).
Storia di Brescia, vol. 2, *Il Dominio Veneto* (1961) (Treccani degli Alfieri, n.p.).
Storia di Milano vol. X, *L'Età della Riforma Cattolica* (Treccani degli Alfieri, n.p. 1957).
Stow, Kenneth, *Theater of Acculturation. The Roman Ghetto in the Sixteenth Century* (Seattle and London, 2001).
Tammasia, Nino, *La famiglia italiana nei secoli decimoquinto e decimosesto* (Milan, Naples, 1910; Rome, 1971 reprint).
Tarabotti, Arcangela, *L' 'Inferno monacale'*, ed. Francesca Medioli (Turin, 1990)
Tedeschi, John, *The Prosecution of Heresy. Collected Studies on the Inquisition in Early Modern Italy* (Binghampton, NY, 1991).
—— 'Il caso di un falso inquisitore', in *Sotto* il segno eds, Del Col and Paroni Bertoja, pp. 137–42.
Tentler, Thomas N., 'The Summa for confessors as an instrument of social control', in *The Pursuit of Holiness,* eds, C. Trinkhaus and Heiko O. Oberman (Leiden, 1974), pp. 103–26.
Terpstra, Nicholas, 'Piety and Punishment: the Lay Conforteria and Civic Justice in sixteenth-century Bologna', *Sixteenth Century Journal,* 22 (1991), pp. 679–94.
——, 'Confraternal Prison Charity and Political Consolidation in sixteenth-century Bologna', *Journal of Modern History,* 66 (1994), pp. 219–48.
——, *Lay Confraternities and Civic Religion in Renaissance Bologna* (Cambridge, 1995).
——, 'Ignatius, Confratello: Confraternities as Modes of Spiritual Community in Early Modern Society', in Comerford and Pabel ed., pp. 163–82.
——, 'Mothers, sisters, and daughters: girls and conservatory guardianship in late Renaissance Florence', *Renaissance Studies,* 17 (2003), pp. 201–29.
Terpstra, Nicholas (ed.), *Politics of Ritual Kinship: Confraternities and Social Order in Early Modern Italy* (Cambridge, 2000).
Tomaro, John B., 'San Carlo Borromeo and the implementation of the Council of Trent', in *San Carlo Borromeo,* eds, Headley and Tomaro (1988), pp. 67–84.
Tomizza, Fulvio, *Heavenly Supper. The Story of Maria Janis,* trans. Annc Jacobson Schutte (Chicago and London, 1991).

Torre, Angelo, 'Faith's Boundaries: Ritual and Territory in Rural Piedmont in the early modern period', in *Politics of Ritual Kinship,* ed. Terpstra pp. 242–61.

Toscani, Xenio, 'Il reclutamento del clero (secoli xvi-xix)', in *Storia d'Italia,* eds, Chittolini and Miccoli, *Annali,* 9 (1986), pp. 575–628.

Tramontin, Silvio, 'Gli inizi dei due seminari di Venezia', *Studi Veneziani,* 7 (1965), pp. 363–77.

Tramontin, Silvio, 'La Visita Apostolica del 1581 a Venezia', *Studi Veneziani,* 9 (1967), pp. 453–533.

Trisco, Robert, 'Carlo Borromeo and the Council of Trent: The Question of Reform', in *San Carlo Borromeo,* eds, Headley and Tomaro, pp. 47–66.

Turchini, Angelo, *Clero e fedeli a Rimini in età post-tridentina* (Rome, 1978).

Ughelli, F., *Italia Sacra, sive de episcopis Italiae…* (Venice, 1717–22; 1979 Bologna photo reprint used).

Valerio, Adriana, 'Donne e celibato ecclesiastico: le concubine del clero', in *Donne,* eds, Galasso and Valerio, pp. 67–90.

Valone, Carolyn, 'Roman Matrons as Patrons: various views of the cloister wall', in *The Crannied Wall,* ed. Monson, pp. 49–72.

Vianello, Andrea, 'I "Fiscali delle miserie". Le origini delle Fraterne dei Poveri e l'assistenza a domicilio a Venezia tra Cinque e Settecento', in *Per Marino Berengo. Studi degli allievi,* eds, Livio Antoniello *et al.* (Milan, 2000), pp. 277–98.

Villani, P., 'La Visita apostolica di Tommaso Orfini nel Regno di Napoli (1566–1568)', *Annuario dell'Istituto storico italiano per la storia,* 8 (1956), pp. 5–79.

Villari, Rosario, *La Rivolta antispagnola* (Bari, 1976 edn).

Voelker, E.C., 'Borromeo' Influences on Sacred Art and Architecture', in *San Carlo Borromeo* eds, J.M. Headley and J.B. Tomaro, pp. 172–87.

Volpe, Francesco, *La parrocchia Cilentina dal xvi al xix secolo* (Rome, 1984).

Waquet, Françoise, *Latin or the empire of a sign. From the sixteenth to the twentieth centuries,* trans. John Howe (London and NY, 2001).

Watkins, Glenn, *Gesualdo. The Man and his Music* (London, 1973).

Weaver, B. Elissa, *Convent Theatre in Early Modern Italy. Spiritual Fun and Learning for Women* (Cambridge, 2002).

Weston-Lewis, Aidan (ed.), *Effigies and Ecstasies: Roman Baroque Sculpture and Design in the Age of Bernini* (Edinburgh, 1988).

Weissman, Ronald F.E., *Ritual Brotherhood in Renaissance Florence* (New York and London, 1982).

Whitfield, C. and Martineau, J. (eds), *Painting in Naples 1606–1705 from Caravaggio to Giordano* (London, 1982).

Wills, Gary, *Venice: Lion City. The Religion of Empire* (NY and London, 2001)

Wisch, Barbara and Ahl, Diane Cole (eds), *Confraternities and the Visual Arts in Renaissance Italy. Ritual, Spectacle, Image* (Cambridge, 2000).

Wittkower, Rudolf, *Art and Architecture in Italy 1600–1750* (Harmondsworth, 1973 rev. edn, used), and same, 6th edn. revised by J. Connors and J. Montagu, 3 vols. (New Haven and London, 1999).

Wöllflin, H. *Renaissance and Baroque,* trans., K. Simon, (London, 1984).

Wright, A.D. 'The Significance of the Council of Trent', *Journal of Ecclesiastical History,* 26 (1975), pp. 353–62.

——, *The Early Modern Papacy. From the Council of Trent to the French Revolution, 1564–1789* (London and NY, 2000).

Zardin, Danilo, 'Relaunching Confraternities in the Tridentine Era: shaping conscience and christianizing society in Milan and Lombardy', in *Ritual Kinship,* ed. Terpstra, pp. 243–61.

——, 'Gregorio Barbarigo, la "crisi" della prima Controriforma e I vescovi del seicento', *Annali di Storia moderna e contemporanea,* 6 (2000), pp. 645–55.

——, 'Monasteri femminili e città (secoli xv–xviii', in *Storia d'Italia,* eds, G. Chittolini and G. Miccoli, *Annali,* 9 (1986) pp. 359–429.

——, *Le Sante vive. Cultura e religiosita femminili nella prime eta moderna* (Turin, 1990).

——, 'Il monastero dei Santi Vitale e Agricola: aspetti di una communità femminile nell'antico regime', in *Vitale e Agricola,* ed. G. Fasoli, pp. 169–82.

Zarri, Gabriella, 'Dalla profezia alla disciplina (1450–1650)', in *Donne e Fede,* eds, Scaraffia and Zarri (1994), pp. 177–225.

——, 'Il matrimonio tridentino', in *Il Concilio di Trento,* eds, Prodi and Reinhard, pp. 437–83.

——, 'Living Saints: a typology of female sanctity in the early sixteenth century', in *Women and Religion in Medieval and Renaissance Italy,* eds, Daniel Bornstein and Roberto Rusconi (Chicago, 1996), pp. 219–303.

——, 'Il "terzo stato", ' in *Tempi e spazi,* eds, Silvana Seidel Menchi *et al.* pp. 311–34.

Zarri, Gabriella (ed.), *Finzione e santità tra medioeva ed età moderna* (Turin, 1991).

Zarri, Gabriella (ed.), *Per lettera. La scrittura epistolare femminile tra archivio e tipografia secoli xv–xvii* (Rome, 1999).

Index

[Note. For space reasons, the Index does not list Bishoprics listed in the Appendix which are not mentioned in the main text. With smaller places the heading 'diocese' may cover a variety of aspects, which receive sub-headings for major bishoprics. 'Protestant' is used, especially in sub-headings, to cover all those showing some significant interest in northern reform ideas, and also Valdesian and Waldensian beliefs. Modern authors are only indexed if there is a major comment on them in the main text. Minor references to non-religious writers and writings, mentioned in discussing libraries or censorship for example, are not indexed.]